THE
HAWKE
MEMOIRS

THE HAWKE MEMOIRS

BOB HAWKE

Published 1996 by Mandarin
a part of Reed Books Australia
22 Salmon Street, Port Melbourne, Victoria 3207
a division of Reed International Books Australia Pty Limited

First published in Australia in 1994 by William Heinemann Australia
Reprinted 1994

Typeset in Janson by J&M Typesetting Services
Printed and bound in Australia by Australian Print Group

National Library of Australia
 cataloguing-in-publication data:

Hawke, Bob, 1929– .
 The Hawke memoirs.

Includes index.
ISBN 1 86330 490 8.

 1. Hawke, Bob, 1929– . 2. Australian Labor Party. 3. Prime ministers — Australia
— Biography. 4. Australia — Politics and government — 1976–1990. I. Title.

994.063092

For my parents,
Ellie and Clem.

CONTENTS

ACKNOWLEDGMENTS

The best lack all conviction; while the worst are full of passionate intensity.

W.B. Yeats, *The Second Coming*

Yeats, like the creators of so many stunning aphorisms, got it half right. Too much of history seems to confirm his dismal perception of human nature. But all my experience attests that the good, and the best, in our societies do not lack conviction, and that a passionate intensity is not the monopoly of the worst among us; nor, unfortunately, do the latter lack all conviction.

I hope this book may lead you to share my interpretation, for it tells of working with thousands of good people, and with many of the best, whom I have seen devote their lives to fighting for a better world.

There is, I believe, an inexorable asymmetry in life. Mistakes are almost inevitably one's own responsibility, but one's worthwhile achievements are rarely posted without the help of others. Foremost has been the invaluable support of Hazel and my children Sue, Stephen and Ros. In my case it is impossible to refer to all those who have helped me with their love, friendship and co-operation. I hope that all such dear friends who are not mentioned specifically – people from the trade unions, politics, business, ethnic organisations, the Jewish community, the public service – will know that they are in my heart if not in this book. This applies very much to those who under the successive direction of Graham Evans, Chris Conybeare, Sandy Hollway and Dennis Richardson served on my staff during my time as Prime Minister; many of them became close and enduring friends. In the same way I thank the many members of my security team and the Lodge staff who became almost part of the family.

All Members of Parliament rely heavily on their electorate officers to discharge their representative duties. My reliance, particularly after becoming Prime Minister, upon Mimi Tamburrino was almost total. She was assisted over the years by other devoted staff and a great band of party activists; but to Mimi, in particular, go my thanks for her unfailing loyalty to me and her dedication to my constituents, to whom, in turn, I extend my gratitude for their continuing support at the ballot box.

I must, however, mention six friends, and their families – in Melbourne, Saul Same, Peter Redlich, Isi Magid and Yvonne Edmonds, and in Sydney, Sam Fiszman and John Saunders – for their unfailing friendship and support. And I also remember the late George Rockey, Sir Peter Abeles' original business partner. George was like a father to me, a source of comfort in adversity but strong in reproof when he thought it necessary. I felt a devastating sense of loss when he died of cancer in 1980.

Sport has been a sustaining passion in my life and in that context I thank Col Cunningham – a character Damon Runyan would have killed for – for thirty years my mate at the races, on the tennis court, the golf course and at the snooker table.

When I undertook to write this book in early 1992, I knew I had a busy period ahead. As events unfolded I found the launching of a new career taking more of my time than expected. I am grateful to my publishers, Paul Hamlyn, a good friend of many years, Sandy Grant and Louise Adler of William Heinemann Australia for their ready acceptance of the delay this involved in producing the manuscript. I particularly thank Louise for her gentle but constant pressure and assistance.

My researcher, Garry Sturgess, was both diligent and patient throughout and I am deeply indebted to him. Jill Saunders, with me throughout my time as Prime Minister and now my Assistant, was heavily involved in the preparation of the book. I thank her sincerely for her invaluable assistance and her determination to clear my diary, for without that, I would never have been able to complete this work. Garry, Jill and Karen Shea, of my office, who typed and retyped the manuscript with competence and unfailing good humour, have been my mainstays. I also sincerely thank my former staff members – Senior Advisers Simon Balderstone, Dr Craig Emerson and Hugh White; Senior Private Secretary, Peter Harris; and Press Secretary, Grant Nihill for providing assistance in various forms.

Although he was not directly involved in helping with the preparation of the manuscript, I could not have found the time nor had the peace of mind needed to produce it, without the assistance constantly provided to Hazel and me in our personal affairs by our good friend Richard Super.

Lastly, I thank Blanche d'Alpuget, whose excellent biography gave the fullest account of my early life. In March this year she put aside her own book to work as my editor as the deadline approached. Her expertise and professionalism were invaluable.

With the help of these men and women I have been blessed with unique opportunities to serve this country, Australia, that I love, unashamedly, with a passionate intensity.

Sydney, May 1994

PREFACE

Looking back at my time as Prime Minister, I think of the state of mind of the early eighties, of the attitudes and assumptions which, with the exception of three years of Labor under Whitlam, had been shaped by three decades of conservative governance. They were attitudes and assumptions which were stultifying Australian life; they had to change if the nation was to grow materially, intellectually and morally and so be able to take its proper place in the world.

At the beginning of the 1980s it was accepted that employers and workers were destined for conflict and confrontation; that rural and city Australia were almost different nations and that Labor was an alien force in rural politics; that education was not a right equally available to the children of the poor as of the rich; and that pensions should be available equally to the asset rich as to the asset impoverished. Superannuation was the preserve of the privileged few. It was also accepted that manufacturing was to be conducted behind high tariff walls with no relevance to earning export income; that high inflation was endemic in Australia and would always be higher than in the major industrial economies; that the countries to our north were properly designated in Eurocentric terms as 'the Far East', not as they are, East

Asia, and that this was a region to be regarded either as a potential threat of war or a place for exotic holidays. It was assumed that in the conduct of our international relations we exhausted our responsibilities by ascertaining the view of the British and the Americans and falling in line with them; and, most reprehensibly, that a condescending attitude to our Aboriginal citizens was somehow justified. Informing all of this was the view, based on our history, that Labor only became the Government of Australia by default.

Overriding these positions was an assumption that the glory days when the world clamoured for and paid high prices for our primary products would return and go on forever, allowing us to play by rules of our own.

Each of these attitudes and assumptions was wrong, and dangerously wrong, in a world that was changing dramatically.

To the great benefit of this nation, by the end of my period in office all of them had been demolished. A new spirit is abroad in the workplaces of Australia, reflected not only in a 60 per cent decline in industrial disputes but in the extensive changes in work practices and the movement towards enterprise bargaining which are lifting Australian productivity to make it increasingly competitive in the international marketplace. There is, in the 1990s, a more constructive integration of rural Australia into the processes of government, and relations between the political and industrial wings of the labour movement and rural Australia are better than ever before. The proportion of children staying on to Year 12 has more than doubled, and no-one is denied access to tertiary or technical education for financial reasons. We have started to give hope to Aboriginal Australians that their special needs and their relationship to the land are recognised and understood, and there is now a basis for a reconciliation founded not on guilt and recrimination but on mutual respect. The level of real social security benefits for those most in need has been substantially increased

– by 14 per cent for a married pensioner couple with two children, 17 per cent for a sole parent with two children and 40 per cent for a long-term unemployed single adult, under my Government. (This compares with real reductions of 2 per cent, 4 per cent and 19 per cent in those categories under the previous Government.) The country no longer tolerates the affront of paying pensions to those obviously capable of providing for themselves. The growth in manufactured exports in the last decade has been almost twice as fast as that of other Western industrialised countries, outstripping all except the United States which has enjoyed a record similar to Australia's. BHP, which was considering closing down its steel industry before we came to office, is now a significant competitive exporter.

By the time I left office we had more than halved the inflation rate we inherited of over 11 per cent, which was double the average level of the seven major OECD economies.[1] It is now down to 1 per cent or well under half the average rate in those countries.

What in 1983 was dismissed as my fanciful dream is daily a clearer reality as Australia becomes more deeply enmeshed with Asia. Sixty per cent of our exports now go to that region, and the proportion of Asians among our international visitors is fast approaching 50 per cent. Our role in facilitating a settlement in Indo-China and in the creation of APEC has established for Australia a place of permanent relevance in this most dynamic region of the world.

As a nation we have created a reputation for innovation in address-ing a range of fundamental issues; for example establishing a third force in world trade negotiations with the Cairns Group and in work-ing for disarmament, the South Pacific Nuclear Free Zone, peace in Indo-China and the ending of apartheid. Politically, the whole country is better off because the Left has been brought into the mainstream of Labor thinking on international affairs. Foreign policy is no longer Labor's Achilles heel, but a source of electoral strength.

Australians have become more economically literate and aware of the harsh competitive realities of the world in which they live. There are still pockets of xenophobia and prejudice but, more and more, we understand that the pursuit of our interests is inextricably related to working with, and not shutting ourselves off from, the rest of the world.

All of these changes have made Australia a better place and have given Labor a new stature. These are the changes I wanted for my country and my party. This is the story of why and how it happened.

I

'A SON OF THE MANSE'

ONE

'It was a pleasure, son.'

I was sitting at my mother's bedside in a Perth private hospital where she had lain in a coma for months and was now clearly in her last days. As I looked at her wasted but still gently determined face I was overwhelmed by the knowledge that no human being had influenced my destiny more. Words seemed pointless, but certain that I would not see her alive again, I picked up her listless hand and whispered my gratitude for all she had done to encourage and equip me for life's journey. To my amazement, one eyelid moved slightly and she spoke those words. They were the last she ever uttered.

This happened in July 1979, almost fifty years after my birth in Bordertown, South Australia on 9th December 1929. Edith Emily Lee, known as Ellie, was a country schoolteacher before marrying my father, Clem. A newly ordained Congregational minister, Clem was kindness personified. Ellie was a woman of passionate commitments. In the armoury of her convictions, which she used to assault the consciousness of those around her, none was more intensely held than her belief in the importance of education. It was an integral part of her religious faith to believe that we each have a responsibility to develop to the limit the talents with which we are endowed.

My earliest recollections are of Clem and Ellie reading aloud to me for hours. No request for a story was ever refused. I absorbed when very young many of the dramatic biblical tales, with David and Goliath being a favourite. The good winning against the odds appealed to me from the beginning.

I also recall being enveloped by love. The purposeful love of my mother was supplemented by what was nothing less than a mutual adoration between my father and me. In his eyes I could do little wrong and if there were aberrations, they were to be explained by mitigating circumstances. Admonitions were rarely delivered – usually at my mother's insistence – and caused him more hurt than me. Clem's paternal attitude reflected a broader gentleness of character. I have met no man as prepared to see good in others and to shoulder their problems and pain.

His was a very practical Christianity. When I was a young man, he said to me, 'Belief in the fatherhood of God necessarily involves believing in the brotherhood of man.' This was Clem's creed for life. I remember the endless stream of the poor and destitute arriving at the manse door in rural South Australia during the Great Depression. No-one ever went away without food, shelter or some form of assistance.

I was not conscious that there was developing in me at this very early stage an unconventional concept of family which was to dominate the rest of my life. It was not simply that Ellie and Clem constantly made our home a haven for others. Beyond that was a growing feeling that love and a sense of bonding with others were something which went beyond the bounds of immediate family; everyone, all humans, were kin.

This atmosphere of love gave me a great sense of security and confidence but no doubt encouraged a precociousness which I am sure was objectionable at times. The parental attitude of those days, that children should be seen but not heard, was not embraced by Ellie and Clem. They always fostered my questioning and expressions of opinion. I apparently caused considerable merriment when, aged three, I made a parish call to cheer up a sick old lady who was unable to get to church. I stood on a chair and preached a sermon. I don't know whether her faith was enhanced, but I'm told her spirits were restored. In political life the pulpit has often been the precursor to the platform.

This web of love and affection became more complex with the death of my brother Neil. He was nine years my senior, but I had had little opportunity to develop a close relationship with him because he had been sent as a full-time boarder to King's College in Adelaide before I was four years old. This, too, was part of Ellie's determination to provide us with the best possible education. Neil was dux of the college, and both my parents, my mother especially, took pride in his achievements. On top of his strong academic record, Neil was a good sportsman, a competition swimmer and cyclist.

The fatal bushfire summer of 1939 which scarred Australia was a time of tragedy for our family for other reasons. Ellie's mother had died on 18th February, and at the funeral Neil's sickly appearance alarmed my parents. In fact he was in the early stage of meningitis. At that time there were no antibiotics and Neil was soon fighting a hopeless battle against a deadly affliction. Ellie and Clem prayed day and night by his bedside, to the point of exhaustion. Neil died on 27th February.

His death transformed our family, turning me, in effect, into his heir. All the love and hopes which had focused on Neil were now transferred to me. Neil had been the apple of my mother's eye, as I was of Clem's. Now, in her grief, all her love and her intense sense of mission to make the world a better place centred on me. My father, meanwhile, bore his own sorrow and hers; I remember him urging me to share my love for him with her, to ease her grief.

Towards the end of 1939, partly to help the healing process, Clem accepted an invitation to take up his ministry in Western Australia, at the Leederville Congregational Church. I was an ardent advocate of acceptance for no better reason, I confess, than the excitement of a train journey across Australia. It seemed an adventure beyond anything I could imagine. Going west was a decision neither my parents nor I ever regretted. I became and remain an unabashed devotee of Perth, then and still – with Sydney – the loveliest city in Australia. We soon came to experience the truth that there are no more friendly people in this country than West Australians, and I became the beneficiary of an outstanding education system. And, most importantly, Hazel was there.

TWO

The war had started by the time we arrived in the West, and after only a short time at Leederville, Clem enlisted as a chaplain in the Australian Imperial Forces. This was exciting and traumatic, for he was both my father and my best friend, and I remember my yearning expectation as I hung over the fence waiting for him to come home on leave.

The year of his enlistment also saw Ellie concentrating on securing the next stage of my education. She wanted me to attend a private school, an idea which, with Clem's support, I successfully resisted. Perth's Modern School was the academically elite institution in West Australian secondary education. Access to this Government co-educational school was by way of a fiercely competitive State-wide examination taken at the end of the final primary year. The top fifty students received Scholarships and the next fifty were awarded Entrances, together making up the first year's intake.

Ellie set her mind on her son being part of that intake as a Scholarship winner. Until then I had found little difficulty in South Australia and at West Leederville in being at the top, or equal top, of my classes. But Ellie's fervour and dedication in masterminding my preparation was a totally new experience for me. She instilled in me the feeling that this was not just another test but a shaping point for my whole career. As with the passionate convictions of most good people, there was enough truth in this to impress me. We adhered to a strict regimen of study, with the schoolteacher in Ellie acting as both guide and disciplinarian. When my name was among the fifty Scholarship winners, I felt pride in myself and pleasure for my mother. My sense of goodwill towards her was very considerable, but distinctly I remember feeling that in this next stage of my life I was going to be much more my own person.

For her part, Ellie seemed to feel that having achieved the goal of a good educational environment for me, she could turn her boundless energies to a range of other interests. Predominant among these was her work with the Women's Christian Temperance Union. As with everything she did, she threw herself into the fight against the demon of alcohol. Her zealotry invited gentle derision from all of us, but she coped with that easily.

My time at Modern School was not one of great application. Scholastically, these were the lazy years and I was rarely out of second gear. There were many interesting contemporaries who acquired subsequent fame. Among the most studious 'swots' were the close friends John Stone and Maxwell Newton. They both achieved excellent results throughout their time at school. Stone, whom I inherited decades later as Secretary of Treasury, exhibited at that early stage all the arrogance and cynical contempt for his fellows which were to characterise his distinguished career as a public servant. In a sense, it was altogether appropriate that he became a Senator as the protégé of a man he despised intensely, Sir Joh Bjelke-Petersen.

As a firm believer in the dictum *de mortuis nil nisi bonum*, I will not unburden myself of all my feelings about Max Newton, with whom I later had several celebrated clashes, including litigation. Newton was a man of tragically failed talent. He was possessed of a very considerable intellect and, when so minded, a massive capacity for hard work and research. He distinguished himself at Cambridge only to scintillate through his time in Treasury and then journalism, with spells at manufacturing batteries and, later, some less salubrious occupations. He had developed cynicism to an art form and seemed determined to work out his lack of ease with the world by prolonged and dedicated bouts of self-destruction. Newton could be very engaging and I always felt that there was a layer of goodness in the man which, perversely, he felt it necessary to suppress. I believe Max Newton made himself into one of the great losses to Australia. If he had been able to identify with or find a spark of compassion for his fellow man, there is no limit to the contribution he could have made to his country.

A friend of Stone and Newton was John Wheeldon. Then and for some time after Modern School, Wheeldon was an ardent conservative and an active member of the Liberal Party, with a fair share of the others' cynicism. This was leavened, however, by a witty ebullience and an enjoyment in interacting with those around him. We were often adversaries in school debates. This was entertaining at the time and made the more pleasurable subsequently by the thought that I may have played a small part in his later conversion to the Labor Party. He served with distinction as a Senator and minister of the Crown in the Whitlam Government.

Another Perth Modern boy was Alan Barblett. He and I were in the same class throughout school and studied law together at the University of Western Australia. Alan was a good student and a remarkable sportsman. He represented Western Australia in Junior tennis and went on from what was initially just a dalliance with hockey to become an Australian and Olympic representative. After successfully practising law, he has distinguished himself as Chairman of the Family Court in Western Australia and is one of Australia's most respected judges. He was best man at my wedding.

Ralph Slatyer, a quiet but brilliant student, also attended Perth Modern. He was well liked by all, a young man who, one sensed, would make his mark in life. Ralph became an outstanding academic scientist and servant of the Australian community as Ambassador to UNESCO and later as Chief Scientist to my Government. In that capacity he made several enduring contributions, especially his concept of the Co-operative Research Centres, which match the best of our academic research capacities to the requirements and resources of industry.

In my early teenage years my health was indifferent, but a transformation occurred after Ellie took me to a naturopath in 1944. He changed my diet to one of high-fibre, natural foods and I developed quickly and strongly. I was physically very active. Cricket had always been a passion, nurtured by hours of practice against Clem or anyone else I could badger into bowling to me. When the Australian team was in England in 1938, I would come home from the little country school to the farm where I was staying while my parents were on a caravan holiday, and go to sleep early so that I could sit up late at night to listen to the simulated broadcast of the Test matches. Bradman was God. I still recall feeling that the world had fallen apart when a young upstart, Len Hutton, broke the Don's world record with his innings of 334 at Leeds. My passion and practice paid off, and I was a member of the School First XI in both my fourth and final years.

I matriculated from Modern School at the end of 1946 with some distinctions but with results which I knew were well below my capacities. I had a few regrets, but on balance I looked back with pleasure and forward with exuberance, confident in my physical and mental ability to handle whatever might be ahead.

Very early ideas of becoming a doctor had long since evaporated, and my academic future lay clearly in the humanities rather than the sciences. I decided on Law, not with any intention of practising, for I found unattractive the idea of being available to argue cases which I was not convinced about or indeed whose merit I might seriously doubt. I was aware of the profession's argument that everyone is entitled to the services of a lawyer whose duty it is to be advocate not judge, but I found this proposition uncongenial. Nevertheless, I believed that a degree in Law would be a useful foundation for whatever path I chose in the future. It was a decision I have never regretted. Hardly a day of my life has passed when, directly or indirectly, I have not been able to use to advantage the knowledge and techniques acquired during my legal studies.

To be a student at the University of Western Australia in 1947 was an unlimited joy. I had gone to secondary school as a very dependent child and now, just turned seventeen and with an undiminished love for my parents, I felt a liberated young man. Their love for me was to remain a rock of comfort but not a constraint. The regimented authoritarianism of school gave way to the idea that, within certain obvious limits, one was free and expected to run one's own race.

This sense of exhilaration was enhanced by the incomparable beauty of the university campus, which was spread over spacious, leafy grounds beside the Swan River. Those who had planned and built it had spent well the endowment of Sir Winthrop Hackett, the newspaper magnate whose generosity had made this the only free university in Australia. This fact partly explains a phenomenon in Australian life often commented on but not to my knowledge ever sensibly analysed. People constantly refer to the large number of West Australians – out of all proportion to the State's population – who have reached positions of eminence in many different walks of life in the eastern States. The explanation is simple and twofold. First, because it was the only free university in Australia, the University of Western Australia tended much more than those in the rest of the country to be able to enrol a high proportion of students with the best talents and greatest desire for a tertiary education. Second, the small economy of Western Australia offered relatively few openings to its talented graduates and, as a result, it was normal to see an exodus from west to east.

The campus throbbed with life. Social, political and religious clubs catered for all tastes, while the sporting environment and facilities were superb. In the immediate postwar period an additional dimension came from the presence at university of many ex-servicemen studying under the Commonwealth Reconstruction Training Scheme. I admired the way in which these men, many without secondary level qualifications, adapted to the unfamiliar discipline of study after the rigours of war. They were generous in their attitude to us young people who had enjoyed such an easy run compared to them. Our contact with the war had been limited to the occasional air raid siren which sent us racing to the sand trenches dug around the school grounds – always 'practice only'. Our apprehensiveness following the bombing of Darwin had changed to nonchalance and turned 'air raids' into an opportunity to flirt with the girls. At university the returned servicemen did not shove their war down your throat but, if asked, were prepared to share their experiences; they were hard workers but when they did relax, they became wonderfully boisterous companions. The taste I got from them of the value and pleasure of older men's company developed, in adulthood, into an affinity with people who were my seniors.

I threw myself into this exciting, liberated environment, becoming active in the Labor Club, the Australian Student Christian movement and in the less formalised but equally stimulating interchange of ideas and argument which dominated the early postwar student scene. Amidst all of this and in the thrill of sporting involvement, studies were interesting, but I felt no compulsion to move out of my relaxed Modern School second gear.

Two-thirds of the way through this first year, however, something happened, suddenly, to change my life forever. Our home in West Leederville was only a few miles in a direct line through King's Park to the university. Public transport was circuitous, involving a trolley bus into the city and another around the Swan River to reach the campus. I used this waste of time as an argument for having a motorcycle, but encountered strong resistance from Ellie, whose natural apprehension of these machines was reinforced by her grief over Neil's death. I persisted, however, and finally, with Dad's support, I became during the second-term holidays the proud owner of a second-hand Panther.

I rode my Panther to the Law Library one day during the vacation but after studying for a while, began to feel unwell. After taking a couple of aspirins in the refectory, I waited briefly then set off for home through King's Park. Inside my windcheater I was carrying a heavy metal stand for the bike. I don't know whether I actually blacked out as I was riding, but I have vague memories of careering off the road. I came to my senses bruised and bleeding, lying in sand and bushes some distance from the twisted, upturned bike. I was in excruciating pain and barely able to move.

After what seem an eternity, a motorist found me and I was raced to hospital where tests indicated that the pain was probably coming from my spleen, ruptured by the metal stand when I landed face down in the bushes. The spleen was removed the next day. For several days I hovered between life and death. Through a blur of agony and fear, I was aware from time to time of the anguished presence of my parents. To the extent that my mind could focus beyond my own pain, I felt unbounded sorrow for them. They grieved for me and reproached themselves for having allowed me to have the motorbike, contemplating the loss of their remaining child at virtually the same age as Neil. Their world, with my life, was in the balance.

Their prayers, supported by those of many throughout the churches, were unceasing. When it was clear I would survive, my parents took this as a further sign of the portents Ellie had claimed to discern before my birth: portents that I was destined for a special life. While I did not embrace her esoteric visions, I firmly believed that God had spared my life. I felt the force of the Parable of the Talents and saw in my attitude to school and university studies the bad servant's waste of his talent. I determined to live life to the full extent of my abilities, to push myself to the limit. Study assumed a much greater importance. It was not a question of spiritual rebirth but a conviction that I had been granted a new life; I was not going to waste it. Where Ellie had on occasion experienced some success in instilling this sense of commitment, the touch of death inscribed it in my consciousness for ever. Some months after the accident, when my recuperation was complete, I became aware of having, as it were, an extra store of energy. I gradually discovered that this additional vitality and stamina would allow me to go for thirty-six hours without sleep, for example, and to undertake enormous workloads. Bountiful energy has remained with me.

THREE

Although my study program had been entirely disrupted I decided not to postpone my examinations in 1947 and passed in all four subjects. Given the circumstances, a pass was a good result, but it posed a problem for obtaining a first class Honours degree. Such degrees were awarded on the basis of the number of distinctions in legal subjects recorded during the four years of the course. I did well in 1948, and in 1949, the first year in which we were eligible for prizes, I won the John Norman Barker Prize for the best third-year Law student. In the final year I needed distinctions in each of the five subjects but missed in one, coming in second to my mate John Toohey, who took out the prizes. This was an eminently fair result as, quite apart from some diversion on my part as President of Societies Council and member of the Students Representative Council (Guild of Undergraduates), John was a better student of, and more devoted to the law, than I. It was my great pleasure as Prime Minister to recommend his appointment to the High Court in 1987; his stature is considerable, his judgments widely acclaimed.

While John and I were competitors academically, he co-operated with me to change the framework of political activity at the University of Western Australia. My sympathies were by nature very much with the Labor Party and there was a strong family influence at work. Clem had been something of a Labor activist in his younger days, but the political standard-bearer in the Hawke family was Clem's younger brother, Albert. After a term in the South Australian Parliament, Albert had come to Western Australia as an organiser for the party, and was elected to the West Australian Parliament as the Member for Northam in 1933. He became Deputy Premier in 1945 and served as Premier from 1953 to 1959. Uncle Albert was very close to Clem, Ellie and me. At least once a week he came to our house for 'tea' and politics was always on the menu. Discussion would continue over a game of bridge after the meal. Albert was a tall, intelligent, friendly man with a passion for sport and an irrepressible sense of humour. He had Clem's decency and compassion, but there was a tougher edge to him which came from his immersion in the hard world of Labor politics. I grew to understand this necessary element in his make-up. We played tennis together regularly and he was a great friend and mentor to me in these formative years.

On arrival at university I had joined the Labor Club, but became cynical during 1947 about its right to the title of 'Labor', since its sympathy for the Communist Party seemed to lead to regular attacks on the Australian Labor Party. I left the Club in 1947 and the next year formed and became the foundation President of the first ALP Club at the university. John Toohey succeeded me as President in 1949. I fully supported and argued for the right of communists and their sympathisers to be active in the political life of the university and the country. This was not merely an academic issue, for by 1951 the Prime Minister, Robert Menzies, was seeking to ban the party. But I was not then, nor at any later stage of my political career, prepared to translate their liberty to be heard into a licence to subvert the Australian Labor Party.

There were hardly enough hours to accommodate the range and

intensity of my interests at university. In sport I represented the University Firsts in both cricket and baseball. After finishing my Law degree, I worked for a few months as a trainee executive with the Vacuum Oil Company but returned to university full-time during 1951 to pursue an Arts degree, majoring in Economics, and to immerse myself more in student politics. This led to my election at the end of 1951 as President of the Guild and, as such, the representative of the student body on the Senate of the university.

By this time Hazel had well and truly entered and was sharing my life. We had become aware of each other through our active involvement in the Congregational Youth Fellowship, but it was for me a distant awareness. I learned later that Hazel was acutely embarrassed by her then rather pimply complexion, but she was there in the back of my mind as a strong and pretty face and – a lustful assessment I've never had cause to change – she had one of the most beautiful pairs of legs I had ever seen.

As I settled into the committed mode of 1948 I began to feel I needed a companion with whom I could share my new purpose and ambition. One bright, clear, winter Sunday, I remembered this vibrant girl, and told Ellie I thought I would ask her to come for a trip to the hills on the Panther – now carefully and, on Ellie's part, reluctantly, resurrected as a necessary part of my university studies. Ellie had already got to know Hazel better than I and I noted with pleasure and some amusement my mother's enthusiastic endorsement of my interest in Hazel, for she had, quite independently, formed a high opinion of her. I rang Hazel, who accepted with an alacrity which flattered me, and so began our partnership. Our mutual attraction and infatuation quickly blossomed into a love which withstood incredible pressures and which sustained me through the highs and lows of a supercharged existence. My passion for her was enhanced by the knowledge that I had acquired a remarkably talented partner.

Hazel was the daughter of Jim Masterson, a self-employed accountant–auditor, and his wife, Edith Laura, a resolute but unpretentious woman. Hazel and her sister Ede enjoyed a loving family environment. Unlike me, she was not encouraged to develop her undoubted academic talents. Her father was a man of quiet good works with whom I was never really comfortable. He was politically conservative, with a traditional view of the role of women. Hazel had been dux every year at school but after three years of secondary education with a commercial emphasis, she was channelled into a position as a secretary–bookkeeper with a small electrical engineering firm. But I was aware, once she came to mix with me in university circles, that she knew she could have easily handled the demands of tertiary education.

We became engaged in early 1950 and our plans for a future together became enmeshed in our ambition for me to win the Rhodes Scholarship. I missed out in my first attempt at the end of 1951 and Hazel agreed that I should try again in 1952, knowing that this would delay by another year the date of our marriage, since in those days Rhodes Scholars had to be single. As she has so frankly written in her autobiography, she underwent the trauma of an abortion in the early part of 1952 so that our plans for the future could go ahead. She showed great courage as she handled the nagging fear of sterility which was with her until the birth of our beautiful daughter Susan nearly five years later.

Hazel identified with my idealism and with much of what I was doing at this time, particularly my work with overseas students. One of the things which impelled me to join the Labor Party was excitement about the massive immigration program that the Federal Labor Government had initiated under the direction of Arthur Calwell. I was passionately convinced of the economic and humanitarian correctness of this policy, and believed it was the responsibility of all Australians to make these newcomers welcome. One aspect of Australia's opening up to the world, and particularly to the region around us, was the access to our universities which it gave to Asian students. Growing numbers of them were coming to the University of Western Australia, especially from Ceylon, Malaya and Singapore.

I was disturbed by the lack of warmth shown to these students, and the loneliness of their lives seemed at least as much our loss as theirs. Hazel joined with me in inviting them to our homes and sharing meals with them in their friendless lodgings. From this experience I moved to establish an International Club within the university, which created, I believe, a much more congenial relationship between students of various nationalities on the campus.

At the end of 1952 I applied again for the Rhodes Scholarship and entered the contest as red-hot favourite, but my confidence was shaken when I reached the final stage. Those of us on the short list gathered at Government House, each ready for his private interview with the selection panel, which was chaired by the Governor, Sir Charles Gairdner. When my turn came things went well until I was asked by a lawyer on the panel what I intended to do after Oxford if I were awarded the scholarship. I said I wasn't sure, but explained that it would be some sort of public service, although not necessarily as a civil servant, and not as a lawyer. This answer did not satisfy him and he repeated the question somewhat tersely. I apologised, saying that I couldn't honestly add to what I had already said. For some reason this annoyed him intensely. My answer simply wasn't good enough, he said, and he put the question to me again. I was worried but by now I was also annoyed. Thinking that I was probably blowing it, I turned to the Governor and said, 'I'm sorry, Your Excellency, I have answered the question truthfully and to the best of my ability without concocting what may be perceived as an acceptable response. I resent the suggestion that I'm avoiding the question and the implication that I'm not being honest, and intend to add nothing more.' The Governor turned the questioning to other matters and the interview soon came to an end. I was shown out to the waiting room.

When all the interviews were over, we marked time anxiously while the committee concluded its deliberations. When the Secretary emerged and said they wished me to come in, I had an overwhelming sense of elation, tempered immediately by the awful thought that perhaps they were going to deliver me a reprimand before calling on the winner. The quick congratulations of the Secretary dispelled this fear. My joy was complete when the Governor strode forward, took me aside and whispered in my ear, as only an English officer and gentleman could, 'Hawke, I thought on the papers you were the one, but any doubt I may have had was removed by the way you dealt with that blithering idiot!'

Soon after winning the scholarship, I went as a member of the Australian delegation to the World Conference of Christian Youth at Kottayam in the southern Indian state of Travencore–Cochin (later Kerala). My years at university had not destroyed my faith but had made me more uncertain and inclined to quest after the truth. I enjoyed as much as any other intellectual pursuit the countless hours spent in animated discussion and argument with Roman Catholic friends. They included John Toohey, Bob Rogers, a tutor in the English Department, and Selwyn Graves, a senior lecturer in Philosophy and a convert to Catholicism. Against the laxness, almost ambivalence, of the Congregational creed, I found the certitude of Catholic doctrine fascinating but intellectually unacceptable. At another level I spent hours in absorbing discussion with the Hindus and Buddhists among my new Asian friends, intrigued by their central tenet of reincarnation.

I found this concept philosophically attractive but politically stultifying. Under the Judaeo-Christian doctrine an individual's eternal eggs are all in the one basket of a single fleeting existence in the infinity of time, which is tough on the unredeemed sinner and a real dud hand for those who go through life without ever hearing God's message. Against this, the concept of recurring opportunity and perfectibility through time seemed to me to make much more sense. But at the same time, in political terms, reincarnation was a recipe for inertia; the lot of the poor and underprivileged was predetermined, therefore it was not for them or the community to change it in this life.

It was not surprising then that the visit to India became another turning point in my life. It marked the beginning of the end of my belief in the organised Christian religion. Some three hundred delegates from around the world had gathered in a centre of Christian influence and affluence which was unique in India. Christianity in this region dated back to the mission of St Thomas in the first century. The communists were stronger here than anywhere else in India because, paradoxically, the Christian schools had helped to create the highest level of literacy in the country. Communist Party literature was everywhere and it was cheap; in addition to propaganda, beautifully bound Russian classics were available at one twentieth of the price of a Bible. The communists had organised a huge rally and an edict went out from the conference organisers that delegates were to have nothing to do with it. I ignored this directive, went to the rally and was taken up on the dais to meet the leaders. Their appeal to the masses was evident and I predicted then, accurately, that Kerala would be the first communist state in the British Commonwealth.

Just a few days after the rally, Christmas celebrations began, and two things happened to complete my disenchantment. A great feast was held in the grounds of the Bishop's residence where, under the eyes of hundreds of poor villagers staring in through the fence, delegates gorged themselves on an array of food. I'm not sure what was going on in their minds, but I know I had no stomach for feasting. Then on Christmas Eve we were invited to parties in the homes of the

Kottayam Christians. People sang hymns and carols but I was appalled by the fervent rendition of 'The World to Christ We Bring, Christ to the World We Bring'. It all seemed so hypocritical; I wandered off into the village.

Although hot during the day, it was cool at night and the people sleeping in the streets had pulled rags around themselves to keep warm. One little kid in particular, with huge eyes in a beautiful face, looked terribly miserable as he lay there next to an older girl. The whole situation suddenly stuck in my gullet. The comfortable Christians in their comfortable houses singing comfortable songs about bringing Christ to the world and the world to Christ, and here was the world. But to the Christians these people seemed totally irrelevant, as the Christians were to them. I went back to the dormitory, grabbed a windcheater and took it down to the girl for her little brother. She put it on him and their eyes lit up as though this was the best thing that had ever happened to them. I kissed them and went back to my bed sick at heart.

Although I talked at length with my parents about the political impressions formed during my visit, and referred to my concerns about the irrelevance of Christianity in India, I did not confide to them my rising sense of alienation. I looked at them with love, knowing how their faith was such a force for good, and I could not bring myself to hurt them by calling into question the basis of their whole lives. I was now aware that my time as a believer in the organised Church was almost at an end. I was sad for any difficulties this would cause Ellie and Clem, but I felt a deep gratitude to them for having instilled in me the basic Christian principles of brotherhood and compassion, which I knew would stay with me for the rest of my life. More than this, Ellie and Clem, on the basis of these principles, had fostered in me beliefs and precepts which were to guide me in my future career. They had an idealistic sense that the world can and should be made a better place, that one should always try to see the good in people, and that the healing of divisions was an important part of life's work. These convictions had become my own.

Meanwhile the Indian experience added zest to the hours of argument about religion and philosophy with Catholic and Asian friends. Our discussions often went late into the night, over many beers. When I told my parents that I had started to drink, I was struck less by Ellie's disappointment than her look of resignation. It seemed to say, 'This was inevitable.' While it was clear they would have preferred it if I had not made this choice, they did not belabour me with their views. Ellie contented herself with the observation that I may not have survived the 1947 accident if my strong body had been polluted by alcohol. For my part I did my best to avoid embarrassing them by evidence of drunkenness.

In 1952, before I had finished my own degree, I was appointed a part-time tutor in the Department of Economics. In August, I arrived in Oxford and for the first time experienced loneliness. I had been a big man on campus in Perth; here I was just another bloody colonial. The university itself was somewhat forbidding; it struck me as ancient and aloof but also as a place of profound sanity. As the memories of that beloved Perth campus came back, the contrast was something like that often made between Sydney and Melbourne. One is like the vivacious woman who throws herself at you and overwhelms with her obvious charms, the other is more refined and with a mysterious attraction which it takes time to explore and fully appreciate.

I had read arguments as to whether University College, my new abode, or another was the oldest college in Oxford. Any doubts vanished as I was taken to my freezing, dilapidated study and cell-like bedroom – nothing could possibly predate this! But I soon came to understand that in the very antiquity of these institutions lies a virtue which more than offsets the physical discomforts they impose upon their transient lodgers. Over the centuries they have been touched by tyranny, have seen and frequently nurtured the spirit of revolution in ideas and action, have observed emperors lose their clothes and outcasts become the source of wisdom. With its liberal tradition, Oxford did not embrace the McCarthyist doctrine which was sweeping the United States and being felt in Australia. McCarthyism promoted guilt by association. At Oxford, it was simply not acceptable to act as though you had said something definitive about a person by citing their politics, race, colour or creed or that of any of their associates.

In this congenial atmosphere I imposed a moratorium on student and party politics, feeling that in one way or another I would be deeply involved in politics on my return to Australia. I started the Bachelor of Arts degree in PPE (Philosophy, Politics and Economics) but in the second term I began to feel frustrated. I seemed to be going over ground already covered in my Australian degrees. The college authorities and the Warden of Rhodes House responded positively when I suggested that my time would be better spent moving on to a second degree which, given the limited time remaining, would have to be a Bachelor of Letters rather than a doctorate.

My immediate commitment to choosing an appropriate area of research gave rise to one of the most bizarre experiences of my whole career, and one that was to have important ramifications in later years. Dr Colin Clark, Director of the Oxford Institute of Agricultural Economics, agreed to be my supervisor when I said I wanted to work in the general area of wage determination in Australia. I had been grateful to find a wealth of material in the library at Rhodes House: full sets of Arbitration Reports, Hansards, the Federation Convention Debates, newspapers of the 1890s covering the disastrous strikes which gave rise to the ALP and arbitration, as well as a wide range of other historical books and material.

No other researcher was mining this treasure trove; as I immersed myself in it with growing excitement, I knew what I wanted to do. The development of the arbitration system and, within it, the instrument of the basic wage, was something uniquely Australian and something which, with my background in law and economics, I was uniquely equipped to research. It was something which had become part of the political and social fabric of our country, and it was virgin territory for a scholar.

I announced to Clark that I had decided that my thesis would be on the development of the federal conciliation and arbitration system, with special reference to the concept of the basic wage. To my amazement he replied, icily, 'That is a matter of no interest to me, and what is more important, it would be of no interest to the University of Oxford.' I could not, then, understand his view and I simply did not believe his declaration about the attitude of the university. I conveyed this to him, succinctly, and left.

Of course, Professor Clark had completely misrepresented the university's position and within a matter of days, with the co-operation of the college and Rhodes House, I secured as supervisor the distinguished Australian, K.C. Wheare, Professor of Government and Public Administration at All Souls. Ken professed his interest, and confessed his innocence of the subject. His enthusiastic suggestion that we would perhaps be able to learn a lot together was put into practice during the rest of my time in Oxford in many hours of lively discussion and over numerous glasses of his dry sherry.

I later discovered the reason for Colin Clark's blatantly dishonest attempt to divert me from this area of research. He had been an economic adviser to the Queensland Government in Australia and, after converting to Catholicism, had embraced the philosophy of the National Catholic Rural Movement (NCRM). Dr Clark had, in fact, been the architect of a framework of economic policies built upon the central tenet of less industrialisation and a massive program of intensive land settlement supported by the concept of 'many more peasants from abroad'. He saw the abandonment of the long-standing system of quarterly automatic adjustments to the basic wage as essential to beating the enemy of inflation. All of this was expounded to and developed with B.A. Santamaria, head of the NCRM, who in turn had the ear of Sir Raymond Kelly, then Chief Judge of the Arbitration Court. A fellow judge, Alf Foster, told me later that Santamaria 'wore the carpet thin' to Kelly's office in the period before the Bench, presided over by Kelly in 1953, gave effect to Clark's prescription by abolishing the adjustment system. Years after I left Oxford, I was able as advocate for the Australian Council of Trade Unions (ACTU) to demolish that fatuous judgment in the Arbitration Commission.

But here I was in early 1954, totally unaware of Clark's deep involvement in this recent travesty, announcing that I wanted to research the fixation of the basic wage, a matter in which he coldly asserted 'no interest'. The last thing Colin Clark wanted was a bright and committed young fellow probing the ground he had contaminated. He sought subsequently to divert attention from his own dishonesty by denigrating my work as a scholar, a tactic later adopted with filial devotion but equal disregard for the facts by his son, Professor Gregory Clark.

I now entered a period of unique pleasure in my life. I was at Oxford on my own terms, literally, for I proceeded to cram the equivalent of two terms work into each of the two non-summer terms, until the end of 1955. The library at Rhodes House became my den from early in the morning until its close in the late afternoon, and the more I dug into this untapped resource the more enthralled I became with my new area of work. For the first time, I passed over that exquisite line in academic endeavour where study becomes pure joy, free of drudgery and duty. It would be an exaggeration to speak in terms of feeling some guiding force, but in a vague, indefinable way I had a sense that my past had prepared me for this task and that my future was being inexorably shaped by what I was doing now.

I have always possessed a strong hedonistic streak, but following the events of late 1947, I had often felt a tension between my enjoyment of extra-curricular activities and the commitment to academic excellence. That tension was now replaced by an energising sense of balance. Study itself had become a source of unalloyed happiness. The knowledge that I could structure my time into long, productive hours from which I gained a total confidence in my mastery of the subject made any time away from study a period of undiluted pleasure.

Hazel had joined me at the end of 1953, and in addition to deriving satisfaction from her secretarial job at the Institute of Statistics, she became immersed in my work, particularly through typing my drafts. By the time she had typed and retyped all the drafts of my thesis, she was the second most knowledgeable person in the world on the Australian arbitration system!

Summer was a time of relaxation. In 1955, one of the all-time great English summers, I played cricket nearly every day. The previous year had been less accommodating but memorable, for I had had the privilege of being selected to go on tour against the Counties and the Marylebone Cricket Club with the Oxford team, captained by Colin Cowdrey. Although I never got beyond twelfth man, I realised every young cricketer's dream by fielding at Lords for a day when one of our team was out of action. Hazel and I travelled widely through England and Europe in a little van we had bought. We were poor and did it on the cheap, but were idyllically happy in those weeks spent soaking up the delights of a Europe which was still, in many ways, as it had been before the war. As a member of the Royal Air Force Volunteer Reserve Squadron attached to the university I also learned to fly and, under the influence of my instructor, who had been the RAF aerobatic champion, engaged in acts of lunacy over the Cotswolds.

In more down-to-earth fashion I inadvertently achieved notoriety as a result of one of the quaint and ancient customs of my college. A system operated at dinner in the Great Hall under which if an offence was committed – in my case coming to dinner without a gown (some bastard had 'borrowed' mine) – one was 'sconced'. This meant having to drink two and a half pints of ale out of an antique pewter pot in less than twenty-five seconds. Failure to do so involved paying for the first drink, plus another two and a half pints. My chance of avoiding payment lay in downing the ale within the limit and hoping that the Sconcemaster – the President of the Junior Common Room – could not beat my time. I was too broke for the fine and necessity became the mother of ingestion. I downed the contents of the pot in eleven seconds, left the Sconcemaster floundering, and entered the Guinness Book of Records with the fastest time ever recorded. This feat was to endear me to some of my fellow Australians more than anything else I ever achieved.

In January 1956 I presented my thesis and, in a brief appearance before the examiners, was proud to be told that it was a first-class piece of work. Reproduced later that year in an abridged form in an Australian academic journal, it remains the standard reference on the subject.

Hazel and I married in Perth in March 1956 then left for Canberra, where I had a scholarship to do further research towards a doctorate in the Law Department at the Australian National University. My arrival constituted a 50 per cent increase in the faculty which consisted of Dr Sam Stoljar, a wise and learned man who became a dear friend, and the Dean, Professor Geoffrey Sawyer, a man of boundless energy and breadth of interests, who also became a friend as well as a supervisor. Geoff encouraged my desire to pursue research at a practical level. I sought and received permission to attend a Special Congress of the ACTU called in 1956 to consider the trade unions' approach to the basic wage after the Arbitration Court's refusal that year to review the 1953 decision. The ACTU was responsible in these major cases for setting the wages framework for Australia. Decisions in the federal tribunal tended to be reflected, directly or indirectly, in the State jurisdictions.

I immediately felt at ease with the friendly yet serious and committed men of the ACTU. The officers sat me on the platform, where I was able to meet all the leading players; they took the opportunity to explore the extent of my knowledge about the basic wage. Out of this came an invitation to assist them in an honorary capacity in the preparation for the 1957 Basic Wage Case. With Professor Sawyer's permission I helped prepare material for Dick Eggleston, the brilliant Melbourne barrister who was then appearing for the ACTU. I worked with a young Economics tutor from the University of Melbourne, Keith Hancock, who, in an intriguing turn of the circle, went on to become a Professor of Economics, Vice-Chancellor of Flinders University and who, thirty years after our joint initiation, was appointed Deputy President of the Australian Industrial Relations Commission by my Government in 1987.

After providing assistance again, in the 1958 Basic Wage Case, I was invited to attend an ACTU dinner at Ushers' Hotel in Sydney. During the evening the President, Albert Monk, manoeuvred the chairs in the lounge bar so that he was sitting next to me. Albert was a reserved man from whom any show of affection was unusual, but he moved closer and put his arm around me. What he had to say was a bolt from the blue – he wanted me to abandon university and come to work full-time at the ACTU as its research officer and advocate.

I thanked him and asked for time to discuss the offer with Hazel and Geoff Sawyer, but my instincts were to accept. The drawbacks were obvious. Hazel and I were living comfortably in a university flat with our beautiful new baby daughter, Susan. My research was going well, I was lecturing part-time in Law at the Canberra University College and had already received interesting offers of permanent academic employment. Accepting the ACTU job would mean not completing the doctorate. It would require us, a couple of small-town kids, accustomed to the cosiness of Perth, Oxford and Canberra, to move to the big unknown of Melbourne.

But here was the chance to bring together in the most practical way all my academic experience in a job in which I could exercise my talents and give expression to my deepest social and political convictions. It would take me into the heart of the labour movement and it would fit precisely the concept of public service I'd had in mind but could not specify to the 'blithering idiot' on the Rhodes selection committee. It was, I sensed, a point of destiny. Hazel and Geoff shared this view. Within weeks we had packed and were on our way to Melbourne, where we would live until, twenty-five years later, we returned to Canberra to live in the Lodge.

11
SERVING THE LABOUR MOVEMENT

FOUR

Thoughts of a future political career in Canberra were, however, far from our minds as we settled into a very modest weatherboard cottage near the beach at Sandringham, financed by the advance of a year's salary as deposit. As a twenty-eight-year-old student, I had no savings and some debt. Life was frugal – Hazel made cupboards out of boxes, we slept on a mattress on the floor and made do with an antiquated, inefficient refrigerator. Hazel enjoyed the new physical environment, which was important, for I was immersed in the challenge of my job.

The Melbourne I came into at the end of the 1950s was the epicentre of the convulsions which had torn the Australian labour movement apart. On the political side, the split had been formalised by the creation of the Democratic Labor Party (DLP). Blessed by Archbishop Daniel Mannix and strategically directed by B.A. Santamaria, the DLP, while not exclusively the preserve of Roman Catholics, could not have survived as a potent political force without the comfort and support provided by the hierarchy of the Church in Victoria.

Santamaria and his Movement believed that the Australian Labor Party was being subverted by the growth of communist influence and control in the trade unions; they formed the DLP when convinced they could not win their fight against communism within the existing political structure. On the industrial side, the Movement kept up an incessant fight against the communists and those ALP officials whom they regarded as co-operative with or sympathetic to communism. Despite some talk of establishing an alternative central body, unions controlled by supporters of the Movement had remained affiliated to the ACTU.

This Melbourne was a cauldron of hatred, a witches' brew of loaded labels, mindless epithets and raw sectarianism. Families were split, with brother set against brother or father, officials within the same union regarding each other as mortal enemies, worshippers in the same Church treated by their co-religionists as lepers, while to be a Mason was to wear a badge of honour in the Victorian branch of the ALP, soon to be guided by the unlovely hands of William Hartley.

The red-brick ACTU headquarters in Lygon Street, Carlton, sat squarely in the middle of this, directly opposite the Trades Hall and immediately between the two segregated hotels – the Lygon (later the John Curtin), home to those trade union officials who were ALP supporters, and the Dover, inhabited by the 'Groupers', members of the Industrial Groups. The Groupers were the industrial battle squads of the Movement, and adherents of the DLP.

I arrived in May of 1958 and was immediately fascinated. The fascination was mutual, with a good dash of scepticism on the part of many of the denizens of this combative environment about whether the young fellow from the groves of Academe would have what it takes. I decided that part of what it would take was not to remain in the seclusion of my office but to mix freely with them in the pub and to visit the factories and workplaces they represented.

The response was quick, warm and genuine, leading to friendships which have lasted a lifetime. I was struck particularly by the phenomenon of the generational 'opportunity gap'. I met scores of older trade union officials of outstanding intellectual abilities who had never had the opportunity to develop their talents at a university; indeed, many of them had received no formal education beyond primary school. These men had been denied the chance to become the surgeons, barristers, engineers or bio-chemists they undoubtedly could have been, but their natural endowments and determination had seen them emerge as prominent trade union leaders.

I think of people like Stan Willis, father of Ralph, who was to become my first Research Assistant and go on to a distinguished parliamentary career. Stan was the gentlest and most self-effacing of men, with a vast and well-read library. He was a worker at the Newport Railway Workshops and a part-time official with the Victorian branch of the Boilermakers' Union who had made himself an internationally recognised authority on industrial deafness. To talk philosophy, politics or religion with Stan was as rewarding as any conversation with an academic; what's more, he was a man whose learning and wisdom was no end in itself, but a backdrop to his constant efforts to help the cause of working men and women.

I think, too, of three communists, each in his way a giant of the trade union movement. One was Jim Healy, the General Secretary of the Waterside Workers' Union. Jim's political philosophy and power in the postwar union movement were a product of his searing experiences on the waterfront during the Depression, when desperate men were forced to offer the favours of their womenfolk in return for a day's employment. He was tough, eloquent, acutely intelligent, charismatic and, as the employers in his industry testified, a man of his word. On the anvil of those experiences where he had witnessed the degradation of the human spirit under an unbridled and uncaring capitalist system, Jim Healy had shaped an intellectual commitment to the philosophy of communism. Moreover, his commitment to the working class was not circumscribed by political prejudice. My last memory of him was in the back bar of the Lygon Hotel. We were having a beer together when, to the amazement of all present, in walked John Maynes, Secretary of the Clerks' Union, hated by the patrons of the Lygon as an arch Grouper. Maynes wanted to talk to Healy about benefits for his members on the waterfront which might arise from negotiations Jim had recently completed. The troops wanted to throw Maynes out, but Jim quietened them, invited John to sit down with us and proceeded to advise him on how to get the best deal for his members.

Another great man was Alec McDonald, who had risen through the ranks to become Secretary of the Queensland Trades and Labour Council and, in that capacity, was a member of the ACTU Executive. Alec, like Jim Healy, was respected across the trade union spectrum and among employers for his intelligence, hard work and the integrity of his negotiating word. He was a thoughtful man with profound analytical powers. From him I derived deep insights into the character of the labour movement. His sheer ability, warmth of personality and sense of humour were sufficient to deflect the barbs of those who felt they had made some contribution to affairs by simply labelling him a communist.

The atheist in him would hate me saying it, but when the gods made George Seelaf they threw away the mould. In the world of rough diamonds, George, Secretary of the Victorian branch of the Meat Industry Employees' Union, was surely the uncut Koh-i-noor. Balding, beetle-browed, hairy-armed and normally looking as though he had just marched off a shift at an abattoir, George never appeared remotely comfortable in anything more formal than slacks and an open-necked shirt. He could murder a suit faster than anyone I've ever known, with the possible exception of Sir Peter Abeles. Some leaders of the Left had to work hard at showing their identity with the workers they claimed to represent. Not George. He was an authentic working-class man, with a passionate commitment to workers in general and the underprivileged in particular. In the time before Medibank and Medicare, he pioneered the concept of health clinics in Footscray where his community work, which he continued to his last days despite the ravages of cancer, had elevated him to god-like status. He was a man of irrepressible good humour and broad vision, as much at ease with professors and captains of industry as he was with the roughest slaughterman. He was always ready to see the good, even in his toughest opponents, and was as close to a secular saint as I have met.

I could never accept the political philosophy of these men, although I can imagine that had I been a young man in the Depression I could well have been a communist. But I hadn't, and instead I enjoyed countless hours of spirited debate with them over more beers than I care to remember. It was a common but nevertheless mindless denigration to simply pin the tag 'communist' on them without bothering to understand either the roots of their conviction or the depth of their commitment to the cause of ordinary working people. To their credit, there were those among their opponents – like John Maynes – who had some understanding of these things.

Besides the men of the Left, there were many across the spectrum, all the way to the far Right, who were clear-cut examples of the generational opportunity gap. Clyde Cameron, boss of the Australian Workers' Union in South Australia and later a federal minister, promoter and then denigrator of both Gough Whitlam and myself, was one who, given the chance, could have been as brilliant a barrister as any in the land. It would have been easy, and natural enough, for these men of great capacity to have a sense of frustration and even bitterness at this new arrival, who had spent more than a decade in three universities developing his skills. But there was none of this.

With a marvellous generosity of spirit, they shared their knowledge and understanding of their industries and of the labour movement with me. They became my tutors and my friends.

Nevertheless, as I began my preparation for the 1959 Basic Wage Case, there was still plenty of scepticism about me in various quarters. Tom Doherty, General Secretary of the Australian Workers' Union (at that stage unaffiliated with the ACTU) ran a headline in *The Worker*: 'From Eggleston to Egghead'; while Judge Foster, sitting on his first basic wage Bench since 1950, got a backdoor message to Albert Monk complaining that he deserved to have the services of senior counsel, not some whippersnapper just out of university. In spite of this my confidence was undiminished; I had faith in my own knowledge and ability and in the assistance I was receiving from three outstanding economists: Horrie Brown and Dr Wilf Salter of the Australian National University, and Professor Eric Russell of the University of Adelaide. By the end of the first day of the case I had the doubtful Judge Foster on side and was enjoying the undivided attention of the whole Bench.

In the event I was able to destroy the legal and economic under-pinning of the 1953 decision which had abolished the automatic adjustments of the basic wage. It was a particular pleasure to demolish in the process the employers' witness, who had been trotted out year after year to give a thoroughly misleading story about company profits and whose evidence up to this point had been uncritically endorsed by the court. The judges accepted that their embrace of the vague concept of 'capacity to pay' had allowed the real value of the basic wage to be eroded in a period of substantial economic growth. Without being prepared formally to restore automatic quarterly adjustments, they did the equivalent by increasing the basic wage by fifteen shillings, bring-ing it above what it would have been if the adjustment system had still applied.

The decision was a massive breakthrough for the trade union movement and was welcomed enthusiastically. My reputation as a tough and
effective advocate was soon enhanced by winning in the 1959 Margins
Case, a 28 per cent increase in the award payments above the basic
wage paid for various levels of skill and experience.

In one year I had achieved my fundamental aim of persuading the
judges to rethink their approach to wage fixation. They had seen wages
essentially as a cost and made decisions almost exclusively on that basis.
My philosophy and my advocacy was based on making them understand that wages are both an income and a cost – an income to the
worker and a cost to the employer. In an economy that was growing in
real terms, it was essential that wages – the only source of income for
the overwhelming majority of workers – should reflect that real growth
if those workers were to share in the growing prosperity of the nation.
By definition, the only way that could be done was to adjust wages for
both productivity *and* prices. The real value of wages must decline if
they were adjusted only for productivity while prices which rose faster
than productivity were ignored. This seemed to me to be a matter of
basic fairness and equity, and I was delighted that I had convinced the
court. In fact, with one exception[2], this principle was consolidated in all
subsequent cases.

Some of the cases had their rough, tough and tense passages.
Justice Frank Gallagher, who became a dear friend, boiled over with
annoyance on one occasion, calling me 'a Domain Demosthenes and
Hyde Park Cicero' – a flourish of rhetoric which later often gave us
reason for a good laugh together. As an advocate I favoured none of the
niceties and euphemisms beloved by lawyers when gently suggesting
an alternative interpretation, or even the possibility of error, to the
Bench. I was enraged by the enormous injustice done to Australian
workers by the 1953 decision, and as the representative of those
workers, I did not feel it within me in those early days to go beyond the

necessary formalities of respect. The Arbitration Court had been manipulated at workers' expense to give effect to an absurd and covert agenda. Its President, Dick Kirby, was innocent of this agenda, but his initial sensitivity to my harsh and uncompromising advocacy changed to a feeling of horror at what had been done. He became determined to redress the wrong. He and his colleagues seemed to sense the cause of my uncompromising passion and became prepared to listen and, as they openly conceded, to learn. The arbitration judges were, with some exceptions, good men. Dick (later Sir Richard) Kirby, was an outstanding Australian.

Any trace of scepticism among officials or members of the trade unions vanished as a result of the 1959 Wage and Margins Cases and I was the new young hero who had turned the system around; they had been going backwards but they now had a chance within the arbitration system to get a share of the increasing real output they were helping to create. I felt a passionate identity with these ordinary Australian people whom I was representing.

They wanted my time, my advice and my company, and they wanted, by sharing themselves and their experience, to have some part in shaping the perceptions and attitudes of a young man who they believed had a future in the labour movement. For my part, I welcomed their interest and enjoyed their adulation. I responded freely to their wishes and to the growing number of invitations from labour groups and organisations in the wider community. Sudden national hero status is not the easiest thing to handle and certainly my behaviour at times was excessive and unintelligent. I did not realise then how much strain I was putting on Hazel and my family – which had expanded with the arrival of Stephen in 1959 and Rosslyn in 1960 – by giving so much time to the labour movement. Nevertheless, Hazel grew to appreciate the importance of the vast network of friends and contacts I built up during this period.

My total commitment to the labour movement made it easy to knock back the financially attractive offers I received from the time of my first successes in 1959. The only temptation to quit the industrial scene to which I succumbed came as a request from the ALP to stand as the candidate for Corio in the 1963 federal election. Labor had come within two seats of winning in 1961 and it was suggested that I had an obligation to use my high profile to try to win the seat from the Liberal incumbent and sporting legend, Hubert Opperman.

The gods were not smiling on Labor but they had a generous grin for me. Against a national 3 per cent swing away from Labor I gained 3 per cent in Corio, not quite the 3.4 per cent needed to win, with my lead over Opperman on primary votes overtaken by the distribution of DLP preferences. During the campaign I witnessed at first hand the hysteria generated by the DLP in this awful period of Labor history. One Saturday afternoon a group of us attended the opening of a new Catholic hall with Senator Pat Keneally, the ALP leader in the Senate. Pat was profoundly anti-communist and a devout Catholic, but had spurned approaches to leave the party and join the DLP. As we walked through the crowd, a group of young children hissed at him: 'Communist, communist!' With tears in his eyes, Pat, famous for his stammer, said to me, 'My G-G-God, Bob, look w-what it's come to.' My heart went out to him, as well as to those poor brainwashed kids.

With Labor losing the election, the result in Corio was the best possible outcome for me. I would have been totally frustrated by years in Opposition. As it was, I had shown some capacity as a vote-winner, done my duty by the party and was now able to return to the work which I loved and which was to prove an infinitely better training ground for high office than the sterility of the Labor Opposition benches in Canberra.

After the jubilant successes of 1959, 1966 was the most crucial of my years as research officer and advocate. In 1965 a majority of judges,

Gallagher, Sweeney and Nimmo, had rebuffed the presiding judge, Kirby, with a judgment that matched the 1953 decision for sheer intellectual incompetence in every area it touched: law, economics and the role of the court. Even the employers, who liked the decision (a six shilling increase in margins) were embarrassed, I thought, by the shoddy reasoning which permeated the judgment. I steeped myself in that judgment as I had in no other and determined to destroy it. It abandoned the new principles established in 1959. Further, I found it utterly offensive that a decent man like Kirby had been publicly humiliated by such a low-grade piece of work. A great wrong had been done and I was determined, from the depths of my soul, to rectify it.

The 1966 case did not start propitiously. The employers' counsel, Jim Robinson – a dour opponent in court but a drinking partner and good companion at the end of proceedings – began to make hay with the report of the Vernon Committee of Economic Inquiry. This committee had been chaired by Sir James Vernon of CSR and consisted of two of Australia's leading economists, Sir John Crawford and Professor Peter Karmel, and two businessmen, K.B. Myer and D.G. Molesworth. Menzies, who had appointed the committee in 1963, tabled its voluminous report in September 1965. The section on wages was manna from heaven for Jim Robinson. It expounded the theory he had been advancing to the court that wages should be adjusted for productivity alone and not prices – the antithesis of the principles I had persuaded the commission[3] to accept. The Vernon Committee's central argument supporting this position was that in the period in which adjustment for prices had not occurred, wages had nevertheless retained a stable share of national income.

Jim embraced the committee's wisdom, extolling the expertise, experience and independence of these wonderful men and creating the impression that the commission would be derelict in its duty if it did not accept their view. The Bench consisted of Wright as presiding judge,

Gallagher from the 1965 majority, Moore and Commissioner Terry Winter. They were undoubtedly impressed by Jim's argument. Our position looked desperate. I knew that something decisive was required.

Next morning I dropped a bombshell – a request for the right to subpoena the Vernon Committee myself. It was a delicious situation. Poor Jim Robinson had been endowing the Vernon Committee with the wisdom of the ages. He had been asking the Bench to put its trust in them and indeed to base its judgment on their view of the world. Now he was resisting with every argument at his command the simple – and of course quite ingenuous – proposal to give the commission the fullest possible opportunity to hear and test the relevance of that view. The Commonwealth, represented by John Kerr QC, vigorously supported him. The irony of it all was not lost on Mr Justice Wright, formerly a long-time employers' counsel, whose sardonic wit was often directed now at his erstwhile clients. I felt confident of getting his vote. I could see I had no chance with Judge Moore, and realised that it all turned therefore on Judge Gallagher who, as the representative of the 1965 majority, had been on the receiving end of my sharpest invective. To his everlasting credit Gallagher voted with Wright to grant my application.

The atmosphere in the packed-out courtroom was electric on 27th May when Sir James Vernon entered the box. In addition to the array of barristers already at the table, Sir James had been provided with two Queen's Counsel, the formidable Jack Smythe, regarded as the pre-eminent counsel on the rules of evidence, and Hal Wootten, together with a number of junior counsel. Those rules of evidence precluded me from cross-examining Sir James Vernon, my own witness, and the morning was taken up with a continuous series of mostly successful objections from Smythe.

By lunchtime my colleagues were frustrated and crestfallen. I urged them to have confidence because I thought I had detected a hint of annoyance on Sir James' part when Smythe, in objecting to an economic question I had put to the witness just before lunch, said to the Bench, 'That is like asking a plumber a question about medicine.' After all, Sir James had agreed to head up a Committee of Inquiry into *the economy* and I thought he would have found the analogy repugnant and the excessive protection offensive.

My intuition was right; I learned subsequently that over lunch Sir James had exploded with anger and told his counsel he was prepared to answer any relevant questions I put to him. That was all we needed. He was an honest witness and by the end of my examination, he had conceded that the committee was wrong on its central point of the stability of the wages share, which had in fact been eroded. The employers rested their hopes on Professor Karmel and let it be known that the eminent economist would put the brash young advocate in his place.

Karmel was also, of course, totally honest and he quickly confirmed that he agreed with every concession Sir James Vernon had made to me. It was all over. I had fulfilled the promise to myself to destroy the 1965 judgment, and in the decision handed down in 1966, the Bench reinstated the principle that wage adjustments must take account of movements in both productivity and prices, a principle never seriously questioned since that time. My undiluted pleasure at this outcome was enhanced by the fact that Ellie and Clem had been in court to witness the travail and the triumph.

For much of the rest of 1966 and early 1967 I was back and forth to Papua New Guinea conducting a case for indigenous public servants in what was still a colony of Australia. I acted for the Territory Public Service Association, which was seeking by arbitration to lift pay scales for a group of employees – Local Officers – which had been set at as little as one-third of those for Europeans doing the same job. This was one of the most stimulating experiences of my whole career, for in addition to learning about the economy of the country I had to establish a proficiency in anthropology, nutrition and the politics of emerging nationalism. In this latter respect I was privileged to have as witnesses and friends the men, including Michael Somare, who were in the process of forming the PANGU party and who were to become the leaders of their new nation in 1976. Although I was disappointed at the marginal improvements we achieved in the ratio of Local Officers' wages to those of their white counterparts, things were never the same again in Papua New Guinea. Albert Mara Kiki, who was to be the foundation President of PANGU, told me: 'You have taught us to stand up for ourselves. You have given us confidence that we can handle the challenges ahead of us when we get our independence.'

By 1966 I had made up my mind to run for the presidency of the ACTU when Albert Monk retired. No-one could be sure when the taciturn and secretive Albert would leave, and he was not about to cast any light on the matter. He was as old as the century and while it was unlikely he would go before the 1967 biennial Congress, it seemed reasonably certain he would not carry on beyond the next in 1969, given his age and the increasing frailty of his health.

As both Secretary and President of the ACTU, Albert Monk had given remarkable service to the trade union movement and the nation for more than forty years. He was a small, unprepossessing man who never claimed any great intellectual prowess, but he was shrewd and in his younger days had demonstrated personal physical courage in some ugly situations. He did not like taking tough decisions and was not by nature a publicist for the movement. To my mind he made two outstanding contributions which have served as a permanent monument to him within the trade union movement and the nation as a whole. First, he kept the ACTU as the one central trade union organisation against successive threats from the Left and Right to establish rival bodies. This was a tribute to his quiet, patient negotiating skills in times of crisis. Second, he gave strong and courageous support to the Labor Government's massive postwar immigration program against the initial opposition of many sections of the trade union movement. Australian workers had never experienced full employment and it is often forgotten that although the massive 30 per cent unemployment levels of the Great Depression had diminished, unemployment at the outbreak of the Second World War was still at least 10 per cent. Many union leaders and the workers whom they represented saw waves of migrants as threats to jobs that had always been scarce. Without the far-sighted leadership and commitment of Monk, it is arguable that the immigration program would not have been able to assume the proportions which have done so much to change Australia for the better.

Normally Albert was very reluctant to give of himself to others. With his permanently startled-looking eyes darting around behind thick glasses, he erected a defensive barrier which was in fact penetrated by only a few intimate friends. I was not in this category but enjoyed good relations with him and was often the beneficiary – usually after a few drinks in the evening – of his reminiscences about a long and influential history in the labour movement. In this sense Albert was closer to me than to Harold Souter, who would be my rival for the office of President.

Harold Souter was the first Bill Hayden in my life. He was well ensconced as Secretary of the ACTU, after having come up through the tradesmen's ranks to work with the metal trades unions, and seemed destined to take the presidency. He was respected as a hard worker and an assiduous administrator but, like Albert Monk, had few intimate friends among his working colleagues. Unlike Albert, he was a non-drinker and never saw these colleagues in anything other than a working environment. This was undoubtedly a handicap for him in the protracted leadership fight.

Harold could not have been kinder to me and Hazel in the early ACTU days and he was supportive of me professionally. But as time went on he became uncomfortable with the prominence I was attaining, and with his constant reminders that I was an 'employee' not an elected official, he sought to circumscribe the invitations I could accept outside my strictly designated area of responsibility. This pettiness should be set against his largeness of vision when the big chips were down. For example, when I asked permission to subpoena the Vernon Committee, Harold assumed that we would be rivals for Albert's job and that if I succeeded in subpoenaing Vernon, it would be an enormous boost to my stature. Yet he did not hesitate for a moment in supporting me and in fact persuaded Albert Monk, who initially found the idea too radical. He had recognised what was in the best interests of the people we represented and, ignoring his own interests, acted accordingly.

Whenever I sought authority for a particular course of action in my professional duties, I never had reason to believe that personal considerations would override Souter's commitment to our constituents. As for his irritating restrictions, I used to accept them, turn a blind eye or, on what I regarded as really important issues, go to Monk as a court of appeal, depending on the circumstances. Albert hated this but more often than not, after much equivocation, would come down on my side.

He was not on my side in the fight for his succession, which now developed into a tough no-holds-barred contest. It was depicted in most of the press at the time as a straight-out fight between the Left, supporting me, and the Right, behind Harold Souter, but it was never quite as simple as that. On the floor of the Congress I could not win without significant support from the Right and, to the limited extent one could speak of such a category, the non-aligned.

The split between the Left and Right in the labour movement in those days had an intensity which makes the spats of today look like kid's stuff. Ideology laced with sectarianism makes a poisonous brew. The Victorian branch of the ALP was by definition 'Left' because the 'Right' had defected to the DLP, and politics in that State were still very much cast in the mould created by the split of the fifties. There was no doubt where I stood on that matter but this did not mean that I embraced the fanaticism of the Bill Hartleys, George Crawfords and their ilk, nor that I was prepared to bar myself from fraternising with those from the Right whose merit I recognised and whose company I enjoyed. This was particularly relevant in NSW, where Santamaria's attempt to split the ALP had been frustrated mainly by the steadfast opposition of a great Australian, Bishop James Carrol – to my mind, a worthy candidate on that account for canonisation. Carrol's gentle demeanour masked a steely determination to ensure that the Church he loved and the party he respected should not be split asunder in NSW as they had been in Victoria.

Having said this, my campaign lieutenants were all men of the Left. Prominent was Ray Geitzelt, the Federal Secretary of the Miscellaneous Workers' Union, whose dynamism had lifted that union from a marginal position in the industrial and political scene to a vastly increased membership and a pace-setting role in wages and conditions of employment. Ray was a *bête noire* of the NSW Right in general and of its emerging strong man, John Ducker, in particular. It gave me pleasure to be instrumental in gradually transforming a poisonous relationship between these two dedicated servants of the labour movement into one of reasonably cordial co-operation.

Our immediate task was to loosen the Right's dominant hold on the Interstate Executive of the ACTU, which would have the authority to appoint an acting President should Albert step down between Congresses. At the 1967 Congress, Ray Geitzelt toppled the very able

Joe Riordan as representative of the Services Group, and the Executive emerged evenly split at eight-all between the pro-Hawke group on the Left and those for Souter on the Right. This setback became a major disaster for the Right when in February 1969 the right-wing Secretary of the South Australian United Trades and Labour Council, Bill Brown, died and was replaced by the Left's Jim Shannon of the Amalgamated Engineering Union.

Within a month Albert Monk had fired the starter's gun by announcing on 8th March that he would retire at the 1969 Congress. Two days later Harold issued a 'Declaratory Statement', the main thrust of which was to attack 'the attempt by disruptive elements' of the pro-communist Left to take over the ACTU. I issued a statement the following day and, noting that the succession was now a public issue, said,

> It seems the main contenders will be Mr Souter and myself. My opponent has seen fit in these circumstances to issue a statement to the Press, and he refers to a 'pro-Communist alliance front' which seeks to take over the trade union movement. I expect I will receive the support of the Left wing of the movement. I know I will receive the support of many unions not normally classified as being on the Left. I expect Mr Souter will receive the support of unions, or branches of unions, under the control of the extreme Right-wing, including the DLP. I don't expect he will reject that support. Nor do I think the fact of that support says anything about his capacities or incapacities relative to my own for the position of President of the ACTU. I hope that the trade union movement will make its decisions on the basis of assessing our respective capacities. I have always regarded the techniques of guilt by association and the tactic of the smear as abhorrent, and I refuse to resort to it myself.

Smear is an inadequate word to describe the tactic followed by some of Harold's supporters. The worst offender by far was Brian Harradine, then Secretary of the Tasmanian Trades and Labour Council and, in that capacity, a member of the ACTU Executive. I think I have never seen a more fanatical zealot of the Right than Brian at that stage of his career. He viewed everything through the distorting prism of anti-communism and his eyes literally blazed with an anger that made Senator McCarthy look a wimp. He ran an article in Santamaria's *News Weekly* accusing 'certain Left-wing and Communist opponents of Souter' of contributing to the deaths of Bill Brown and Jim Kenney (the Secretary of the NSW Labour Council and Senior Vice-President of the ACTU who had died between the 1967 Congress and the first meeting of the new Executive) and went further by referring on television to the 'psychological murder' of Kenney and Brown. Harradine wisely declined the challenge of Ray Geitzelt, Jim Shannon and Charlie Fitzgibbon to identify them as 'psychological murderers' so that they could sue for defamation. Many on the Right were appalled by his behaviour and I believe that Brian himself, now a much mellower and more likeable independent Senator from Tasmania (he was expelled from the ALP in 1975), would regret that unsavoury contribution from his ultra-fanatical period. Certainly we enjoyed a cordial and co-operative relationship during the whole of my time in Parliament.

The fight for the presidency may not have done much for fraternal goodwill, but it was good for the ACTU coffers. Unions previously reluctant for financial reasons to reflect their full memberships in affiliation dues, suddenly discovered their proper records and many small unions which had not been affiliated were persuaded to join. In the event, 101 more delegates attended the Congress in Sydney's Paddington Town Hall than had been present in 1967, and when they voted on 11th September, I was elected President of the ACTU by 399 to 350.

FIVE

In my acceptance speech to the Congress I said, 'I will not be the President merely of those who worked and voted for me. I will be the President of the whole of the ACTU – equally of those who exercised their democratic right to work for another result ... I will seek genuinely to work in harmony with all sections of this movement.' Many on the extreme Left didn't want to believe this, and many on the Right didn't believe it but, most importantly, I did. Before long, no-one in the labour movement had any reason to doubt that these words were a true reflection of my philosophy.

My broad objective of reconciliation started with Harold Souter. I could not, of course, make him overjoyed at the outcome, although in a strange way, I think he was not entirely unhappy at not having to assume the onerous burden of publicly representing the ACTU in Australia and internationally. I made it clear to him that I valued his commitment to the trade union movement, his diligent work as an administrator, and that I wanted to work in full collaboration with him. He was generous in his response. He told me I was now the boss, that the asperities of the election were behind us, and that I would receive his total support. It would be silly to deny that we had any differences in the ten years before his retirement in 1979, but we were both true to our word, and this was an important element in restoring a greater sense of cohesion in the ACTU.

The 'Hawke eight' on the Executive were Joe Anderson, Federal Secretary of the Painters' Union; Jim Coleman, Secretary of the West Australian Trades and Labour Council; Jack Devereux, head of the Metal Workers; Jack Egerton, President of the Queensland Trades and Labour Council (Alec McDonald had died on the eve of the 1969 Congress); Charlie Fitzgibbon, Federal Secretary of the Waterside Workers' Federation; Ray Geitzelt; Fred Hall, Federal Secretary of the Meat Industry Employees' Union and Jack Petrie, Federal Secretary of the Storemen and Packers' Union.

With Ray Geitzelt, Charlie Fitzgibbon was the driving force of this group. Like Ray, Charlie was another who in a later generation with the appropriate opportunities could have had a brilliant professional career. There were reverse parallels between Charlie's succession to Jim Healey and my own battle for the ACTU presidency. In a bitter fight he had beaten the Left candidate, the communist industrial officer and advocate, Norm Docker. Norm was also a man of outstanding abilities, and after Charlie's victory, they formed the most formidable union negotiating team in the country. They understood the inevitable change occurring in the stevedoring industry around the world, largely as a result of containerisation, and were determined to secure maximum benefits for their dwindling but still industrially strategic membership. They did this with a combination of intellect, meticulous research, education of their members and superb advocacy. It was a pleasure to be associated with them in a number of negotiations and to witness the impact of their professionalism on both the employers' representatives and the arbitral authorities. Charlie was a vibrant, articulate leader whose contributions to debate were always incisive. He was a true internationalist who benefited his own country and beyond.

Cliff Dolan, Federal Secretary of the Electrical Trades' Union, had been a strong supporter of my push for the presidency, but was not successful in gaining a place on the Executive himself until 1971. The NSW Right directed at Cliff the special venom it reserves for those it regards as deserters from the ranks. Formerly part of the establishment in NSW, Cliff had broadened his horizons during the 1960s – a result, in part, of the many nights he spent as our guest in Sandringham, when we would yarn for hours about the issues of the day including, particularly in the earlier period, the war in Vietnam. Perhaps more than anything else this was the catalyst for Cliff's move to the Left. As this journey proceeded over the years, it carried him beyond my own position on a number of issues, and on nothing was this more obvious and painful for each of us than uranium mining and nuclear-powered electricity generation. Cliff often exasperated his friends and invited the derision of his enemies with his long and turgid expositions. But to make judgments on the basis of this characteristic does him less than justice. He laid no claims to being an intellectual, but he was a thinker, and a man of integrity. He was a true friend and a selfless servant of the labour movement.

My respect was not confined to these men of the Left. The Right had people of talent on the Executive, none more outstanding than John Ducker, Secretary of the NSW Labour Council. John was a migrant from Yorkshire with an accent you could cut with an axe. This has only slightly diminished over the years and he is still referred to by friend and foe as 'Bruvver Ducker'. John had worked his way up to Secretary after beginning as an organiser in the Federated Ironworkers' Association. He was a protégé of its Federal Secretary, Laurie Short, himself an object of hate in the extreme Left. John later consolidated his power base by becoming the President of the NSW branch of the ALP.

My first acquaintance with John was when he was a witness in the 1959 Margins Case, one of several people giving evidence on the level and extent of over-award payments in the metal trades industry. I was struck then by his confident, even aggressive, self-assurance and his preparedness to draw a long bow in the interests of those he repre-sented – characteristics which reassured his allies and infuriated his opponents. There was endless speculation whether, if the split had occurred in NSW, John would have found himself in the DLP. To my mind this was an irrelevant puzzle. Despite our many differences on particular issues, I respected his toughness, intelligence, aggressive commitment to the political and industrial labour movement and, not least, his delightful sense of humour and occasionally devastating repartee. He became a good friend and loyal supporter.

I was committed to breaking down the antagonism between the two groups on the Executive which had produced the long period of debil-itating deadlock. I was impartial in the chairing of meetings and in being available for representatives of either side. Where previously they had drunk in separate hotels after meetings, I sought to bring them together, and in fact made a practice of having a dinner during the Executive week at our home in Sandringham, to which they were all invited. This process worked and as time went on, the overwhelm-ing majority of decisions on the ACTU Executive became unanimous.

Another objective was broadening the constituency and role of the ACTU. As to the former, one of the continuing sources of conflict with Albert Monk and Harold Souter had been my increasingly close relationship with the white-collar organisations. I believed they should be dealt with co-operatively as a genuine part of the broad trade union movement and indeed should be encouraged to affiliate with the ACTU. Albert and Harold resisted this all the way, basically, I think, because they were reluctant to change a structure with which they were comfortable and, in the latter stages, because they no doubt suspected it was just part of a power play for the presidency.

Their suspicion was unfounded. When I became President, I set myself the goal of making good the promise of achieving one organically united trade union movement in Australia. We broadened and deepened our areas of co-operation with the Australian Council of Salaried and Professional Associations (ACSPA) and the Commonwealth and Government Employees' Organisation (CAGEO). The goal was achieved with the affiliation to the ACTU of ACSPA at the 1979 Congress and of CAGEO in 1981.

My greatest ally in this endeavour was Barney (Rees) Williams, the Secretary of the Bank Employees' Union in Victoria and the major force in establishing ACSPA. He lived in our street in Sandringham and was Secretary of the local branch of the ALP. I find it difficult to do justice to the greatness of this man. The word selfless can be applied to many people in the labour movement, but in the whole of my experience no-one deserved the description more than Barney. While remaining deeply committed to his family and a devout Catholic, he gave his life to the movement and never sought any personal aggrandisement in return. When unionism was a dirty word in the banking industry, he educated employees into understanding, and the banks into accepting, that there was a relevant and honourable role for workers acting together – an association by any name was still a union, and Barney made it a very effective one indeed. He remained undaunted by the rebuffs he received at the hands of Albert, Harold and others in the ACTU hierarchy and consistently returned rudeness with reason. Without his determination and guiding hand, the movement towards amalgamation of blue- and white-collar workers in Australia could have been aborted or at least greatly prolonged.

Barney Williams' contribution to the political wing of the labour movement was no less significant. He had incurred the wrath of the DLP for remaining loyal to the ALP, a loyalty reflected in years of effort dedicated to keeping the flickering light of the Sandringham branch alive. After the DLP, it was the turn of Bill Hartley and his hard Left cohorts to attack him. Disgusted by their extremes of policy and intolerant sectarianism, including their position against State aid to Catholic schools, Barney become a leading figure in a reform group within the ALP known as the Participants. It was substantially his work which provided the solid basis for Gough Whitlam's intervention, through the Federal Executive, into Victoria in 1971. Without the sacking of the Hartley clique, and its replacement by a more moderate State Executive, the federal Labor victory of 1972 would not have been possible. If there is a pantheon of Labor heroes, Barney Williams deserves his place on one of the higher pedestals.

My determination to expand the activities of the ACTU into the commercial area sprang from a conviction developed during the years as research officer that Australia, under what was now twenty years of conservative rule, had become a society of double standards. Wages are both an income and a cost.[4] Prices similarly are both an income and a cost – income to the employer and a cost to the worker. Our society insisted, in the public interest, that workers justify their claims for increases in wages by going through the legal processes of the arbitration tribunals.[5] On the other hand, businesses were free to set whatever price the market would bear. Competitive theory was stood on its head by the pervasive practice of retail price maintenance, under which manufacturers simply refused to supply retailers who would not undertake to sell at the price set by the manufacturer.

As research officer preparing ACTU economic submissions, I had hammered both the inequity and inefficiency of this situation, urging the Government to outlaw retail price maintenance. The Government always rejected my submissions. I had more success with the Arbitration Commission, which I persuaded to adjust wages for both productivity and prices. But this was a second-best outcome. Much better for workers and the country, and indeed for employers them-selves, if Australia could get a lower price- and cost-structure through a more competitive system.

What I had not been able to achieve by argument as research officer, I was now, as President, in a position to attempt by other means. The opportunity came towards the end of 1970 when Lionel Revelman, owner with his brother George, of Bourkes Store, put a proposal to me that the ACTU enter into a partnership with them. The Revelman brothers were among the first large discounters in Australia. Lionel's proposal was aimed at getting the ACTU's help in breaking the manu-facturers' boycott on Bourkes for refusing to comply with retail price maintenance requirements; in return, Lionel offered the ACTU income and a later opportunity to acquire Bourkes. His proposal also offered new and substantially enlarged accommodation in the Bourkes' building on the corner of Elizabeth and Latrobe Streets, a vast improvement on our poky offices in Lygon Street.

The Executive accepted the proposal and with Bourkes–ACTU I now had an instrument with which to tackle retail price maintenance head-on. During the early part of 1971, I tried to talk reason to the manufacturers. Most of them continued to hold out, supported publicly and privately by the Prime Minister, Billy McMahon, who accused me of 'lawlessness' and made threats about not allowing me 'to run the country'. The most hardline company was Dunlop, headed by its chairman, Eric Dunshea. He refused to budge, so on 17th March, St Patrick's Day, I announced that our affiliated unions would be stopping the movement of all goods to and from the whole group of Dunlop companies in Victoria.

McMahon, long on rhetoric but short on action, turned a deaf ear to Dunshea's plea for support. Within less than two days, Dunshea, on the instruction of his London directors, capitulated and rang to tell me that the Dunlop companies would be supplying our store. I was elated but did not want to embarrass him further. He was kind enough to say about my conduct of the joint press conference held to announce the Dunlop decision:

> I thought he was going to humiliate me and I'd have to sit there while he rubbed salt in my wounds. But he was like a son protecting his own father. He answered most of the questions for me, before the Press could get stuck into me; and he avoided the use of the term 'surrender'. He'd conducted all our negoti- ations as if we were in a boxing ring – everything was in the open, there were no behind-the-door deals. Then, in the hour I dreaded most, he was like that – he made it as gentle, easy and honourable as any person could.[6]

I have never found any satisfaction in humiliating a defeated oppo- nent. The important thing for me was that with the Dunlop decision opposition from all the other non-supplying companies collapsed and I was able to tell Australia that retail price maintenance had been abol- ished. All retailers throughout the country were the beneficiaries; Bourkes–ACTU in the longer run enjoyed no particular prosperity, for the lack of any special commitment to it by trade unionists and its rela- tively unfavourable location told against it. But the great satisfaction was in knowing that through our purposeful action in this joint venture, the ACTU had destroyed a pernicious practice and saved Australians literally hundreds of millions of dollars annually. After the years of frustration it was an exquisite pleasure.

The public clearly approved of this extension of the ACTU role under the new presidency, but it was far more divided on the stand I took later in the year in opposing the Springbok Rugby Union tour of Australia. My revulsion at apartheid and all its manifestations was reinforced by the strong policy position of the International

Confederation of Free Trade Unions to which the ACTU was affiliated. Without the support of all our affiliated unions, and in the face of strong opposition by the McMahon Government, we were not able to stop the tour. But the opposition which we, together with other like-minded groups, were able to engender against the tour meant that no other team from South Africa selected on the basis of racial discrimination ever visited this country again. I coped easily enough with the various forms of abuse, but found it harder to bear the vilification to which our children were subject at school. Hazel and I tried to explain to them the whole range of fears, emotions and mindlessness which go to make up racial prejudice; the repudiation of intolerance became as much a part of their character as ours.

While I was developing the role of the ACTU in these ways, Bill McMahon and his ministers were clamouring for us to stick to industrial matters and stay out of what they were pleased to call 'political issues', which were the sole prerogative of government. I was never prepared to accept this specious dichotomy; as the nation moved into the federal election year of 1972, the hypocrisy of the Government became increasingly apparent as it sought to use me and the ACTU as a stalking horse to meet the threat of an ALP reinvigorated under the leadership of Gough Whitlam.

A protracted dispute with the oil industry over the 35-hour week was exacerbated by the intervention of the Government. McMahon saw the possibility of petrol queues and a breakdown of essential services as an ideal context for calling a 'law and order, who's running the country?' election. He and his ministers urged the oil companies to give no ground, and issued a steady stream of inflammatory anti-union statements; I learned later that he had canvassed with the industry the possibility of using troops to run the refineries but had been warned against it. On the other hand, some of the extreme-Left elements in the unions were more than happy to accommodate this desire for mayhem, as the prospect of a reforming Labor government didn't fit into their ideological scheme of things.

Through all this I was working prodigiously long hours with a bad back. Despite a brief collapse which had me operating from home for a few days, I maintained a constant dialogue with unionists, the commission and certain contacts which I had managed to open up within the oil companies. This was the beginning of my friendship with that great Australian, Ted Harris, former Davis Cup broadcaster, and then a senior executive with Ampol. Ted cleared the way for me to see Mac Leonard, the head of the company. All this paid off, and towards the end of July I was able to announce a plan guaranteeing the maintenance of essential services through the exemption of some refineries from strike action.

This did not suit the Government strategy at all and the Prime Minister arranged a crisis Cabinet to decide whether Parliament should be recalled. So far in Australia's history Parliament had only been recalled for the abdication of Edward VIII, the declaration of war against Japan, and the dispatch of troops to Korea. Even the news media, which were normally supportive of the Government, recognised the proposal as opportunism gone mad. I sensed some uncertainty of purpose when Phillip Lynch, the Minister for Labour and National Service, rang and pleaded that I meet with him in his office. I told him that his Government had been playing politics, were worse than the oil companies and I refused his request, adding that if they believed they could bash us into submission then they had better think again. Lynch rang back suggesting a meeting at a hotel; I responded that if they wanted to see us, then they could do so in the ACTU office. The crisis Cabinet folded, and Lynch with the Attorney-General, Ivor Greenwood, and the Minister for Shipping and Transport, Peter Nixon, were detailed to come to the ACTU.

The embarrassed ministers had to run the gauntlet of a massive media contingent but, once in the meeting, I did not attempt to humiliate them but tried to establish the facts, including the fundamental point that their behaviour was delaying the settlement of the dispute. I asked them to get their noses out of it and let me get on with resolving the matter, which, I said, would be in everyone's interests except perhaps those of their electoral strategists. They conducted themselves well and must have taken the right message back to Canberra. Within a matter of days work in the refineries had been resumed and negotiations in the Arbitration Commission led to a settlement and a new two-year agreement.

Whitlam won the election on 2nd December 1972, ending Labor's twenty-three barren years in Opposition. It was the beginning of a fascinating strand in my period as President of the ACTU. I had supported the 1971 federal intervention in Victoria and had become a Victorian delegate to, and Vice-President of the Federal Executive of the party. In doing so I had incurred the wrath of the Hartley-led Socialist Left, but this was as much a badge of honour as any cause for concern. More important, and certainly at times more difficult, was coming to terms with the fact that the unions, and the ACTU in particular, were no longer the only effective voice of working men and women in Australia. The ALP had been politically neutered for years by its own bitter internal fighting and often irrelevant policies, and had created a vacuum of effective opposition. This had come to be filled by the industrial wing of the labour movement. Whitlam began to change this after his election as Leader in 1967 and, while I had an affection for Arthur Calwell, I welcomed and respected the new sense of purpose and direction. I threw myself into the campaign. Within the party it was recognised that, apart from Gough and the Federal Secretary, Mick Young, no-one worked harder for the long-awaited victory than I.

I had premonitions before the election that, in the euphoria of its occupancy of the Treasury benches, the new Labor Government could neglect the fundamental task of effective economic management. There were already signs that the new Government would not have the advantage of the steady, international, low-inflation economic expansion which had generally provided a congenial environment for growth in postwar Australia. At the last Federal Executive before the election, which we were now confident of winning, I had warned: 'Whatever great social changes you make, and whatever good initiatives you take in the international arena, this Labor Government will live or die on its handling of the economy.'

I buttonholed Gough about the need for him to acquire some economic expertise himself and offered to arrange for people from the ANU to help, arguing that he had a brilliant barrister's mind and would quickly pick up the basic concepts and interrelationships. He toyed with the idea very briefly and then did nothing about it, reminding me that he had economic advisers. This was hardly illuminating information; the whole point of the exercise was for him to be in a better position to evaluate their advice and to play an informed role in economic decision-making. There was no doubting Gough's brilliance, but the simple truth is he was frightened by economics and finance. Mick Young was always amused by the countless hours Gough spent poring over and personally indexing the Parliamentary Hansards. I was more annoyed than amused, believing that this time would have been better spent in the way I had suggested; certainly the Labor Government would have been much less likely to sow the seeds of its own destruction via its fiscal profligacy and the financial scandal of the Loans Affair, which emerged in the absence of an economically knowledgeable and involved Prime Minister.

Early relations between the Whitlam Government and the ACTU were complicated by the personality and prejudices of the Minister for

Labour, Clyde Cameron. He was a man of immense abilities; it is arguable that without his acumen and tough support Gough could not have mounted the successful 1971 intervention in Victoria – the necessary prelude to victory in 1972. Gough owed Clyde, they both knew it and, initially, they both felt that Clyde had received his just reward.

Cameron's talents were great but they were measurable. His capacity for hatred, however, was boundless. I can remember no-one whose personality has been so consumed by hatred, which, along with envy and jealousy, is the most corrosive of all the emotions. He had the trappings to go with it: venomous sarcasm, a deadly sense of humour, a thin smile which played around his mouth and a fascinating capacity to look a person in the eye and, well aware that the person knew he was lying, tell the most outrageous porky.

Clyde had promised the presidency of the Arbitration Commission to his mate Jack Sweeney, a Sydney barrister. I told Clyde this was not on, as the obvious successor to Sir Richard Kirby was John Moore. Moore was the senior Deputy President, with unrivalled experience in major cases and all aspects of conciliation and arbitration; he enjoyed the confidence of unions, employers and governments. Jack Sweeney was a nice fellow and a good lawyer but was not entitled to be mentioned in the same breath as Moore for this critically important position. Clyde, however, would not listen to my arguments and told me the matter was settled. I informed him that the appointment was too vital to be left to his whim and that I would raise the matter with Whitlam. Whitlam accepted my argument, Moore was appointed and Clyde wasn't sure which of us, Gough or me, he hated more, a dilemma he has been wrestling with ever since.

This did not augur well for good working relations between the Government and the ACTU. Cameron's introduction of significant changes to the Conciliation and Arbitration Act in the Parliament without the ACTU having sighted the Bill led to Harold Souter's caustic observation: 'We were better off under the Liberals. At least they used to talk to us first.' The formal structure for consultation was the Australian Labor Advisory Council but it had lapsed into disuse after Whitlam and other ministers made it clear by their lateness or non-attendance that they did not take it seriously.

The final straw for many of my trade union colleagues was Whitlam's 1973 decision to cut tariffs by 25 per cent without a word of prior consultation with the ACTU. I agreed with the principle of the decision and did what I could publicly to support it; I was privately appalled at the Government's political ineptitude in not trying to secure a degree of understanding and support in the trade unions before undertaking such a radical step.

The pressures on me in this sort of situation were compounded by my election as Federal President of the ALP in June of 1973. This was not a duty imposed on me but an honour I sought. I had a keen sense of the distinction of being the organisational head of this great party and Australian institution; and of being, at the age of forty-three, the leader of both the industrial and political wings of the labour movement.

I readily admit I was proud to have the job, but I also believed at the time that I could strengthen relations between the two wings and enhance the ALP's electoral standing through occupying both positions. There was no shortage of contrary opinions and when confronted with them, my reply usually was: 'If you can't ride two horses at once, you shouldn't be in the bloody circus!' Like many glib responses this contained enough substance to subdue some questioners, but it didn't do justice to the genuine concerns held by some of my friends as well as opponents. With the benefit of that most useful analytical instrument, hindsight, I would not now assert with such certainty the merit of holding the two positions simultaneously – at least not for five years, as I did from 1973 to 1978.

Looking back, I still think the advantages outweighed the disadvantages. It was certainly an advantage to be able to go into the critical 1974 double-dissolution election in support of the Whitlam Government in this dual capacity. Although I have mentioned the trade unions' problems with the Labor Government, we were still proud of much of what it had done both domestically and in Australia's international relations. And despite difficulties with Cameron, unionists were indebted to his far-sightedness in championing the cause of trade union education. Meanwhile, wearing my two hats I was able to help Gough harness the base Labor vote in 1974. In what was a close-fought election one of the more amusing incidents of the campaign was provided by the publication of the March Quarter Consumer Price Index figures. The figures were good for Labor but by no means indicated that inflation was under control. This did not stop Frank Crean, the Treasurer – a committed Christian and to my mind one of the most decent men in the labour movement – from making a meal of them in his role as one of the speakers supporting Gough and me at a packed meeting in the Springvale Town Hall. To listen to Frank, we had won the battle and inflation was a thing of the past. When he sat down next to me after his speech I said, 'You are a good Christian gentleman, aren't you, Frank – that was a bit rich, wasn't it?' He gave a warm smile and replied, 'The Lord allows a little latitude in a good cause, Bob.' The latitude worked and Labor scraped back in with a reduced majority of just five seats.

From the May 1974 election it was all downhill for Whitlam. The Government compounded the difficulties created by the first oil price shock of late 1973 with its own fiscal irresponsibility. Expenditure burgeoned to an unprecedented and unsustainable proportion of gross domestic product. At the beginning of the decade, Jim Cairns had been a magnificent figure in rallying the conscience of the country against the folly of Vietnam; as Treasurer and Deputy Prime Minister he became a joke.

In January 1975 Whitlam made a hurried return from overseas to look at the devastation caused to the city of Darwin by Cyclone Tracy then resumed his forty-day international odyssey, leaving Cairns as Acting Prime Minister. I led a union delegation to meet Cairns in his Melbourne office at Treasury Place and we were kept waiting and waiting. His adviser, Brian Brogan, was uncomfortable and I suggested that we start the meeting without Jim, who could be brought up to speed when he arrived. Brian agreed but as we attempted to proceed we were continually interrupted by Brian, who would excuse himself, duck off and then return looking exceedingly worried. After several such interruptions, I said, 'For Christ's sake, let's end this bloody farce! Many of these blokes have come from interstate, their time is not unlimited. Let's call this off and see if we can meet in the near future.' Brian, indicating that he understood my frustration, asked me to step out to another office for a moment. I did so, to be told: 'Bob, I know how you feel, but we've lost the Acting Prime Minister. We've got a cable from overseas which has to be dealt with but he and Junie[7] have slipped security and we simply don't know where they are!'

I felt an overwhelming despair and sadness that a Labor Prime Minister and Deputy Prime Minister had their priorities all wrong; one stayed away for too long and the other may as well not have been there. I think my sense of doom about the fate of the Government dated from this time. Any doubt was removed in May when Gough made one of the stupidest political decisions in living memory; he agreed to Lance Barnard's request to retire from Parliament with the reward of the ambassadorship to Sweden. Lance was a good and loyal servant of the party, deserving and capable of filling such an appointment at an appropriate time. But anyone out of the kindergarten of politics should have known that this was not such a time.

I was overseas, on my way to the International Labour Organisation (ILO) meetings in Geneva, when the news broke. I had no hesitation in publicly thundering my opposition to the proposal in the outside hope that there might be a change of heart. One did not have to be a political genius to recognise the disaster staring Labor in the face. Lance had a high personal vote in his Tasmanian seat of Bass, the rural sector was in open revolt against Whitlam and the textile industry in the Bass electorate was in grave difficulties, which it attributed wholly to Whitlam's tariff cuts. I told colleagues and had it conveyed to Whitlam that we were certain to lose the seat with a double-digit swing against Labor. Gough's anger at the message and its author was not diminished by the fact that Labor did suffer a 15 per cent swing in losing the by-election on 26th June. This result was more than enough to nurture the Liberals' belief in their divine right to rule; the seeds of 11th November had been sown.

Against the gathering storm clouds, I tried to use the 1975 ACTU September Congress to make the unions understand the serious economic and political crises we were facing. I pointed to the massive deterioration in employment, economic growth and inflation since the 1973 Congress, while emphasising the worldwide character of these phenomena, irrespective of the complexion of government. Unions should act responsibly by limiting wage claims to levels set by index-ation; and the Government for its part should act in a way – in partic-ular by not increasing indirect taxes and charges – that would maximise the opportunity for co-operation. Such co-operation, I argued, was essential; at the same time we had to retain our commitment to the right of free collective bargaining, an essential characteristic of a democratic society. I wanted to get across the message that the lotus days were over. The trade unions should have the right to bargain in pursuit of their members' interests but in exercising that right, they should recognise the rights and interests of others. They should also recognise the responsibility of government to act firmly to protect the interests of the community as a whole. It was a message for the

Government as much as for the unions. Congress accepted my arguments; despite disillusionment, the unions still wanted the Government to survive and, on these terms, were prepared to collaborate with it.

But not only were the lotus days over. Time was fast running out for the Whitlam Government and, indeed, from the end of the Congress on 19th September, it would survive for only another fifty-three days. Under Malcolm Fraser, the Opposition refused to pass Supply in the Senate. The atmosphere of crisis steadily mounted, as Labor, tragically, had provided its opponents with a weapon of giant dimensions in the form of the Khemlani Loans Affair. The Government had allowed itself to be conned by this unimpressive little shyster into believing he could raise billions of dollars on favourable terms to finance schemes for a national pipeline grid. When the story broke the Australian Government became an international laughing stock; its days were numbered. After this bizarre episode was over, I found myself one night alone with Khemlani in the first-class cabin of a Pan Am flight out of Bangkok to Europe. I had never met or spoken with the man before and arranged with the hostess to have him come over to sit next to me. Not surprisingly, he denied my accusation that he was a two-bit fraud and then proceeded to confirm this by raving on in preposterous detail about a fairy-tale scheme for raising tens of billions of dollars for some other unidentified government. It is a mystery how otherwise intelligent men could have allowed this charlatan to be the instrument of their destruction.

But the mistakes of the Whitlam Government provided no justification for the disgraceful events which culminated in Whitlam's dismissal by the Governor-General, Sir John Kerr on 11th November 1975. I had had a long discussion with Gough in Melbourne the previous day, and believed I had persuaded him that the right course to break the deadlock in the Senate was to call a half-Senate election. Unbeknown to us, however, his fate had already been sealed in discussions between the conniving trio of Malcolm Fraser, Kerr and Sir Garfield Barwick, Chief Justice of the High Court.

Sir John Kerr's improper and treacherous decision added a certain piquancy to my relations with Gough. When Gough, without consulting his colleagues, had announced Kerr's appointment as Governor-General, I had been appalled and told him so at the first opportunity. I said Kerr had been sympathetic to the DLP, could not be trusted and was altogether a lousy appointment. Gough, as usual not too favourably impressed when his judgment was questioned, countered aggressively, 'All right, comrade, whom would *you* have appointed?' I replied that as it was not my responsibility, I had not given it any thought; but on thinking about it and assuming that he wanted a lawyer, I said an obvious choice would have been Dick Eggleston QC, a leader of the Victorian Bar, whom Menzies had blackballed from appointment to the High Court because of his work with the ACTU. After Whitlam's dismissal by Kerr, one of the first and best letters to the Melbourne *Age* condemning the legal impropriety of the decision was from Eggleston. To his great credit Whitlam recalled our conversation and said to me, 'Comrade, you were right!' And when it came to my capacity for judgment, he had no doubt that I was absolutely right in 1983 in offering him – as I did with pleasure – the post of ambassador to UNESCO in Paris, a position he filled with distinction.

Gough's mistake about Kerr was of no moment as I plunged with him into this weirdest of all campaigns. With his approval, but to the annoyance of the hard Left, I used my influence to prevent national industrial stoppages in protest against the dismissal. My view was clear. Fraser and his cohorts had acted improperly and unconstitutionally and we were not going to play their game by attempting to settle the issue in the streets. I said it was much better to harness the movement's financial resources and donate a day's pay, or more, to the campaign fund, for it was going to be a hard and expensive fight.

The rallies Gough and I addressed around Australia were larger and more passionately enthusiastic than anything we could remember. The ranks of traditional Labor supporters were swollen by thousands who were outraged by this unprecedented flouting of Constitutional law and convention. But one could soon sense that the rallies were not an accurate reflection of the mood of the electorate. Whatever they may have felt about how it had been created, the voters seized the opportunity on 13th December to throw the Whitlam Government out and give Malcolm Fraser a massive majority of fifty-five seats.

I was in the national tally room in Canberra, and when Gough arrived to concede defeat, all my past points of annoyance with him fell away. I simply felt a sense of enormous sadness for this giant of a man who had done many good things in office, and without whom Labor would not in fact have won office. David Combe, the Federal Secretary of the party, rang me the next morning to say that Gough wanted to see me at the Lodge. Gough, as he had done in 1974, kindly said that no-one could have done more in the campaign than I. He thanked me and then surprised me by saying that I had to come into the Parliament and take over the leadership of the party. His first choice had been Bill Hayden – who had performed admirably during six months as Treasurer in attempting to get economic policy on course – but Bill had declined. I was flattered, of course, and said I would discuss the matter with close colleagues, although I knew that the disposition of the leadership was not in his hands. My interests weren't served when the story was leaked. All hell broke loose in the Caucus and much of the accumulated resentment at the power and influence of my dual presidential role came to the surface. I was not offended by this, for I realised that at times I could have shown a better appreciation of

Caucus feelings when, as ALP President, I had pronounced on issues where I thought the party's interests were at stake. I also accepted that Caucus members could have felt annoyed when, with my ACTU hat on, I had found it necessary to say or do things with which they were uncomfortable. My intentions were honourable but I was not surprised that some of them equated this occasional insensitivity towards their feelings with arrogance. But, above all, Caucus members felt that no-one was entitled to the leadership of the party without first serving an apprenticeship in the Parliament, and this was a reasonable point of view. In the event, Gough had second thoughts, submitted himself again and was re-elected as Leader.

Within weeks Whitlam's leadership was on the line and, again, I was centrally involved. To appreciate the full drama of these events, it is necessary to understand another aspect of my role as President of the ACTU. As President I had full responsibility for the conduct of its international relations, a state of affairs I had inherited from Monk; once, in reply to a question from a foreign trade union delegation as to the size of the ACTU's International Department, I had to admit: 'You are looking at it.'

Much of this work centred on Geneva, in my capacity as a Workers' Representative on the governing body of the tripartite International Labour Organisation, although I also travelled extensively to the Asian region, Europe, the Soviet Union and the United States. Dramatic developments in the Middle East, culminating in the invasion of Israel by Egypt and Syria on 6th October 1973, made this region the focus of international tension; the Organisation of Petroleum Exporting Countries (OPEC) trebled oil prices by the year's end which intensi-fied this focus and was a seminal event in changing for the worse the course of economic history for the rest of the century. Costs and prices across the world escalated and the massive increase in debt burden fell most heavily on non-oil-producing Third World countries.

Nations, like individuals, have never been backward in looking for scapegoats in times of difficulty. In one of the more perverse chapters in history, the aggressors and their allies nominated the victim of their aggression, Israel, for this role and an increasing number of insensitive and selfish nations acquiesced in this obscenity.

My direct personal involvement with the region had begun in 1971 when I visited Israel as the inaugural Sam Cohen Memorial Lecturer. Cohen, an outstanding Melbourne barrister and prominent Left-wing Senator, collapsed and died during the campaign for the 1969 federal election; his widow Judith, friends in the Jewish community and other supporters established a fund in his name to send people to Israel who would then deliver a public lecture on their return.

On the day I set out to fly to Tel Aviv I had no idea I was beginning an aspect of my career that more than any other was to stretch my emotions to their limits. I was to reach black despair, driven for the only time in my life to contemplating suicide when the duplicity of Soviet officials led me to give false hope of release to a group of Russian Jews. At the other extreme, I was later to experience the exquisite joy of being instrumental in freeing some of the same people from the tyranny and persecution of Soviet dictatorship. My contact with Israel was to find me being a secret emissary between countries in conflict in the region, and on their behalf and on my own initiative becoming a point of liaison between the Soviet Union and the United States. It was to bring threats to my life and safety, and to those of Hazel and our children. It brought me to the point of questioning whether I could remain a member of the party I loved but whose leadership was practising what I perceived as immoral partisanship under the guise of so-called 'even-handedness'. Nor could I anticipate the paradox that this 1971 journey to honour a hero of the Victorian Left was to be the beginning of a central strand of the Left's hatred for me and their determination to keep me out of the Federal Parliament.

SIX

My first visit to Israel transformed my interest in that country into fascination. The dry, dusty landscape dotted with ancient olive trees evoked all the memories of those biblical stories which had enthralled me as a child. The cocky insouciance of the Israelis creates a barrier for many outsiders; but if you match it with a fair amount of your own – as I did – it can be the medium for endless hours of vibrant discussion and debate. The trade union movement, the Histadrut, predated the State of Israel and played a dominant role in the economy through its industrial and financial enterprises. It worked in collaboration with the Labor Party which had been in government since the creation of Israel in 1948.

All this was part of my fascination but did not go to the heart of the matter. During the Second World War two out of every five Jews on earth were slaughtered for no other reason than that they were Jews. The crime was Hitler's but the world which had stood by and allowed the Holocaust to develop was also guilty. The world recognised this guilt and began the redemption of that crime after the war by action in the United Nations through the work of the Special Committee on Palestine. On 29th November 1947 the General Assembly approved, by more than the required two-thirds majority, the recommendation of this committee to partition Palestine into independent Jewish and Arab States. The decision would not have been possible without the strong support of the Soviet Union and the USA, the first two major powers to recognise the State of Israel immediately after its proclamation on 14th May 1948. Member states across the political spectrum voted in favour of the resolution. The sense of deep moral obligation was, interestingly, best put in the 1947 debate by the Soviet representative Andrei Gromyko:

> It will be unjust if we do not take account of this aspiration of the Jews to a state of their own and if we deny to the Jews the right to realise this aspiration. The denial of this right to the Jewish people cannot be justified, especially if we take into account everything that the Jewish people underwent during the Second World War.

My intense empathy with this sense of collective guilt and responsibility was more than an intellectual response. I also had a sense of personal shame in recollecting that as a young student I had not recognised and stood up against occasional instances of anti-Semitic behaviour. In sum therefore, I knew that the world community had created and invested its conscience in the State of Israel in response to the agony of the Jewish people, and I felt a special identity with that State and those people. These feelings were enhanced by my pride in the leading role Australia had played in the emergence of Israel. Dr Evatt, our Minister for External Affairs and Chairman of the General Assembly, had been a driving force as Chairman of the Select Committee on Palestine.

Israel's neighbouring Arab states did not accept the UN decision and within hours of the proclamation, their armies attacked the new State.

This was to be the first of four occasions – 1948, 1956, 1967 and 1973 – when these states either launched or prepared to launch military attacks which led to wars threatening Israel's survival. In all that period and beyond, the Palestine Liberation Organisation (PLO), in specific written articles of its basic constitutional document and in the actions of its terrorists, was committed to the elimination of Israel.

With an hypocrisy that defied intelligent analysis but was well fashioned to provide a peg of comfort upon which oil-conscious nations and others could hang their own fears and prejudices, the Arab states and the PLO paraded the plight of the Palestinians. There should be no doubt about the tragic reality of this problem nor the responsibility for it. When the Arab states invaded the tiny State of Israel – 15 000 square kilometres or one-eighth of the total area known as Palestine on both sides of the Jordan and which had been recognised at the end of the First World War as the territory for the Jewish National Home – they urged Palestinians living there to flee temporarily from the state they intended to destroy.[8]

After the armistice in 1949, some of these people returned to Israel but many joined their brothers on the West Bank and the Gaza Strip to live in the squalor of the refugee camps. For nineteen years, from 1948 to 1967 when Israel occupied these territories in the Six-Day War, there was nothing to prevent the Arab states from establishing a State of Palestine there, precisely as envisaged by the United Nations November 1947 Resolution. Nothing, that is, except the explicit determination of these states and the PLO to eliminate the State of Israel entirely.[9]

Compassion should know no boundaries of geography, race or creed. I have always felt a deep concern for the plight of the Palestinians, who have been denied an honourable resolution of their aspirations by the evil intentions of their own leaders, abetted at later stages by the intransigence of some conservative Israeli leaders. I have always made my position on this absolutely clear, saying in a 1975 speech to the ILO:

> In making a passionate defence of Israel no-one is more conscious than I am of the fundamental problems of the Palestinian people and I believe that they have a right to a state, a right to peaceful existence in that area of the world, but not at the expense of the obliteration of Israel.

It is a matter of continuing satisfaction to me that, despite the grotesque misrepresentations by the extreme Left in this country, my position on these matters has been understood and appreciated by moderate Arab leaders and by the Arab community within Australia. Before I became Prime Minister, as well as during that period, I was the welcome guest of the leadership in Egypt and Jordan and was able to act as a trusted intermediary bilaterally and within the ILO. In Australia I have continued to enjoy a warm relationship with the various Arab communities.

Israeli leaders and the Jewish community in Australia have also understood and appreciated where I stand on this issue. I think the most emotional experience of my whole career was a meeting with Golda Meir, the Israeli Prime Minister in 1973. The Yom Kippur War launched by the Arab states against Israel had just ended and I was the first non-Israeli to go across the Syrian lines on the Golan Heights. I spent much of the morning inspecting the scores of brand new Soviet tanks smashed by Israeli forces. Evidence of the carnage due to this pointless conflict was all around me. I was then driven down to Jerusalem to the Prime Minister's office. This magnificent, strong woman and dear friend broke down and wept as she embraced me; when we were alone together, she told me of the awful dilemma she had faced. As in 1967, Israeli intelligence had alerted her to the imminent Arab attack. And, as in 1967, advice was given that the Israelis should make a pre-emptive strike which could shorten the war and save Israeli lives. Golda desperately wanted to do this but, in the end, refrained through fear that the Americans would not maintain the supply of equipment and ammunition necessary to see the war through to a successful conclusion. She was wracked by emotion, blaming herself for the deaths of some of the 2500 young Israelis killed in the war.

As I sought to comfort her we talked of the future. Golda agreed that there could be no peace for her people until there was an honourable settlement of the problems and aspirations of the Palestinian people. She agreed that this must happen within the framework of UN Resolution 242, passed after the 1967 Six-Day War, which envisioned Israel's withdrawal from occupied territories to positions behind secure and internationally recognised borders.

Again, as I had done in 1971, I went to the Soviet Union at her request to argue the case for such an outcome and to renew my earlier pressure for a more liberal approach to Jews wishing to emigrate to Israel. My contact, as before, was Alexander Shelepin, head of the trade union movement, one of the top ten in the power structure and sometimes spoken of as a possible successor to Brezhnev. I argued that the Soviet Union, like Israel, was a creation of the twentieth century; like Israel, it had been attacked at the very time of its creation and again in the Second World War, and it should understand better than any other nation Israel's passionate concern for its territorial integrity and security. I developed these arguments at length with Shelepin who listened intently and promised to convey them to those who made the decisions in these matters. I have no way of knowing whether he did and if so, whether this played any part in his removal from power within six months of our meeting.

Against the background of this deep commitment, involvement and knowledge, I could not remain silent when after yet another attempt by the Arab states to obliterate Israel in the 1973 Yom Kippur War, Gough Whitlam and the rest of the parliamentary leadership enunciated a policy of 'even-handedness' in regard to the Middle East. Israel was the only democracy in the region. It was governed by a Labor Party with which we enjoyed fraternal relations; in fact it took democracy to the extreme of allowing representation in the Knesset of a Communist Party oriented to the Soviet Union, the major supplier of military hardware to the Arab states bent upon the destruction of Israel.

I made my position clear, not as President of either the ACTU or the ALP, in an address to the Biennial Conference of the Zionist Federation of Australia and New Zealand on 26th January 1974 at the Maccabean Hall in Darlinghurst, Sydney. The meeting was held with massive security surveillance, for there had been warnings of trouble. When I rose to speak a cord seemed to form between me and the audience, charging the atmosphere with emotion. I repudiated the policy of 'even-handedness' as morally repugnant and inconsistent with ALP policy, which required the Arab states to recognise Israel's sovereignty and right to exist declaring, '... as an individual Australian, I know that I am not an island and I know that if we allow the bell to be tolled for Israel it will have tolled for me, for us all, and we will all to that extent again have been diminished.'[10]

I was more than ready to argue the case with Hartley and some of the Left who wanted me disciplined by the Federal Executive. Nothing came of this and although Whitlam was not pleased with my public exposure of our differences on the issue, we were able to work together through the 1974 and 1975 elections.

Our relations, however, could never be the same after the events which unfolded in early 1976. In February Jack Egerton, a Queensland representative on the ALP Federal Executive, and the Assistant Federal Secretary, Ken Bennett, alerted me to a situation which, at first, I literally could not believe. During the 1975 election campaign

Bill Hartley, with the agreement of Whitlam and David Combe, the Federal Secretary, had attempted to arrange a $500 000 gift to the campaign funds from the Government of Iraq's Baath Socialist Party. Hartley worked as a press correspondent in Australia for the Iraqi Government and I was not surprised in the least at his complicity. He had earlier written publicly of the 'splendid militancy ... of socialist Libya and Iraq ...'. The 'splendid militancy' of the Iraqi Government had seen it involved in every attempt to destroy the State of Israel and in supporting terrorists in the region and around the world. It was the same splendidly militant Iraqi Government which on 29th January 1969 had invited its citizens 'to come and enjoy the feast' when it publicly hanged nineteen Jews in the squares of Baghdad.

Hartley, in his fanaticism, obviously saw the enmeshment of the ALP with Iraq through this proposed transaction as highly desirable. But that Whitlam, who was aware of the abhorrent nature of this régime, should acquiesce appalled me beyond measure. As for David Combe, a close friend, I was intensely annoyed but was prepared to put it down to the thoughtless reaction of a Secretary who was strapped for funds.

I believed that Whitlam could not survive the scandal, but I agreed with the officers who recommended to the specially convened Federal Executive meeting that Hartley be expelled and Whitlam and Combe severely reprimanded. Thankfully the money had never arrived, but everyone agreed that this did not detract from what was a totally inexcusable decision. A suggestion made at the beginning of the Executive that I would not be able to occupy the chair impartially was not accepted and I then presided over what for me was the saddest meeting of my whole career in the ALP. The three had agreed that they bore equal responsibility and when Whitlam sought to distance himself at an early stage from Combe, David said to Ducker and me during an adjournment, 'If we're breaking the principle of equal culpability, then the gloves are off. I'm going in to give fresh evidence.' Ducker spoke to Whitlam, who then made it clear to the Executive that he accepted the principle. I took great pride in David Combe's praise for my handling of the Executive over the two days and his belief that this prevented the outbreak of factional war.[11]

In the event, the Executive decision was that the three be severely reprimanded. Again the question was raised whether I would be able to conduct impartially the massive press conference which was awaiting the end of our meeting. That I did so – admittedly under enormous emotional stress – is perhaps best attested to by the fact that when the press conference concluded, Hartley congratulated me and said that he could not have been given fairer treatment. However, the censure by his colleagues did not diminish his fanaticism, and he continued to lead the Left's determined campaign against me in the party.

SEVEN

During my ten years as research officer and advocate I had been responsible for all the ACTU's wage cases, economic analyses and submissions to government. As President, I had been appointed in 1973 to the Board of the Reserve Bank and remained there until 1980. This appointment was one of two by the Whitlam Government which gave me the opportunity to develop an even more detailed insight into the Australian economy. The other was to a Committee of Inquiry into Australia's manufacturing industry. The committee was headed by Gordon Jackson, then chief executive of CSR Pty Ltd. Members of the committee were Rod Carnegie, head of the mining house CRA, Brian Inglis, head of the Ford Motor Company and Neil Currie, Secretary of the Department of Industry and Commerce. The committee was well serviced professionally and Jackson was a cordial and efficient chairman who made the best use of the considerable resources available to him. The Fraser Government appointed me to its follow-up committee headed by Sir John Crawford, one of Australia's greatest public servants and economists. He brought to his task the same capacity as Jackson for getting the best out of people; he had in addition a more profound knowledge of the Australian economy and the international trading environment than anyone I had known. We became good friends and he remained a source of sound advice for me until his death in 1984.

The well-researched reports and recommendations of the two committees were not reflected in specific decisions of the Whitlam or Fraser Governments, but they bore later fruit. From my invaluable experience on these committees I came to a detailed understanding of both the weaknesses of, and the opportunities for, Australian manufacturing industry. I was determined, if given the opportunity, to put that knowledge to good effect.

As President of the ACTU I continued Albert Monk's commitment to Australia's immigration program through active participation on the relevant official councils and advisory bodies. My early excitement with the program never diminished. I saw Australia becoming an economically stronger and more culturally enriched nation as the impact of these millions of new arrivals permeated every aspect of our society, in the things we could produce, the art we appreciated, the sports we played, the foods we ate and what we drank. I was committed to this new multicultural Australia and determined to do whatever I could to strengthen Australia's understanding of its virtues.

By strengthening the financial resources of the ACTU, I gradually built up the staff from the handful I had inherited. I was determined that as I involved the ACTU more deeply and broadly in a range of economic and social issues it would have the professional capacity to service those officers and constituents who were responsible for presenting our policies in these areas. We led the way in making this a period which saw a radical transformation in the operations of the trade union movement. My own success as a research officer and advocate had encouraged many unions to recruit academically qualified young people. During the seventies a pattern emerged where many of them had their second graduation – from employed researchers to elected officials. It was a tribute to the traditional officials who had come off the job, and to their members, that they recognised the need to blend their practical experience with the professional academic competence these people could bring to an increasingly complex and competitive economic and social environment. They welcomed and nurtured the newcomers who married their own enthusiasm and ambition to a sensitivity towards the traditions of the unions and the movement they were joining.

We encouraged trade union education by the use of our own resources and later in conjunction with Cameron's Trade Union Training Authority (TUTA). Our aim was to extend the knowledge and increase the efficiency of officials in discharging their traditional negotiating functions. This was clearly in the interests of union members, but it would also benefit all employees and the community generally. The more facts the protagonists carry into a dispute the less room they have to be burdened with prejudices. I argued this point with originally sceptical employers' organisations. They and particularly their chief spokesman at the time, George Polites, deserve recognition for accepting the essential truth of the argument and co-operating actively in the work of TUTA.

When I finally left the ACTU after twenty-two years I derived as much satisfaction as anything else from the knowledge that I had helped to change the face, the structure and the competence of the Australian trade union movement. I remembered with affection and pride those men of high talent, but no academic qualification, who in the earliest days had put their trust in me. Many of them had now passed on, but I was sure they would have had a special satisfaction in seeing the movement they loved being big enough to build on their vision and to strengthen itself by bringing in so many of the new generation who had used the opportunities they had never been given to develop their talents. I saw this new strength at the ACTU level in the brilliantly talented young Bill Kelty, who became Assistant Secretary in 1977, and I saw it reflected in appointments within scores of our affiliated unions. I knew that the Australian trade union movement was going to be well equipped to meet the challenges of the eighties.

The periodic speculation about whether or not I would move to federal politics intensified after the 1975 election. As the ACTU President I of course had to deal with the Fraser Government, a fact which seemed to escape or was deliberately misrepresented by my enemies on the Left. Fraser seemed fascinated by me but I can't say the feeling was mutual. Like the hard Left, he tended to think in stereotypes; to them I was in his pocket, to him I was in theirs. But he respected my abilities and gave the impression he took me and the ACTU more seriously than did his Opposition in Parliament.

Meetings with Malcolm Fraser were in two parts. He was always well briefed for the formal agenda and could make informed contributions to discussion. In these meetings original thinking was not his forte but his capacity for hard work always ensured that he was across the issues and that the meeting dealt with all items on the agenda. He clearly enjoyed these interchanges but when the agenda was completed it was a different story. He had a very limited capacity to sustain conversation on other matters. I wondered at first whether this was because of some problem he had with me but found it to be the general experience of others.

Many have put this Fraser characteristic down to aloofness and arrogance. I think this misses the point about his unique background before entering Parliament. To my knowledge, no Member in the history of the Federal Parliament has ever come to that position with a virtually complete lack of exposure to average Australian citizens, as did Malcolm Fraser in 1955. He went as a boarder to Melbourne

Grammar and from there straight to Oxford University. He returned to the farm and then went into Parliament. All this may have bred an aloof arrogance, but the simple fact is that Fraser as Prime Minister was ill at ease with his fellow Australians because he had never got to know them.

As events confirmed the economic analysis I had presented to the 1975 ACTU Congress, I attempted during the early part of Fraser's administration to persuade him to adopt a more co-operative approach to economic management. I thought it was madness to have an un-restrained free-for-all in wages and prices, and was prepared to face the unions up to the issue of wage restraint if the Prime Minister would reciprocate in the area of prices and tax policy; I argued that improve-ment in real after-tax income could be achieved more efficiently in everyone's interests – workers, employers and the community gener-ally – than by encouraging the pursuit of the highest possible level of money wage increases.

I got nowhere with Fraser. He was committed to a what-the-market-will-bear philosophy for the price of everything except labour. In that area he threatened wage freezes and more punitive legislation to inhibit trade union bargaining power. I would not accept this double standard; but my satisfaction in successfully leading the union fight against it was tempered by the knowledge that Australia was getting a second-best outcome. The resultant explosion of wages and prices at the end of the seventies and beginning of the eighties imposed a special characteristic on the accompanying recession; for the first time in our history Australia experienced simultaneous double-digit inflation and unemployment. It was a high price to pay for the absence of an effec-tive income policy and an ideological prejudice about the trade unions.

During this period much of my time was taken up in the settlement of major industrial disputes. Undoubtedly one of the factors in my growing popularity in national opinion polls was the consistent success

I was able to achieve as a negotiator. The public had a better perception of the complex dynamics of these disputes than did those cynics who peddled the line that I sat by on the sidelines until an impasse had been reached and then, in some magical way which they never explained, imposed a solution. The truth is, of course, that no two disputes were ever exactly the same in character. But one feature common to all of them was that the unions directly involved, and their members, understandably believed that they had the primary responsibility for the carriage of the dispute. This was in fact correct, although there was a recognition in practice and in the rules of the ACTU that we should be notified when the interests of other unions could be affected by a dispute. Some unions were more ready than others to observe the spirit of this provision, and the reality was that it was almost impossible to do anything effectively until there was at least some degree of co-operation from the unions – or, in some cases, a part of the union.

At times this was frustrating, for one could see opportunities for an honourable settlement being missed. But the essential ingredients of successful negotiation, in addition to intelligence, are patience, honesty and the authority to make decisions. People must be able to believe you and to know that you have the authority either to make a decision yourself or to initiate the process which will produce a decision.

One of the ugliest disputes I had to settle concerned the export of live sheep to the Middle East, which almost led to bloodshed between farmers and unionists on the wharves in South Australia.[12] In this dispute, as with many others, I had good reason to be thankful to Tony Street, Fraser's Minister for Labour and Immigration. Street was more loyal to Malcolm Fraser than any other minister; he was a small, slight man, dwarfed by Fraser physically, but yielding nothing to him in other respects. He did not, however, share the Prime Minister's ideological extremism and his natural bent was towards consultation and co-operation rather than confrontation. Fraser repaid Street's loyalty by gutting his portfolio responsibilities when Street had the honesty in the Parliament to acknowledge certain negative aspects of the employment market. I was with Street and Polites on a tripartite mission to Japan when this happened and although he was devastated by Fraser's action he would not say a word in criticism of him. In the live sheep dispute Fraser had left the running to Street, who in turn had allowed me free rein to resolve the matter. In some generous comments about my role, Sir Richard Kirby said, 'I think for the country as a whole, we had a very lucky escape in 1978.'

That year was to see two constructive achievements in the international arena, but it also set the scene for the most personally devastating failure of my whole career. In 1978 I accepted an official invitation to visit Jordan. While I did not seek permission from the Israelis, I discussed the offer with them. I dispelled their initial scepticism and with their authority became one of only a handful of non-Israelis to have acted as an unofficial conduit between Israel and the Arabs.

I had walked across the Allenby Bridge into Jordan with a mixture of trepidation and hope, but my apprehensions were dispelled at once by the warmth of the welcome extended to me and the opportunities for lengthy and constructive discussions with Crown Prince Hassan who was in charge of the country in the absence of his brother, the King. We established an immediate rapport. I was impressed by his knowledge and by his physical courage when he drove with me into a crowded and squalid refugee camp well ahead of his bodyguards and mixed freely with the inhabitants. His empathy with the refugees did not preclude him from understanding Israel's position. He asked me to convey to the Israelis Jordan's view that Israel had a right to a secure existence alongside a Palestinian entity, which could be some form of confederation with Jordan. Most significantly, Hassan talked of the possibility of an economic federation between Jordan and Israel after a peace settlement. These attitudes were particularly reassuring to Israel when later in the year negotiations began with Egypt on a normalisation of relations which would involve handing back the Sinai. For me it provided a basis of friendship and confidence that was to be extremely useful in the future.

At the ILO in 1978 we were able to avert a disaster for that organisation over the application by the UN Council for Namibia for that country to be admitted as a full member of the ILO. South Africa continued its illegal occupation of Namibia, which it designated South West Africa, but the ILO was faced by what seemed the insuperable difficulty of a detailed opinion from its legal counsel, Francis Wolf. The essence of the opinion was 'that Namibia cannot be admitted as a member of the ILO until it attains independence'. I did not question Wolf's legal competence but was adamant that the ILO's good standing should not founder on such niceties. Wolf was generous in his account of what then happened:

By any legal definition, Namibia was not a State, and only States may be members of the ILO. The difficulty was that virtually all members of the ILO wanted Namibia to be admitted – many of them passionately so, for one-third of our members are Africans. The problem appeared insoluble and for the ILO secretariat was an extreme embarrassment. Bob Hawke appreciated that a political disaster was looming for the Organisation. He got himself elected to a small sub-committee of the Selection Committee, which organises the work of the International Labour Conference, and there he produced a draft proposal of great ingenuity: it did not refute the ILO's formal legal opinion, but stepped around it. The crux of Bob's draft was that the ILO 'should not let the illegal action of South

Africa frustrate the aspirations of the Namibian people'. It was a masterstroke! What he had done was to change the question around: instead of being asked to vote *for* an illegality (violation of the ILO Constitution, by calling a non-State a State), the Conference would be asked to vote *against* an illegality (South African occupation).[13]

I gained the unanimous support of the Workers' Group, then addressed the plenary session of the conference, which voted 386 to nil, with fifty abstentions, to admit Namibia to the ILO.

Whatever exultation I felt over these achievements as a negotiator in the international arena was smashed the following year. In May 1979 I visited the Soviet Union again to argue the case for more lenient treatment of the Jewish 'refuseniks'. My commitment to these people was reinforced by meeting them in their miserable apartments. Their nobility of spirit overwhelmed me. Here were professors, engineers, men and women of outstanding talent relegated to menial occupations, prevented from freely practising their religion, their children denied access to university. They were pariahs in a squalid society. Yet through all this their indomitable faith imbued their sadness with a warmth and a sense of optimism which moved me beyond measure. I felt a personal convergence with them and was utterly determined to do everything in my power to honour that faith and justify their hope in me.

I argued their case in hours of prolonged discussion and argument with the Soviet authorities, invoking morality and the Soviets' own self-interest. I exhausted myself emotionally and pushed myself to the limit physically with the compulsory vodka and cognac consumption which, in those days, was used by Soviet officials as a weapon in the process of negotiating and dealing with visitors – particularly visitors who sought concessions from them.

Ecstasy is the only word to describe adequately the reaction when I was able to meet again with the refuseniks in one of their apartments and share the news that I had been told my requests on their behalf would be granted. I had asked the Soviet officials if I could telephone the news to friends waiting in Rome; they agreed and facilitated the call. At the airport the next morning I showed Peter Pimenov, the powerful Secretary of the Soviet Trade Unions' Council, a proposed press release that had been prepared overnight by Professor Alexander Lerner, the leader of the refuseniks:

> We welcome the position which we believe has been conveyed on behalf of the Soviet Authorities in regard to the emigration of Jews from their country. Our understanding of this position, as conveyed at the end of last week to an Australian Trade Union Official, Mr Bob Hawke, was summarised to three issues. First, people who have had their application for visas denied for more than five years will be granted exit permits. Second, the twelve in prison or in exile will be released. Third, as to the future, five years will be recognised as the maximum period for refusal of exit permits, consistent with the concern of the Soviet Authorities for security in regard to State secrets. We understand that the processes necessary to give effect to these changes are to be initiated in the near future. These changes are of profound importance and when given effect to, will call for appropriate positive response on our part.

In front of a number of Soviet officials and the Australian Ambassador, I asked Pimenov what I could do with this and he replied that I could do as I wished. I flew with Hazel to Rome, more exhausted than I could ever recall, but with an exhilaration only exceeded by that of the magnificent friends we had left behind in Moscow. By the time I arrived, washed out, in Rome the world had the story, for Lerner had distributed the statement in Moscow. The international leaders of the Jewish community in Rome to whom I reported the next day were overwhelming in their gratitude, including Isi Liebler, a good friend from Melbourne, who has done more for the cause of Soviet Jewry than anyone I know. I set off for the annual conference of the ILO in Geneva where Pimenov was to give me the list of those to whom visas would be issued.

As soon as I caught sight of Pimenov at the ILO I could sense disaster. He avoided me and authorised a statement that I had 'misunderstood' what had been said in Moscow. Pimenov was fluent in English. We had previously had many discussions but when I buttonholed him he refused to speak English, or to use an interpreter. I was approached a short time after by a Soviet apparatchik, Arapov, whose status I suspected; ILO officials later confirmed that he was a KGB operative. His line to me was that the matter was still being worked on in Moscow at the highest level. He then linked the outcome to the Salt II Agreement that had been signed just a few days earlier in Vienna by President Carter and Brezhnev. The condition the Soviet Union now placed on delivering on the Moscow undertaking was that I use my influence on the Jewish community in the United States to pressure the Senate to ratify Salt II without amendments; Arapov would confirm this arrangement either before I left Geneva or, on my return to Australia, by a message from the Soviet Embassy in Canberra, which would be simply: 'Go on, Bob.'

There was no confirmation in Geneva nor was the message ever delivered in Canberra. Subsequent professional analysis suggested that the Soviets may have thought it desirable to get a message of hope for the refuseniks out of Moscow before the Carter–Brezhnev meeting to prevent possible public protests by Jews in Vienna, and that the Geneva manoeuvres were designed to stop me using the ILO as a forum in which to attack the Soviets. I have never experienced such a sense of utter desolation. That I had been played for a sucker by the Soviets was of no moment. That I had, albeit in good faith, raised and then dashed the hopes of these great human beings brought me to a point of desperation where I questioned the value of continuing my own life. I had never seen anything to match the joy in their eyes, and the thought of their despair tormented me. Although this passed, the sense of responsibility for their anguish was not extinguished until eight years later when, as Prime Minister, I secured the release of some of these very same people.[14]

In the latter years of my ACTU presidency the question of uranium mining dominated political debate and made a fool of the trade union movement. The strong pro-mining position I adopted further alienated the Left and reinforced their determination to keep me out of Parliament.

The labour movement in Australia has never been able to get its act together on uranium. Under the Whitlam Government the Mary Kathleen mine in Queensland was developed and Jim Cairns travelled abroad to sell our uranium to the rest of the world. But in the mid-seventies the end of the Vietnam War created a vacuum for crusaders who quickly filled it with uranium. Those who had supported its mining and sale, or had been silent, now saw uranium as *the* moral issue of our time. A waffly resolution in 1977 fulminated against the evil of uranium mining and nuclear energy but left an escape clause for a future Labor government. Successive party conferences moved from one illogicality to another. The resolutions always started off from the high moral ground, denouncing as a matter of principle each and every part of the nuclear energy cycle; but then came the exemptions – first Mary Kathleen, then Nabarlek and Ranger, and then Roxby Downs.

What was designated immoral and unprincipled could then be lived with in each of these cases for reasons of expediency.

The early implications of this farce at the political level were hypothetical, for the party was in Opposition. But within the ACTU it was a much more practical question, for members of our affiliated unions were engaged in the mining and transport of uranium. I was able to divert the Left's attempts at the 1977 ACTU Congress to impose a total ban, but the matter was squarely on the agenda again in 1979 for what was to be my final Congress as ACTU President.

My mother, Ellie, passed away on Friday, 8th September, three days before Congress opened. I was distraught, but delivered the presidential address on Monday and then flew to Perth with Hazel for the funeral on the following day. I grieved as I kissed Ellie goodbye and comforted Clem, returning to Melbourne emotionally drained. I concentrated on recharging myself for what I knew would be a volatile debate on uranium on Thursday. Bill Kelty was sure the Executive recommendation supporting the operation of the existing mines would be rejected and offered to lead the debate so that I should not suffer a personal defeat. I declined his decent gesture.

My position on uranium mining is simple. While I may wish that uranium had never been discovered, it is a fact of life, as is its use around the world to produce a substantial proportion of energy for peaceful purposes. Australia has the strictest supply safeguards in the world, and the International Atomic Energy Agency has declared that the safety of the international nuclear fuel cycle would be diminished if our place as a supplier were taken by less scrupulous countries. As a member of the Non-Proliferation Treaty – a fundamental instrument in Labor's international disarmament policies – we are bound to provide uranium for the generation of power for peaceful purposes. Since the overwhelming majority of social democratic parties of the

Left around the world embrace this position, the zealots within the Australian Left could not base their position on any international political authority.

I expounded these principles with passion and an emotional intensity I had never employed before at an ACTU Congress. I knew what harsh industrial reality lay beyond the arguments of principle – the Congress could not deliver on any resolution calling for a ban of the mining and export of uranium. Union members would defy such a decision and make it easy for the Government to circumvent its purpose; I did not endear myself to union officials by telling them that they neither understood nor represented the views of their rank and file membership. The ferocity of my intervention in opening and closing the debate reflected a strong and carefully arrived at intellectual conviction on the issue coupled with the emotional strain of being alienated on this issue from my daughter Susan and son Stephen. Sue was, in fact, among the anti-uranium agitators in the Congress precincts. I was also intensely angry that the Congress was about to lower the credibility of the ACTU.

In closing my reply to the debate I warned delegates that if they voted for the Left-sponsored amendment for a ban on the mining and export of uranium, they should not be deluded that they had achieved anything except making the ACTU a laughing stock. The Congress carried the amendment 512 to 318. In a little over two years, rank and file pressure forced the ACTU to waive the bans which those delegates so exultantly imagined they had imposed in 1979.

All the pressures on me at the 1979 Congress were compounded by the fact that nominations for pre-selection of candidates for the 1980 federal election were to close in another two weeks. The decision about which I had agonised, and so many had speculated, for so long, had to be made before the end of the month. What had for so many years seemed inevitable was now by no means straightforward. I had absorbed at an early age my mother's premonitions about a career of influence and power that would lead to the prime ministership. From my early teens a suppressed sense of excitement had developed in me that I should equip myself to make this wild dream come true. I could achieve at the national level what Albert Hawke had done in Western Australia.

Now, after I had spent more than twenty years as its research officer, advocate and President, the ACTU had become very much more than a stepping stone to Parliament. I loved the working men and women of Australia and, in representing them through the ACTU, was 'in government' permanently; there was always something positive to be done on their behalf either at home or internationally. This contrasted starkly for me with the sterility of the Opposition benches which the ALP had occupied for so long and which the Socialist Left seemed determined to make Labor's permanent habitat.

I was increasingly frustrated that the party generally and the decent elements of the Left would not act against Hartley and the extremists of the Socialist Left in Victoria. The ALP was not their home but their hiding place, from which they disseminated ideological positions on domestic and international issues alien to the philosophy of Labor and inimical to its electoral fortunes. I initiated a move to expel Hartley in January 1979. The numbers were there on the Federal Executive until Frank Wilkes, the parliamentary leader in Victoria, retracted his agreement to support the expulsion. Frank did this in good faith, believing that the resultant furore would prejudice his chances in the forthcoming State election. His judgment was wrong – he lost the election and then the leadership.

Hartley was the spokesman in Australia for Libya and Iraq. At the Victorian State ALP Conference in March 1979, he extended his circle of virtuous friends. In a speech enthusiastically embracing Ayatollah Khomeni as the new head of state in Iran, Hartley extolled the revolution there as another glorious example of the triumph of democratic forces in the Third World. It was all too much. I launched a scathing attack on the Hartley group as a 'telephone box minority' who were nevertheless 'a canker' within the party which, if left untreated, would destroy our electoral credibility.

My attack was on Hartley, for I loathed everything he stood for and what he was doing to the party. But it was also directed in a sense at the rest of the party; I wanted to shock them into asking themselves how long in good conscience they could tolerate this evil albatross around their necks. Certainly these considerations were part of my thinking as I wrestled with the question of whether to nominate for pre-selection. I did not feel happy about representing a party which continued to accommodate a group of fanatical extremists.

There were strong arguments for remaining as President of the ACTU. My position was secure and offered a continuing opportunity for constructive action – so much so that it was often referred to as the most powerful position in the country after the prime ministership. I was also being urged to become the chief spokesman for workers around the world as successor to my good friend, Joe Morris, the head of the Canadian trade unions, who was about to retire as Chairman of the Workers' Group at the ILO. Joe was flattering in his argument as to why I should accept the honour of this prestigious and powerful position which was there for the taking. He touched a responsive chord in me with the passionate assertion that trade union officials were better people to live and deal with than politicians. I have never approved of the widespread habit of knocking politicians but I did agree with Joe's assessment. Politicians seemed to me, generally, a much more bitchy, jealous lot than their trade union counterparts. I found that politicians, after an argument with you, could carry a personal grudge for years; in the trade union movement you could have a blazing row and then put it behind you while you got on together with the job in hand. I think this difference, again, was in part a function of the trade unions always 'being in government', while our parliamentary colleagues accumulated the frustrations of semi-permanent Opposition.

Parliament itself never excited me. I had seen it close-up over many years and could never quite understand why so many people fought so hard to have a career in that frenzied, artificial environment. The only point of standing for Parliament was to play a part in getting Labor into government and I believed that I was most likely to do that as Leader. Labor had been thrashed again in 1977 under Whitlam, and Bill Hayden had been given the opportunity he deserved to lead the party. If Bill won the 1980 election – and I would do my utmost to see that he did – then I would become a minister. That simply would not match the satisfaction and interest of the ACTU presidency. If we lost the election, then I knew – and so did everybody else, including Bill Hayden – that unless something changed to make him look more likely to lead Labor to victory in 1983, I would be challenging him for his job. My own confidence in my ability to take on this task was supported by polls regularly showing me as preferred leader of the party. Polls were one thing but the leadership would be decided in the Caucus, not by popular vote. I have always thought the riddle: 'What is the difference between a cactus and the Caucus? – With the cactus all the pricks are on the outside — unfair to the Caucus; but I knew that in this tight little club I had quite a few enemies and no solid base of support.

In the turmoil of these conflicting considerations there was a temptation to take the easy course and stay with the ACTU. But in the end there was no choice. I know that some will find this language presumptuous and it would therefore be easier not to use it, but the truth is that I felt a sense of destiny; I felt that everything I had done to this point had prepared me for this step. Hazel agreed that I would go to the grave never forgiving myself if I baulked at this final hurdle.

At a heavily attended press conference on 23rd September 1979, I announced I would be a candidate for pre-selection for the seat of Wills. I said that my aim was 'to help provide a position which will match the thoughts and aspirations of the great majority of Australian men and women, which will help weld Australians together'. In case the Socialist Left had any doubts about my intentions, I added: 'We cannot be a vehicle for advancing the fantasies of any extremist group.' My supporters, led by the energetic Bill Landeryou – who had transformed the Storemen and Packers' Union in Victoria into a potent industrial and political force – had done their work well. On 14th October, despite frantic campaigning by the Socialist Left, I won the vote on the pre-selection panel by thirty-eight to twenty-nine over Gerry Hand, who was later to become a minister in my Government, a good friend and a strong supporter.

As the endorsed Labor candidate for Wills, a safe seat in Melbourne's industrial northern suburbs, my entry to Parliament was assured for whenever Fraser chose to call the 1980 election. With the die cast, I took time in the weeks and months ahead to analyse my strengths and weaknesses, to assess, as honestly as it is possible to do of one's self, what sort of person it was who was now perhaps moving towards the prime ministership. I needed to examine and confirm in my mind the legitimacy of the ambition sustained for so long, burning at times, wavering and dormant at others, but never extinct.

The surest foundation of my confidence was a sense of identity with and understanding of the Australian people. Much has been written about this relationship, but most of it misses the simple point that I have a genuine affection for Australians. I have watched many in political life who gave the impression that, for them, meeting and mixing with members of the public was a necessary chore and rarely a source of stimulation. But of all the things which had sustained me through twenty-two years in the labour movement, the bonding with ordinary people through constant association provided the oxygen for my political existence.

I was fascinated by how the Australian character had evolved after the Second World War as we experienced one of the most massive immigration programs in history. While still not at peace in our own minds with the Aborigines, who had been dispossessed by our forebears, many of us now struggled in turn to come to terms with the millions of immigrants who were seen as a threat to our way of life. Where others felt uncomfortable with reconciling these three elements, I easily recognised their important and unique contributions to our national character: the ancient dignity of the Aborigines and the challenge posed by their latter-day degradation; the Anglo-Celtic predominance, which had provided the institutions of parliamentary democracy and freedom under the law, and had adapted a class-ridden tradition to produce in this vast continent a people with a cocky insouciance, a society where mateship and the concept of 'a fair go' were more than myths; and finally, the enrichment of that national character by the new citizens who came to us from more than 140 countries around the world. For me, this was not just historical and demographic fact. It was what made our country unique and inspired in me a dedicated love for Australia and Australians, a love best reflected perhaps by the surge of excitement I always experience when flying back to Australia feeling that I am returning to the best country on earth. As I mixed with Australians from all walks of life and of every station, they came to reciprocate the sincerity of my feelings. They respected my talents and could identify with my weaknesses. They recognised that I had been given opportunities to equip myself in an extraordinary way but appreciated my identification with their aspirations and interests. I felt comfortable with the Australian people, I understood them, and out of the rapport between us, I derived both strength and the certainty that I could speak for them.

This rapport was in turn the basis of the second asset – a capacity for bringing people together. As ACTU advocate I was rightly perceived in an adversarial role, as the protagonist for organised labour and necessarily the antagonist of its opponents. These public perceptions changed quite rapidly after I became ACTU President. I was no less committed to my constituency than before, but I saw the achievement of its aspirations calling as much upon the reasonableness of the conciliator as the vehemence of the partisan. I enjoyed and developed an expertise in the dynamics of conflict resolution. In major national industrial disputes, all the unions involved rarely had identical positions and it required endless patience to draw them together to consolidate a negotiating platform. Fortunately this was usually true of the employers' side as well and often the secret of successfully resolving a dispute was to discern a reasonable opening among their ranks and to marry it to what I saw as the acceptable limit of the unions' claims. In assessing that limit I would take into account the unions' position and what I saw as the community interest, not merely in ending a serious dispute, but in having an industrial environment after the dispute in which the two sides would be able to live and work together reasonably.

This attitude reflected my profoundly held conviction that consensus, or its first cousin – agreement – are better stimulants for productive behaviour than conflict or imposed régimes. The whole process was a fascinating, mutually beneficial exercise. Once people on both sides accepted the integrity of this approach, I received constructive responses which eased the difficult task of resolving what often appeared to be intractable disputes. And for my part I learned a great deal about human nature and the character of leading players on the industrial stage.

One individual who stands out in my mind in this respect is Laurie Carmichael, then a prominent official with the Amalgamated Engineering Union[15], the main left-wing union in the critically important metal trades industry. Laurie was a member of the Communist Party and an industrial militant, with his reputation as an ogre deriving as much from his manner as from the frequent extremism of his demands. His Salvation Army background showed in a declamatory style which would have done him proud at a revivalist meeting. Laurie's trade union colleagues often cringed when he harangued them in a negotiating session, as much as the employers did when he hurled the occasional barbed insult across the table. When a dispute developed into its penultimate stage Laurie was always the one hanging out for something more in the settlement and was not averse to suggesting we were selling out too easily. But when we had made the collective decision which had to be endorsed by rank-and-file meetings around the country, he would always take on the toughest assignments and identify himself, and his organisation, with the proposed terms of settlement.

The more I came to know Laurie Carmichael, the more I came to respect him. The private man was one who had a profound knowledge and love of classical music and a dedication to gardening. As he became disaffected with communism, he turned his fertile mind more and more towards how, from a committed trade union point of view, a competitive capitalist market economy could be made to work with greater efficiency and equity. He travelled and studied extensively overseas to see how the best overseas practices could be adapted to meet the challenges facing Australia; to this end he co-operated with employers both informally and on a number of official committees in the fields of manufacturing industry and technical education. To me Laurie Carmichael dramatically exemplifies how much more fruitfully the talents of individuals can be harnessed in an environment of constructive co-operation than of adversarial conflict.

My third source of confidence in myself as a future Prime Minister was the knowledge that I had been given a unique opportunity to understand the Australian economy. The tenuous understanding afforded by an undergraduate degree of all the linkages, domestic and international, which affect our economy had been enlarged by detailed work as the national union advocate, and then fleshed out through my membership of the Reserve Bank Board and the Jackson and Crawford Committees. I believed I would come to the prime ministership better equipped in economic competence than any predecessor. Similarly, I was confident that I could bring to the position not only an abiding interest in but also a considerable grasp of international affairs in general and of our region in particular.

Finally, after thirty-three years' immersion in its often turbulent waters I knew, better than most, the strengths and weaknesses of the Labor Party. Although I had no illusions about the depth of feeling against me in sections of the Left, I had no antagonism to the faction as a whole and had many good friends within it. I believed that many of the best motivated people in the party were in the Left, but my concern was that too many of its policies had been dictated by extremists who were simply out of touch with the realities of the nation and of the world in which we lived. I knew that on many issues I would have to fight them, and that those confrontations could be bruising and bitter. But I believed that, given time, I would be able to make the Left an important part of a cohesive Hawke Labor government.

The Right was certainly not inhabited by uniformly attractive characters either but they had the redeeming characteristic of wanting to win; and, in politics, winning ultimately means being in government. The Right's single-minded determination to win every issue at every level – the branch, the State Conference, the Federal Conference and Executive – often presented itself as pragmatism with an ugly face. This was the other side of one's dilemma with the Left. I often castigated them for providing the most pathetic sight in politics – squatting under the banyan tree wrapped in the warm euphoria of their

EIGHT

The 1980 election set the stage for the subsequent fight for the leadership between Bill Hayden and myself. The party organisation believed on the basis of its research that Bill did not have sufficient clout with the electorate to carry the campaign on his own. It decided to give equal prominence in the election advertising to Neville Wran, then the popular Premier of New South Wales, Bill and me.

This was embarrassing for Hayden but it was a measure of this complex character that he accepted the facts and threw himself with us into an arduous election campaign to defeat the Fraser Government. I knew that victory for Labor in this election could spell the end for my own aspirations to the prime ministership, but I did everything possible to help Labor win. As we posed in Sydney's Botanical Gardens for the first photographs of the campaign the jokes about Labor's 'troika' rang a little hollow in everyone's ears, but we were all committed to making this conveyance an effective vehicle for victory.

It is doubtful that Labor was ever going to do well enough to overturn the Coalition's hefty forty-eight seat majority, but any chance of this disappeared with some ill-disciplined comments about capital gains by Senator Peter Walsh. These opened the way for a massive fear campaign by the Coalition that Labor, if elected, would introduce a capital gains tax which would include the family home. In the event, we achieved a 4.2 per cent swing which produced a gain of thirteen seats, leaving Fraser with a seventy-four to fifty-one majority in the House of Representatives. Walsh was one of Bill Hayden's fiercest supporters and while self-doubt has never been one of his distinguishing characteristics, I wondered later whether he did not deeply regret the lapse which perhaps cost his champion what turned out to be his only chance of becoming Prime Minister.

From the beginning I was given a privileged run in the Parliament. In line with Bill Hayden's public pre-election commitment that I would go straight to the front bench, the Caucus elected me to the shadow ministry and Bill gave me responsibility for Industrial Relations, Employment and Youth Affairs. This rare, immediate elevation was sufficiently obvious and appropriate to silence the mutterings among a few die-hards, particularly as the decision had the full support of the very popular Mick Young, who had previously held these responsibilities.

I was allocated a good room in a back corner of the first floor of the old Parliament House and here Jean Sinclair and I quickly established a functional and by the standards of that rather decrepit, over-crowded building cosy operation. We recruited an able and enthusiastic young economist, David McKenzie, and were soon regarded as an efficient, dedicated and friendly team.

Much of the credit for this was due to Jean, who had been with me as a personal assistant at the ACTU since 1972 and had become my right arm. Jean was a petite, very intelligent woman, born in England, who, after graduating from the University of Melbourne had worked with Rod Carnegie at McKinsey's before Rod went on to CRA. She was married to Gus Sinclair, a gentle and learned academic. Jean was independently wealthy and her decision to work with a leading light in the labour movement caused raised eyebrows among her friends and relations. She was a remarkably efficient manager and administrator who within a very short space of time transformed what had been the chaos of my personal office as ACTU President into an orderly operation. She was remarkably adroit in dealing with people; she could put at ease and be at ease with the highest and humblest in the land. In the often bitter tribalism of Labor's factional politics, her personality and obvious commitment made her a point of access for all sides. But fierce loyalty to me did not prevent her from voicing criticism privately when she felt it necessary.

I had a special affection for Jean. In 1991, already dying from cancer, she battled on, putting aside her illness to work through the Centenary ALP Federal Conference, held in Hobart in July. When she died two months later I lost a friend and the labour movement lost one of its most dedicated servants. The success of my career owes much to this fair-minded and courageous woman and, beyond her, to the steady support she received from her husband, Gus.

On coming to work in the Parliament I was intrigued to see the way in which Members became seduced by what they seemed to see as the mystique of the place. This attraction to both premises and processes escaped me entirely. The Federal Parliament had moved to Canberra from Melbourne in 1927 to occupy what was to be temporary accommodation until a new and permanent Parliament House was built. Here we were fifty-three years later in the same building, which had been added to inadequately from time to time and which provided staff conditions and auxiliary services which would have been condemned under every Factories and Shops Act in the country.

The processes were still more ancient and, in their way, even more confining of the human spirit. As a spectator I had never been enamoured of the forms of the House, and my direct exposure to them then and for a decade later did nothing to diminish that response. As a frontbencher I had plenty of opportunity to be involved in the action. For the backbencher, parliamentary life seemed to me a frustrating experience. The overwhelming part of what happened in the House itself was pre-ordained, with virtually no significant role for the backbencher. The Government was committed to the legislation it introduced, and amendments which might be made to that legislation following debate in the House were the exception rather than the rule. Even in Question Time, questions to ministers from backbenchers on either side were normally prepared for them by the ministry or the Opposition executive.

However stultifying these procedures were for Opposition backbenchers, the lot of Government backbenchers seemed the most frustrating of all. At least backbenchers in Opposition were free to attack the Government and give rein to their real feelings, although even here they were inhibited by party discipline if they happened to disagree with their own colleagues. Government backbenchers often had reservations about particular aspects of Bills or other official business before the House, but only in the most exceptional circumstances could they give expression to such views. Ultimately, their role was to be there when the bells rang to ensure that the Government position prevailed. In this sense the proceedings in the House were essentially a charade, with everyone knowing in advance what the outcome would be. I never really came to terms with this uncongenical atmosphere, compared with that of the Arbitration Court or the public meeting, in which I revelled.

I do not mean to imply that I found Members of Parliament to be anything other than hard-working and conscientious. With the obvious exceptions to be expected in such a large group, my parliamentary colleagues were diligent men and women who put in long hours in the discharge of their duties. I was impressed in particular by the way Bill Hayden had the committee system operating. In all important areas, hard and constructive work was under way to prepare policies to take to the next election and it was a pleasure to participate in these undramatic but necessary labours.

Preparing sound policies was, however, a necessary but insufficient condition for winning office. As time went by and the party became hungrier for office but less certain of winning it, my ambition coincided increasingly with that of the Caucus. By mid-1982, Caucus and party dissatisfaction with Bill's leadership had intensified and my own aspirations stiffened accordingly. The stakes were too high for sentimentality and I became increasingly tough-minded. In pressing my claim for leadership I tried as hard as I could not to attack Bill personally. My major argument in 1982 was that I believed profoundly that I had the best chance of winning government for Labor. Internal party polling and independent electoral soundings made it crystal clear that I was right. Among voters in marginal seats I was preferred as Prime Minister against all other contenders by embarrassingly high differentials. Against the incumbent, Malcolm Fraser, my lead was more than 20 per cent. Against Bill it was more than 30 per cent. Labor's internal party research confirmed the public polls.

Naturally it was impossible to push my own case without any reference to Hayden. In talking with shadow ministers and other Caucus colleagues I emphasised what I saw as my advantages and at times this inevitably involved comparisons with what I perceived was Bill's incapacity to ensure electoral victory. I had, nonetheless, a keen sense of the value of Bill's work during his hard-slog period of leadership. Since becoming leader after Labor's thrashing in 1977 he had taken the party through the bleak aftermath of two successive election debacles and had fought to rid the party of the tax-and-spend, interventionist, fiscally irresponsible image which had contributed to these disasters. I had no desire to denigrate Bill or belittle his contribution.

Equally, I did not allow my respect for his achievements to obscure the fact that we had not won in 1980 and that even with the country sunk in recession and bitterly divided under Fraser, the chances of victory in 1983 were uncertain, and receding. I knew that under my leadership Labor could win, and win well. In politics, winning is not everything, but it is the beginning of everything. Without power there is no achieving anything.

The crunch for Hayden's leadership came in June and July 1982. First came his extraordinary stumble on visits by nuclear ships. It would be 'totally undesirable for Australia or any ports of Australia to become nuclear weapons arsenals or storage or transit points,' he declared on 9th June. His interpretation of party policy necessarily banned all warships of our ANZUS partner, the United States, from our ports. Bill's deputy and Shadow Foreign Minister, Lionel Bowen, brought him back to the bold print by noting that ALP policy had always allowed ship visits without any declaration by the Americans that the ships were nuclear-free.

Malcolm Fraser had a field day with this, warning that Hayden's policy would mean the end of the ANZUS Treaty. What might have been seen as prime ministerial exaggeration was given a sharp cutting edge by the fact that an ANZUS Council meeting was held in Canberra as this imbroglio was unfolding. In fact two senior US delegates to the meeting went to Hayden with the direct warning that his latest gloss on ALP policy would jeopardise ANZUS.

The Americans then went public. The Deputy Secretary of State, Walter Stoessel, declared ships visits were critical to the maintenance of ANZUS. Bill had indulged in an extravagant impulse, wrong in substance and politically untenable. He had no alternative but to climb down ignominiously, which he did almost immediately after Stoessel's press conference on 22nd June. This somersault ended two taxing weeks for Hayden and the Labor Party. They were critical weeks because they exacerbated incipient dissatisfaction with Bill's leadership and raised the spectre of yet another defeat at the polls.

Soon after the ships contretemps, in the week beginning 5th July, the party held its biennial National Conference at the Lakeside Hotel in Canberra. Shortly before the conference Bill signalled his intention to seek a change in the party's anti-uranium policy. In 1977 the National Conference in Perth had pledged the party's opposition to the mining, processing or exporting of uranium. Not content with that, it had bound a future Labor Government to the repudiation of uranium-mining contracts entered into by the Fraser Government. As National President of the party at the time, I had strongly opposed this position. My objection had been one of the reasons for a bid to remove me from the presidency in 1977.

Now, in 1982, in the run-up to an election, Bill well understood the political lunacy of the policy. But in contrast to his aberrant position on nuclear ships, of which the Left had thoroughly approved, this bid to change the party's uranium policy – the Left's litmus test of political correctness – infuriated them. The Left were Bill's strongest supporters and, at that stage, my most vehement opponents. For them, changing uranium policy was not on. But for some of them, changing leaders was.

Clearly I, too, supported a change in policy but Bill's move cracked the monolithic basis of the Left's allegiance to him. In late June I was startled to receive a phone call in my Coburg office from Tom Uren. Tom was the father figure of the parliamentary Left, the principal proponent of the anti-uranium platform and one of the prime movers against my presidency in 1977. On the floor of the House he had once thundered that I would never lead the Labor Party.

Tom was incensed by Hayden's machinations to ditch the anti-uranium platform and by a press interview in which Bill had said that the existing platform allowed a Labor Government to approve uranium exports under certain conditions. Uren said to me, 'At least we know where you bloody well stand on the issue!' I made it clear that I supported Hayden's desire to change the policy and would do all that I could to secure that change. I told Tom that if the policy remained unchanged I would, reluctantly, support it. He said, 'Hayden is finished, he's a dead-duck leader,' and indicated that he would be moving to secure the support of the Left for me to replace Hayden.

I was of course excited but uncertain about just where Tom was coming from or whether he could deliver. It was a time for Labor's old stayers to be unpredictable. Earlier that day I had listened to former Whitlam minister Clyde Cameron, a Hayden admirer, talk up my leadership stakes on national radio. 'We've got to face facts,' he said. 'The public opinion polls show that Bob Hawke now commands more support than any other politician ever registered in these public surveys, and Labor would romp home with Hawke as Leader.' Cameron's fear was the prospect of a snap election and the party being 'caught with its pants down with a Leader that can't win enough public support to take us to victory'.

With these questions teasing delegates' minds, the National Conference became enmeshed in the leadership issue. Policy was not ignored and the conference did result in the dilution of the party platform on uranium mining, following a debate which showed the Labor Party at its best and at its worst – with convictions strongly and genuinely held and passionately articulated by some, and ill-founded, blind ideology presented as holy writ by others. It was a close decision. The Left called for a division and those voting to change the platform were jeered, hissed and even spat upon as they crossed the conference floor.

Leadership speculation swept the hotel. Publicly, I had made my position clear in the lead-up to the conference. Asked about Cameron's remarks I simply replied, 'Leadership of the party and the electoral welfare of the party is a matter for the Caucus.' As it turned out, Bill himself provided the trigger for a vote; on Thursday afternoon, 8th July, he told me and announced publicly that he was calling a special Caucus meeting on 16th July.

It was time for the parliamentary party to fish or cut bait. In particular, certain key individuals had to decide exactly where they stood. One of these was Paul Keating. Although his faction, the New South Wales Right, was not signed, sealed and delivered at the time Bill called on the challenge, it was clear that the majority of the faction would come my way. This they did as the week wore on. But Keating did not. He was the one critical hold-out, agonising over his decision. Some of his delay may have arisen from a faint residual loyalty or affection for Bill, but looming much larger for him was the question of how the coming vote would affect his own leadership ambitions. Paul's essential concern was that if anyone were to replace Hayden it should be him. He had no doubt contemplated a range of possible scenarios for his own succession. Hayden would scrape into the prime ministership, stay a term or two, and Paul would take over. More likely, Bill would lose the next election and then Paul would take over. Whatever his precise appraisal, Keating considered himself next in line.

My arrival on the scene threw a sizeable spanner in the works. Paul is not given to hiding his resentment easily and some of his glib one-liners were inevitably passed on to me. He had not, he said, tilled the soil for all this time (he had been in Parliament for thirteen years), to let someone else in to take over. It rankled with Paul that I had just arrived in the parliamentary party and was going to get what he saw as an armchair ride to the leadership and the prime ministership. That did not sit as comfortably with him as it did with others of comparable, or greater, experience.

He knew he had considerable talent but the stretch of his ambitions exceeded his grasp. At thirty-seven, he was a young bright front-bencher with an interest in and considerable knowledge of mineral resources and a talent for knock-down parliamentary debate. He was certainly not yet well rounded or mature enough for leadership.

In any event, the reality was that the New South Wales Right, and its leadership, had a clear view about winning government and about my capacity to deliver that. By now the leadership of the Right was firmly established in the redoubtable person of Graham Frederick Richardson. I give him his full name here because Graham's father, Freddy, had been a good friend and colleague when he was NSW Secretary of the Postal Workers' Union. Freddy died at a relatively young age from a heart attack. Our association had created a warm link between Graham and me, a bond which was strengthened by Graham's perception that I had treated him well when, as a lowly organiser with the NSW party, he was sent to be my chauffeur during election campaigns in the early seventies. By 1976 he had become Secretary of the party in NSW and had established an authority and influence in the Ducker tradition. This rested upon an acute political intelligence and an amiable and gregarious spirit which never masked his steely toughness. He had an incomparable network in the political and industrial wings of the labour movement. Admired by his supporters, respected and even feared by his opponents, Richardson was already a formidable figure in Labor politics.

In that mysterious way of the NSW Right, the strength of their view was conveyed to Keating. Just how they put it, I am not sure. One has to be initiated into the rites of the Right to know exactly how they operate; I never have been. It is a closed group with unwritten rules of its own. But it was put strongly and convincingly and Paul obeyed the tribal dictum.

The public announcement of his support came after a long, gruelling session at the Boulevard Hotel, my Sydney base at the time. My parliamentary colleagues Senators Gareth Evans and Robert Ray, the Member for Melbourne Ports, Clyde Holding, and Simon Crean, then the Federal Secretary of the Storemen and Packers' Union and Vice-President of the ACTU, were all in attendance. All were members of the Centre Unity faction of the Victorian Right. Richardson was there with Mick Young, the Member for Port Adelaide, ALP Vice-President and Chairman of the National Campaign Committee. Keating was the reluctant last man aboard, an appropriate description, for I think it was at this meeting that the caustic numbers-man, Robert Ray, warned him, 'When the boat leaves the wharf, you had better be on it because we've got most of your crew on board already.'

That was indeed a powerful argument. As parliamentary leader of the NSW Right, Keating could hardly stand in splendid isolation from his party organisation and the bulk of his factional colleagues in the Parliament. To retain credibility he had to come along, albeit with considerable prodding from his colleagues. Fear of isolation was not his only consideration. Although his calculations were slowed by his own ambition, he understood two things well. First, that no-one shared his conviction of his own right to the succession, and second, that Labor's chances of winning government would be better served with me as leader than with Bill. Paul had spent thirteen years in Parliament, ten of them in Opposition. He was as hungry for office as the rest of the party and it was time to sublimate his own aspirations, at least for now.

Arriving at this position had been made easier for him by the maladroit and malcontent manoeuvring of the Left. Tom Uren, who had acted unilaterally and without any broad Left support, hastily retreated to the Hayden fold. A Left delegation waited upon Hayden and me in turn, making it quite clear in the process that they saw Bill as the lesser of two evils. Then the extra-parliamentary far Left chose to interfere. Laurie Carmichael, still identified with the Communist Party, declared for Bill.

The oiliest contribution, however, came from the former communist, John Halfpenny, who was preparing to deposit his lead in the saddlebag of the ALP. Just one day before the Boulevard gathering the new conscience of the party pontificated on national radio: 'We feel that Bill Hayden would make a better Leader of the Labor Party because he has a deeper, a more honest commitment to the labour movement and the policies of the Labor Party.'

This gratuitous intervention inflamed the non-Left forces in the party, particularly the NSW Right, providing the peg upon which Paul could publicly hang his support for my leadership bid. As the media gathered in the Boulevard foyer, Paul read over a statement drafted, inevitably, by Gareth Evans, added a few twists of his own, and headed for the lifts.

'The Left has now made it clear that it is resiling from any commitment tendered to Bob Hawke on its behalf,' Paul read to the media throng. 'It made this decision after having been brought into line by interests outside the ALP. The Centre Unity group in NSW finds the involvement by Messrs Carmichael and Halfpenny in the leadership of the Labor Party totally unacceptable,' he continued. Then came the reluctant conclusion: 'The New South Wales members will take the view that the best interests of the Labor Party, and the millions of Australians who deserve and need a Labor victory and the end of Fraserism, will be best served by Bob Hawke now becoming leader.'

This shoring up of the Right, however, was not enough to get me across the line. When the votes were counted in the Caucus room on Friday, 16th July, Bill Hayden had forty-two votes to my thirty-seven – I had needed a switch of another three votes.

It was clear to everyone, to Bill and his closest advisers, that the margin was too narrow to be decisive. I regretted losing, but I had been given an important lesson in the ways of politics and politicians. Votes I had expected to come my way had not. The Left had given me a wink which I had mistakenly taken to be a nod. Although I am by nature an optimist and I trust people, the vote reinforced to some degree the advice of my closest supporters, who were men more seasoned than I in vote-counting. That advice, which they had proffered over and over again, was that when it came to vote-counting, the only person you could absolutely rely on was someone who looked you straight in the eye and said he or she was not going to vote for you. It was a lesson I never completely learned.

Meanwhile, my regret at losing was tempered by the knowledge that I had mounted a challenge of substance. The vote had done nothing to shake my belief that I offered the most certain chance of leading Labor to victory and of leading a successful government. This left a difficult line to tread. I could not delude myself or my colleagues that my leadership aspirations had been extinguished. Nonetheless, Bill had survived, he was in charge and I was determined to do all I could to help the party within that framework.

Bill, too, adopted a positive attitude in the immediate aftermath of the vote. He acknowledged that I had established a right of succession and, in a moment of light relief at our joint press conference, appointed me to the party's powerful electoral strategy committee. It was the high point of Bill's commitment to face forward and get on with the job.

What happened over the ensuing months had less to do with me than it did with him. Talk of another challenge all but subsided and whenever media speculation stirred I jumped on it from a great height. But in Bill's mind all shadows had substance, and my shadow loomed largest of all. A sort of siege mentality developed, making it almost inevitable that serious mistakes of judgment would occur.

Through the 1982 Spring Session the Labor Opposition trounced the Government using the rich lode of material unearthed by the Costigan Royal Commission. In one of the classic rebounds of federal political history, the commission, which had been set up by the Government to embarrass the labour movement with an investigation of the Ship Painters' and Dockers' Union, became a millstone around Fraser's neck. Costigan's investigations led him into the shadowlands of tax avoidance and evasion, which he described as 'the fastest growing industry' in the period of the Fraser Government. As to the Liberal Party itself, the Commissioner named a number of prominent party members and supporters as tax avoiders.

Day after day we were in a dominant position in the Parliament – until Bill went too far. He personally attacked John Reid, an ex-director of BHP and prominent establishment figure, as a tax avoider. The unfounded charge was bad judgment and bad politics, and it backfired. Bill had to withdraw, damaging himself and the party, and seriously stalling our momentum. While I knew that he had acted in good faith, I also knew that the incident had a devastating effect on his confidence.

This was most painfully evident on Thursday, 2nd December in Melbourne, the beginning of a three-day period which effectively signalled the end of Bill Hayden's hopes of retaining the leadership. On that day he, his deputy, Lionel Bowen, the Shadow Treasurer, Ralph Willis, and I met with the ACTU Executive in their Melbourne headquarters to discuss the Wages Accord which Ralph and I had been hammering out with them over many months. The situation was complicated by the fact that in November Fraser had announced a six-month wage pause; Bill had read into the ACTU reaction to it a greater preparedness on their part to parley with the conservatives than to talk reasonably with their natural ally, the Labor Party. Overlaying this view was his suspicion that my successor as ACTU President, Cliff Dolan, and his colleagues were playing their hand in a way calculated to embarrass him and therefore to advantage me.

In this atmosphere of paranoia our meeting with the Executive contained plenty of robust exchanges, including several between me and the ACTU representatives. One in particular with Jan Marsh, the ACTU advocate, who totally repudiated my proposition that we should consider a return to the concept of a basic wage and margins had the Chairman on the edge of his seat.

I saw all of this as good clean fun, a tough negotiation about a tough issue but one that was resolvable given time and enough goodwill. But, ill at ease with the issues, suspicious by nature and walled in by his own demons, Bill could not see it that way. The union movement was shifting the goalposts on him and, come what may, he was going to blow the whistle. His determination to do so, however, was for the moment hidden from his colleagues. The meeting concluded with the Accord process apparently back on course, with both sides committed to smoothing out their differences and finalising an agreement as soon as possible.

The media were waiting, and through the thin partitions of the ACTU building had got an inkling of a rowdy meeting. Confronted with the suggestion of a massive split between the ACTU and the parliamentary Labor Party, Cliff Dolan calmed the waters. He conceded that there had been some animated discussion but that we had agreed to continue processing the Accord and would attempt to finalise it in the near future. He reiterated this message under repeated questioning then returned to continue the meeting.

Now it was Hayden's turn to face the media. My parliamentary colleagues and I watched incredulously as he proceeded to chop up the waters. According to him, everything was in disarray, the Accord was in a blowhole and the waves were crashing in.

In the event they did crash in, with Friday morning's press proclaiming a split between the ACTU and the ALP over the Accord. The timing could not have been worse. The very next day, voters in the Victorian federal seat of Flinders were to cast their ballots in a crucial by-election. Although Flinders was traditionally a blue-ribbon Liberal seat, simultaneous double-digit unemployment and inflation, coupled with high interest rates, had brought it within Labor's grasp. Hayden, however, campaigned without confidence and in the aftermath of headlines proclaiming a split between Labor and the unions, Labor got 3.3 of the 5.5 per cent swing needed to win the seat. Although we did not have a strong candidate, we should have won or at the least have gone much closer to winning. Pre-poll and post-poll analysis went to the issue of leadership; a piece by Robert Haupt in *The Age* suggested the outcome would have been different if I had been leader.

The loss of Flinders at this critical juncture, with talk of a looming federal election, concentrated the mind of the party and made a switch of leadership to me inevitable. Bass and Flinders, two of our most famous early explorers, who encountered much turbulent water as they explored Australia's eastern and southern coastline, lent their names to two electorates which have marked turning points in the fortunes of the Australian Labor Party. The disaster in Bass in the 1975 by-election had signed the death warrant of the Whitlam Government. Seven years later, the result in Flinders ensured the beginning of a long period of Labor ascendancy.

Bill Hayden was not about to relinquish his position without one last throw. In mid-January 1983 he reshuffled his front bench, offering Paul Keating the job of Shadow Treasurer, a bitter blow to my friend Ralph Willis, who had held the position for five years. Paul, agitated and in a deep dilemma about what to do, desperately sought reassurance and advice. He phoned me with the news between one and two in the morning of 14th January and asked my opinion. I told him the answer was clear. The decision had been made and he should not only live with it but should do his absolute best to make it work. His agitation was understandable, for the new portfolio meant a very big change and a huge responsibility for him. It was little wonder he was uncertain and far from keen on the idea. He was Shadow Minister for Minerals and Energy and absolutely on top of that responsibility. He had made all the contacts and had achieved a detailed mastery of a complex area.

Paul was also suspicious of Bill's reasons for offering him the job. Clearly it was a last-ditch effort by Hayden to maintain his leadership, and Paul saw the position of Shadow Treasurer as something of a poisoned chalice. One did not need to be brilliant to surmise that Bill, fighting for his political future, sought to divide and rule – and reward and punish – by offering Ralph's job to Paul. I hesitate to use the word Machiavellian but Bill's thinking was many-tiered. Labor was not succeeding in selling its economic message as a party of growth. Thus, the change could also be seen as waiving Ralph's undoubted mastery of the subject for Paul's salesmanship. No doubt Bill also saw it as a way to weaken the relationship between Ralph and me, and that between the two of us and the ACTU. His other problem was factional. The NSW Right had declared for me over him. In offering the Shadow Treasurer's job to Paul, Bill sought to lock in the support of one of the tribe's favourite sons, the President of the party in New South Wales. He was also trading on the fact that Paul's support for me was less than wholehearted.

Hayden's frantic, last-minute manoeuvre came too late. Played earlier, perhaps straight after the July challenge, it may have proved a trump card. Played so late, it was plainly a trick card in a last desperate hand.

I knew that we were in the end-game when a couple of days later Senator John Button and the backbench MHR, Michael Duffy, both Victorian Independents in the Caucus, came to see me at my Sandringham home. Their message was simple – I had to take over the leadership. Button, a close friend and previously a strong supporter of Bill, assumed the responsibility of talking to Hayden and keeping me informed of developments.

Button saw Hayden twice in Brisbane but made little headway. On 28th January he finally committed his thoughts to writing in a tough 'Dear Bill' letter. It was a painful experience for both men as Button, in a series of bullet-like points, shot the heart out of Bill's leadership. 'I believe that you cannot win the next election. In July last year I had doubts about this. Since the last leadership contest, it seems to me that your level of performance as party leader has declined considerably ... It has been my view that with the recent economic performance by the Government, we should have been 10–15 per cent ahead ... You have, unhappily, a difficulty in working with colleagues, but it in no way diminishes their respect for your political career. I believe that respect and affection would be greatly enhanced if you stepped down ...'

After this, events moved swiftly. Button met with Hayden again on 1st February in Brisbane, following their attendance at the funeral of a former Labor Prime Minister, Frank Forde. Forde had led the party during the brief interregnum between the death of John Curtin on 5th July 1945, and the election of Ben Chifley on 12th July. Like Hayden, Forde had harboured ambitions to stay on in the job and once asked the Labor MHR for Parkes, Les Haylen, about his chances: 'I told him frankly what the position was. It was brutal, but it was the kindest thing to do. His face went deathly white, the veins on his neck stood out in an effort to suppress his emotions,' Haylen related.[16] This time Button was the bearer of 'brutal but fair' (Hayden's words) news to a Labor leader. Hayden agreed to step down the following Friday.

During the course of the week, however, he received word of the Prime Minister's frenetic behind-the-scenes tactics to speed to the polls while Labor was in the throes of a leadership struggle. Fearing the possible humiliation of having to resign after Fraser had called an election, Bill expedited his plans. He would announce his resignation during a meeting of the Shadow Cabinet in Brisbane on Thursday, 3rd February 1983.

The scene was set at the drab Commonwealth offices in Ann Street for one of the most extraordinarily dramatic days in Australian political history. From all appearances the meeting of the executive began normally, with Bill in the chair and business continuing as usual. For those with an inkling of what had gone on behind the scenes and for what was about to occur, the atmosphere was surreal.

At mid-morning Bill adjourned the meeting and Lionel Bowen, John Button and I accompanied him to his twelfth floor office where the conditions of the transition were hammered out. It was a shattering experience for Bill and painful for the rest of us. Although he was mentally prepared for this moment, Hayden's anguish and disappointment were palpable; having worked so hard to prepare Labor for government he was being told by his friend and colleague, John Button, that as we got towards the final furlong he could not lead the party home. John's opinion was shared by Lionel Bowen, Bill's loyal deputy. Typically, Lionel had kept his feelings about the leadership tight and never uttered a word against Bill publicly, nor denigrated the leader behind his back. But Lionel, too, had concluded that Bill had to go.

The solemnity of the occasion weighed on all of us. We four were deciding not only the future leadership of the party but our individual futures, particularly Bill's. And his future course bore on the future of others. Just as Bill had had his heart set on leading the party to the next election, Lionel Bowen was set on being Foreign Minister in a future Labor government. As Deputy Leader he was entitled to select his portfolio. With Bill now denied his prize, he eyed off Lionel's, and wanted it. As if the occasion wasn't heart-wrenching enough, a heated argument broke out between Bill and Lionel about the Foreign Affairs portfolio. The fight got very personal, with each giving the other a precise summation of their respective characters. Lionel objected to Bill taking Foreign Affairs from him and to some of the other demands about the future that Bill wanted as a pre-condition for resignation.

At the height of the tension, sometime after 11 a.m. Brisbane time, a messenger came to the door. 'I want to tell you that Malcolm Fraser has gone out to see the Governor-General.'

The squabbling ceased for a moment and there was a burst of laughter; we knew that the only reason Malcolm would visit the Governor-General at that time of day was to seek a double dissolution. We returned to the brokering. Lionel, being Lionel, made it clear that while he wasn't happy about giving up Foreign Affairs he was not going to allow that to stand in the way of change.

Bill had other conditions. Although he was a broken man, the way he fought for what he wanted was admirable and I respected his deter-mination. Reflecting his disappointment, he wanted to retire from politics after a brief interlude. In that event he asked to be Australia's High Commissioner in London. If that was what he wanted, he could have it – he was a worthy representative of the country's interests. This request, though, was driven by pain; to Bill's perpetual credit, the terri-ble depression which made him consider leaving politics lifted later and in time was replaced by commitment to the incoming Hawke Labor Government.

After reducing the transition agreement to writing we returned to the conference room downstairs where Bill announced his resignation to the Shadow Cabinet. In the emotional tumult which followed, the exuberance of my long-time supporters was mixed with the special sympathy for Bill of the die-hard Haydenites. But dominating everything was the exultation that we were about to take on Fraser and beat the hell out of him. Tom Uren indicated that the total support of the Left for my accession would make the necessary Caucus meeting a formality. This time I knew he spoke with authority.

In all this euphoria – the euphoria of future expectations – Bill was a sad and lonely figure of a past that hadn't worked out. He showed enormous courage but it was asking too much of human nature that there should be no touch of rancour in him. Thus, in announcing to the public his decision to stand down, he observed that 'a drover's dog could lead the Labor Party to victory the way the country is and the way the opinion polls are showing up for the Labor Party'. It was a pity he couldn't have kept the drover's dog kennelled within his deep disappointment, but, given his drained and highly emotional state, it was a fairly modest contribution to the record of political spleen. Certainly, I experienced far worse in the years ahead.

Leadership challenges often provoke bitterness, even hatred in some, but there was none of that in my feeling towards Bill Hayden. To the hard-headed and cynical it may appear hypocritical, but on that day my own jubilation was mixed with real sadness for the man I had defeated. I was the immediate cause of his pain. In the world of politics, at least, I hurt him more than anybody else had ever done. My understanding of this was confirmed later when I first discussed, at his request, appointing him to the position of Governor-General of Australia, and we had an intimate discussion about the trauma of 1982 and 1983 and, particularly, of that day in Brisbane.[17]

For Hayden, those events had opened up wounds from childhood. He had been reared in dirt-poor Mabel Street, South Brisbane, on the wrong side of the tracks; his earliest memories were of frequent beltings with a rubber hose by his drunken father. I couldn't help but compare this with the atmosphere of love with which I had been surrounded during all my formative years.

Difficult beginnings had coiled Bill like a spring and driven him forward, first into the police force, then into Federal Parliament where, to his great credit, he acquired a degree in Economics while working as a sitting Member. As Minister for Social Security in the Whitlam Government he tenaciously engineered a national comprehensive medical insurance scheme. Then in the dying days of the Whitlam era, at a time of diabolical economic and political strife for the Government, he was thrown in at the deep-end as the nation's Treasurer. In that job he impressed everyone with his toughness and determination.

So, here was a man building himself up in every way; every way, that is, except one – he did not trust people. He had taken to heart his mother's advice: 'Bill, don't trust anyone.' By the 1980s Hayden's distrust of people loomed as a serious disadvantage. He obviously trusted his wife, Dallas, but his life in politics was marred by his suspicious attitude towards others. His ability to apply himself diligently to improving his academic capacities, his knowledge and technical expertise so as to equip himself for leadership wasn't matched by expertise with people.

Maybe the prime ministership would have despatched his anxieties. He would have seen it as proof positive to everyone, his family, his acquaintances, the world, that whatever his background was, whatever limitations he had, or thought he had, or others may have thought he had, he had made it in his own right, and there he was – Prime Minister. Being deprived of that final proof was a painful experience. I am not saying that Hayden's life was in any way just about proving himself. Bill had a commitment to Labor principles and he wanted to change Australia for the better, but there was a strand running through all his endeavours in which he was declaring: 'I am worthy of any job in this country.' And he was.

NINE

For all the pain 3rd February 1983 caused Hayden and his family, that day in Brisbane was a tumult of many other emotions, and larger national concerns. For me, it seemed a moment of destiny, as if the whole of my life had been lived in anticipation of, and preparation for, that day. I felt an enormous sense of excitement and pleasure in our out-manoeuvring of the Tories. The bloodless switch from Hayden to me had taken Malcolm Fraser completely by surprise. His schoolboy boast about catching Labor with its pants down had rankled with the party, which remembered 1975 when Sir John Kerr's constitutional coup against the Whitlam Government had given Fraser an illegitimate leg-up to power. Now it was our turn.

Imagine our piquant sense of excitement at having captured Fraser and his Government unawares. At 12.20 p.m. when he arrived at Government House seeking a double dissolution from the Governor-General, Fraser thought he was fighting Bill Hayden as Opposition Leader. Twenty minutes later, as events unfolded in Brisbane, it turned out he was fighting me.

Malcolm's whole purpose in calling an early election had been to stop Labor switching leaders. Certainly that was his thinking when senior Liberals met at the Lodge on Wednesday, 2nd February. His strategy was to get to Government House as quickly as possible, to lock Labor into Hayden. The tactic was not new. In 1977 Fraser had rushed to the polls a year early to prevent any challenge to the then-Leader of the Labor Party, Gough Whitlam. Malcolm was always precipitate in electoral contests; 1983 was the fourth election he had engineered in just over seven years. In calling it, he was trying to dictate to the Labor Party in the same fashion in which he ran the Coalition, and, unfortunately, the country.

As a politician he deeply feared meeting me in a head-to-head contest on the hustings. It was a fear of some years' standing, dating back to the time before I entered the Parliament when he had denounced various proposals I floated in my 1979 Boyer lectures.[18] What upset him, particularly, was my suggestion that some Cabinet posts should be offered to men and women of talent who were outside the Parliament. Malcolm is discomforted by new ideas, certainly, but his main reaction then, I think, was that I would somehow wheedle myself into government without being elected. Ironically, he had managed his own transition to the prime ministership on 11th November 1975 without an election by the Australian people.

Now that I was in the Parliament, duly elected by the people of Wills, Malcolm was determined to stymie the timing of my succession to the Labor leadership. In going early, he was also trying to prolong his own prime ministership. His dash to Yarralumla, to be sure, had its admirers. The Melbourne *Age* gasped at his 'tactical brilliance'. But to more prescient observers, the Prime Minister's manoeuvre was a tangle of belts and braces coiled around his imperious ankles.

Not everyone had it wrong at *The Age*. The cartoonist Tandberg drew a triumphant Malcolm Fraser calling, off-stage as it were, 'Bill, I've caught you with your pants down!' 'It's Bob!' I yell. Underneath, a dejected Fraser stands in polka-dotted briefs, his trousers six feet five inches down, hobbling him.

Some in the Coalition, too, were sceptical of Malcolm's tactical brilliance. When the Governor-General, Sir Ninian Stephen, sent Malcolm away to prepare a fuller explanation of his reasons for a double dissolution, the Coalition leadership, aware now that I was to be the Leader of the Opposition, toyed with the idea of withdrawing the request. By that stage, however, events were too far advanced and Malcolm was snared in his own worst political nightmare – fighting me. All of this added spice to that truly unforgettable day, one of the most dramatic, surely, in the political history of our nation.

The 3rd February 1983 was not only extraordinary because the Labor Party had changed its Leader and the Coalition had called an election; it was also extraordinary for being a watershed, a day on which healing began both within the Labor Party and, more broadly, within the country. Labor scented triumph for the first time since it had been hijacked out of government on 11th November 1975. The leadership crisis had been resolved, not without pain, but without bloodshed. All sectors of the party, even those disappointed by the change of leadership, were pulling behind me. The attitude of Hayden's closest supporters was that if he could live with the leadership change and resign in the interests of the party, then who were they to nurture resentment? Besides, they were also caught up in the excitement that, with the election less than a month away, Labor was on the edge of victory.

For the country generally, this was a critical time. The economy was in deep recession, the mood of the people depressed. Although Australia was a much smaller economy in those days, unemployment topped 10 per cent. Inflation was higher still, hovering around 11 per cent, well above the OECD average. Our rate of growth in per capita income was also well down on comparable countries, and had been so throughout most of the Fraser period. The deficit was growing by alarming proportions, although by just how much we would not discover until after we were in government.

When announcing the double dissolution Malcolm Fraser said, 'We don't need to sit back and wait for the rest of the world.' The irony was that we had fallen so far behind the world during the seven years of his Government that our task was now to catch up.

The indicators of the state of our economic well-being were one thing; they did not reveal the dispirited mood of the country, the extent to which we were divided against ourselves and set at each others' throats. There was no way to measure the great divide existing in Australia between employer and employee, rich and poor, male and female, young and old, city and country.

We were a nation beset by confrontation and 'isms': sectarianism, racism, sexism, ageism. Much of this was, of course, endemic and dated back to our beginnings as a penal colony. These violent origins didn't help us to live easily together in this part of the world. The tyranny of distance made us sometimes xenophobic and wary of outsiders and of each other. Without extending the analysis of how we came to be the way we were as a nation, it was clear that thirty years of Tory rule, broken only by a brief interregnum of Labor government from 1972 to 1975, had done little to bond Australians together. From 1975 the polarisation of Australian society had become more pronounced. Malcolm Fraser himself was a symbol of division in this country, his stony features projecting the very image of confrontation.

Nowhere was his legacy of confrontation more clearly seen than in industrial relations. So riven by strife had this field become under Fraser, that on 30th January 1983, four days before Hayden cleared the way for my leadership, I addressed the Summer School of the Australian Institute of Political Science on the subject 'Industrial Confrontation: Can We Survive It?' I pointed out how the Fraser Government had used industrial relations as an electoral plaything, fuelling industrial conflict through a mass of legislation attacking the rights of Australian working men and women in both the public and private sectors.

In the public sector, laws passed in 1977 gave the Federal Government sweeping arbitrary powers to stand down, suspend or dismiss Commonwealth public servants involved in, or affected by, industrial action. In 1978, these laws were condemned by the Freedom of Association Committee of the International Labor Organisation. In the private sector, the Fraser Government used social services legislation to prevent the payment of benefits to people engaged in or affected by industrial action. Obsessed by a divisive and punitive philosophy, the Government even denied unemployment benefits to those thrown out of work by the action of others.

I said much more about the Government's industrial relations in that speech, but the essential point I made was that the time for provocation, confrontation, and the exacerbation of division in Australia was over. We had to make a new beginning. The task was one of bringing the country together.

The speech turned out to be seminal, for in the course of it I floated a concept for moving towards a sense of national unity. As the party's industrial relations spokesman I called for the convening of a national economic summit in which employers, unionists, governments and others would meet and forge their way towards a common understanding. I pledged the full resources of the Federal Government and its instrumentalities (the Treasury, the Reserve Bank, the Industries Assistance Commission, and other relevant departments) to assist in laying bare the economic realities both at home and abroad. The simple question, I suggested, was whether Australia could continue riven and divided – or were we able to be a nation in accord?

I relished the challenge of presenting the starkness of this alternative to the Australian people. I knew I would do it well. I have always enjoyed campaigning. At that stage I had done more election campaigns than most people in the party. But I had always been, in a sense, fashioning and firing the bullets for others. Now I was leading the cannonade. The twist, I suppose, was that the cannonade was aimed at urging people to drop their weapons, and move forward in peaceful co-operation.

Our theme for the campaign was reconciliation, recovery, reconstruction – the three r's. The ideas of recovery and reconstruction had been kicking about in the Labor Party for some time. They had multiple authors and had emerged against a backdrop of high and growing unemployment, high inflation and interest rates, and flat or declining economic growth.

The theme of national reconciliation, however, was my own contribution to the trilogy and the glue that bonded all three elements together. This was encapsulated at an executive meeting of the party held at Labor's New South Wales' headquarters in Sussex Street, Sydney. Bill Hayden was still Opposition Leader at that stage and I recall that he and others talked endlessly about their ideas of how Labor should go into the next election. I jotted down three words – *reconciliation, recovery, reconstruction* – on a scrap of paper and shoved them under John Button's nose. 'That's the guts of what the election and our Government has got to be about.' Button nodded.

Later, I outlined my ideas more fully in a paper which I prepared for Labor's campaign committee meeting on 20th January 1983.[19] I argued that the Fraser period had eroded any sense of common national purpose. The community had a desire for healing, for a sense of common purpose in the face of increasing social disintegration. My theme of reconciliation was backed by three powerful arguments: 'It's right; it represents what the electorate wants; and in itself, it's cost-free.'

The country had to be reconciled. Without reconciliation there would be no recovery, there could be no reconstruction. Reconciliation, then, and consensus – a word that has become almost synonymous with my style – were vital to me as we marched toward government.

Ironically, the hard heads in the Australian Labor Party, concentrated mainly in the New South Wales Right, still needed convincing of the virtues of consensus. They thought that the themes of reconciliation, recovery and reconstruction were good alliteration and useful window- dressing, but nothing more. Even my friend, the Labor great, Neville Wran, Premier of New South Wales and ALP President at the time, was sceptical: 'If the greedy bastards wanted spiritualism, they'd join the fucking Hare Krishnas,' he told a campaign meeting in Sydney the day after I became, practically but not formally, the leader of the party. (I was formally elected, unopposed, parliamentary Leader of the Australian Labor Party on Tuesday, 8th February 1983.)

There was a sense in which the hardened party professionals had been blinded by the internecine strife which characterised parliamentary politics in Australia. Like others in the community accustomed to division, they, too, needed to have their eyes opened to fresh possibilities. The theme of reconciliation and consensus offered the country a new start.

I came to Canberra in 1980, unencumbered by years of political baggage, with a background of brokering peace on the industrial front and accustomed to finding ways through threatened impasses. I often thanked my lucky stars that I had not been elected to Parliament in 1963. Who knows what twenty years in Parliament, with all but three of them in Opposition, would have done to my sense of what was possible for Australia in 1983? Or what it would have done to me?

In any event, the notion of consensus wasn't all hope and fresh air. One of its basic underpinnings was reaching an Accord with the trade union movement. The Accord would be central to Labor's alternative economic strategy for getting Australia out of recession. In essence, it was based on shifting the focus of wage bargaining away from money wages towards a social wage based on real wages after taxation and government expenditure. It was also aimed ultimately at introducing superannuation schemes throughout the workforce.

There is little doubt that wage increases at that time, particularly the wages explosion ignited by Fraser in 1982, had come at the cost of increasing unemployment. Wage restraint, then, was fundamental to job security for those in work, and to job creation for those out of work. The primary objective of the Accord was to secure policies which would result in faster economic growth and a reduction in unemployment.

I had, in fact, begun the Accord negotiations before leaving the presidency of the Australian Council of Trade Unions and pursued these negotiations in Parliament in partnership with fellow Opposition frontbencher, Ralph Willis. Between us we knew the Australian labour movement inside out. In particular, our close relationship with the trade union leadership was fundamental in striking the Accord.

At the ACTU we were negotiating with Simon Crean and Bill Kelty, both of whom helped enormously to develop and maintain the Accord. Crean and Kelty are qualified economists. They understood the Accord not merely as an instrument for responsible wages determination but as a unique mechanism for achieving positive economic and social outcomes which would otherwise be impossible.

The Accord, painstakingly pieced together through years of Opposition, anchored consensus to a firmer base than mere aspiration and spiritualism. Even so, there were those in the party who remained sceptical. Indeed one of the few hiccups in the 1983 campaign came when the Shadow Treasurer, Paul Keating, told his favourite radio talk-back host, Sydney broadcaster John Laws, that he was unsure about the workability of the Accord. I was in Townsville, in north Queensland, when I learned of his *faux pas*. I was furious and my anger went a little beyond 'Oh, Paul! Why did you say that?'

One forgives and forgets these things, but it raised doubts in many minds at the time about Paul's ability as putative Treasurer in a Labor government. Earlier, he had put in what he himself conceded was a very poor performance at the launch of the party's economic policy on 10th February. He was nervous and plainly out of his depth, and gave perhaps the worst display I have seen him give; but then later that day he did very well in a debate with the Coalition Treasurer, John Howard, on national television. Now he had given me fresh cause for concern.

Fraser seized on the slip with the fervour of a drowning man desperate for rescue, but happily, by that stage in the campaign Labor's fortunes were strong enough to withstand this mistake.

Malcolm was in the grip of panic. His flailing had culminated a couple of days earlier at a rally he addressed in Melbourne, when years of anti-Labor rhetoric spilled over into uncontrolled hysteria. Desperate to paint Labor as profligate and fiscally loose, he went over the top. He warned that people's hard-earned savings would no longer be safe: 'Under Labor it'd be safer under your bed than it would be in the banks,' he threatened. 'They would be robbing the savings of the people to pay for their mad and extravagant promises.'

I was thoroughly enjoying myself. I knew then that Fraser was finished and I had great pleasure in laughing away his ludicrous warning. Reviving memories of the Coalition's hysterical McCarthyist tactic of earlier years of trying to associate Labor with the communists, I told my fellow Australians, 'They can't put [their savings] under the bed, because that's where the commies are!'

As we entered the final phase of the 1983 campaign my rapport with the Australian people was at its height. There have been various attempts to analyse this relationship. Writers and journalists have fumbled around in what they claim is my own and the nation's psyche to deliver hyperbolic analyses; they have spoken of ancient and inchoate forces, as if something mystical was at work. To me, the explanation for the rapport I have always felt with my fellow Australians, and they with me, is much simpler. My mother and father were always doing pastoral work. They were forever talking to people, persuading, charming, ministering, always trying to win hearts and minds for the Church. They expressed a deep commitment to others. That commitment had both religious and political elements which seemed to sit together very comfortably in a non-conformist Congregational Church. There was none of the exclusivity and taboo prevalent in other church denominations of the time, none of the deliberate closing of doors to those of other faiths. The non-conformist church ethic, with its commitment to and acceptance of one's fellows, bred in me an openness that made me eager to engage with people from all walks of life.

In addition, I was heavily influenced throughout my youth by my uncle, Albert Hawke. Albert was a born politician. He was hail-fellow-well-met, with a hello for everyone, a good sense of humour and a love of playing the crowd. Years of exposure to his 'people skills' helped them rub off on me. I knew that he and my parents expected a lot of me, and I have tried never to step away from meeting the commitment they inspired in me to serve others.

It is not enough, however, to cast everything in terms of family history and obligation. The simple fact is that I like people. I like to listen to people and I am a good listener. I understand and respect what people have to say and the beliefs they hold.

In 1983, as I travelled the length and breadth of the continent calling for an end to division and a fresh start, I was aware of an enormous reservoir of goodwill towards me. One of my many public psychoanalysts has said that I walk everywhere in a warm tropical breeze, as if this was somehow a bad thing. In fact, I do. The Australian people are a warm, generous race and I revelled in meeting them in all their various contexts: on the factory floor, in country towns, in suburban shopping malls, in the outback, in the cities, in boardrooms, in pubs, in their homes – everywhere. I felt confident as I travelled about that people knew me. It is not as though I had suddenly jumped out of the ground. Before the 1983 campaign I had been in public life for a quarter of a century. I did not burst upon the scene as a complete enigma. I had always been accessible and no-one, I believe, saw me as placing myself above the mob. Australians detest snobbery and anybody who seems 'up himself'.

That Australians regarded me as one of them, and I felt part of them, was one of the great psychic rewards of the 1983 campaign, and of my subsequent years as Prime Minister. When campaigning in 1983 I was determined to promote Labor as a party which would govern for all Australians. This did not mean that each and every citizen would necessarily have to agree with all our policies. But I was determined to be the leader for the whole nation.

In 1983 a bitter and divisive environmental controversy was raging over the proposed building of the Gordon-below-Franklin dam in Tasmania. The dam threatened to flood a large part of the Gordon and the lower Franklin Rivers, irreversibly damaging a key part of the world's natural heritage. Through much of 1982 there were serious clashes between the forces for and against the dam. In particular, a blockade on the Gordon, and on the Crotty Road leading towards the dam site, organised mainly by the Tasmanian Wilderness Society, showed the extent of the animosity generated by the dispute. Many of the environmental protesters risked life and limb as they battled bull-dozers, dam workers and those whose livelihoods depended upon the building of the dam. There were some fifteen hundred arrests.

Labor had declared itself against the Franklin dam at the 1982 National Conference. Although only a handful of votes had decided the issue, by February 1983 our pledge to the Australian people was clear and unambiguous. A Labor government would use all the powers at its disposal to ensure that the dam was abandoned, I told electors during my campaign speech from the Sydney Opera House on 16th February 1983. I added that Tasmania would not be economically disadvantaged by this decision.

Research polls showed us that whereas mainland Australia was firmly against building the dam, the majority of Tasmanians, seeing in the Franklin proposal valuable opportunities for employment, wanted the project to go ahead. I did everything I could to persuade Tasmanians of the wisdom of our no-dams policy. In the course of a short, hectic campaign I twice visited the Tasmanian capital, Hobart, in an effort to turn local voters around. In one speech at the Hobart Town Hall I spoke for an hour and a half, exhorting all those present to go out and convince two other voters to vote Labor, and for those two voters to convince two more. My staff despaired at the energy I devoted to what our research showed was a hopeless task. But the need to reach out – to build, in this case to build bridges not dams – was forever on my mind. This openness and receptivity to argument and discussion was the method by which Labor intended to govern. 'It's not a matter of having to choose between environment and development,' I said during my policy speech. 'With sensible policies, and a willing-ness to resolve problems through negotiation and consensus, Australia can have both.'

As it turned out, my exhortations to the Tasmanian people were not enough. Tasmania held out against the national swing which swept Labor to power on 5th March with a twenty-five seat majority; while all other States and Territories swung to Labor, in some cases by huge margins (Western Australia – 8.3 per cent, the Australian Capital Territory – 6.9 per cent) with the national average being just under 4 per cent, our vote in Tasmania dropped by 3.5 per cent. The reduced vote in Tasmania was not to be used as a pretext for changing policies. On claiming victory just after midnight on 6th March 1983 I stated, 'The dam will not go ahead.' Our electoral showing in Tasmania was a reminder that the politics of consensus and of reconciliation didn't end at the ballot box, but began there.

It is usual for Prime Ministers-elect to claim victory at the national tally room. There, supporters, well-wishers, barrackers and excited revellers would cheer in the new Prime Minister and his Government. There were certainly scenes of great excitement later in the night as I toured the various media booths in the tally room at the Canberra Showgrounds. But the actual claiming of victory was made in the studios of the national broadcaster, the Australian Broadcasting Corporation, not in the tally room.

There is no doubt that we had won an historic victory. But the atmosphere in my suite at the Lakeside Hotel in Canberra as staffers and close family and friends watched the results being posted was more subdued than might have been expected. All of us had been through the triumphs and disappointments of an earlier period when, in 1972, the Whitlam Government had swept to power in a wave of euphoria and then, in 1975, was tipped out of power so ignominiously – first by a constitutional coup then by a thrashing at the polls. So our win in 1983 was tempered by a good deal more realism than the Whitlam victory of a decade earlier. We also knew that we were participants in and witnesses of a great event in Australian political history. That encourages sobriety rather than euphoria. The most unrestrained enthusiasm was shown by my father, Clem. After just a few hours' sleep this very proud old gentleman was down in the foyer of the hotel at 8.00 a.m. telling anyone who cared to listen what a great Prime Minister the country had acquired. Clem remained my most ardent supporter until his death at Christmas 1989, aged ninety-one.

For me, there was an element of premonition in the victory. At no stage after that historic day in Brisbane on 3rd February 1983 did I have any doubt about the outcome of the election, or that I would be Prime Minister come 5th March. So sitting in a chair watching the swings go up for Labor, my mood was one of calm certainty. Now began the task of governing.

The victory heralded an enormous change in the life of my family. It is sometimes thought that political leaders somehow exist in a vacuum, without a family life. But during the 1983 campaign our daughter Ros was married, and on the very day of the election, 5th March, my father celebrated his eighty-fifth birthday. His birthday, and the great achievement that day represented in my life, inevitably reminded us of the absence of my mother, Ellie. She had had this wild dream, this vision about her son. I remember thinking how marvellous it would have been if she had been alive to see her ambition and commitment realised. Hazel and I were also aware of the huge transformation which 5th March would make to our daily lives. All of these factors made the occasion joyous, but solemn too. For that reason, it seemed more appropriate for me to claim victory in a straight-to-camera piece without interview, without the hurly-burly of microphones being thrust in my face; in short, without the tumultuous scenes one often encounters in the national tally room.

But while the personal and political drama of gaining office carries its own solemnity and weight, it is of a different order, and far lighter than that involved in losing office. For Labor loyalists, 'the big bastard' had gone, and we were in government. For Malcolm Fraser it meant taking 'total responsibility for the timing of the federal election … total responsibility for the conduct of that election … total responsibility for the defeat of the government'. *The Age* cartoonist Tandberg, who had so accurately captured Malcolm with his pants down on 4th February, returned again to capture just as accurately the vanquished Fraser. His cartoon in the morning's press was of an Easter Island statue with a tear in its eye.

The prime ministership had begun and ended badly for Malcolm. His leadership was tainted by November 1975. Snatching government in those bitter circumstances required that, if he were to succeed, he had to show a capacity for reconciliation. But given his lonely, patrician background, it's not surprising that he lacked that very capacity.

Fraser's lack of exposure to the country he came to govern was virtually unique in Australian public life. It's little wonder he was ill at ease with people. I recall seeing him at the annual Australian Rules grand final breakfast staged by the North Melbourne Football Club, so unable to sustain a conversation that people just wandered off. Even utterly gregarious types who could amuse themselves talking to trees if need be would run out of things to say in Malcolm's presence.

This inability to mix affected Fraser's ability to be a leader and made his leadership counterproductive. He was a dominating Prime Minister who stuck his nose into every area of government. His ministers were always being second-guessed and overridden. A brilliant mind, equipped with Malcolm's application and hard work, might have succeeded. But Malcolm lacked that, and his Government, in the event, lacked a cohesive sense of direction. The paradox of his seven years in office is that he came to power as the hard, brutal man of Australian politics who would be prepared to take tough decisions. For five years as Prime Minister, he controlled both Houses of Parliament.

The fact that he held such power but did not exercise it magnified his party's massive and continuing disappointment with him.

Yet for all the criticisms one can make of Malcolm Fraser, he had one great positive feature – he was totally intolerant of racism. He wasn't a late convert either. At one stage the Federal ALP office made a check back through his speeches to his earliest days in public life. He was always absolutely rock solid on the issue. I always respected Fraser for his colour blindness, and I saw in him, in this respect, a fellow spirit. That is why I later proposed him for important international positions within the Commonwealth.

III

RECONCILIATION, RECOVERY, RECONSTRUCTION

TEN

I had no intention of imitating the frenetic early days of the Whitlam Government, when the artificial duumvirate of Gough and his deputy, Lance Barnard, churned out forty decisions in less than a fortnight. However, the doomed Fraser ministry had thrown up a major crisis which required my immediate attention and decision.

During the campaign the Minister for Industry and Commerce, Andrew Peacock, constrained neither by principle nor the slightest knowledge of the subject, predicted a 15 per cent devaluation of the Australian dollar should Labor come to power. Fraser had added to market nervousness with his farcical 'money under the bed' statement.

Markets lacked today's sophistication and the Coalition's fear-mongering set off a flight of capital. After Peacock opened the flood-gates with his irresponsible speculation on 17th February, $2700 million fled the country. By the standards of the time this was a huge sum. Fanned by the Coalition, rumours swept the market that a Labor government would regulate foreign investment to prevent people taking their money out of Australia. If the rumours were wrong, investors reasoned, they could return their capital after the election; so why run the risk of having it locked up?

During the campaign I had done what I could to soothe the markets. I carefully and consistently refused to enter into speculation about the exchange rate and fielded calls from the United States, reassuring investors of Australia's soundness under Labor. But the leader of Her Majesty's Loyal Opposition can only do so much when faced with a disloyal Government intent on talking the country down.

The capital flight was enormously costly to Australian taxpayers, and to domestic borrowers. In those days we had a managed exchange rate system. Those wishing to take money out of Australia had either to borrow money here and convert it to foreign currency, or to sell securities or assets in Australia and convert them into foreign currency. The heavy borrowings and the selling of assets put upward pressure on interest rates. Not only that, the Reserve Bank of Australia was obliged to clear the market every day. In the lead-up to the election, and immediately afterwards, there were daily trades of one and two hundred million dollars' worth of Australian currency being sold. As the Reserve Bank had to buy Australian dollars at a fixed rate this imposed an enormous cost on the Australian taxpayer. Malcolm Fraser, his Treasurer, John Howard, and Andrew Peacock had effectively delivered the taxpayer into the arms of speculators, the main movers of money out of the country.

Come Sunday, 6th March, the Coalition, having created the problem, were no longer around to deal with it. Their tactic had failed with the voters but, unfortunately, had worked with the money movers. That Sunday I was still at the Lakeside Hotel, briefly the headquarters of the Government-elect. Preliminary discussions about the currency crisis took place early on Sunday afternoon when the Treasury mandarin, John Stone, and one of his deputies, Dick Rye, briefed Paul Keating and several senior Labor Party staffers on the state of the Australian economy.

Space was at a premium at the Lakeside that day and the meeting took place in the hotel's saloon bar. This classy venue was apparently chosen after the party ruled out the hotel manager's interesting suggestion that the group might like to hold their discussion in the hotel foyer.

The meeting, minus Stone and Rye, adjourned to my suite. Before discussing the subject of devaluation, I wanted to nail down the size of the deficit left to us by the outgoing Government. Late in the campaign a tip-off had alerted me to the possibility of a Budget deficit considerably higher than that disclosed by the Government. I was well aware of the implications of a high deficit for our election program. On the day before the election, an opportunity arose to express my concern about a possibly inflated deficit. Addressing the National Press Club, I was asked if changed circumstances would result in Labor climbing down from its election promises. I confirmed that agreed outcomes at the summit would of course affect our economic policies. I remember saying that I would be 'very, very interested' in Treasury assessments of the deficit.

Now, the day of reckoning had arrived. When Paul and his team reported in from the saloon bar meeting I asked Dr Barry Hughes – an economist with the University of Adelaide and later a consultant to Paul Keating – for the Treasury readout on the 1982–83 deficit. '$4.3 billion,' he replied. The figure was not significantly larger than the $4 billion estimate of the deficit supplied by the Fraser Government. That surprised me in view of the information I had received about a larger deficit, but before I could pursue this Hughes chipped in: 'Don't you want to know what the projection is for 1983–84?' Of course I did. '$9.6 billion,' he declared.

This figure was contained in the infamous Treasury minute handed over at their earlier meeting by John Stone, disclosing what was then the largest projected Federal Budget deficit in history. The minute said:

> The magnitude of the fiscal imbalance is unprecedented in Australia during peace time, as is the level of Government spending. The budget balance is projected to deteriorate from near zero to more than 6 per cent of GDP in a two-year period. The speed and magnitude of that deterioration is almost without precedent among the major OECD countries in the post-war period.

I knew that we had struck political gold, that my tip-off was correct. At the same time I was painfully aware of the implications of the figure for our program, and for our economic management of the country. When Stone and Rye dropped by shortly afterwards they were preaching to a Prime Minister who did not need to be convinced. Stone was nevertheless intent on getting his message across: with the deficit blowing out to that degree, there was no room for profligacy. His concepts of profligacy and mine were entirely different and I had no intention of entering a new Stone Age, but the basic facts were unavoidable.

That $9.6 billion figure became a stick with which we were justifiably able to beat the Liberal–National Party Opposition for several years. Fraser had sat on the figure, refusing to disclose it to the Australian public even though, as I know, he was urged to do so by a senior Liberal Party minister. Having told people for six years to tighten their belts, he had opened the fiscal throttle full-bore in the seventh year as the scent of an election gathered in his nostrils.

Compounding its deception in not having disclosed the $9.6 billion figure, the former Government later attempted to argue that the Treasury figure represented the 'first bids' of Government departments. The outgoing Prime Minister claimed that 'competent ministers would have knocked $3 billion off that figure before it was ever presented to Cabinet'. In fact, the Treasury projections made no allowance for any such bids.

Stone's Treasury minute and his briefing that Sunday afternoon on the size of the projected deficit materially affected much of the Government's deliberations during the course of 1983: its preparation for the summit, the May statement, the June Premiers' Conference, and the Budget itself. But overshadowing the Budget deficit, and clamouring for our immediate attention that day, was the currency.

Knowing Stone's position on this issue was not crucial to my thinking but I was intrigued as to what his attitude would be. His uncompromising fight-inflation-first mentality would make him wary of cheapening the dollar and I expected him to be concerned about any diminution in the power of the group of three (Stone, the Governor of the Reserve Bank and the Deputy Secretary of the Prime Minister's Department) responsible for managing the country's exchange rate. But, to his credit, Stone generally favoured a devaluation, although he wisely cautioned a wait-and-see policy over the next twenty-four hours while we kept a close watch on the currency. If speculation against the Australian dollar continued, the next question was how big a devaluation was needed to kill it. Opinion was divided. My department and Treasury argued for 5 per cent. The Reserve Bank advocated 10 per cent, arguing for a hit big enough to convince the markets that this was a oncer with no second instalments.

Throughout Monday we tick-tacked with the Bank. Early reports showed little capital movement and some thought the crisis might have abated. In the afternoon the outflow quickened. Towards dusk, two symbols combined to remind me how much life had changed in two days. Not only was I deliberating on the value of the Australian dollar, but the deliberations had shifted from the Lakeside Hotel in

Canberra to Kirribilli House, the Prime Minister's official residence in Sydney.

Shortly after our arrival we received word from the Governor of the Reserve Bank, Bob Johnston, that $200 million had left the country that day. He advised that devaluation was imperative. From Canberra, Stone agreed that the time for wait-and-see had passed.

A principal concern for me was the impact that devaluation would have on the fledgling Accord struck with the trade union movement. The Accord was a co-operative bargain aimed at wage restraint. But the immediate consequence of devaluation is to push up inflation because of the increased price of imports. Should the union movement follow up these movements with higher wage claims, the Accord would be doomed and so, too, would the devaluation. Wage increases would put further pressure on the currency, and we would have entered a cycle of devaluation, inflation, devaluation.

So, beginning on the Sunday, I kept in close contact with the leadership of the ACTU, notably with the Council's secretary Bill Kelty. I was assured that in this first test of the Accord the union movement would take a reasonable view about the impact of the devaluation. We shared a common understanding that the inflationary effects of the devaluation would be diminished by the deteriorating position of the economy at that time.

We were thus poised to make our first big decision in government. Paradoxically, it was easy. The best advice taken on the best evidence led to only one conclusion – devaluation. Once convinced, I have never worried about taking tough decisions. If it is necessary, you do it. And so, standing in the drawing room at Kirribilli House shortly before dinner we decided to devalue the dollar. After some further discussion over the entrée I concluded and it was agreed that the devaluation should be 10 per cent.

Graham Freudenberg, who had accompanied us from Canberra, captured the essence of the evening. He had known 'the certain grandeur' and the bitter defeat of the Whitlam period and after the devastation of November and December 1975 thought that he had seen the last of Kirribilli House. For him the occasion symbolised the drama of a resurrection: Labor was back in charge! Graham, an historian and devotee of Labor, was determined to be part of the action. Just to make sure, he had, in his own inimitable fashion, invited himself to dinner. It was no impromptu invitation. He said to Hazel during the campaign, 'If we win government, there is just one thing I ask as my reward – to be invited back to Kirribilli to dinner after all these years.'

As we came to the end of the meal he stood up and, with a Whitlamesque sweep of his hands, gestured that he wished – indeed, intended – to say something.[20]

'No episode associated with the Labor Party is complete without its speeches,' he began. 'We're addicted to speech-making, so it is obviously incumbent on me as the survivor from the Whitlam days to say a few words at this historic gathering at Kirribilli House on this 7th March 1983, the second day of our return to government.' At this, he turned his attention to Hazel, thanking her for the privilege of 'sharing this, your first meal in your official Sydney residence'. After waxing lyrical about her gracious hospitality, he looked across to me.

'Bob,' he said, 'the people of Australia have elected you to the most important position that it is possible for an Australian to hold – Prime Minister. This is indeed a great honour, as I'm sure you realise.' He extolled my capacities to match the honour and meet the challenge. He was, though, merely gilding the way to his peroration, and the most memorable of the evening's *bons mots*: 'Now, back at Kirribilli, I am reminded of the words of Pope Leo X in the 1500s, the last Pope really before the Reformation – "God has given us the papacy, now, let us enjoy it!"'

There was nothing cynical or opportunistic about our enjoyment. In fact as we left the table it spilled over into the pleasure of work, the building for the future. Paul Keating's adviser, John Langmore, and I worked from nine until midnight on the organisation of the economic summit: its structure, who should be invited and the agenda. Peter Sheehan, economic adviser to the Victorian Government, had also joined us for dinner that night and he moved off with Paul Keating to work on a statement about the devaluation.

It was thirsty work and during the course of it the incident referred to in Hazel's autobiography occurred.[21] Hoping to rustle up a cup of tea, I pressed the only button I could see on the sitting room wall. Within seconds two security police burst in on us prepared to defend the Prime Minister against an assassin. Panic quickly dissolved into laughter and amused goodwill towards the new tenant.

In the early hours of Tuesday morning, around 5.00 a.m., the devaluation of the Australian dollar occurred. There was a gap in the twenty-four hour clock during which all major foreign exchange markets around the world were asleep. Through this gap we snuck in the devaluation. Ironically, although the devaluation was our call, aimed at handling the results of their recklessness, the formal decision was the last to be made by the Fraser Government. John Howard was still technically Treasurer and as we dealt with him I couldn't help but feel that Australia's interests would have been better served if his inclinations had prevailed over those of his leader.

That morning I flew back to Canberra and during the trip I read over the press release prepared after dinner, principally by Peter Sheehan, settled by him and John Langmore and cleared by Paul. I was outraged when I picked up a fundamental arithmetical mistake which would have proved highly embarrassing to the new Government. I fumed to Hazel about what I regarded as gross incompetence. To me, it was a telling reminder of how easily carelessness could bring us undone. At the same time, it was reassuring to know I had the technical capacity to pick up such errors.

The arithmetical slip had another consequence. Subtly, informally, without any aggressive canvassing of his candidature, Peter Sheehan was one of a number of individuals being touted for the position of Secretary of the Treasury. Whatever merit there may have been in that option, it was completely closed off after that slip. He was soon back in Melbourne, once again heading up the Victorian Government's Department of Management and Budget. With the deficit blowing out to record levels, big-spending Keynesian economists were not the need of the day. Over the coming weeks there would be some skirmishing between market-oriented economists and traditional Keynesians, but in my mind the debate was already over.

Heading for Canberra that day, I came under heavy pressure to rid Treasury of John Stone, who was an object of hatred for many in the Labor Party. John Langmore in particular was keen for me to move Stone to Defence. He rattled off a list of candidates, including Sheehan, for the Treasury post, although none, he conceded, was a stand-out choice for the job.

For my part I never thought of Stone as indispensable. No-one is. In my view he had not been a model public servant under the Tories. His sharp tongue and public expression of policy judgments during Fraser's term in office should not have been tolerated by his political masters. What's more, he was enormously cynical about the Accord and the upcoming national economic summit. On the other hand, he was an experienced Secretary of Treasury, he had got there on merit, and it was sensible for an incoming government not to be unnecessarily disruptive. My whole concept was one of trying to knit the country together, not of creating unnecessary fights. I was also prepared to give people a go. My long acquaintance with Stone had not endeared him to me – and I knew the feeling was mutual – but I took the view, as I did with everyone, that a person is innocent until proven guilty.

I was advised for example to sack Sir Robert Cotton, Australia's Ambassador to the United States, a Fraser appointee, an ex-Liberal Member of Parliament and former minister. Why should he go? I asked. I had seen Cotton in action. To me, he was a dedicated servant of the country, trying to do his best for Australia. To take another example, people said I shouldn't use Malcolm Fraser's driver, Noel Hansen. 'Bugger that!' I said. I kept Noel and he proved not only a great driver but also a good friend. I started from the presumption that people in the bureaucracy were loyal public servants who understood that there had been a change of government and that they had a duty to serve the new Government as faithfully as they had served the old. So Stone kept the Treasury job. Whether Paul Keating would stay on as his political boss was another judgment I had to make in those first few days of government.

ELEVEN

One of the most fascinating responsibilities of the Prime Minister is the allocation of ministerial portfolios and Cabinet positions after an election. I exercised this responsibility on four occasions – in 1983, 1984, 1987 and 1990 – and it is one of the few duties that did not seem to become simpler with experience.

In part this is because with Labor, as distinct from the Coalition parties who leave it entirely to the Prime Minister, half the job is done by the Caucus. The Caucus elects those who are going to be in the ministry. The arguments are endless as to which is the better system and there are certainly points to be made in favour of both. There is no doubt that on each of the four occasions if it had been my choice alone the composition of the ministry would not have been the same as that delivered to me by the Caucus. But the difference would have been at the margin. By and large the Caucus acts responsibly in recognising talent and experience, while taking into account considerations of faction and geography. The factions themselves, with increasing efficiency and co-operation during my time in office, facilitated this process and were amenable to my suggestions.

It is interesting to note that after Labor's unexpected victory in 1993 the Caucus gave Paul Keating virtually a free hand in the selection of the ministry. The experience of the next nine months, culminating in an extensive reshuffle in December that year, has led the Caucus to make it clear it will not repeat the experiment.

In 1983 my overwhelming feeling was one of gratitude to this strange and marvellous beast, the Australian Labor Party, for the quality of the people it had thrown up into the Federal Parliament and who were then presented to me by the Caucus as the material for the first Hawke ministry. In some mysterious and unco-ordinated way the various State and Territory branches of the party, engaged as they were over many years in the bitterest of factional conflict, still managed to pre-select a range of candidates of outstanding calibre. It was no surprise to me that observers as detached from Labor as Professor Hewson[22] rated these early Hawke ministries as the best in the whole postwar period – I would, in fact, match them against any since Federation.

There was talent in abundance among the twenty-six elected by the Caucus but there were still sensitive decisions to be made as to how best to use that talent and to balance aspirations and experience. I was happy with the tradition that the Deputy Prime Minister and the Leader in the Senate should have the right to nominate their preferred portfolio. Lionel Bowen, re-elected by the Caucus as Deputy Leader and denied his opportunity as Foreign Minister by the deal with Bill Hayden, chose to take the Trade portfolio and to assist me in Commonwealth–State relations. Lionel was the ideal deputy. His loyalty was absolute and he had experience in local and State government, as well as having held several portfolios in the Whitlam Government. An affable, active, shrewd man, with a delightful, self-effacing sense of humour and an uncanny capacity for accurately judging character, Lionel was with, but not of, the NSW Right. Respected across the factions, he became an avuncular figure for many of the newer Members of the Parliament. He struck a particularly close relationship with Michael Duffy from Victoria, whom I appointed

Minister for Communications. The two shared a passion for horse-racing which gave us a common bond, and it was line-ball between them as to who was the worst tipster. If their ministerial tenure had depended upon the quality of the 'good oil' they occasionally confided to me they would have finished on the back bench.

John Button, the Leader in the Senate, took some time to decide what portfolio he wanted. He surprised many of us when he finally settled on Industry and Commerce. It was an inspired choice for as the minister responsible for these important areas he became one of the early success stories of the Government. Not quick to action, he consulted widely and obtained the confidence of his portfolio's constituencies; as a result he was able to bring about significant and necessary changes in Australia's industrial structure.

My appointment of Button as Minister assisting Duffy in Communications – I thought it an inspired move – was less successful. As fellow Independents in the maelstrom of Victorian factional politics, the two had developed an understanding and empathy which did not carry over into their new co-habitation in Communications. They did not regard it as entirely necessary to contain their differences and I was often entertained by their pungent expositions of the other's intellectual inadequacies and character deficiencies.

At that stage I was by no means convinced that Paul Keating was the best qualified for the post of Treasurer. He was very new to the job, unsure of his grasp, and he had twice blundered during the campaign. He had little knowledge of taxation policy, which was particularly worrying, as tax reform was a major plank in our program. Paul's uncertainty on tax issues had resulted in tax policy being carved out of the Shadow Treasurer's brief when Hayden reshuffled his front bench in January.

To be fair to Paul, the Treasury position is a very complex one. Paul had established a considerable reputation in the minerals area and he certainly knew more about that than most people in Australia. But to move from that relatively confined subject to the much broader canvas of Treasury was an enormous challenge for anyone. The fact that Paul didn't bring a relevant academic background was not a bar, but it was a factor which caused some concern to both of us.

The obvious competitor for the Treasury portfolio was Ralph Willis. Unlike Paul, Ralph was at home with the facts and the language of the economy. He had the academic background, practical experience as Shadow Treasurer, and he was a developer and promoter of the Accord, the centrepiece of our economic strategy. Having worked with Ralph at the ACTU I well knew his capacity and his nature. I also knew how much Bill Hayden's decision to replace him with Keating had hurt Ralph, one of a number of disappointments he came to absorb over the years.

Nevertheless Ralph, like Paul, was not then the character he is today. He was a gentle, sensitive person who lacked the firepower he subsequently developed. Paul's lack of confidence at that stage stemmed from his comparative economic illiteracy. Ralph, on the other hand, had all the technical skills but seemed to lack tough personal confidence, or at least the ability to project it. Keating, as Hayden had recognised, was the better salesman.

In the end Paul's potential as a publicist tipped my hand in his direction, although with some reluctance. Other factors, too, weighed in his favour. Paul was the parliamentary leader of the New South Wales Right, whose support I had relied upon in my bid for the leadership. We had also campaigned with him as Shadow Treasurer and there was a measure of expectation in the electorate, or sectors of it, that Paul would serve as Treasurer in the Labor Government.

In any case I had to decide on the best overall use of talent and on the smoothest course to effective government. There were other key economic portfolios besides Treasury and I had no doubt that

Ralph Willis, would be a magnificent Minister for Employment and Industrial Relations, a judgment which turned out to be correct.

As for Paul, I was confident he would grow into the Treasurer's job and I was willing to act as his mentor and assist him as much as I possibly could. The very first days of government had underlined the extent of decision-making left to the Prime Minister in consultation with the Treasurer. I told Paul that we would continue 'to do the job together' and urged him to get good, competent people around him and to get his head down. I assured him that while he was learning the ropes he would have my ready support. For a long time he was nervous, but to his credit he applied himself assiduously to learning not just the detail but also the ambience of the Treasurership. He acquired an excellent range of very able personal staff both from within and outside Treasury. He developed the capacity to absorb the thinking, language and ideas of these people and of Treasury officials whom he trusted. They naturally responded and became a source of strength in helping him to become undoubtedly one of the best Treasurers in Australia's history.

Although much has been written and said about the conflict which exploded between Paul Keating and me in the latter stages of my prime ministership, the true story of our relations for the greater part of that period is that it had more to do with commonality of purpose than with conflict. It was a commonality of purpose which, after early doubts by some of the Left, increasingly became the commonality of purpose of my entire Government.

I say 'my Government' because it was the Hawke Government, not the Hawke–Keating Government. To say otherwise is to misstate history just as roundly as if we were to describe John Curtin's prime ministership in the 1940s as the Curtin–Chifley Government, even though no-one doubts the powerful role played in the Curtin Government by the Treasurer, Ben Chifley. I do not make this point simply out of personal pride; rather I wish to emphasise that the Hawke Labor Government was a team which became the most successful long-term Labor Government because of the range of talent it exercised in a collective fashion.

Paul Keating was vitally important. But so were others. In the economic field, besides Ralph Willis, the contributions of John Dawkins and Peter Walsh were outstanding. Dawkins, quick, abrasive but an adventurous lateral thinker, made formidable contributions to trade policy and, in education, built imaginatively on the solid foundations laid by Susan Ryan. In the area of social welfare and health, the path-breaking work of Don Grimes and Neal Blewett was developed sympathetically by Brian Howe and, later, Graham Richardson. Bill Hayden was a courageous and innovative Foreign Minister. His replacement, Gareth Evans, who had the most acute mind of any of my ministers, has gone on to become the best and most widely respected Foreign Minister in the country's history. And there has been no better Defence Minister or Primary Industry Minister than Kim Beazley and John Kerin respectively. In the increasingly important area of the environment Barry Cohen did substantial work. Graham Richardson, who surprised everyone with his 'road to Damascus' conversion, built spectacularly on this foundation. In the difficult area of Aboriginal Affairs, first Clyde Holding, then Gerry Hand and later Robert Tickner were committed to advancing the status, dignity and empowerment of Aboriginal people, objectives which I am glad to see have been enthusiastically embraced by my successor. Barry Jones, in his own effusive fashion, began to give science the prominence it deserves, while Tom Uren's enthusiasm gave Local Government a federal stature it had never before had. And Arthur Geizelt, whose appointment as Minister for Veterans' Affairs was initially greeted with dismay by the ex-service communities, soon endeared himself to them by his dedication to their welfare.[23] John Brown did more for tourism and sport than had been achieved in any previous government.

This is not, of course, an exhaustive list; my point here is simply to establish the breadth and depth of the collective talent which was available to me during my period as Prime Minister and for which I was consistently and consciously grateful.

I was keenly aware, too, that I stood on the shoulders of many greats in Labor history and particularly, in my mind, on the shoulders of John Curtin, who had fashioned consensus and unity at a critical juncture in Australia's national development. I am often reminded in this context of a story told by the late Reginald Pollard[24] about John Curtin. Curtin was being farewelled in the refreshment rooms of the Old Parliament House on the eve of a trip abroad. Labor Members wished him godspeed and a successful trip. In reply Curtin said, 'I am what I am, John Curtin from Creswick, Victoria, a policeman's son.'

Curtin then related a story by Jack London in which the sole survivor of a shipwreck scrambles from a raft onto a rock and thence to shore on a desert island. He looks all around him, and there's not a soul in sight. So he stands erect and pushes his chest out and slaps his hand upon it. 'Alone I did it,' he yells. As his cry echoes around the jungle, a booming voice replies, 'Ah! But who made the raft?'

And so, alone, certainly I did not do it. The sweat of Opposition provided the raft of policies upon which we won government, and freakish coincidence and changing social circumstances provided the talented ministers whom it fell to my good fortune to lead. But like Curtin, who led the party during war, when history and tradition and the times combined to place maximum stress on institutions and personalities and on the party itself, my own contribution to the raft was in holding it together when it could well have splintered, broken up, and drifted off into irrelevance. My personality, experience, and style of leadership leaned always towards unity and consensus. Historical labels which play up the tension between the Prime Minister and the Treasurer, or treat the two as a duumvirate which dominated the party and the Government to the exclusion of other voices, ignore the raft and its occupants and the fundamental unity of purpose which, under my guidance, held it together.

I was determined to have a personal staff of the highest calibre and in this regard was assisted by Neville Wran's generosity and my own early optimism about securing the leadership. The Labor Party as a whole owed a great debt to Wran; after the devastation of 1975 he was able to show with his 1976 victory in NSW that Labor was still alive and capable of governing. The longevity of his Government, his professionalism and style, were an important stepping stone for the Hawke Labor Government. Wran had assembled around him an intelligent and experienced staff who knew the ropes of government; when I became Leader Neville said to me, 'Look, regard my staff as a smorgasbord.'

I took him at his word and immediately plucked out Peter Barron as my political adviser and Graham Freudenberg as my speech writer. Peter is an astute political intelligence. He is a short, thick-set, plump-ish fellow, who only has to look at a sandwich to put on weight; his benign bulldog appearance is deceptive. Rank, including my own, meant little to him and his unrivalled capacity for robust and direct expression did not always endear him to those with whom he dealt. He had been an invaluable source of advice to me during the campaign and I was delighted that he was prepared to make the transition with us.

Graham Freudenberg was a crucial link with Labor history and with the past leadership of the party. He was Arthur Calwell's speech writer in the 1960s and then, when Gough Whitlam took over as Labor leader, Graham became famous in Labor folklore for the symbiotic relationship which developed between leader and wordsmith. Graham

– known with universal affection as 'Freudy' – is one of the icons of the labour movement. Short, with horn-rimmed glasses and dark complexion, he lives for Labor. His erratic working habits are notorious and are the bane of the secretaries who must take his dictation as he paces the room, drawing on an ever-present cigarette and often imbibing a cleansing ale. Mornings are basically non-events for Freudy, who uses them merely to recover from the labours of the night. His efforts are prodigious when required and, although he often cuts it fine, he has never missed a deadline.

The relationship between Prime Minister and speechwriter is a fascinating phenomenon. The mutual dependency is enormous as is the need for understanding of each other's style of thinking and natural method of expression. I was fortunate in my experience with all of those who had this, at times, uneviable job. There was only one unhappy episode, and that had nothing to do with Freudy. On one Sunday in my electorate in Melbourne I had two functions to address. The schedule was unbelievably hectic and I just had time to grab the speech from one of my assistants before going up on the platform in a Coburg park to speak to the assembled throng. I wasn't too far into it before I realised I had been given the wrong speech and had to call upon my experience of extemporary delivery. It seemed to wash well enough for me to temper the generous remarks I was preparing to deliver to my staff who hadn't realised the cock-up that had occurred.

I was a little more fortunate than my predecessor, Malcolm Fraser, of whom a story is told which, I am assured, is not apocryphal. Fraser had had a hell of a row with his speechwriter. The Prime Minister had to deliver an address in Melbourne that night and, again, in the rush of events it was put in his hands just before he went on stage. Malcolm read the first two pages and then turned them over to be confronted with a sheet which was blank except for the words: 'Now you are on your own, you bastard.'

Graham and I went back a long way. I had known him since 1963 and over the years he had seen me at my best and worst. In earlier days he saw drink bring out the demon in me and later made fond comparisons between myself and Curtin, two characters from the West who struggled with alcohol, gave it up, and became Prime Minister.

Graham, with his deep knowledge of Labor history, told me that Frank Anstey, in the late 1920s Deputy Leader of the ALP and Curtin's mentor, said that Curtin would be literally in the gutter when drunk. 'John Curtin sober was the finest bloke alive. John Curtin drunk was a vicious cur,' Anstey said. Sober, certainly, I do not claim Curtin's mantle, but there is no doubt that excessive drink sometimes brought out an unpleasant personality change which, had I continued to drink, would have made me unfit to be Prime Minister. But Graham stuck by me and he was, in fact, the first person I appointed to my staff.

The appointment had a history. Shortly after the 1972 election, Graham and I were celebrating at Sydney's Four Seasons restaurant. Hazel was there, Mick Young, John Ducker, and other Labor stalwarts. We were all euphoric and speeches were made. In the midst of this Graham said, 'Bob, the time will come when you will be leader of the party and you will be Prime Minister and I will be your speech writer.' And so, on 3rd February 1983, the day I became de facto leader of the Labor Party, I phoned Graham. 'Do you remember what you said at the Four Seasons in 1972?' I asked him. 'Yes,' he said. 'Does the offer still stand?' I asked. 'Yes,' he replied.

While Graham helped me to keep faith with Labor's history, Peter Barron was an important link with the Right, the dominant faction within the Labor Party – and in particular, with the New South Wales branch. Robert Hogg, from the Victorian Left of the party, also joined my staff in those early days and was an effective factional counterpoint to Peter.

Bob was a shrewd political operator and had been largely instrumental in establishing the conditions for Labor's return to power in Victoria in 1982. A man of strong opinions but with a preparedness to conciliate, Hogg was less aggressively upfront in his presentation than Peter Barron. Their relations were often strained but to their credit they normally subsumed their antipathies in pursuit of the Government's interests.

It was important to me that my staff should reflect the modern, internationalist orientation that I intended to bring to government. I had, rather presumptuously, begun the selection process in 1981 in Washington where I had been impressed by the Counsellor at the Australian Embassy, Graham Evans. He was intelligent, tough-minded and a cool and efficient organiser. I told him I hoped to become Leader of the party and secured from him an indication that he would be interested in joining me should that eventuate. After doing some advanced academic work in international economics, Graham had returned to the International Division of Treasury. He immediately accepted the invitation to become my Principal Private Secretary.

Graham had captained the Australian embassy cricket team in the Philippines and at one time had recruited Australian National University economist Dr Ross Garnaut to open the bowling for Australia against Hong Kong. Off the field, the two cricketers had common interests in Australia's foreign policy, especially international economic policy in the Asia–Pacific region. They both abhorred Australia's excessive protectionism.

Graham recommended Ross as a first-rate candidate for my economics adviser and, incidently, as a mean fast bowler. I took an immediate shine to the idea as I had known Ross from my days as a member of Sir John Crawford's Study Group on Structural Adjustment (the Crawford Committee). Garnaut had close contact with Crawford during that period and attended study group meetings which dealt with the trading opportunities for Australia which were emerging from the rapid economic growth of East Asia. His emphasis was towards transforming Australian industry by tapping into the extensive industrialisation sweeping the East Asian region. His fundamental theme was that export expansion needed to be supported in Australia by import liberalisation. In other words he was an unabashed free-trader and exactly the person I was looking for as an economics adviser.

But the Crawford group had deliberated some time ago and it was important to test out Ross's views to make sure that we were compatible. I invited him to Parliament House for a chat, where he confirmed our shared anti-protectionist views and our agreement that the pace of movement in that direction would depend on the emergence from recovery.

As it turned out, work on reducing protectionist barriers began very early in the life of the Government. Development of the plan to save the steel industry by marrying regional assistance with the removal of quotas on steel started almost immediately, and Ross was a critically important contributor to the plan. Malcolm Fraser had slapped quotas on steel imports in the latter stages of his Government, and the economic conventional wisdom at the time was 'quotas on, never off'. In 1983, my Government took them off. So in hiring Ross Garnaut I was not simply tilting in the direction of free trade for the sake of appearances. I aimed to do something about it from the very beginning.

While interviewing Garnaut for the position of economic adviser, one further point arose. Ross was worried that the economic policies upon which Labor was elected were too expansionary. He ran through a check list of difficulties confronting the Australian economy at that juncture. The international commodity price outlook was bleak, world food markets were worsening due to European agricultural protection and subsidy policies, and mineral prices were down. But I was able to reassure him that in the context of a $9.6 billion prospective deficit, fiscal expansionism was not on the agenda.

Graham Evans was also responsible for introducing an individual who became one of the real characters of the Prime Minister's Office. Graham suggested I consider for the position of international adviser one John Bowan, whom he had known and respected for his work in the Department of Foreign Affairs and the Office of National Assessment. I was immediately attracted to John. He had a good mind, extensive knowledge of the whole field of international affairs and what I regarded as sound positions on a range of relevant issues, all laced with a wry sense of humour. Bowan brought many bonuses with him. He had a passion for and encyclopedic knowledge of classical music and every known form of sport – a resource which came to be much appreciated and drawn upon by Hazel and me. I think John must have averaged about two hours sleep a night, for he read and analysed every cable and relevant document, listened to every classical music performance and watched any sporting event that happened to be televised. A gem of a man.

Geoff Walsh, a journalist employed by the Federal ALP, had, without need of invitation, flown straight to my side when I became Leader, and he rounded off the senior appointments to my personal staff when he assumed the position of Senior Press Officer. Geoff's amicable disposition and professional competence guaranteed the respect of the press gallery, while his deep knowledge of Australian politics added another dimension to his value within the office.

I therefore had the ministry and the personal staff to undertake the challenging task of government. And importantly, I had an obsession to change Australia for the better and a strategy for achieving that goal. The country and the people whom I loved, and whom I was now privileged to lead, were in a parlous condition. Australia was gripped by double-digit inflation and unemployment in a recession which had no underlying imperative or purpose of structural change. Our secondary industry was ossified and cosseted behind high, self-defeating protective barriers; we had no real understanding of our place in the world or of the opportunities which change in our region was offering. We were, properly, part of the Western alliance but it was an association devoid of the collateral independence of mind which in any way could put an Australian mark on the events that would shape the lives of our children.

Educational opportunity was still the privilege of the well-to-do families, with Australia having, by international standards, an abysmal level of school retention rates. We had a social security system grossly unrelated to needs, while the admirable concept of universal health cover initiated by the Whitlam Government had been eroded under seven years of conservative rule. The needs of the most underprivileged Australians, the Aboriginal people, were relatively neglected. Above all, we had become a society of conflict. We had lost our faith and trust in one another and had ceased to recognise that our greatest hope for growth lay in acknowledging the legitimacy of the aspirations of others as well as our own.

I knew that all of this could not be changed in one term. From the very beginning I was determined to lay the foundations for a long-term Labor Government. I was committed to avoiding the pattern of the past where Labor came to power for a brief flickering period and was then relegated to Opposition and doomed once more to a long night of irrelevance. Labor had been in power for fewer than nineteen of the eighty-two years of federation. I was not, however, interested in office for the sake of office. Australia needed change and for that to happen Labor had to become a natural party of government in the eyes of the electorate. I believed that I could give Labor that status and was determined to do so.

The Whitlam Government did many good things but its strengths were not economic. I was determined that the Hawke Labor Government would distinguish itself as a better economic manager than its predecessors and would establish a clear superiority in that respect over our Opposition. I intended to turn the Government's performance as an economic manager into an asset rather than a liability.

If we were to manage the economy efficiently we had to manage ourselves competently. Here again the Whitlam Government was an object lesson in what not to do. Whitlam presided over a Cabinet which was in a permanent shambles. It included the full ministry of twenty-seven and was far too big and unwieldy. Beyond that, the Government was continuously rent by a lack of Cabinet solidarity. Unhappy with what the Cabinet decided, ministers raced off to the Caucus and unravelled Cabinet decisions. The making and unmaking of policy was conducted in the media with maximum bloodshed for the Government and the party.

This made no sense and was extremely debilitating for Gough's Government. So right from the beginning, I insisted and it was accepted that we should enshrine the principle of Cabinet solidarity. The size of the Cabinet was reduced to thirteen, picked by me from the Caucus-elected ministry. Very few Prime Ministers, if any, encouraged the breadth and depth of Cabinet discussion that I did. But once we made a decision, ministers were bound by it. There was no second guessing and no recourse to the Caucus.

There it was – the team, the staff and the strategy. My immediate task was to lay the foundation for all that we were hoping to do – the reconciliation, recovery and reconstruction of Australia.

TWELVE

Long before I was in Parliament I had had the idea of a National Economic Summit aimed at establishing a social compact between Australia's main constituent groups: governments, business and labour, in particular, but also a wide range of community organisations.

The idea of uniting the country around commonly agreed values and goals on the basis of a shared understanding of economic realities was the centrepiece of my thinking for the future of Australia. Although I had mentioned the idea earlier, I floated it in some detail in the 1979 Boyer Lectures on the Resolution of Conflict broadcast on the ABC's Radio National.

After calling on the Government to convene such a summit, I had said, 'Co-operation can only be the product of understanding; confrontation and conflict are the inevitable and disastrous alternatives.' If crucial then, how much more crucial in early 1983? Now, however, I was more than commentator. And so at the launch of Labor's economic strategy on 10th February 1983, I announced that a national economic conference would be convened within a month.

Now that we were in government, planning began immediately. As John Langmore and I put our heads together in the sitting room of

Kirribilli House in the late and early hours of 7th–8th March 1983 we were concerned not only with planning the summit but also with what was to come out of it. The summit to me was a step in a process which was to unfold throughout the life of the Government. In an aide-mémoire jotted down early on 8th March I noted that I was keen to foster ways in which consultation of the type envisaged for the National Summit could be perpetuated.

As well as showing the nuts and bolts of forward planning, my aide-mémoire refers to the broad aspirations of the newly elected Government. As I read the words again after all these years I have a sense of excitement and pride at the vision and the reality that emerged from them: 'Essentially the Government is concerned to manage the economy in a way which reflects the consensus of all sectors of the community and is based on an assumption of mutuality of interests and widespread goodwill between all Australians.'

From the very outset I wanted the summit to be an expression of the entire community. A corporatist cozying-up of the big three – big government, big business, and big unions – was not my idea of a summit. It had to be much broader than that; it had to include representation from small business, the professions, the welfare sector, and State and local government. That late night at Kirribilli House planning the summit was but one of several spent by me and many other people over the coming weeks. In that first month of government there were almost nightly meetings in my office at Parliament House as we kicked around the ideas for the summit and kept account of how we were progressing. We were elected on 5th March 1983, sworn in on 11th March, and the summit was scheduled for the week beginning 11th April 1983. There was no time to lose.

The bureaucratic effort required for the summit was prodigious and I asked the Department of Prime Minister and Cabinet to assume the major responsibility for its organisation through a Conference

Secretariat. I also established a Conference Technical Committee responsible for preparing reports on the Australian economy and prognostications for its possible recovery. The reports were to include specialist information obtained from wherever it could be found, and whatever expert advice was forthcoming from employer groups, the union movement, and the universities.

On the day we were sworn into government I invited to the summit representatives of all levels of government, major employer and other business groups, together with a number of prominent Australian businessmen, the trade union movement, professional groups, the Australian Council of Social Services (ACOSS), other welfare organisations and the Churches. On that day, too, I wrote to Sir Geoffrey Yeend, Secretary of my department, stressing the summit's importance to the Government and calling on the department's help both in staffing the Secretariat and in contributing to the work of the Conference Technical Committee and its various working parties.

There was no time for the Government and the bureaucracy to tip-toe around each other and to allow churlish suspicion to foster a poisonous atmosphere of mutual distrust. Immediately, we started pulling together on a great enterprise, and as we worked together, sleeves up and late into the night, there was an instant rapport. One of the great spin-offs of that early period in government was the melding of the new Government with the career public servants. Of course there were disagreements. The summit was an experiment and the preferred course, not only for many public servants but also many new ministers and their personal staff, was for known and charted waters. It was clear to me, for example, that the only place where one could hold such a conference was in the Chamber of the House of Representatives. But acceptance of this idea required some education. The summit itself was daring enough, but to have it in the Chamber – never! 'You can't have it in the Chamber, Prime Minister!' went the conformist strain of opinion. 'Why can't I have it in the Chamber?' I asked. 'But it's not done, it has never been done.' 'Well, it's going to be done,' I said. 'But Prime Minister ...' 'It's going to be done!' and that was the end of the argument.

Planning for the summit proceeded apace with the wind of endeavour behind it, but with an air of scepticism wafting across the sails. Some of the scepticism blew from the captain's own cabin. Peter Barron and Graham Freudenberg were prepared to humour me but, in essence, they shared Neville Wran's view that the summit, consensus and the Accord were a bit of nice nonsense got up for Hare Krishnas. For them, as for others, the blinding light of faith was a little in the distance. Lacking their atheism but agnostic, nonetheless, was my economics adviser, Ross Garnaut. He needed no convincing of the rationale behind the summit and the Accord. From his unique vantage point as a specialist in East Asian trade he viewed with horror the colossal damage done to Australia in the previous decade by the confrontational conduct of economic policy in general, and industrial relations in particular. Shocking industrial disputation, poor growth in productivity, endemic inflation and a reputation as an unreliable trading partner were all part of the legacy. Ross lived in hope of a better way but whether the summit, and what it stood for, would provide the answer was another matter.

There was a smattering of like views across my department where there were those with hope but few true believers. In Treasury, from Stone down, the orthodox view saw the summit as a distraction, probably not even worth trying. The Treasurer himself was sceptical about the summit and its concomitant, the Accord, but was less dogmatic than his department; he hoped it would work but had little faith that it would. Strangely, though, the air of scepticism pervading the planning of the summit did nothing to prevent maximum effort being devoted to it. It was a peculiar phenomenon in some ways. The sceptics said,

'Oh well! we're humouring the Prime Minister. He promised the summit in the election and now we have to do it.' And in the aftermath of a massive election victory, where goodwill abounded, it was part and parcel of the euphoria of the time to accommodate the new man at the helm.

As I saw it, the Prime Minister was humouring the sceptics – a number of my parliamentary colleagues, a fair swag of the bureaucracy, and most of the journalists – because I knew that the summit would work. Indeed it was a fascinating and rewarding experience to see the scepticism being shed, layer by layer, as we plunged into the planning and then the summit itself.

My own confidence was not blind faith; the summit would be a success but only if we settled some fundamental economic questions in advance. Chief among them was the size of the deficit. Simple arithmetic showed the potential for disaster. Taking Fraser's projected deficit of $9.6 billion and adding the cost of Labor's election policies catapulted an already unacceptable figure to around $12–13 billion. A deficit of that order was a Whitlam-style ticket out of government. The frightening thing was that there were those within the Labor Party and within the Government who advocated buying that ticket. Horrified by the unemployment figures, as we all were, they argued that the Government should honour all its election pledges and spend away, soaking up the jobless with a huge injection of Commonwealth money.

Spend, spend, spend was an easy argument to make but it was a chimera. First, the Australian economy imposed intrinsic limits on how far a government could spend without the deficit blowing out almost irretrievably. Beyond that there was the important question of market confidence, which it was fashionable in some circles to treat with disdain, but this could only be done at a devastating cost. Our starting point with the money markets was not good. Historically, they regarded Labor as something of an ogre. Fortunately, we had managed to still some anxiety by our decisive devaluation. We now faced a new test as the markets pondered the issue of our fiscal rectitude.

Every day upwards of $300 billion moved across the world's foreign exchange markets. Daily movement across the Australian exchange reached billions of dollars – less than the $20 billion plus in the 1990s – but still an enormous number in 1983.

I was acutely aware – more so I think than most of my colleagues, particularly the fiscal expansionists – that if the world's foreign exchange dealers took a set against the new Australian Government then the game was up. If the world decides it does not trust you then it can ruin you. No Australian Government, even one as well led and as well constituted as the Hawke Government in 1983, could turn its back on market realities of that order. I wasn't going to be the servant of the markets but I was not, gratuitously, going to give them an excuse to destroy us.

Naturally there were some tough and willing arguments in the Cabinet room and in the Caucus between those who would allow the deficit to billow and those of us bent on sucking it in, but these were quickly over. The pattern of the Government was to support the Prime Minister. In any event the weight of numbers was clearly for restraint – the figures and market realities both demanded it.

What we needed quickly was our own projected Budget deficit estimate for the 1983–84 year. One thing that could wreck the summit and all my hopes for it was the use of that forum as a bargaining shop for the funding of pet projects, or for deliberations to become bogged down in an open-ended discussion where Keynesian expansionists could argue for unlimited Government spending. We needed to write into all summit documents a deficit figure for our first Budget significantly below the Coalition's $9.6 billion. Substantial work on this began in the first week of government. In mid-March the Cabinet established the Expenditure Review Committee (ERC) to fine tooth comb Government expenditure and to advise the Cabinet on spending priorities. The new Hawke Government was not spendthrift but it was nevertheless a Labor government in the true sense of the word. Social equity and equal opportunity were central goals, reflecting a deep concern for the truly disadvantaged.

The ERC had none of the crimping, mean-minded brutality of Fraser's Razor Gang[25] which, ironically enough, had allowed Government outlays to balloon to around 30 per cent of Australia's gross domestic product. My ERC had a pound-wise philosophy, slicing away the desperate give-aways of Fraser's last Budget to make way for the essential elements of the Labor program: re-introduction of a National Health Insurance Scheme, raised living standards for pensioners, greater benefits for unemployed youth, direct Commonwealth funding for public housing, major job creating initiatives, increased education allowances, and a major boost in spending for Aboriginal Affairs. The ERC accepted a projected Budget deficit of $8.5 billion. This figure was inserted into the summit papers and relentlessly pursued in the Government's May Statement, the first Premiers' Conference and Loan Council meeting on 30th June–1st July 1983, and was tightly adhered to in our first Budget. In fact higher than anticipated growth through the course of the year brought the final deficit for 1983–84 in at just over $8 billion.

So successful was the ERC in vetting expenditure and ordering priorities that it became a permanent feature of the Government and the engine room of our economic policies. The original membership of the ERC is instructive: the Treasurer, Paul Keating; Employment and Industrial Relations Minister, Ralph Willis; the Finance Minister, John Dawkins; Resources and Energy Minister, Peter Walsh; and myself. Aside from Keating, who covered his then-patchy economic expertise with good political skills and a fast learning curve, individual

1.*(top left)*
With my father, Clem
Hawke, and older
brother Neil.

2.*(top right)*
I was born in Bordertown
and we lived in rural South
Australia until moving to
Perth in 1939.

3&4.*(above and right)*
My mother, Ellie.

5.*(facing page)*
The proud winner of
a scholarship to Perth's
Modern School.

6.*(above)*
Selling hot cross buns.

7.*(left)*
With my uncle, Albert
Hawke (*centre*) and Harvard
Bowman (*right*).

8. *(above left)*
Off the Cape of Good
Hope en route to Oxford.

9. *(left)*
Receiving congratulations on
winning a Rhodes Scholarship.

10. *(above)*
I knew that I stood on the shoulders
of Labor greats, especially John Curtin.

11.*(facing page)*
As ACTU research officer
and advocate in the early 1960s.

12.*(left)*
Elected ACTU President in
1969.

13.*(below)*
With Ros, Jan Marsh of the
ACTU and Hazel on the beach
in the early 1970s.

14. *(right)*
Father of the Year in 1971.

15. *(below)*
With Yemcham Meshel,
President of Histadrut, 1971.

16. *(far right)*
Dedication of a forest
in my honour in Israel.

17. *(below right)*
With Shimon Peres,
Israeli Defence Minister.

18.*(left)*
Sport — one of my great
passions.

19.*(above)*
Studying the form guide.

20.*(right)*
There was never time for enough
cricket.

21.*(far right)*
Playing the trombone.

22. *(above left)*
With ALP's Federal Executive
(*left to right*) Senator Ken Wriedt,
Prime Minister Gough Whitlam,
Party Secretary David Combe and
myself as Federal President.

23. *(left)*
With Andrew Peacock in the 1970s.

24. *(above)*
The ACTU's 50th anniversary dinner
(left to right) Sir John Moore, Harold
Souler, myself, George Polites, Gough
Whitlam and Sir Richard Kirby.

25.*(above)*
Addressing the crowd outside Parliament
House after the dismissal of the Whitlam
Labor Government in 1975.

26.*(facing page)*
The press conference with Bill Hayden
when I won the first ballot to lead the
Labor Party.

27. With my father, Clem, in 1987.

members of the ERC had impressive formal economic credentials. As a body, the ERC easily had the weight to carry the Cabinet and the Caucus. Its natural authority was augmented by hard work and thoroughness; over time ERC members became exceedingly knowledgeable about the operations of government, to the point where they were able to hold their own with – and were, for that reason, respected by – the veteran public servants who served and dealt with them.

There was, moreover, a recognition on the part of the Cabinet and the Caucus that fiscal rectitude was not an end in itself. Part of their task was to clear arteries blocked by old and misdirected spending programs to make way for fresh initiatives protective of those most in need.

The membership of the ERC also demonstrated the cohesion and unity with which the Government began and continued. In the leadership battle Walsh and Dawkins were staunch Hayden supporters. Keating had held out, and Willis was a victim of Bill's final power-play. All that was forgotten. Now we worked cheek by jowl to ensure the success of the new Government. Grudges were the furthest thing from my mind when assessing how best to harness the talents of the parliamentary party and from the beginning Walsh and Dawkins were appointed by me as vital participants in the Government's most powerful committee.

Bill Hayden was also showing his enthusiasm for the new Government. In March he asked me to appoint him to the Economic Policy Committee of Cabinet. Naturally I obliged and when the committee was established on 16th March 1983, the same day as the ERC, Bill was a member. Its role was to fix the broader macro-economic agenda of the Government by mapping out the shape of the Budget and advising on monetary policy. However, it quickly became evident that the ERC, as spending watchdog, could not work in a vacuum. Its task was integral to broader economic policy formulation. Becoming quickly and inevitably involved in both roles, the ERC subsumed the job of the Economic Policy Committee and the latter was, to some extent, stillborn. Co-operation became the hallmark of the Government: co-operation among colleagues, co-operation with, and within, the bureaucracy, co-operation between sectional groups and interests previously implacably opposed to one another.

In those early days a remarkable feature of this co-operation was the opening of the Government's doors to the union movement. The carpets to government had always been well worn by business but rarely by the union movement. With the general exception of the Whitlam period, from the advent of Sir Robert Menzies' government in 1949 until the 1983 election, governments and unions certainly saw each other in Sir Winston Churchill's description of Russia as 'a riddle wrapped in a mystery inside an enigma'. Now, the riddle, the mystery and the enigma were being unwrapped.

In the run-up to the summit ACTU economists were thrown together with Treasury forecasters to argue through various Treasury scenarios about the impact of wage increases on unemployment. Treasury hammered the ACTU with the theory of real-wage overhang and the savage relationship between a wages explosion and unemployment. The ACTU acquainted Treasury with the theory in practice. They well knew the cycle: economic growth, a big wage increase, inflation, a fiscal or monetary crunch, and mounting unemployment. They knew first-hand what was at stake – their financial base as dues fell away, the prestige of their organisation as unions became the whipping post for the country's ills, and, of course, their bargaining power.

Now, with the prospect of yet another wages explosion as the lifting of Fraser's wages pause approached (historically one had always followed the other), the union movement was ahead of the game. Like the Government, Ralph Willis and myself in particular, they believed in the Accord and began their sensitivity training of sceptical Treasury bureaucrats.

There were many humorists, sceptics, agnostics and doomsayers back then but few true believers. In March the former Whitlam minister, Clyde Cameron, flashed into my life again with a categoric and gloomy prediction: 'Your economic conference will fail; the participants won't be able to deliver and will be addressing the record. If you can succeed in making a worthwhile compact with the unions, you'll go down in history as the greatest Australian Prime Minister ever. I would love the opportunity of saying "Well done!"' I'm still waiting for Clyde's 'Well done!' His letter, however, was typical of the prevailing mood of the cognoscenti. I believed, the union movement believed, the Australian public believed, but cynics abounded.

Just as Treasury and union officials were bent now on a common purpose, so, too, unions and business were about to shake hands at the summit. They had traditionally met as opponents on the industrial battlefield when the lines were drawn. The summit was a new experience. As 11th April approached the chemistry of the summit promised to be weird and wonderful. How, for example, would the captains of industry cope with sitting down to morning tea with the stubborn, irascible Ivan Hodgson, Federal Secretary of the Transport Workers' Union? Well, the chemistry did work, even in that case. It was fascinating to observe the ninety-eight delegates and nineteen observers at the week-long event. Time and again leading industrialists would take me aside, having just dined or chatted over coffee with a trade unionist, and say, 'You know, Bob, this is the first time I've really talked to a trade union leader; they're not bad blokes.' 'Oh, really!' I would reply. 'Glad you think so.' Then it would be a trade unionist's turn to buttonhole me: 'You know, Bob, that mate of yours, Sir Peter Abeles, isn't a bad bloke, is he?' Besides Peter, they spoke of

John Utz (Wormald International), Sir Eric McClintock (Woolworths), Sir Roderick Carnegie (CRA), Bob White (Bank of NSW) and others of the assembled captains of industry not as the ogres they had imagined but as decent, responsible men.

Those simple observations excited me because, after all, that was what the whole thing was about.

I had been insisting for some years that employers and trade unionists had an essential commonality of interests. Trade unionists had a legitimate aspiration for better wages and working conditions; employers had a legitimate aspiration to improve profitability and growth. The aspirations of both were, in fact, concordant and the most likely way for each to achieve those aspirations was by co-operatively recognising the interests of the other.

'So often in our affairs the emphasis has been upon the competing struggle between wage and salary earners and business, and residually, welfare recipients,' I said in my welcoming speech to all participants and observers of the summit. 'I believe we must come to put the emphasis upon the fact that they all have a common goal and therefore a common interest,' I continued. 'They all seek the same thing – through time, an improvement of their standards of living. The indispensable condition for the achievement of this common legitimate goal is real economic growth – an increase in the per capita output of goods and services.'

During the week of the summit, rhetoric became reality. The leaders of industry and of labour glimpsed a better way. Many years down the track, John Prescott, head of Broken Hill Proprietary Limited's Steel Division at the time and later Managing Director of the company, gave me an insight into the sea change of attitudes swept in by the summit. Thanking me for the new approach I had brought into the steel industry in particular, but to the economy generally, he said, 'In BHP we preferred it if our workers left their brains at the gate. Now, in this new atmosphere of industrial relations we realise that is absurd. They are, in a sense, our best resource. If we are going to do well as a company then it makes sense to work with our employees co-operatively.' As I listened to John, I recognised in his words the resonating spirit of the summit.

The changes to Australia's industrial culture as a result of the summit were profound. During the summit, the Accord signed in the euphoria of the election campaign was cemented into place; it endures to this day. In that campaign, I had made the commitment that Labor would create five hundred thousand new jobs in the first three years of government. Job creation was fundamental to our program. But integral to it, and to market confidence, was a scaling back of inflation. Labor's strategy, propounded through the summit, was to fight unemployment and inflation simultaneously, and at the summit the union movement confirmed its commitment to that fight. This took the employers somewhat by surprise, for they were not quite used to the idea of trade unionists agreeing to wage restraint, let alone urging it. But the employers also rose to the occasion, for the first time accepting publicly the joining of a reduction in unemployment with the reduction of inflation as equally legitimate objects of Government policy.

The proof of the pudding came in October that year when the Commonwealth Conciliation and Arbitration Commission granted workers a wage rise in accordance with the 4.3 per cent increase in the Consumer Price Index. As a result the vast bulk of unions gave the commission a written undertaking foregoing additional claims. With that, Australia became one of the few Western industrialised countries to escape a wages pause without a subsequent wages blow-out. Employers generally accepted this as a reasonable outcome in accord with the spirit of the summit.

Other successful outcomes of the Accord processes followed throughout the coming decade. In 1986, when the dollar fell and the price of imports shot up, wage rises were again quarantined. Similarly, during the boom of the late eighties wages were contained. As a result the Hawke Government's Accord agreement and the decisions made under it effectively snapped the back of inflationary expectations in Australia. It is an outcome that can be traced all the way back to the National Economic Summit of April 1983.

While I have never subscribed to the theory that the level of industrial disputation, of itself, tells you anything definitive about a country's condition, Australia undoubtedly suffered from far too many disputes. From the summit on, time lost in industrial disputes continued to fall dramatically.[26] From being regarded internationally as an impediment to investment in our country, Australia's industrial relations record gradually became a positive factor which stood favourable comparison with the rest of the world.

There were more immediate spin-offs from the summit. Employers, a little dazzled by some of the leading lights of the union movement, such as Bill Kelty and Charlie Fitzgibbon, and comparing the relative cohesiveness and sophistication of the ACTU with their own disarray, broadened their horizons. The interaction among business groups at the summit led eventually to the formation of the Business Council of Australia. Whereas business had traditionally approached government as self-interested lobbyists pressing for specific or sectoral favour, from here on the dialogue with government became far more comprehensive and meaningful.

Employers and trade unions were large building blocks in the reconstruction of the country. But they were only part of the mix. Welfare organisations and the churches were also present. It was my goal to expose conference participants to a detailed appraisal of the economics of their country. As they read and understood the detailed papers prepared and distributed for the summit, welfare and church representatives deepened their understanding of what could and could not be done for those to whom they were most committed. Their compassion, of course, remained undiminished but the language of deficits and of macro-economic constraints introduced more realism into their approach. They came to understand that government was not a cornucopia out of which money could be drawn to satisfy every cause.

The State Premiers were also there. The economic realities facing the country were laid bare for them, too, so that when the Treasurer and I met with the States in mid-1983 much of the pain had gone out of our discussion. For the first time since the Second World War, the Premiers agreed to a joint communiqué on national economic policy. They subscribed there to our deficit figure of $8.5 billion, agreeing that any figure significantly above that would threaten the viability of Australia's recovery.

The summit delivered practical outcomes. The Economic Planning and Advisory Council (EPAC) was established. The Council, unprecedented in Australia, institutionalised co-operation between Federal and State Governments, business, unions, the rural sector and community groups. EPAC first met in July. Its main role is to analyse medium and long-term economic performance in Australia, and factors influencing that performance. In tandem with EPAC, the Government legislated for a Prices Surveillance Authority which had been part of the Accord arrangements cemented at the summit.

Australians knew that the carping, bitterly confrontationist society which had arisen out of the Fraser period was not a true representation of the national character. We knew that we were better than that; and the summit proved it. Televised nationally and extensively reported, it restored the faith of Australians in themselves and in their nation.

During the election campaign I had often compared the supreme crisis of the early 1940s with the deepening recession of 1982–83. Of course the recession did not threaten the very survival of the nation as it did in 1942. But in some respects the recession posed a greater challenge to the resourcefulness of our people. In 1942 we battled a foreign enemy, clear and identifiable. The challenge in 1983 came from within. In opening the summit on 11th April, I said:

> More than forty years ago, one of the very greatest of all Australians stood in this place in this historic Chamber to give this message to the people of Australia. On that occasion, 16th December 1941, John Curtin said, 'Our Australian mode of life, our conditions, our seasons, all that go to make up the national conditions of living, make us better equipped [for the purpose of meeting this crisis] than are the peoples of many other countries ... the qualitative capacity of our population compensates in large measure for the shortage of our numbers ... I, like each of you, have seen this country at work, engaged in pleasure, and experiencing adversity; I have seen it face good times and evil times, but I have never known a time in which the inherent quality of Australia has to be used so unstintingly as at this hour.'

I concluded my opening address to the conference:

> I do not believe for one moment that the essential quality of our people has in any way declined since 1941. On the contrary, it has been enriched and strengthened by the contribution of the millions of our fellow citizens drawn from nearly every country and race around the world. If we at this conference dedicate ourselves to provide leadership to this great people, I have absolute confidence that they will respond with the united effort and a renewed determination to beat this crisis and to build an even better future for this great nation, Australia.

By the end of the summit there was no doubt that the delegates had so dedicated themselves. At the end all but one rose to applaud the final communiqué; the solitary exception – the lonely and irrelevant Premier of Queensland, Sir Joh Bjelke-Petersen – pointed up the unparalleled success of the summit.

The sceptics were converted. I recall one of the more sophisticated and articulate of them, the Canberra press corps veteran Mungo McCallum, an immense but often wasted talent, coming up to me and saying, 'Hawkie, I thought it was all bullshit – but it worked.' His excitement excited me.

So well did it work that the ripple effect of the summit success was felt internationally. Foreign governments were anxious to emulate the idea. In 1984 the incoming Labor Government of David Lange in New Zealand followed Australia's lead. In March 1985, Canada's new Prime Minister, Brian Mulroney, invited me to deliver the keynote address at his country's National Economic Conference, the concept of which was based squarely on our own. In 1989 I sent a tripartite delegation to the Republic of Korea to brief the new Government of President Roh Tae Woo at their request about the Accord, which was integral to the summit. In December 1992, soon after his election victory, United States President-elect Bill Clinton paid us his tribute by holding an Australian-style summit.

International interest was particularly intense in the immediate aftermath of the summit. At that time summit participant Bryan Kelman, General Manager of CSR Limited, toured the financial centres of Europe: Basel, Zurich, Paris, Brussels, Frankfurt and London. There, Bryan and senior CSR colleagues met with the chief executives or chairmen of over twenty different banks, including all the major European ones. His main interest, naturally enough, was to discuss the fortunes of his company. But being the first summiteer to venture into these circles, the going was hard. 'At many meetings it was difficult to get a chance to talk about CSR!' he wrote to me. 'Practically everyone to whom we spoke was very well informed, from their local media or from their Australian representatives, as to what had transpired at the summit conference and that was the subject that they wanted to discuss.'

'The interest expressed was quite extraordinary,' Bryan continued. 'Many of the Swiss bankers volunteered the opinion that a strong and unified Labor Government would be better placed than a Coalition Government to guide Australia through the economic difficulties ahead.'

This was the mood everywhere, and Bryan's letter was but an instance of it. And very importantly for me and the Government, the success of the summit was not lost upon Treasurer Paul Keating. He quickly dropped his reservations about the Accord and, like his saintly namesake, embraced it with the fervour of a convert. This was to be a factor of supreme importance in his burgeoning confidence and success as Treasurer. I was delighted to see the beginnings of an increasingly close association between him and the ACTU in general and Bill Kelty in particular.

THIRTEEN

Favourable winds were filling the Government sails. Share prices were taking off, bond rates were falling, there were signs of hope and fresh confidence everywhere. We eagerly awaited the opening of the new Parliament on 21st April. But just ahead out of sight, a submerged reef threatened to splinter the Government even before we could collect ourselves, for the very first time, on the front benches of the Parliament.

Day one of government had brought my former classmate, John Stone, to the door with news about the deficit. Now it was the turn of another student from the University of Western Australia, Harvey Barnett, to startle me with grim news. Barnett, the Director-General of Australian Security Intelligence Organisation (ASIO), came to see me in my Parliament House office on 20th April 1983.

It was the second time I had seen Harvey since becoming Prime Minister; he had briefed me on ASIO's work on 8th March at Kirribilli. That meeting had been a relaxed occasion. My first glimpse of the spy-chief was when I bounded down the stairs wearing only swimmers – it was a beautiful sunny day – to say goodbye to my old friend, George Polites, Director-General of the Confederation of Australian Industry.

Barnett came forward and immediately offered to have Polites taken home by an ASIO car. George burst out laughing; the idea of being hauled away from the Prime Minister's residence by spooks struck him as hilarious, and he made a pantomime of being under arrest.

I dashed off to change so Barnett and I could talk. He confirmed what I already knew about the modern ASIO. Routine political demonstrations were exempt from their watch; trade unions, environmental groups and Aboriginal groups were, despite furphies to the contrary, no part of ASIO's work now. International terrorism and the operations of foreign intelligence services in Australia were a different matter and Barnett outlined ASIO's efforts to prevent terrorist outbreaks and to keep tabs on those who would spy on us. There was nothing remarkable about what he had to say, it was routine intelligence. The significance of that first meeting lay in its conviviality and in the opportunity it gave me to assess Barnett.

Historically, Labor and ASIO deeply distrusted one another. In 1954, with a federal election imminent, ASIO coaxed and in fact paid for the defection of Soviet diplomat Vladimir Petrov. The Coalition Government of Robert Menzies ruthlessly and dishonestly exploited the defection and the issue of Soviet espionage in Australia against the ALP. Labor's pre-poll lead evaporated and the Coalition won the election. In 1973, with the Labor Party in power, it was ASIO's turn to be on the receiving end. On 16th March, Lionel Murphy, the Attorney-General and Minister responsible for ASIO, took a posse of Federal Police and raided ASIO's St Kilda Road headquarters in Melbourne.

When Barnett and I met on that brilliant day at Kirribilli we were both prepared to put that history behind us. In me, the ASIO chief was dealing with a Prime Minister who believed in security. For reasons I give in detail later, in 1983 the Cold War and threatened global conflagration made the world a dangerous place. In Barnett I confronted a security chief anxious to demonstrate his loyalty to the new Government. He told me how much he looked forward to working with us. Indeed, he had circulated to ASIO staff a memorandum saying that our election gave ASIO an opportunity to prove that it could work just as well with Labor as with a Coalition government.

So when he visited me at Parliament House six weeks later there was none of the old baggage cluttering the room. That was just as well because, this time, Barnett was not offering routine intelligence but startling news. 'I have an unpleasant duty to perform,' he said. 'I have information that you might not wish to hear about David Combe.'

After more than seven years as National Secretary of the Australian Labor Party, Combe had left in July 1981 and was now working as a lobbyist in Canberra. As well as being a respected figure within the labour movement generally, David was a close friend of mine and many other ministers. The worry was, as Barnett began to disclose the contents of his brief, that David was also becoming all too close to a Soviet diplomat called Valeri Ivanov, who had been positively identified by ASIO as a career officer of the KGB.

Barnett was not by nature a drama merchant. Speaking from notes, his exposition was calm and clear and appeared compelling. The only intelligent thing to do was to start by taking him at face value. At face value, what I was presented with was a KGB operation to penetrate the Labor Government by seeking to use a favoured son of the party as both an intelligence provider to a foreign government and an agent of influence for that government.

Barnett spelled out in some detail the extent to which Ivanov had sought to cultivate Combe. In November 1982 David had attended a Union of Friendship Societies' conference in Moscow as an Australian delegate of the Australia–USSR Society (AUS), a trip which Ivanov had effectively engineered. Upon David's return to Australia, ASIO noted the increased scale and number of meetings Ivanov had with him. A three-hour conversation between Ivanov and Combe at Ivanov's home on 4th March and a further meeting on 3rd April 1983 brought matters to a head for ASIO and prompted Barnett's presence in my office.

In a remarkable operation ASIO had recorded the meetings between Ivanov and Combe with a listening device in the ceiling of Ivanov's residence and from this had produced a verbatim transcript of about forty pages of the dinner meeting on 4th March. While the thrust of the conversation was troubling in itself, with Ivanov apparently propositioning Combe to work commercially for the Soviet Union, assessing trading possibilities between Russia and Australia, what alarmed ASIO was the way in which the relationship appeared to be moving rapidly beyond simple commerce.

The meeting on 3rd April had concluded, according to ASIO's reading of the conversation, with David Combe agreeing with Ivanov that future contacts should be made secretly. With this proposed move to a clandestine relationship Barnett warned me that ASIO's ability to stay abreast of its development could not be guaranteed. He advised that the time had come for action.

Naturally, his revelations staggered me. I had no illusions about the Soviets and knew this behaviour was typical. But to have David caught in their web posed a security problem for the country and a grave political problem for the Government. The Opposition parties would begin watching us for the least sign of softness towards the Soviets and towards our party's former Federal Secretary. And the media, I could see all too clearly, would be screaming 'Spy Scandal'.

On the other hand, as the media and the Opposition bayed for blood, I would, no doubt, have to contend within my own party with the conspiracy theorists automatically suspicious of ASIO's motives. On top of that there was rightly bound to be internal party debate about the implications for the civil liberties of individuals from any action we took.

As Barnett briefed me, a recent incident involving David flashed through my mind. He had arranged an appointment between me and the Northern Territory Chief Minister, Paul Everingham. He introduced Everingham to me and, to my surprise, stayed while Everingham and I conferred. I was a little annoyed at this presumption but I said nothing as I had no wish to embarrass him in front of his client. When leaving, he did so with a light-hearted flourish about the amount of money he was earning as a lobbyist. If that was an example of how freely David thought he could operate with me, then the doors of my Government would seem to be wide open to him. This was ASIO's fear. They imagined him playing his very easy access to the Government to the hilt, to the benefit of the Soviets.

Given the seriousness of what Barnett was saying, there could be no going off half-cocked. I wanted to know all the facts before I made a decision and I demanded assurance in the information given to me. I wasn't interested in opinions or hunches. And I wanted time for reflection and the opportunity to thrash things through with appropriate colleagues – members of the National and International Security sub-committee of Cabinet (NISC).

Even so, it was clear that events were heading towards Ivanov's expulsion at the very least. One option put forward by Barnett was that this be done quietly, with an unpublicised instruction for Ivanov to leave the country. I suspected, however, that such an instruction would be quiet one day and a blaring headline the next.

My political judgment of the Government's interests coincided with ASIO's assessment of their own. Their counter-espionage operation apparently constituted the first time in the Western world that eavesdropping on a Soviet diplomat's home had rendered useful intelligence.

If there was to be an expulsion, ASIO wanted the kudos for it. For years ASIO had weathered taunts from the right-wing National Civic Council that it had been penetrated by the Soviets and was incapable of catching a spy. Ivanov's expulsion would put paid to that.

I had the feeling that I would need Barnett again before the evening was out and I asked him to remain on stand-by at the Lakeside Hotel where he was staying. In the interim I gathered together the bulk of the NISC: the Foreign Minister, Bill Hayden; the Attorney-General, Senator Gareth Evans; the Special Minister of State, Mick Young; and myself. The remaining two members of the committee (the Deputy Prime Minister and Minister for Trade, Lionel Bowen, and the Defence Minister, Gordon Scholes) were unavailable.

I briefed them on the contents of Barnett's conversation. Like me, they were staggered at the possible implications for the Government. Around 9.00 p.m. I called Barnett in. He fielded questions about Combe's visit to the Soviet Union and the possibility that David might have been recruited for Soviet intelligence work while he was in Moscow. He could only point to the red-carpet treatment Combe had received there but he knew nothing beyond that.

There was no doubt, however, that Ivanov was a KGB agent and ASIO had detailed knowledge of his background and the extent of his activities here. I now needed little convincing on this point. 'We should kick this bastard out,' I said. 'If you kick him out it will damage Australia–Soviet relations,' Barnett dutifully cautioned. 'Fuck the Russians,' I replied. This heartened Barnett and took his breath away at the same time. I don't think he quite expected to encounter a Labor Prime Minister as adamant on security issues. Bill Hayden was apprehensive. He wanted Ivanov out of the country but quieter than quiet, without so much as a word to the Soviets. To Mick Young, this was a nonsensical idea.

'You can't have your bloody cake and eat it too, Bill,' Mick remonstrated. It was the sort of down-to-earth, commonsense approach that made Mick invaluable on such occasions. He was very often an anchor to reality, bringing back to earth conversation which was drifting into the ephemeral. Ironically, Mick's straight-talking folksiness was also to be his undoing. Within months, he, too, would be ensnared by the events now unfolding.

Although we kicked the issues around that night, we were not yet in a position to make a decision. I asked Barnett to brief the full NISC first thing the following morning. The midnight oil burnt from many windows in Canberra that night – in Parliament House, at the Lodge and at ASIO's Canberra offices.

It was a bleary-eyed team that heard Barnett run through his briefing notes for the third time. This time, however, he was questioned aggressively by Lionel Bowen about an issue straight out of left field. Lionel had a particular concern about an obscure Soviet citizen whose visa had been extended, Lionel alleged, through ASIO's connivance. Barnett had no idea what he was talking about and neither did the rest of us.

Lionel is a remarkable mixture. He has a great capacity for acuity and succinct summation, at times shooting off his points with deadly accuracy. At other times, and this was one of them, he could ramble in a way that made his colleagues struggle to get hold of his meaning. Nonetheless, Lionel was the Deputy Prime Minister, a member of the NISC and if he had a problem, then we all had a problem, even if we couldn't figure out exactly what it was. So I asked Barnett for a fuller briefing, this time with ASIO's investigating officers present.

They were summoned from Melbourne and brought with them all relevant documentary evidence. The meeting of the NISC reconvened in the Cabinet room at 12.40 p.m. At that point the head of ASIO's counter-espionage department dealt with Lionel's suspicions about the Soviet citizen whose visa was extended. ASIO had nothing to do with it. The citizen, who oversaw the servicing of Soviet tractors sold in Australia, had applied for an extension of his visa through the Department of Immigration and Ethnic Affairs and his application had been dealt with in a routine manner.

We were now back on the main track. The decision was taken to expel Ivanov and the following afternoon, 22nd April at 2.00 p.m., Bill Hayden met with the Soviet Ambassador, Nikolai Sudarikov, and told him that Ivanov had one week to leave the country. Sudarikov was informed that a succession of incidents had led the Government to conclude that Ivanov was a professional intelligence officer of the Committee for State Security (KGB).

That took care of Ivanov. David Combe was a different matter. However compromising, stupid or greedy his behaviour had been, David and the party went back a long way. He was also a close friend of mine. On the very day the NISC sealed Ivanov's fate and discussed the scope of David's relationship with him, Combe had watched the opening of Parliament from a seat in the gallery reserved for a member of my family. One could make clear-headed, rational decisions about the necessary fate of David Combe but one couldn't make them without pain.

A legal opinion from the Attorney-General's Department told us that on the evidence available David had committed no criminal offence. With Ivanov about to leave the country on 28th April the dangerous circumstance that may have led to such an offence was removed, or almost. There was still the possibility that Ivanov may try to contact him before leaving Australia, or that another agent might take over the cultivation of Combe where Ivanov had left off. As soon as it became obvious that neither Ivanov nor a substitute were going to contact Combe, I ordered the removal of all forms of surveillance on him. The surveillance lasted from 21st April until 4th May. That it should have been necessary in the first place was part of the torment of the whole distasteful episode.

A large part of the agony was the Cabinet's decision of 26th April 1983 to bar Combe's access to ministers. Security and political imperatives demanded this. In Adelaide to coincide with a session of the Constitutional Convention, the Cabinet met on a nervous knife-edge. There was an air of shock and trauma about the reactions of some of my colleagues, as if the sky were about to fall in on the Government. This was instructive to me, a study in the stresses and strains of government and the way in which people coped – some, obviously, rather better than others.

My own position could be likened to that of a surgeon forced to operate upon himself – each cut hurt. David and I had worked together for a long time and our views on many subjects were *ad idem*. Having to cut him clear of the Government was indescribably hurtful. All the same, I did not doubt for a second what had to be done. A Prime Minister cannot deal with a crisis blinkered by sentimental attachments. In personal decision-making, yes, but in making decisions for the nation, the Government, and the party, no. If I thought otherwise I would have been in the wrong job entirely, and I did not believe that for a moment. This did not, however, anaesthetise me to the pain of the decision.

While the Cabinet deliberated in Adelaide on the fate of a dear friend, a strange coincidence was being played out in Melbourne. My younger daughter, Rosslyn, was due to deliver our first grandchild at our house in Sandringham, with Hazel present to help and to let me know the news immediately. When an official told me there was a call from Melbourne I dashed out of Cabinet to be informed by a delighted Hazel that we had become grandparents to a healthy little boy, named David. It was also the fortieth birthday of David Combe.

The decision to cut off Combe's access to the Government was received with bitterness and I rapidly became a target of vilification among the prejudiced and the uninformed. I was accused of being a bastard who had dumped his mate and behaved cruelly towards him.

And there was more trouble brewing. I was soon forced to apply the scalpel to yet another mate, more beloved even than David – Mick Young. Although Combe's involvement with Ivanov was meant to be a tightly kept secret, rumours of it were circulating widely. As it turned out, the source of them was a member of the NISC.

On 21st April Mick Young had hooked up with his old mate, lobbyist Eric Walsh (a former press secretary to Gough Whitlam) and, in the car park of Canberra's 19th Hole Motel, he foreshadowed Ivanov's expulsion and the link between the Soviet spy and David Combe. When knowledge of this conversation came to light in mid-July I immediately sought Mick's resignation as Special Minister of State. *That bastard Hawke had struck again.* This time he had reached past the human shape of David Combe and into the heavens – he had torn down one of the gods of the labour movement, Mick Young.

There was hell to pay. To the conspiracy theorists, I was confirmed as the worst sort of ogre. To civil libertarians, I had once again breached due process. To those who viewed government as an institution of men, not of laws, and above all, of mateship, I had wantonly savaged a friend. But mateship was exactly the problem, and Mick knew it; part of Mick's hurt and the anger he felt towards me came, ultimately, from knowing that he had done what he should not have done. I was closer to Mick than to anybody else in the Cabinet and in the parliamentary party at large. Making decisions about the plight of David Combe was traumatic enough. Demanding Mick's resignation was the hardest thing I had to do in government.

A cold front settled on our relationship. We had met almost daily; now, almost never. Where there had once been warmth, there was ice.

To Mick's great credit, our friendship would resume and he would fight his way back into the ministry. But for the time being our friendship lay frozen in the bitterness of his reaction.

In the meantime the media and the Opposition were howling like wolves around the rumours that Mick had helped set off. On 10th May they sank their teeth into the Combe–Ivanov relationship and began tearing away at it. Up until this time I had done everything possible to ensure that Combe's name was not linked to Ivanov's expulsion. But, as I explained to the Parliament on 12th May 1983, once 'Mr Combe's name was raised by the Opposition and not by us, [this Government] immediately did every possible thing it could do to ensure that Mr Combe had an unparalleled and historically unprecedented opportunity of knowing why the Government had acted as it did'.

David Combe had been taken through the evidence of his relationship with Ivanov by the Director-General of ASIO and reluctantly accepted our decision to stop the Government dealing with him as a professional lobbyist. During Question Time on 12th May I announced a full judicial inquiry into Australia's security organisations, naming Justice Robert Hope as the Royal Commissioner. Hope had inquired into the nation's intelligence and security forces in the mid-seventies and was the obvious man for the job. He was now asked to report on the circumstances surrounding Ivanov's expulsion, his involvement with Combe, and the actions taken by the Federal Government. If I had been wrong, if ASIO had miscued or over-reached, if Combe's rights had been abused, then a Royal Commission could sheet home the blame. Equally, the Government's actions could be independently endorsed.

I was confident that the Government would be vindicated. ASIO, I was convinced, had good intelligence and we had handled it in the only way possible. Had we let the relationship between Combe and Ivanov slide on, who knows what would have happened? David was on a slippery slope. Better we take the blame for ostensibly compromising his civil liberties than that Ivanov take the credit for compromising Combe completely. For whatever David intended from the relationship, Ivanov intended nothing good from it, only David's ruin.

While ASIO had provided the Government with good intelligence, they had not run a perfect operation and it had peripheral aspects which left a lot to be desired. They made one inexcusable mistake. On 3rd May an ASIO officer told John Enfield, Deputy Secretary of Prime Minister and Cabinet, responsible for security, that my senior adviser Bob Hogg had had breakfast with David Combe on the previous day.

This was staggering information as I had specifically instructed Bob not to meet with Combe. And of course he had done no such thing. ASIO had got it wrong. Combe's ASIO case officer had taken a suggestion by David Combe to Labor Party pollster and managing director of Australian National Opinion Polls, Rod Cameron, that Hogg join them for an early breakfast at the Lakeside Hotel, as evidence that Hogg had in fact attended the breakfast. Hogg had not even been asked to the breakfast. Since when, I wanted to know, did conjecture become fact? I rang Barnett at his home in Melbourne that night in an absolute fury. 'How dare your officers give me false information!' I raged at him. If they had got this wrong, what else might they have mistaken? I demanded that Barnett come to Canberra immediately so that I could personally review the evidence and, in that light, assess afresh the steps we had taken on 21st April.

When the Director-General arrived in Canberra I dressed him down again. His apology was 'abject', the word he used himself. He asked if he could personally apologise to Bob Hogg. I appreciated this, and so did Hogg. Nevertheless, I was determined to review all the material he brought with him. It seemed to measure up but I was still not satisfied, and in Melbourne on Sunday, 8th May I checked off

ASIO's transcript of Combe and Ivanov's dinner conversation of 4th March against the tape recording. Although I did find some minor mistakes they were not exculpatory of Combe. On one occasion ASIO noted Combe's question to Ivanov as 'your brief talk to me'. The question was in fact 'your brief to talk to me', the word 'to' that I had picked up giving the remark a quite different meaning. ASIO's 'brief talk' was, indeed, gentler on Combe than the correct 'brief to talk'. In general, though, the transcripts bore out the tape recordings.

The ASIO tapes did not show David in a good light, but it would be some time before their contents became public. Meanwhile, David, most of the media, and sections of our own party turned the real significance of Combe–Ivanov on its head and used it to impugn the Prime Minister, the Government and ASIO. ASIO was accused of malfeasance and of conspiring to entrap David Combe. Ivanov, well, he was just a straight trade officer and diplomat. But the Government was riding roughshod over David Combe's civil liberties.

From the time the Royal Commission opened its doors in Canberra's Hinkler building on 1st June until I took the stand on 3rd August, Combe and his sympathisers whipped up the expectation that the day the Prime Minister was brought to account outside the Cabinet he dominated on this issue, he would be cast down and Combe exonerated.

I was in the witness box for three days and rigorously cross-examined for more than a day. With each answer the Government's case was driven home. Ivanov was a KGB agent whose cultivation of David Combe had reached a clear point of danger to national security. He sought to make his relationship with Combe clandestine and the moment was imminent when Combe could be 'irretrievably compromised'.

I noted that Combe had unique access to all members of the Government, and although he himself believed Ivanov was from the KGB, did not report it. Combe's half-baked defence was delivered back to his counsel as mincemeat. After his day of defeat in cross-examination, David's counsel, Barker, of Lindy Chamberlain fame, drowned his sorrows in a somewhat bucolic fashion and turned up the next morning looking much the worse for wear.

One account of the questioning comes from Harvey Barnett's auto-biography.[27] 'Mr Hawke was in devastating form before a captive audience … he was unbending in his responses to cross-examination and became testy when, like Toynbee's theory of history, it tended to become cyclical in form. Even Combe supporters in the media ranks were silent and embarrassed at the scorn he heaped on the Combe legal camp.'

One such supporter was lawyer–journalist, David Marr, whose book on the Combe imbroglio, *The Ivanov Trail*, was published in May 1984. '[It] set in cement, if not in concrete, Marr's constant theme that Combe had been crucified by the Hawke government which had made the basic error of listening to the National Security Services warnings. It was a thinly veiled attack on Prime Minister Hawke,' Barnett noted of Marr's work.[28]

But even Marr had to admit: 'Hawke was an exceptional witness in the experience of any of the barristers at the Commission. He could always see the question coming.'[29] This was not surprising. I knew that the Government had acted surely and with propriety. Intellectually, I had no fear of those who were cross-examining me and I had all the facts at my fingertips. Although it was an emotional ordeal I faced my inquisitors with confidence.

That confidence was not misplaced, as Justice Hope made clear when he reported the findings of the Royal Commission on 6th December 1983. Ivanov was a KGB agent actively cultivating Combe to act, knowingly or unknowingly, as an agent of influence for the Soviet Government, Hope concluded. What is more, the danger of

Ivanov succeeding with Combe was probably real, he found. As to the Government, the Prime Minister and other members of the NISC had been right to conclude that Ivanov's cultivation of Combe had serious national security implications. The decision to block Combe's access to ministers was likewise justified. ASIO, too, had acted correctly. It must have been galling for much of the nation's press to carry banner headlines the following morning such as: 'Hope vindicates Hawke's handling of the spy case'.

When Hope's report hit the media between the eyes they had to report it accurately. This was progress indeed. 'It was a long while before some parts of the press were able to spell Mr. Combe's name correctly,' Hope wrote. Now the media had that little detail correct they had also at last, caught up on the true story: the Government had got it right.

Still missing, however, was the media's ability to handle the sub-plot; even today a canard insists that the Hawke Labor Government administered Australia by preferring its 'mates'. Yet here, in the Combe–Ivanov imbroglio, the Government gave the clearest demonstration that good government came first, with mates and all others standing equally thereafter.

Excruciatingly painful steps were taken to establish that this was a professional, unsentimental, non-mates Government. Friendships make for smooth, orderly, convivial, harmonious government but they destroy good government when placed ahead of it. As with so many decisions taken early in the life of the Government, this one set the tone for how we intended to govern through the eighties and into the next decade.

The Combe–Ivanov episode was also an early introduction to the pressures of being Prime Minister and, indeed, to the loneliness that sometimes comes with holding the nation's top job. It was a tense time for me and for my family. Just how tense is reflected in a humorous incident involving Hazel during this period. Familiar with all the talk of a Russian spy, the KGB, GRU (Soviet Military Intelligence), ASIO and the spooky ambience of the whole affair, Hazel was in the Lodge one night hoping to settle her nerves with some quiet reading. She was alone in that great big barn of a house, still unfamiliar with it, sitting with her back to the glass doors of one of the drawing rooms. Suddenly, there was an almighty explosion. *Rifle-fire*, she thought. Her instinctive reaction was to duck low in the chair and swing around quickly in search of a hole in the curtain left by the bullet.

But then she looked up to see tiny particles of dust hanging in the air like gunsmoke around one of the 1960s metal lampshades. A rapid fracture of the metal due to the heat of the light had caused the bang. She was able to laugh, but the dust of this episode took years to settle for many of the central players.

FOURTEEN

Looking back, it is perhaps difficult to comprehend today the significance of the Combe–Ivanov trauma. The world in 1983 was very
different and so was the Labor Party's view of the world. The whole
sorry affair strengthened my determination to do what I could in
government to change both.

In January 1942 John Curtin had ushered in a new era in Australia's
international relations with the ringing declaration: 'Without any
inhibition of any kind, I make it quite clear that Australia looks to
America, free of any pangs as to our traditional links and kinship with
the United Kingdom.' The forging of this relationship with the
United States was the foundation of his prime ministership and of
Australia's salvation during the Second World War. But after the war a
persistent strain of anti-Americanism developed within large areas of
the Labor Party. As the Iron Curtain descended and international
affairs became denominated in the policies of the Cold War, these
elements in Australia and in most democratic parties of the Left
displayed a lack of intellectual rigour in discriminating between the
massive and dangerous evil of the Soviet régime and the mistakes of
practice and policy of the world's greatest democracy, the United States.

In the Australian labour movement there were two strands to this inelegant mindlessness. On the one hand there was the illusion of the label. The Soviet Union described itself as 'socialist' and for that reason alone, although the evidence of history screamed against the linkage, elements of the democratic Left believed in a natural affinity with the USSR and assumed there was an inherent decency in its policies. The facts, of course, supported precisely the opposite interpretation. Soviet Communism ranked with Nazism and Fascism as one of the greatest scourges of the twentieth century. Stalin murdered more of his own people – some twenty million – than any dictator in history, and to him and his successors until Gorbachev the concept of the rights and liberty of the individual was anathema. In their theory and in their practice, wherever they had intruded into the affairs of other countries, they had demonstrated that social democrats were their mortal foes.

On the other hand, the United States did enough during the Cold War period to fuel the fires of paranoia. It often failed to distinguish between strategic imperatives and implicit support for the policies of rotten régimes. The lunacy of the McCarthy period was followed by the savage and unwinnable prosecution of the war in Vietnam. That war brought US and Australian troops together in the jungles of Vietnam but profoundly divided each of their populations at home.

I was a vocal opponent of the war and of US policy in Vietnam but my attitude towards America remained positive. To me, the overriding importance of Australia's alliance with the United States was clear. The United States, whatever its mistakes, was the bulwark of the free world's defence against the threat then posed by the Soviet Union.

The Left of the Party had a different perspective; it was the United States that was suspect. For them, the Combe–Ivanov affair released all the pent-up prejudice and passion and let loose all the fear about United States imperialism. In this demonology, nothing loomed larger than the United States–Australia joint facilities at North West Cape, Nurrungar and Pine Gap. For those who opposed them, these were not joint facilities but 'United States bases'. The facts, of course, were irrelevant to the prejudiced, but they are indisputable.

North West Cape in Western Australia was established as a communications relay station for ships and submarines of the United States Navy and is also used by the Royal Australian Navy. Narrungar in South Australia and Pine Gap in the Northern Territory are satellite ground stations and together provide early warning of missile launches, monitoring of nuclear explosions and intelligence collection aimed at verifying arms control and disarmament treaties. With no combat personnel or combat equipment present, no military stores or workshops, no plant or machinery or laboratories for research, development, production or maintenance of any weapons or combat systems of any type, they are not military bases but facilities – and they are joint facilities.

Ordinary Australians, I knew, had no time for those who larded the language with anti-American polemic. And, to the extent that they identified this attitude with the Labor Party, the party was damaged by it. Electorally, through the fifties and sixties particularly, the tag of anti-Americanism had been one of the elements which kept the party from government. Now that we were in government I believed Australians hoped to see again the party of Curtin, and I was determined that their hopes would be realised.

The Combe–Ivanov affair showed early in the life of the Government that we were prepared to deal with security issues without fear or favour. It demonstrated to the public that Labor would never compromise on national security. What's more, if Labor softness on national security had been of concern to our own security forces or to the foreign services with whom they dealt, those of the US in particular, from Combe–Ivanov onwards that concern was wiped away.

Despite the intensity and the bitterness of the Left's early reactions I had a strong belief in my capacity, if not to persuade them immediately to my own position, at least to neutralise their readiness to detract from what I intended to be the broad new thrusts of Australian foreign policy. My confidence was founded on a number of factors, not least the dangerous realities of that period in which we came to government.

During the Carter presidency (1977–80) the United States had been significantly humiliated by the Soviet Union under the leadership of Leonid Brezhnev, and by other countries, especially Iran. The strategic balance had moved in the Soviets' favour. In 1979 they had invaded Afghanistan and installed a puppet régime which gave final shape to an arc of instability and Soviet influence stretching through Asia from the Middle East to Indo-China. At the same time the Soviets were meddling in Africa and along with their surrogate, Cuba, were pouring weapons and men into Angola.

The Soviet presence and influence was growing visibly in the Asia–Pacific region, particularly with the building of bases in Vietnam which enabled the extension of their air and naval power into the vital sea lanes of that region. Nearer to home they were establishing closer diplomatic and economic relations, including rights for operation of their fishing vessels, with a number of South Pacific island states. They were firing test missiles into the Pacific without inhibition.

Ronald Reagan, elected President of the United States in 1980, tagged the USSR 'the evil empire' and made it clear that America would no longer acquiesce in its expansionism. Reagan initiated a substantial increase in US defence spending which he regarded as necessary to recover the strategic advantage lost under his predecessor. By 1983 the white-heat intensity of the super-power confrontation had diminished slightly but the Soviet threat remained real and the risk of global nuclear war hung like a pall over all human endeavour.

After I became Prime Minister I was moved by the thousands of letters I continued to receive from children and young people. The overwhelming theme of these letters was concern for the environment and, in particular, fear of a nuclear holocaust. Was it all worthwhile, they wanted to know? Should they worry about applying themselves to study if their world was going to be blown apart?

I replied to all their letters and tried to ease their concerns but I was sad, for I knew I couldn't look them in the eye and say there was no reason to fear. But I did know that I could look at my own party squarely, emphasise the harsh and dangerous realities of our time and say that there were things that this Labor Government could, should and would do to help make the world a safer place. I believed my colleagues would want to do this, and I believed they would come to understand that we could only do this on the basis of comprehending those realities. Prejudice would get us nowhere.

My confidence was based in part upon the knowledge that the Hawke Government would be taking initiatives which were not only independent of our alliance with the United States but were at odds with the US position. I did not believe the Americans held a monopoly on wisdom nor a monopsonistic power over our support on every issue in the international arena. I knew that while the Left would not see these initiatives as flowing logically from my view of the world, they would nevertheless find them intrinsically attractive. I trusted that in time they would come to recognise them as part of a pattern based on both an appreciation of global realities and of fundamental Labor principles.

Buttressing this confidence was the knowledge that in George Shultz, the United States Secretary of State, I had a friend of long standing. As the fledgling Labor Government unfolded these initiatives it was going to be important that the Americans understood clearly that they neither were, nor were intended to be, a threat to the principles upon which the alliance between us was based. Rather the US needed to see this range of initiatives as a logically connected series of concepts calculated to strengthen the cause of freedom and peace with security. I knew that in Shultz I had a highly intelligent and sympathetic ear and conduit to the President of the United States.

I first met George Shultz in 1976 at a specially arranged dinner at the Southern Cross Hotel in Melbourne. I was President of the ACTU and he was the head of Bechtel Corporation, a California-based international construction conglomerate with major projects in the region including the Bougainville CRA copper mine in Papua New Guinea. As Bechtel was a large employer of Australian labour, and an enlightened one at that, it was natural that George, who was already something of a Secretary of State for his corporation, should meet with me. The worldwide spread of Bechtel's activities gave him a many-layered understanding of international affairs. He had a unique blend of academic and governmental experience in my own fields, having been a Professor of Labor Relations, Secretary of Labor and Secretary to the Treasury. Over the years I grew to appreciate him as a wise and decent man and could well understand the accolade bestowed on him by Henry Kissinger. Kissinger, who is not known for heaping praise on his contemporaries, wrote of Shultz: 'I met no one in public life for whom I developed greater respect and affection ... If I could choose one American to whom I would entrust the nation's fate in a crisis, it would be George Shultz.'[30] My relationship with George was another example of the comfort I've had, from boyhood days when Clem was my best friend, in being able to draw on the experience and wisdom of people older than myself.

Our Melbourne meeting was a forerunner to others here and in the United States. And so when I became Prime Minister it was obviously an enormous benefit for me and for this country to have the US Secretary of State as a personal friend. George willingly smoothed the path of Australian–US relations with other members of the Reagan Administration. It probably helped that Caspar Weinberger, Reagan's Secretary of Defense, had been Bechtel's chief legal counsel. Caspar, influenced by George's goodwill towards me, relaxed his usually reserved manner and a warm, solid friendship developed between us over time.

More important, of course, than George's initial intercession with Cap was the entrée he offered to the President himself. It was obvious from Reagan's very first communication to me, a letter of congratulations on the election victory, that the Secretary of State had spoken well of me to the President. Reagan's letter went beyond mere diplomatic formalities: 'As you shoulder the many burdens of government, I want you to know that, as a friend and ally, I intend to work closely with you, as I did with your predecessor, in pursuit of our many shared goals,' he wrote. 'In order that we may put this relationship on a more personal basis, I hope that you will be able in the not distant future to visit Washington.'

As a result of this invitation I included the United States in my first overseas trip as Prime Minister. I went first to Papua New Guinea and Indonesia, to establish in the public mind the priority my Government attached to the Asia–Pacific region. We were then to fly to Washington from Geneva where it was my honour to be the first Australian Prime Minister to address the International Labour Organisation.

Both the ILO and I seemed to treat the occasion as a homecoming. I remember being tempted to begin my speech with 'As I was saying before I was interrupted …' for so much of what I had to say continued the themes I had hammered during the seventies when I was a worker delegate and member of the Governing Body. One theme in my speech was resonant of past times. It concerned the freedom of association and the suppression of trade union rights in all ILO regions. I singled out South Africa: '… the repression of trade union

rights is a keystone in the monstrous edifice of apartheid,' I told delegates, who were then dealing with the ILO's report on apartheid. Time
and time again during my prime ministership I was to address international forums on the evils of apartheid. It was not, in my judgment,
an issue sufficiently high on the agenda of the United States, but for
my part I dedicated myself, particularly in the context of the Commonwealth Heads of Government, to mobilising international pressure on
the South African Government to dismantle that abhorrent system.[31] I
linked this aspect of repression in South Africa to the suppression of
Solidarity in Poland. Solidarity represented the budding of freedom in
the Eastern Bloc countries, and the Soviet Union was bent upon its
destruction.

An amusing diversion occurred in the midst of these grim considerations in Geneva. I had invited the Keatings to accompany Hazel and
me on the visit to the United States. On the last night in Geneva, Paul
and I had dinner with Rupert Murdoch at the famous *Parc des Eaux
Vives* restaurant. Murdoch was waxing eloquent about his financial
progress and was particularly enthusiastic about his plans for satellite
television in Europe, which he saw as a licence to print money. As the
dollar signs continued to dance in his eyes, the conversation began to
bore me. I took the plunge: 'Rupert, will there ever come a stage in
your life when you reckon you've made enough money and got enough
power? After all we're only on this beautiful, fascinating globe for a
fleeting fraction of a second in the whole scheme of things. I mean, is
there ever going to come a time when you say – I'm going to save the
rest of my time to enjoy this world and my family?' Murdoch looked at
me as though I was slightly deranged then resumed the musings of
Midas. I excused myself to go and meet some old Genevan friends,
leaving Paul and Rupert to it. I don't know who paid the bill.

When we arrived in Washington the next day the welcome in the
manicured grounds of the White House could not have been warmer.

No sooner had Australia's Ambassador, Bob Cotton, completed his round of formal introductions than George Shultz stepped forward: 'Mr President,' he said to Ronald Reagan, 'the Prime Minister is a friend of mine from the old days, we've had frequent discussions and I know him well. Mr President, I commend him to you.' Instantly, President and Prime Minister were Ron and Bob. This was easy, for Ronald Reagan is a warm, friendly man. He had strong, deeply entrenched conservative views but at no stage did the ideological divide between him and his opponents lead to personal rancour.

In the five visits I made to the United States during Reagan's presidency I did not meet a single political opponent who disliked the man personally. House Speaker, Democrat (the late) Tip O'Neill, was one of the President's most trenchant political critics and best typified the feeling for Reagan when he said, 'Bob, this President is the most conservative son-of-a-bitch I've seen in that position in my time in politics, but goddamit, I can't help liking the guy!'

Although I knew that significant intellectual exchange was not Ron's forte I had treated with scepticism the rumours about his use in formal meetings of a series of hand-held cards as discussion prompters. But when I sat down in the White House across the table from the President, who was flanked on either side by members of his Cabinet, I was astonished to see that he actually did operate this way. After the preliminary introductions and courtesies Ron said, 'Well, Bob, you are our welcome guest, would you like to open up the discussions? Feel free to raise any matters you like.' I responded with some observations and questions about the strength and durability of the United States' economic recovery. The President, with an ease which obviously came from long practice, thumbed through a number of cards held in the palm of his hand, found the appropriate one, read a couple of generalised sentences and then, turning to the Secretary of Treasury, Donald Regan, said, 'Don, this is your area, perhaps you would like to respond to Bob.' A useful discussion between the Secretary and me flowed from this unlikely beginning. My next intervention covered the field of international affairs. Again Ron found the appropriate card, made a couple of broad observations, then passed the baton to George Shultz.

Many people have found President Reagan's conduct of meetings in this manner a subject of hilarity, and have ridiculed him for it.

To me this is a superficial reaction, for at no stage had Reagan masqueraded before the American people as an intellectual or as someone deeply versed in economics or international affairs. What they saw was what they got, a nice guy. There was a refreshing candour in Reagan's approach. He did not pretend to have knowledge or expertise that he didn't in fact possess. After making his chosen introductory remarks he would in effect say: 'over to the experts'. He followed the discussions closely and occasionally intervened. His modus operandi contrasted starkly, and favourably, with some other national leaders who rabbited on, pretending a comprehension that their very conversation belied.

While Reagan did not have a black belt for detail or for intellectual prowess, he was rock solid on the elementary verities that would shape the world to be passed on to future generations – the virtues of the free world over the authoritarian societies and command economies of the Soviet system. In the circumstances of the time this made Reagan a very significant President.

The international arms race was costing the global economy a staggering $700 billion annually, the bulk of this spending being concentrated in the Soviet Union and America. The price of this military madness was far higher in the USSR than in America when taken as a percentage of gross national product. Reagan, in this context, didn't hold the cards in the palm of his hand. He laid them squarely on the table and told the Soviets the stakes had been raised. There would be no more relatively cheap takeovers. The United States regarded seriously the Soviets' hegemonistic ambitions, proof of which were everywhere to be seen. If the USSR wanted to sustain those ambitions, then Reagan would make sure they paid a high economic price. He crystallised more acutely than ever before what had underpinned United States policy towards the Soviet Union in the Cold War period. This policy constituted one of the greatest wagers of the twentieth century; if the United States by the maintenance of its own military power and appropriate alliances could prevent the outbreak of major conflict, the competitive free market system would expose, beat and ultimately destroy the command system of Soviet communism.

Reagan's significance as a President in world terms was not simply that he played the strong hand. It was that, having displayed the strength which he believed was necessary to confront the Soviet threat, he was then prepared to listen to his advisers, particularly Shultz, who judged Gorbachev a leader worthy of serious dialogue. Looking back on that period one can say that without Reagan there would not have been the Gorbachev to whom history will rightly attribute such a significant role in ending the Cold War. Reagan and Gorbachev, so different in so many ways, needed each other.

Ronald Reagan's preparedness to move from bellicose anti-Soviet rhetoric to participation in a dialogue which led to the end of the Soviet system is something which should be borne in mind by those who ridicule him.

In 1983 the ending of the Cold War may have appeared a distant, uncertain dream, with Australia having no place whatsoever in the dreamscape. In the event this was not the case. Australia, through ANZUS and more specifically through the joint facilities, had its part to play in helping to turn that dream into a reality. The ANZUS Treaty and Australia's hosting of the joint facilities were natural discussion points in our talks.

ANZUS was then thirty years old and in need of review. I raised this with Reagan who responded sympathetically. Shortly afterwards, on 12th July, he wrote to me:

> I am personally convinced, as I am sure you are, that a fundamental consequence of the review process will be agreement that the ANZUS alliance remains not only relevant to our mutual security, but also is more important than ever in the face of increasing Soviet military power in the Pacific and elsewhere ... I trust all will also agree that ANZUS is a vital and integral element of the security of all western and democratic nations – that their security is, in the final analysis, intertwined, indivisible and global.

To me, this was fundamental. I proposed the review not to derogate from the importance of ANZUS but to strengthen the alliance and enhance its relevance.

Reagan and I also discussed the joint facilities. In my view the risks involved in Australia's hosting of the joint defence facilities were outweighed by our interests in global nuclear deterrence and in maintaining the global strategic balance. In 1974 the installations in Australia had been brought under the joint administration of Australia and the United States. Even so, our interests could always be enhanced by improved consultative processes. It seemed to me, too, that Australian sovereignty was best served by piercing the veil of secrecy that had grown up around the operation of the facilities. Secrecy had led to a great deal of misunderstanding about the purposes of the establishments at Pine Gap, Nurrungar, and North West Cape.

So, in accordance with party policy and my own conviction, we pressed the United States administration to agree to a public disclosure of the general nature and functions of the joint facilities. We could not in good conscience act unilaterally as our allies had been assured for over a decade that Australia would preserve the secrecy of the installations. What we sought was a jointly agreed form of words which left the Soviets none the wiser as to the technical functions of the three jointly operated facilities but nevertheless gave the Australian public enough general information to reassure them of their strategic necessity. We thrashed these things through with the United States and then on 6th June 1984, in the Parliament, I was able to make a comprehensive public statement on the facilities.

At the time of my first meeting with Ronald Reagan in June 1983 the United States had launched its Strategic Defense Initiative (SDI), a futuristic defence research project popularly known as 'Star Wars'. The joint facilities were no part of this research. Yet the Star Wars program was broadly caught up in the alliance relationship. At the end of a convivial lunch at the White House, Ronald Reagan was at his most charming, but I told him that we were not convinced we should have anything to do with the program. The President suggested that he should have some of his senior people talk to us in detail about it. He sent his top SDI experts down to New York to talk to me and my officials before we left the United States. I was still not convinced either of the feasibility of the SDI concept or that it was appropriate for Australia to be associated with it. We never changed that position.

By the end of the visit my basic objectives had been achieved and recognised. I had established our commitment to the Australian–US alliance and an effective working relationship with both the Administration and the Congress. The Chairman of the Senate Foreign Relations Committee, Senator Percy from Illinois, had interrupted the business of the Senate to escort me on to the floor of the Chamber to introduce me to his colleagues, seven of whom, as he pointed out, were fellow Rhodes Scholars.

In all of this, in moving to put the relationship on a better and more realistic footing than ever before, I had been at pains to emphasise the primacy of Australia's interests. In addressing the National Press Club in Washington I said that our aim was to pursue 'an independent and self-respecting foreign policy, based on a cool and objective assessment – hard-headed if you like – of Australia's genuine national interest'.

The groundwork was now well laid with our major ally and its leadership to pursue that national interest in a world which I felt was, almost imperceptibly, becoming susceptible to radical change.

FIFTEEN

The Liberal–National Party Governments of the past had been long on rhetorical commitment to the US alliance but short on conceptual or practical contributions to the ultimate objectives of that alliance. The Coalition seemed to believe that by identifying the threat of the Soviet Union and inveighing against its evils they had exhausted their obligations to the alliance and its principles. They had earned for Australia the tag of reliable ally, but irrelevant cipher in the broader game plan.

Our Government saw the recognition of the Soviet threat as but a beginning of our national responsibility. While recommitting Australia to our major defence alliance and to its renovation, we were determined to play a significant part in the causes of peace and disarmament which were what we saw as the ultimate objectives of the alliance.

We recognised that whatever the strengths of our economic and social programs at home, they would be futile if a nuclear conflagration occurred. We therefore sought security for all states at the lowest possible level of armament, stability in the nuclear balance, and adequate verification arrangements. To strengthen our capacity to play an effective role in these matters we appointed, in 1983, Australia's first

Ambassador for Disarmament to represent our point of view in international forums, especially the Conference on Disarmament in Geneva.

Wherever possible Australia put its money where its mouth was. The Government funded a Peace Research Centre at the Australian National University in Canberra. We gave financial support to the United Nations Institute for Disarmament Research. We helped finance the world disarmament campaign which aims to increase public understanding of United Nations disarmament objectives.

From the beginning we determined that the cause of peace and disarmament was too important to be left to the superpowers to settle between themselves. Each country had a high stake in preventing nuclear war, but Australia had augmented its stake in the disarmament debate by accepting the presence of the joint facilities on her soil. This made us a direct player as well as an interested observer.

Our pursuit of disarmament objectives throughout the course of my prime ministership created a role for Australia vastly disproportionate to our size or military might. In the United Nations, in the Conference on Disarmament, and in bilateral discussions with the nuclear weapons states, Australia became one of the most active proponents of a comprehensive nuclear test ban treaty (CTB), aimed at outlawing all nuclear testing by all states. Starting in 1983 Australia was a prime mover in the reconvening of the Conference on Disarmament's *ad hoc* committee on a nuclear test ban. And each year from 1983 Australia and New Zealand jointly pressed their resolution in the United Nations General Assembly in support of a comprehensive test ban.

A comprehensive test ban treaty is still to be achieved. Not so the Nuclear Non-Proliferation Treaty (NPT), now more than a quarter of a century old. Here, too, we were indefatigable in pressing the significance of the NPT. Within the party I used the authority of the prime ministership to educate opinion, this time about the implications of the

NPT for Australia as a uranium exporting country. In 1982 the party had only narrowly (fifty-three to forty-six) pulled back from a policy of repudiating Australia's existing uranium exporting contracts. In government, many on the Left and Centre still clung to an anti-uranium mining stance.

But as I constantly emphasised, the Nuclear Non-Proliferation Treaty to which Australia was a signatory presupposed a bargain. By eschewing nuclear weaponry, non-nuclear weapon states were entitled under the treaty to receive assistance from other signatories in gaining the benefits of nuclear energy for peaceful purposes. By signing the NPT, Australia became obligated to supply uranium to buyer states who were signatories.

It had long been my view that the peaceful use of uranium for electric power generation was an increasing fact of international life.[32] Australia, therefore, was better in the uranium exporting business than out of it. Being in it meant that we could participate in ensuring the safety and security of the nuclear fuel cycle. To me this made more sense than leaving the supply of uranium to countries far less stringent about the observance of safeguards.

Support for the NPT was only part of the peace and disarmament strategy designed and laid out during my time in office. Bilaterally, Australia coaxed, cajoled and pestered the superpowers to reduce nuclear weapon stockpiles and to press ahead with Strategic Arms Reduction talks (START) and Intermediate Range Nuclear Forces talks (INF).

In the non-nuclear field Australia played a leading role in seeking to outlaw the use of chemical weapons. The Cabinet resolved on 22nd November 1983, together with other arms control and disarmament measures, to support an international ban on them. Horrifying images of diggers and other soldiers gassed on the battlefields of France had seared the Australian psyche when chemical weapons were first used in

World War I. Australia had a stake, this time a poignant historical stake, in speaking out loudly on this aspect of disarmament.

In 1988 I launched the Chemical Weapons Regional Initiative. In 1989 Australia hosted the Government–industry conference against chemical weapons. Earlier, in 1985, we convened the 'Australia Group', an association of like-minded Western governments seeking to synchronise and strengthen the steps they had taken individually to improve export controls on substances used to make chemical weapons.

In this and in other disarmament issues, Australia was playing a role far greater than that indicated by its size in the community of nations. I look back with pride on a comment made early in 1987 in Geneva by the Secretary-General of the Conference on Disarmament, Miljan Komatina. 'Prime Minister,' he said, 'if other countries had done as much as Australia is doing in this area, the world would be closer to comprehensive and effective disarmament than it is.' He stressed the political commitment we had demonstrated and praised the dedication and professionalism of our diplomatic representatives.

Quite a few of our foreign policy stands, particularly on disarmament and chemical weapons, were not favoured by the Americans. We were the soundest of allies but we were not unquestioning subordinates. If we disagreed with the United States, whether on bilateral or multilateral issues, we would say so and argue our case both publicly and privately. For example, the US objected initially to the establishment of a South Pacific Nuclear Free Zone (SPNFZ), an initiative I began when I was host Prime Minister to a meeting of the South Pacific Forum in Canberra in August 1983.[33] The concept was unanimously supported by all Forum members. Two years later, at the Forum meeting in the Cook Islands in August 1985, all of them signed the Treaty of Raratonga prohibiting the testing, production, acquisition, possession or stationing of nuclear weapons in the Pacific.

I discussed the concept of the SPNFZ with President Reagan on my visit to Washington in June 1983. In July he wrote to me in terms characteristic of the new relationship saying that our close association was based on honesty with each other where we differed. He accepted the integrity of our position on the issue, which he agreed should be discussed at the forthcoming ANZUS meeting. He emphasised, however, that wider global considerations made it impossible for the United States to support or endorse the proposal.

That remains substantially the US position, although years of inter-cession and dialogue on my part, particularly with George Shultz, gradually made the US less uncomfortable with the idea. As I explained to Shultz, the SPNFZ was very like the Treaty of Tlatelolco which the US themselves had signed and which provided for a nuclear weapons-free zone in Latin America.

Like Tlatelolco, US transit and overflight of the high seas remained uninhibited in the SPNFZ. The right of US naval forces to visit our ports, possibly with nuclear-powered ships, remained. And under the treaty South Pacific Forum countries retained their unqualified sover-eign rights to decide for themselves their security arrangements and what access they gave to their ports and airfields for vessels and aircraft of other countries. The SPNFZ was not a diplomatic booby-trap which would lead to a domino-like toppling of the US navy's access rights to strategically vital ports, particularly in Japan. As I reiterated these points US resistance became increasingly passive. In the best of all possible worlds the US no doubt wished they had never heard of the SPNFZ. But they did not seek to stand in our way and there was no attempt to persuade us not to go ahead with our efforts to shape the treaty. Nor did they actively seek to dissuade Forum member countries from becoming involved.

Sometimes my intercessions with the US Secretary of State were more aggressive. I attacked the conduct of US foreign policy in the

South Pacific which, in my judgment, had been delegated by default to the United States Tuna Boat Association. The predatory and sometimes piratical conduct of these marauders in the hitherto relatively tranquil Pacific waters was destroying the livelihoods of local fishermen while denying adequate compensation to South Pacific countries and eroding their respect for the United States.

I explained to George Shultz the intensity of feeling which Forum leaders had displayed at Raratonga when they watched an Australian Broadcasting Corporation documentary on the activities of the American tuna fishermen. If ever there was anything calculated to make these states more susceptible to Soviet overtures, it was this. I told George, 'I can't believe how the United States is stuffing up policy and its own interests in the Pacific by allowing this to continue.' The United States changed its policy and negotiated an acceptable Fisheries Treaty with the relevant Pacific countries. This was a measure both of the constructive rapport established with George Shultz and of the health of the alliance. It was very much an alliance of equals. Not equals in power, but equals in terms of the right to be critical, each of the other, and to be heard with respect.

Australia's initiatives on the SPNFZ and on US fishing policy in the Pacific reflected a foundational element in our foreign policy – a commitment to the Asia–Pacific region and an awareness of our place within it. In this context one of the most important initiatives of my entire prime ministership was our diplomatic effort to help bring about a lasting peace in the tragic, conflict-ridden country of Cambodia. For a generation Cambodia had suffered under civil war and the terrifying 'killing fields' of the Khmer Rouge and Pol Pot. In 1979 invasion by neighbouring Vietnam was followed by another civil war, when an unlikely coalition of otherwise opposed groups united against Vietnam's puppet government.

In my view Australia had both an historical obligation and a future stake in Indo-China. Australia had been party to the emergence of the present turmoil. Although Labor was bitterly opposed to foreign intervention during the Vietnam War, Australian troops nevertheless served there. Our involvement had represented, in the starkest form, the mindless sycophancy to the Americans and misunderstanding of the region which had characterised much of the Coalition's policy towards Asia. But we had been involved and I didn't want to see the 504 Australian lives that had been lost in the war become some *caput mortuum* of a tragic and futile exercise. As to our future stake, the Vietnamese invasion of Cambodia and the crisis it generated represented the greatest threat to the stability of the region. The Cambodian people were bleeding, and Indo-China continued to be the focus of intense superpower rivalry. Superimposed upon the general pattern of the Cold War conflict was the tension between China and the Soviet Union and Vietnam's own leadership pretensions in the region which were being sustained by Soviet support and presence. On coming to government I believed we owed it to the people of the region and to Australia to play a positive role in attempting to secure a saner future. I conveyed this view directly to the Foreign Minister, Bill Hayden, in the earliest days of government. I told Bill that Australia, without exaggerating its capacity or influence, was well placed to assume this role.

While Labor's position during the war gave us standing with the Vietnamese, we had a firm alliance with the United States, which was demonstrably strengthening. Any Opposition jibes that we were acting as lackeys for the communists could be deflected for what they were – cheap shots from a discredited crew.

Bill and I agreed that under our Government our involvement with the South-East Asian region should be enhanced. Australia was particularly close to the ASEAN (Association of South East Asian Nations) countries.[34] And thanks to the intelligent approach of my two immediate predecessors, Whitlam and Fraser, we enjoyed good relations with China.

Both Hayden and I were acutely aware of the obstacles ahead. ASEAN had arisen from the instability in Indo-China and the intrusion of the Soviet Union and China into the affairs of the region; its members remained suspicious of Vietnam and the two communist giants. The antagonism between China and Vietnam stretched back a thousand years. Cambodia itself remained sunk in conflict, with an uneasy alliance of forces arranged against the puppet Hun Sen régime. Our knowledge of and closeness to the regional players had its advantages, but understanding the range of their conflicting interests meant that Australia's diplomacy would have to be deft in the extreme. This requirement threw the attitude of the United States into sharp relief, for pursuing this initiative meant talking with Vietnam. My suggestion that Australia play a role in Indo-China was welcome to Bill who, while certainly not anti-American, did not have the same degree of commitment to the alliance as I. I think he had harboured some reservations that I would be reluctant to pursue foreign policy objectives of which the United States might disapprove. My proposal convinced him that while the US relationship was important to me, I would not be blinkered by it. His faith in me was enhanced and his own confidence lifted in what he could hope to achieve as Foreign Minister.

The Americans were certainly concerned by what was being proposed, both as to its substance and because Bill Hayden would have carriage of the initiative. The scars of the Vietnam War are deeply etched in the American psyche and it was almost impossible for the United States administration to be entirely rational about their recent enemy. Bad blood was kept hot by the unresolved issue of US servicemen missing in action. And, entirely reasonably, the United States was concerned at what they regarded as Vietnam's surrogate role in facilitating the projections of Soviet power from bases in their country, particularly at Cam Ranh Bay.

In those days the Americans did not have the same degree of confidence in Bill as they had in me. He carried the legacy of having been a minister in the Whitlam Government which had often antagonised the United States administration, and his criticism of US foreign policy through the years still rankled with them. More recently there was his blunder in interpreting party policy in such a way as to bar US naval ships from visiting Australian ports.[35]

I laid the groundwork, publicly, for our approach when addressing the National Press Club in Washington in June: 'As to Vietnam itself, it seems to Australia that it is neither in Vietnam's interest, nor in our interest, nor in anybody's interest that Vietnam should be isolated from the affairs and opportunities of the region. Such regional isolation could only mean even more complete orientation of Vietnam towards the Soviet bloc.'

But the following month in Washington, when Bill Hayden started talking about Indo-China at the first ANZUS meeting, tempers flared, leading to a contretemps between him and George Shultz. George apparently criticised our proposal as naïve and uncharacteristically gave the proceedings a personal flavour by jabbing at Bill with an observation to the effect: 'If you think you're going to succeed, then that is just stupid.' Hayden responded with a tough verbal assault and a strong defence of our position. When I met George Shultz later he mentioned Bill's prickliness and the brusqueness of his approach. I asked George not to make the mistake of treating Bill as an enemy. 'He's not. He is committed to the Western alliance and is as cognisant as anyone of the Soviet threat,' I said.

The US continued for a while to complain about the way Bill expressed his views but in time a warm and mutually respectful relationship developed between Hayden and the Americans. As they became more exposed to his thinking they came to appreciate his value. Hayden, too, warmed to them and was able to work effectively with them.

Meanwhile we pressed on with our Indo-China initiative. George Shultz, I'm sure, thought not only Bill Hayden naïve on this score but also his old mate, Bob. However there was never any suspicion about our motives, misguided though he thought we were. Our approach was based on the withdrawal of Vietnamese forces from Cambodia and an act of self-determination by the Cambodian people. Beyond that, we argued, it was vital that the territorial integrity of all nations of the region be guaranteed and their boundaries be respected. The intercession by Australia aroused opposition and suspicion in many quarters – not just in the United States but also among members of ASEAN. But Bill Hayden was tireless. With my full backing, he worked his way through this minefield of fears until suspicion gradually evaporated.

The rest is almost history, as Australia moved from perceived interloper to respected prime mover of the settlement diplomacy in Indo-China. In September 1988 Gareth Evans took over the hard slog of Cambodian peace-brokering from Hayden and pursued it with a gusto, brilliance and eye for detail that led to his nomination for the Nobel Peace prize in 1992.

This nomination was an appropriate tribute to Gareth and to our Government. Australia's proposal of November 1989 – two months after the Vietnamese withdrawal – involved the United Nations taking a direct role in the civil administration of Cambodia and the presence of UN Forces preceeding the holding of free and fair elections. The Australian Government can claim more credit than any other for a long-term, consistent and constructive commitment to the processes which have produced the current opportunity for peace throughout Indo-China.

I knew that for Australia to be listened to with respect as we addressed issues of security and peace in our region, we had to have a credible and relevant defence capacity. Since President Nixon's famous off-the-cuff remarks to the press at the Officers' Club in Guam in July 1969, which came to be known as the 'Nixon Doctrine', the United States had been advocating regional defence self-reliance. In its refined form, the doctrine asserted three propositions: the United States would honour all its treaty commitments; it would provide a shield if a nuclear power threatened the freedom of an allied nation, or one whose survival was considered vital to United States security and the security of the region as a whole; and 'In cases involving other types of aggression we shall furnish military and economic assistance when requested, and as appropriate. But we shall look to the nation directly threatened to assume the primary responsibility of providing the manpower for its defence.'

This matched our own defence policy. We did not want the false security and the humiliation of forever being under the protection of a larger ally, whether the United Kingdom, as in days gone by, or the United States. Oddly, our wish to take the Americans at their word, made our allies edgy. At the first ANZUS meeting in Washington Bill Hayden was his no-nonsense self when he made it clear that Australia had for too long coasted on our relationship with the United States, always ready to invoke the alliance as if it were the beginning and end of our defence obligations. He announced that the time had come for Australia to look more to itself. 'Allies but not acolytes' was how he expressed it.

In order to look after our own defence we had to look at Australia's place in the region. Defence, as the Nixon Doctrine said, began at home. We needed to assess what exactly this meant in terms of our military capabilities. One thing I knew it did not mean was the proposal made by the Coalition for a new multi-million dollar aircraft-carrier, a status-symbol serving as flagship for yesterday's policy of forward defence. In a television interview the morning after the 1983 election I made it clear that this dream was over.

It seemed absurd that Australia should be still considering a carrier at a time when the Coalition had run down basic military supplies to an extraordinarily low ebb. It was Labor's task to rebuild the stores. In addition to not being properly provisioned, the morale of our forces had been sapped by the Fraser Government's bid to make defence salaries the first test of their wages freeze.

We wanted to give the defence forces and the nation a new sense of direction but I could not immediately tap the best talent to shape this new course – Kim Beazley. In Opposition, Gordon Scholes had been the Shadow Minister for Defence. Gordon was a former engine-driver and Victorian amateur heavy-weight boxing champion, a stolid and conscientious performer who readily conceded he did not have Kim's brilliance and understanding of defence and international issues. I could not appoint Kim immediately to a portfolio with Cabinet rank, but as well as making him Minister of Civil Aviation I made him Minister assisting Gordon in Defence. I appointed Kim as Minister for Defence after the 1984 election.

He brought to the job a first-class mind, a specialised academic background and a total fascination with all things military, from the most abstruse strategic concept to all the hardware of war. Senior officers of our own and foreign forces were in awe of his detailed grasp of their domain. They simply did not expect this of politicians. The highest compliments to his ability came in separate, unsolicited comments to me from Shultz and Weinberger that they had not dealt anywhere with a more impressive Defence Minister than Beazley.

With no obvious immediate threat we had to peer into the future and plan our defence according to a range of contingencies. Australia's sparsely populated, undeveloped, strategically vulnerable north stood out to us and to analyst, Paul Dibb, as the major consideration.[36] Dibb reported to the Government on Australia's defence capabilities in 1986. Questions that confronted us included: how, left to our own devices, would we best train, equip and man our forces to cope with a push from the north; and what intelligence, surveillance and other adjuncts would we need? Dibb addressed only the issue of capabilities. Then in 1987, in the Defence White Paper, the Government configured the self-reliance concept with our alliance arrangements.

We matched the White Paper with the most massive peace-time reorganisation of the defence forces in Australian history. We increasingly provided each arm of our services with the most sophisticated and relevant equipment, while training concentrated on handling, maintenance and deployment of that equipment. Reflecting the shift in focus, we opened up new airfields in the north[37] and developed our own over-the-horizon radar. In round terms we spend about $10 billion a year on defence. It is both a lot and a little to defend such a vast land mass. We sought, always, to get the biggest bang for the defence buck, even if this meant spending much of it on silent vigilance.

Our new, more self-reliant defence posture reflected Australia's geographical realities. Meanwhile our external economic policy needed to reflect the same realities – that to our north was the fastest growing economic region in the world. Japan was already one of the world's main economic engine rooms; the four 'tigers' – Singapore, Hong Kong, Taiwan and South Korea – were achieving phenomenal rates of growth; the ASEAN countries other than Singapore, and with the possible exception of the Philippines, were poised to emulate the tigers; and China, under Deng's reformist policies since 1978, was the giant of the future. For too long Australians had perceived Asia as a threat. The time had come to see it as an opportunity.

We had, as a country, to wrap our minds around the fact that this was where the future of Australia would lie. Drumming in the message was an essential part of my prime ministership from March 1983 until December 1991. Some were sceptical about my early insistence that we become 'enmeshed with Asia', but by the time I left office it had become a stock phrase. My successor, who in his early years as Treasurer had no real interest in Asia and was reluctant to visit the region, embraced the term. No doubt all his successors will too.

Enmeshment with Asia was not just words. It was a whole new mind set, a different way of thinking about the region and about ourselves. Enmeshment meant change, radical change. It was a case of change or be left behind, with our living standards declining, our economy and way of life stagnant, our citizens envious and, in the long term, left to become the poor white trash of Asia.

That was where we were heading. By the 1980s Australia's agricultural and resources economy had run smack into the wall of declining commodity prices brought about by the subsidising activities of the European Community and fierce international competition from the United States and other producers. The only course was to restructure, diversify and internationalise our economy. The focus had to be on contributing to, and benefiting from, the phenomenal economic growth of our region. We had to develop an export culture, with Asia firmly in our sights. We had to improve the skills and flexibility of our workforce.

Throughout that first year in government education was a constant theme. We needed increased retention rates in schools and quality and performance. In a speech to the National Technology Conference in Canberra on 26th September 1983 I emphasised the theme of training and retraining our workforce and the need for improvements in the education system, especially in basic numeracy and literary skills, including computer literacy.

Our first Budget increased spending on trade skills, youth and special training by 22 per cent. This was the beginning of a series of education reforms. By the time I left office there were, in absolute and relative terms, more Australians at schools, in TAFE and training courses and in universities than ever before. From 1982 to 1990, Year 12 retention rates rose from 36 per cent to 64 per cent. Now, three out of every four children starting school go on to complete Year 12.

Becoming enmeshed with Asia implied other changes. Australia could not identify its economic destiny with Asia and at the same time be in any way racist in its immigration or trade policies. The White Australia policy had been abandoned in the 1960s thanks to the good sense of both the Coalition and Labor. But in 1984 the subject of Asian immigration spilled into the Federal Parliament in a bitter debate. The Opposition Leader, Andrew Peacock, glimpsed a cheap opportunity and took it: 'We want to see that the European nature of this nation continues in the sense that there is balance in the migration intake,' he told the Parliament on 8th May 1984. These were euphemisms for discrimination. I responded by driving home both the moral and economic imperatives that should determine our thinking.[38]

On this subject and so many others – education, defence, industry, agriculture, sport, and tourism – I spoke not only the language of change but of interconnection between foreign policy and domestic policy. In particular, I hammered the importance of working for a free global trading environment. The internationalist influence in my office – Graham Evans, John Bowan and particularly Ross Garnaut – was a constant source of support in shaping this agenda. In October 1989, Ross, having by then served as our Ambassador to China, handed me the now famous Garnaut Report, *Australia and the North East Asian Ascendancy*. The report embodied his consistent philosophy and impact on the Government since his earliest days with us:

As a nation of substantial but limited weight, we have relevance to international discussions affecting our future, but not the capacity to secure objectives through the exercise of national power. As a 'middle power' we must rely on persuading other countries, and influential groups within these countries, that it is in their own interest to move in directions that are consistent with our own interests.[39]

From 1983 onwards, with Garnaut's guidance, we pursued these objectives. The world economy was becoming increasingly integrated. The free flow of international trade was critical to Australia's future as a trading nation. Right from the outset we began coalition-building among similarly placed countries with the object of forcing a greater liberalisation of international trade.

The pre-conditions for co-operative effort were readily apparent. At the time almost 40 per cent of the Western Pacific region's trade was intra-regional. Indeed, intra-regional trade was growing faster than world trade as a whole. Investment, commercial and political ties in the region were strengthening and countries of the region would continue to feed on each other's growth. Why not, then, club together to advance generally agreed objectives? I made my first formal international move in this direction on a visit to Thailand in November 1983 where I spoke to the Australia–Thai Chamber of Commerce.

The proposed new round of international trade negotiations due to begin in 1987 was concentrating my mind. The mooted focus of the new General Agreement on Tarriffs and Trade (GATT) round was on reducing non-tariff barriers to trade in industry and, for the first time, in agriculture. These were problem areas for Australia and many other countries in the Western Pacific region. GATT was dominated by the established industrialised countries. The interests of food exporters like Australia and Thailand, and of the newly industrialised countries generally, were being denied, I told the Chamber. Australia, the ASEAN countries, New Zealand and the market economies of North-East Asia needed to apply their full and united weight to making sure that the new GATT negotiations were about genuine trade liberalisation. There was a vacuum, I suggested, and we in this region had to step into it and, together, advance our legitimate interests.

Useful meetings with countries in the region followed which were the forerunners to our initiative in convening the Cairns Group of free-traders in agriculture in 1986, and later still, in 1989, the Asia–Pacific Economic Co-operation (APEC) group. It was all part of the same conceptual thrust – that force of argument and coalition-building among countries of the region could, over time, help to bring about a freer multilateral trading environment.

Free trade was more than good economics. It was a pre-condition to ensuring a more peaceful world. A world sunk in protectionism and economic autarky is a world much closer to war. So within the region and more widely, the major role we played in shaping the issues and processes likely to lead to a freer trading environment was integral to our wider foreign policy objectives.

We wanted to contribute to the emergence of that more peaceful world as we dedicated ourselves to reforming Australia into a modern, efficient member of the international community of nations.

SIXTEEN

It was untenable to promote the cause of free trade abroad and yet be deaf to it at home. From the outset my Government committed itself to lowering tariffs and other barriers to free trade. It was equally ridiculous to talk of modernisation, globalisation and openness when Australia lay closed at its borders, the arteries of its financial life suffering from a sclerosis of regulation and bureaucratic red tape. The world was kicking at Australia's door; to stand there with our hands pressed against it was folly.

The ideology of financial deregulation had been partly spelled out in a major inquiry into Australia's financial sector headed by the late Sir Keith Campbell, Chief Executive of the Hooker Corporation. His 1981 report advocated a swag of deregulatory measures. He recommended the floating of the Australian dollar so that market forces would determine its value. In addition he called for the removal of foreign exchange controls so that capital could flow freely into and out of the country. Campbell had created an identity crisis for the Coalition. Would the self-proclaimed free-market Government accept his advice? Of course it did not. Some minor piecemeal reforms followed but, in essence, the report was spurned. Even today the former Prime Minister, Malcolm Fraser, still opposes the floating of the Australian dollar.

In this area Fraser is out of touch with reality. But in 1981, and while in Opposition, so too was the Australian Labor Party, at least when it came to the world of financial deregulation. Our traditions and party certitudes made it inevitable that we would baulk at embracing the free market too readily. After all, it was only comparatively recently that the party had unshackled itself from its commitment to socialise the commanding heights of the economy. Campbell therefore also challenged Labor's identity.

Initially the party opposed him. I had a different view and so did some of my senior colleagues, notably John Dawkins and Peter Walsh – all three of us West Australians. Paul Keating, leavened by his contact with the mining industry, also had a market-oriented outlook. At that stage Paul was not an ardent deregulator but he had an open mind. I knew, too, that he shared my desire for a modern, relevant party committed to economic growth rather than merely more equitable shares of a diminished cake.

In the week immediately following the summit, on 20th April 1983, I wrote to him about commissioning a group to report on the recommendations of Campbell's committee of inquiry. What we needed was a short, sharp inquiry as a top-up to Campbell's report, now more than two years old. More importantly, we needed to shake the Campbell report free of its Fraser Government origins. Our own inquiry into Campbell's recommendations would give us a chance to dress Campbell in Labor cloth. If we were to educate the party about the necessities of financial deregulation we needed to embrace it as our own, but Campbell had first to be presented in our own terms of reference.

The group we appointed to review the Australian financial system, under the chairmanship of the Mutual Life and Citizens Assurance Company's Vic Martin, was directed to have regard to '[t]he government's social and economic objectives, particularly the need for an adequate supply of finance at a reasonable cost for the housing, rural and small business sectors, and their implications for the financial system'.

When the Martin Committee reported, its broad endorsement of Campbell came as no surprise. When you gathered intelligent people together (in this case, Martin himself, Treasury's Richard Beetham, Reserve Banker Des Cleary, and Economics professor Keith Hancock) and pointed them to Campbell, a report that endorsed deregulation was almost certain. To expect otherwise would have been to turn one's back on market realities – that is, on the globalisation of the world economy, with rapid-fire electronic transfers of hundreds of billions of dollars occurring daily across the foreign exchange markets.

Vic Martin's report was an important step in getting the Labor Party to jettison irrelevant old platitudes. This was particularly so when it came to changing party policy to allow the entry of foreign banks into Australia. When it came to other deregulatory moves which were to revolutionise Australia, events moved too swiftly for philosophical dalliance. No sooner had we devalued in March than the dollar was again under upward pressure. In the week following the devaluation the dollar climbed by 3 per cent. Throughout the coming months it clawed back much of what we had dramatically slashed away in our first big decision of government. Before the devaluation capital had fled the country. Afterwards it surged towards us.

In August the surge gathered momentum as US interest rates fell and the American dollar weakened. This continued through September and intensified in October. International investors were eyeing Australia lustfully. They looked to take profits from an appreciating Australian dollar and to avoid losses from a declining US dollar.

All this was playing havoc with our method of fixing the value of the Australian currency. Since late 1976 three senior Government officials (the Governor of the Reserve Bank, the head of Treasury, and the Deputy Secretary of the Department of Prime Minister and Cabinet) daily set the value of our dollar against the value of a trade-weighted basket of currencies. As the year wore on the craziness of this system became more and more apparent. By September the value of the dollar was moving up and down, but mainly up, in a losing game of cat and mouse aimed at stopping the flow of money into Australia. Speculators sought to predict what the officials would do when they linked up each morning to set the dollar's rate – whether they would raise it, lower it or leave it alone. The officials played their own game of elaborate trickery by moving the currency in a direction counter to what they guessed the speculators guessed they would do. It was all futile – the money kept rushing in.

With it came more and more destabilisation. From the outset the Government had determined to run a firm monetary policy. During the summit we had announced the largest Commonwealth bond tender yet. Others followed, all aimed at dampening down excess liquidity linked to the Budget deficit. But the inflowing surge of capital was playing hell with our monetary policy. Our regulated exchange rate system meant that the Reserve Bank was the necessary purchaser of foreign exchange offered for sale in Australia. The Reserve Bank had to match every dollar which flowed in by creating domestic currency. The monetarisation of capital inflow was adding greatly to Australia's money supply. This was no good for inflation, the competitiveness of Australian industry or short-term interest rates, which were dancing around unpredictably.

Put simply, the regulated exchange rate system wasn't working. The answer? Deregulate. Let the dollar float and rid the system of exchange controls.

The theoretical arguments for these radical steps were fashioned early on. In this, as with so much else throughout that first year in government, the engine room driving economic change in Australia was my personal office. Ross Garnaut was continuously bending my ear about the instability engendered by the crawling peg mechanism for fixing our dollar's value. My Principal Private Secretary, Graham Evans, backed him. Eddie Visbord, the most senior economist in my department, had long advocated a float. With more fresh air than ever granted to him under Fraser, Eddie filled his lungs and joined forces with Ross and Graham to press for a more open, competitive Australia, subject not to the artificial disciplines of Treasury, the Reserve Bank and the committee of three, but to the disciplines of the free market.

They had little trouble convincing me of the grounds for both the float and the lifting of exchange controls. I had been a member of the Reserve Bank Board for many years and had heard the arguments on numerous occasions. But floating the dollar and deregulating exchange controls was not one of your everyday moves. It was not a question of coming to government and within a week or a month saying, 'Bang! That's it!' As a government we were keen to avoid frightening the horses, so we waited until theory and circumstances converged.

From about May onwards we were watching and waiting. By about October it was time to act. The Reserve Bank (that is, the taxpayer) was losing money hand over fist – hundreds of millions of dollars in fact – as speculators took advantage of the one-way bet offered to them. What we faced was a mini-crisis. In late October I called a meeting in my office in the old Parliament House. At that time Paul Keating's parliamentary offices were immediately below. Relations between our two offices were extraordinarily convivial, and my office was always ready to help the new Treasurer, to talk, to thrash things out, to solve problems and to guide, if necessary.

Paul was frequently bounding into my suite, staff in tow, to discuss whatever was on his mind or on the mind of his staffers. Although I made it my business to be accessible to all my ministers, I indulged him like no other. For a start, as a novice Treasurer he faced an enormous task. As Leader of the Government it was my duty to help out as much as I could. I am fourteen years Paul's senior and there may also have been an avuncular aspect to the relationship. Paul's very boyish enthusiasm was such that I was often caught in alternate moods of not knowing whether to pat him on the head or wave a disapproving finger at him. I think we both got a bit of fun out of this style of relationship in the early days.

However our meeting on 27th October added new elements to those more informal occasions. Usually Paul led the charge of staff up the stairs to my office. On this occasion, with Treasury's senior officers present and the Secretary, John Stone, at their head, one got the impression that he was more in their tow than they in his, and this complicated matters. In my view, and that of my office, the time for grabbing the currency by the scruff of the neck, floating it and freeing it, was imminent. But the upper echelons of Treasury were implacably opposed to this course. Paul was understandably nervous. His instincts were, I think, for what he would call 'painting the big picture' and doing the bold thing, but his trepidation and lack of expertise left him still in thrall to his department and confined, for the time being at least, to John Stone's much smaller canvas.

This was an interesting feature of Paul's early days as Treasurer. More than most ministers at this stage, he was overwhelmingly reliant on experts – his own staff and Treasury officials – a reliance largely dictated by the breadth and complexity of the Treasurer's job. He used the experts to bring himself up to speed with the portfolio and then to maintain the pace. He was quick to establish rapport with his department and he was a great user of ideas. That is not to say that he did not have ideas of his own – he did. But the forceful expression of his own ideas came later. Just now, he was learning to swim.

But floating the dollar was a little too ambitious at this stage. One got the impression that Paul Keating wished to take hold of the rope we were holding out, but that John Stone had grabbed his legs and was holding on for grim death. And Paul would not kick free.

At that October meeting Stone's vociferous opposition and Paul's obvious reluctance were at odds with the desire of my office to float the dollar immediately so the decision was delayed. A compromise was fashioned but one which, inevitably, prefigured the final outcome. We decided to float the forward rate of the dollar. Surprisingly, Stone seized on that; at least it avoided a full float. But pulling the Reserve Bank away from underwriting the forward foreign exchange markets meant that the dollar must soon float free. Perhaps Stone was grasping at straws; maybe he felt that his persuasive powers would so spellbind the Government that the evil day would be forever postponed.

I knew there was no hope of that. This was a curtain-raiser and one which served our purpose. By only floating the forward rate we were preparing the market ahead of time for a full float. Absorbing some of the shock by making a technical adjustment was a good outcome to the meeting. The following day in a speech to the Australian Merchant Bankers' Association I announced our decision to float the forward rate, noting: 'the banks will be permitted greater freedom to hold balances abroad and to borrow for the purpose of matching forward transactions.'

As to the dollar's spot rate, I announced that the Reserve Bank would in future set its exchange rate for the US dollar at the end of the day. This was designed to discourage speculative capital flows during the course of the day. It was absurdly artificial to fix an early morning rate and hold it constant during the day when exchange rates for major currencies were being traded in the Asian markets. Indeed the very process of setting a rate and providing a target for the market was driving the Australian dollar up. 'These changes, though largely technical, should assist in moderating the volatility of day-to-day flows of funds across the foreign exchanges,' I told the bankers. Even in those early days, before the float although presaging it, I was intent on pointing out that however the rate of the Australian dollar was fixed we got, in effect, the dollar that we deserved. In the end the value of the Australian dollar and the flows of funds across the exchanges would not be determined by a particular system. I said, 'the final determining factor will be the relative performance of the Australian economy.'

This meant, as far as the Government was concerned, running a tight fiscal, monetary and wages policy and pursuing measures aimed at long-term growth in productivity. Bluntly, you get what you pay for.

A fortnight or so of relative quiet followed the changes of 28th October, but by mid-November the speculators were stirring again and by December rumours of a jump in the dollar's value were sweeping the markets. Money was queuing at Australia's door. In the first week in December the Reserve Bank spent $1.4 billion on foreign exchange purchases.

Then on 8th December, the last day of a hectic parliamentary year, a time traditionally reserved for partying and letting down the hair, the Reserve Bank phoned with news that something like $800 billion was perched on our doorstep ready to hit Australia the following morning. The party was over – at least for Paul and me, our staff and departments and the Reserve Bank.

Paul did a lot of bounding up and down stairs that afternoon, evening and into the night. We were acutely aware even then that each step we took, each time we talked, each telephone call we made and received was an important part of history – our own, the Government's, and the nation's. Each time he mounted the stairs he did so with the worry of Stone's opposition to a float etched on his brow. Clearly, he had to be coaxed and talked along. In the meantime Stone was waging a frantic rearguard action. At times he bypassed Keating entirely, ringing my office directly to lobby and plead with my staff not to respond to the present crisis by going ahead with a float. His grab bag of arguments against the float would be put on display again the following day.

Meetings continued in my office late into Thursday night. There was a large cast of characters: Ross Garnaut, Graham Evans and Peter Barron from my office, Eddie Visbord from the Department of Prime Minister and Cabinet and, of course, Paul Keating and his staffers. Discussion centred on the need to manage the immediate crisis and the need to 'Float, now!' But underlying the talks was the Treasurer's reluctance. He accepted that the float had to come sometime but he was cautious about steamrolling his head of department.

Paul's need to manage the relationship with John Stone was not something to be dismissed lightly. John was an experienced Treasury operative with an international reputation and he was better on board the ship than over the side thrashing about discontentedly. Both Paul and the Government could do without the drag. But one couldn't procrastinate forever and it had got to the point where Stone's objections were becoming unacceptable. Even so, when Paul left my office at around midnight, nothing had been decided. My staffers and I continued to confer. At about 1.00 a.m. I sent a staffer down to Keating's office. The message was: 'We've just got to do it.'

What we had to do was to take the immediate heat from the crisis and close the market for the following day, Friday, 9th December. Inherent in this decision was the near certainty that we would both float the dollar and release controls on capital flows in and out of the country. It seemed inconceivable that we would take the radical step of closing the markets on Friday only to open them on the Monday with nothing changed. That would be a recipe for chaos.

Nevertheless, if in the interval brought by Friday's closure of the markets opponents of deregulation could conclusively demonstrate that we were set on a ruinous course, then there was time enough to convince us. But their arguments would have to be good. The only alternative to floating seemed to be further tampering with the exchange rate mechanism and the institution of further, draconian, controls to forestall the deluge of money heading our way.

In an increasingly shrinking world where Australia was arguing for open markets and freedom of trade, this seemed a bizarre course. But maybe Stone and his two Deputy Secretaries, Dick Rye and Des Moore, could persuade us that bizarre was indeed best or maybe they had other measures up their sleeves.

In the early hours of the morning I instructed Paul Keating to ring the Governor of the Reserve Bank, Bob Johnston, in Sydney and to summon him and his senior officers to Canberra on the first available flight on Friday. Soon after 10.00 a.m. Paul and I, together with our staff and senior officers of the Reserve Bank of Australia and the Department of Treasury, met in the Cabinet room. It was an encounter with history. I remember it distinctly, as, I am sure, do many of those who were present. Several took extensive notes.

It was a fascinating meeting. I sat where I always sat, at the head of the table. Paul Keating was sitting over on the left where he normally sat as Treasurer. Stone sat along from me on my left, and the other Treasury officials, Rye and Moore, were next to Keating. Down from them sat the Reserve Bankers: the Governor and Deputy Governor, Bob Johnston and Don Sanders, and the Chief Manager of Financial Markets, John Phillips.

The bankers led the charge. They were heartily sick of riding the tiger of an exchange rate pegged daily. At the end of each day they were left with the price tag on inward flows, holding their breath about tomorrow and the next day and every day thereafter. The time had come to let the dollar roam free and to let money move in and out of Australia unshackled by regulations, they said. The Bank had an entire department, 181 staff, furiously pushing paper, making decisions about the country's financial life. The bureaucratic procedures were a tangle of red tape. Australians could buy overseas companies but not overseas shares. They needed permission to deposit their money in an overseas bank. Australian investment companies weren't free simply to deposit their funds abroad. Local borrowings from overseas banks or other institutions were vetted and scrutinised, while overseas contracts could not be signed without Reserve Bank approval. One can imagine the uncertainty this added to complex deal-making where parties could negotiate for months, arrive at an agreement, and then come to a full stop because they needed further approval from a central bank. As to the exchange régime, the Reserve Bankers were at the end of their patience.

Floating the dollar and deregulating the exchange controls were not something the Reserve Bank had dreamed up overnight in reaction to the latest crisis. They had been working on a change of policy for months and came to Canberra with a 'war book'. This book went beyond arguing for deregulation and into the specifics of how exactly to do it: foreign governments had to be notified, rules and regulations changed, and all according to a strict timetable.

With the markets closed, the bankers had come to Canberra in a winning position, assuming the inevitable. They wanted to get on with things. In their view if there was any more proof needed that the system had broken down, it had been provided by the last nine days. During that time the Reserve Bank had virtually washed its hands of its part in the committee setting the daily rate of the Australian dollar and watched as speculators made an ass of the system, in the process pocketing millions of taxpayer dollars. Whatever happened to our currency, if allowed to float freely it could not be any worse than what was happening at present, the Reserve Bank Governor, Bob Johnston, argued. Bob is a man with a naturally soothing presence. Here we were facing a crisis and he was calming it away with a radical solution.

While the Bank officials were strong proponents of the float and had considered the question from every angle, they did not pretend to tell us definitively what would happen to the dollar's value. But it was clear to them that the point of no return had been reached. Their best hunch was that the dollar would float down. The Bank had witnessed the force of foreign money driving the dollar up and, it reasoned, by withdrawing and leaving the market without a floor, the inflow would either dry up or buyers other than the Reserve Bank would step forward. Either way the speculators would be frightened off. And whether the dollar went up or down was but a measure of the state of the economy. The lesson was: fix the economy, not the value of the dollar.

To John Stone and his acquiescent deputy secretaries, Johnston and his fellow Reserve Bankers were talking heresy. Australia was a small country and one could not simply open it up and let the forces of international finance rip into it, he argued. The Government needed to keep all of its armoury, and pegging the dollar and controlling foreign exchange were two of our biggest weapons.

Although Stone was, in general, a forceful presence and very sure of himself, in the Cabinet room that day his voice often dropped to such a low mumble that on several occasions I had to ask him to speak up. His mumbling, however, did not disguise what I considered to be an emotive, almost desperate, edge to his argument. While the Reserve Bank couldn't be definitive about where the dollar would move in the event of a float, this was not the case with Stone. He argued that the dollar would shoot up in value and wreck Australia's competitive position.

We were facing a fundamental decision and Stone was entitled to his day in court. As was my practice in deliberations of this sort, I listened intently and asked many questions. Stone's presentation made no head-way with me. Yes, Australia was a small economy. But this led me to the opposite conclusion to his. With hundreds of billions of dollars wash-ing around the world every day it was futile to believe that our little economy could say to the rest of the world: 'Listen and learn, this is going to be our exchange rate today, like it or lump it.' Australia had neither the reserves nor the capacity in other respects, including the fixing of interest rates, to sustain a fixed rate. And in the meantime our exchange rate régime was placing intolerable strains on the conduct of macro-economic policy. As to the dollar going through the roof, as Stone predicted, the advice coming from my department and office staff, Ross Garnaut in particular, contradicted this. They agreed with the Reserve Bank's best guess that the dollar would lose value, thus enhancing Australia's competitiveness.

In any event I happened to agree with Johnston; that, up or down, the old system had passed its use-by date. And if we couldn't live with a floating rate, then we would have to change the fundamentals of the economy which underpinned it. By this stage Stone was well and truly adrift. He had the support of his two Deputy Secretaries but that was all. As for Paul, he was now, if I may put it this way, prepared to float without the Stone.

After some two hours the issues had been well and truly canvassed and I ended the discussion. I told Stone and his adversaries, 'I want you now to go away and deal with the mechanics of floating the dollar and removing exchange controls.'

The party began to move off but Stone was determined to have the last word with me. 'Prime Minister,' he said, 'you'll regret this; you'll come to see this as a terrible decision. It will rank in history with Prime Minister Whitlam's decision to slash tariffs by 25 per cent across the board.' The comparison was ludicrous. Part of his argument was that floating the dollar would cause it to escalate in value. But when

Whitlam cut tariffs the dollar fell. Perhaps he was speaking merely of the political implications of the decision. Whitlam's move had triggered a fire-storm of criticism. Was that his point?

It was a bizarre interlude but not the only light moment. Someone joked that the Treasury was all for deregulation and the free market, except in those areas where it exercised control. The irony of Stone's viewpoint at one stage became too much for me. Politically, John was way out to the Right in Genghis Khan territory. Yet here he was arguing for control and regulation like some diehard leftie. The Left hated Stone. I recall saying something like this to him: 'You know I have a great affection for the Left of my party. But it's only a few weeks to Christmas and I can't in good conscience take their favourite ogre away by telling them what you've been saying here today.'

I have deliberately cast the steps we took on that dramatic day in terms of inevitability. The float and deregulation of the exchange controls were inevitable – inevitable, that is, for a government prepared to grasp the nettle and make the decisions which circumstances and the interests of the country demanded. This had not been the way of our predecessors. The question of floating the dollar had arisen during Fraser's time on the recommendation of his own commissioned inquiry, but the Coalition chose, as they did on so many issues, to cling to the cliff face, too frightened to look above or beneath. To them, floating the dollar and deregulating were not inevitable. To John Stone in the Cabinet room that day it was not inevitable.

And to the waiting Canberra press gallery it was not inevitable. They knew that the market had been closed. They knew that the Reserve Bankers were in town and that there was a crisis meeting in the Cabinet room. It didn't take an Einstein to work out what in general was going on. Journalists started a book on the likely outcome of our meeting. Would we do nothing, change the exchange rate, introduce tougher controls, float the dollar or what? Of course they would say today that the decision to float was inevitable but the longest odds offered that day by the media were for a float. Our decision took them by surprise.

Having cut loose from Stone, Paul Keating threw himself into the announcement of the float with characteristic gusto. It had been a slow and heart-burning business but he had arrived, and so had Australia. Many years later, again with the fervour of the convert, he put it well to a close confidante:

> One of the things is that the born-to-rule brigade – the Coalition – have never lived with the discipline of a floating exchange rate. They think their mere presence will affect how the world markets treat them. It won't matter a tinker's curse. The float is the decision where Australia truly made its debut into the world and said, OK, we're now an international citizen.[40]

The dollar floated to general acclaim and with none of the dire consequences predicted by Stone. Far from going through the roof, it floated down. Although it fluctuated, only once, briefly, did it attain the heights of the pre-float days. Rather than wreck the competitiveness of Australian industry, the reverse was true. The economy became more competitive, more sophisticated, more diversified and much bigger.

Indeed the success of the float and other deregulatory measures had everyone jumping on the bandwagon, including John Stone. In May 1984, while still Treasury Secretary, he led an Australian delegation to a Paris meeting of the Economic Development Review Committee of the Organisation for Economic Co-operation and Development (OECD). Upon being cross-examined about the committee's draft report on the Australian economy he urged the committee to:

pay more attention to the decision by the Government in December 1983 to float the Australian dollar and, in some ways even more importantly, effectively to abolish Australia's long-established system of exchange controls ... I think it is not an exaggeration to describe these decisions as constituting the most important single step in economic policy to be taken by any Australian government in the post war period ... There is no doubt in my mind that, over time, they will work very much to the end of 'locking' Australia into the wider world, with all the benefits – and no doubt problems also – which that will entail ... Moreover ... the decision to float the Australian dollar will ... enhance the authorities' ability to control the money supply and hence – if the will is there to do so – inflation.[41]

He repeated his remarks in the Shann Memorial Lecture of 1984: 'I personally believe that the decisions taken by the present government on 9th December last will stand as its greatest achievement when all else has been forgotten.' Stone's lecture was called '1929 and all that ...' As he noted in that lecture, and one cannot disagree with him, '1929 was, as we all know, a memorable year. For example, it was the year in which our present Prime Minister was born ...'[42] He might have added that the day we took the decision to float the dollar was my birthday.

Of course John was talking tongue in cheek. The Government's relationship with the Secretary of the Treasury was not a marriage made in heaven nor one that could last on earth. This lecture was delivered on 27th August 1984. Less than a fortnight earlier, on 15th August shortly before 11 a.m., Stone had arranged for a bottle of 1979 Veuve Clicquot and two glasses to be delivered to Paul Keating's office in the Department of Treasury where Stone was meeting with the Treasurer. When the bubbly arrived Stone handed Paul a letter formally signalling his intention to resign.

It's easy to target Stone when it comes to the dollar float and the other measures we took on that December day. He was wrong on that occasion as he later conceded without, I must say, disclosing the depth of his opposition to the decision at the time. Nevertheless he served us conscientiously during an important period when his expertise and his international standing and experience benefited the Government. Then, when the strain of disagreement between him and the Government became too intense, he did the honourable thing and resigned with flair and grace.

Although Stone remained an important figure right up until the preparation of the 1984 Budget, the dollar float marked a watershed date in his relationship with the Government and, more particularly, in Paul Keating's relationship with him. By 9th December Paul at last had the confidence to break free. He was becoming his own man in Treasury and that was a profound relief to those of us who had seen him somewhat daunted by the enormous demands of the job. The decision to float and deregulate, and the actual and perceived success of the decision gave Paul a burst of confidence. He started to make his own way up the mountain, throwing his hook far above him and making the distance in between with alacrity. In short, he was becoming the confident Treasurer whom we came to know, but perhaps not always to love.

This development allowed me and my office to play much less of a hand-holding role and, as Prime Minister, I was able to entrust far more responsibility for the carriage of economic policy to the Treasurer, where it belonged. As was my way with all the ministries I remained across all the important policy issues but the relationship became more equal and, with growing confidence, I gave Paul a freer rein.

This was essentially my style of leadership. I was a trusting, non-interventionist leader who allowed ministers their heads, not least because they had good heads, and because experience had taught me that talented people work best when they are respected and left alone to do their jobs. I provided leadership by identifying the important issues, talking to my ministers about them, then keeping in touch with them as they developed policy. The extraordinary success of the Hawke Government, its achievements, its cohesiveness and relative lack of rancour, its longevity – the longest in Labor's history and the second longest in the nation's history – confirmed to me, constantly, that this style of leadership works.

A Labor government is a rare breed of horse. You don't ride it by cracking the whip and jabbing your spurs into its flanks. You coax it, soothe it, talk to it, ease it along and point the way ahead. This style of leadership had its precedents in the Curtin Government of 1941–45 and the Chifley Government of 1945–49. John Curtin and his successor as Prime Minister, Ben Chifley, understood the value of consensus and the need to harness the strengths of each minister and party member so that they all ran their best race but ran it as a team.

When I look across the period of my own prime ministership it is difficult to find many ministers with whom this style did not work to the maximum advantage of the Government. Critics may point to the resignation of Stewart West from Cabinet. On 3rd November 1983 Stewart, then Minister for Immigration and Ethnic Affairs and a member of the party's left wing, resigned because he could not in good conscience abide by our Cabinet decision to allow the mining of uranium at Roxby Downs in South Australia. He remained a member of the ministry and his letter of resignation made it clear he did not intend to be a spoiler: 'I understand Cabinet arrangements regarding solidarity,' he wrote to me. 'Under the terms of that Cabinet arrangement I understand that I can no longer serve in the Cabinet. I, of course, remain ready and willing and expect to continue to serve the Labor Government as a member of the ministry.'

West's resignation had nothing to do with leadership. Neither a dictatorial nor consensual approach would have stood between Stewart and his conscience. And as was my policy as chairman of the Cabinet, he was given every opportunity to argue his case round and about as often and as long as he could within the Cabinet room. He did this but he could not convince us or the Caucus of the rightness of his view. On 7th November 1983 the Caucus adopted the Cabinet's recommendation on Roxby Downs by fifty-five votes to forty-six.

If there was one case where it could be said that my kind of leadership failed it was with Paul Keating, but more of that later. For the moment, we had just floated the dollar, Paul's confidence was up and the Prime Minister–Treasurer relationship was entering its most productive period.

Throughout 1984–85 we pursued further deregulatory measures. We needed to unshackle the Australian economy, to modernise it and to internationalise it. To do this we needed to break Labor's traditional and residual opposition to free-market economics. This was no easy matter, particularly when it came to banking deregulation. Labor had an ingrained distaste for banks and in the late 1940s Ben Chifley had attempted to nationalise them. The fear and hysteria whipped up by the conservative forces on this issue played a large part in his election loss in 1949. Bitterness towards the banks lingered in our party. Chifley had been opposed to opening up Australia to foreign banks – they were double anathema.

The world of Ben Chifley was not, however, the world of the 1980s. Ahead of us lay the polemical exercise of persuading the Labor Party to abandon the tired certitudes of an earlier age and to prepare for the future. The party platform had to be changed. Paul Keating rose magnificently to the task. With my backing and his confidence rising, he threw his range of skills – vivid language, charm, derision, humour, hyperbole, hard sell – into turning the Labor Party around on the subject of foreign bank entry.

The paramount forum for this task was the National Conference of the Australian Labor Party held in Canberra in July 1984. Banking is pre-eminently a Treasury function and Paul had the responsibility for changing party policy. On and off the floor, he threw himself into the hard slog of persuading delegates that the old way was the losing way. In the new international environment Australia could not afford to show itself abroad as fearing competition from foreign banks. At home, consumers could not afford the inefficiency and expense of the arrangements which kept everything snug and secure for the big four: Westpac, the National Australia Bank, the ANZ Banking Group and the Commonwealth Bank.

Paul's great rhetorical weapon, used with devastating effect, was to grab hold of the traditional debate and turn it upside down by using what we had agreed was one of our sharpest arguments. By refusing foreign bank entry Labor was comforting the existing banks. What had these banks ever done for Labor? The existing banks were traditional enemies of the Labor Party and, if anything, were institutionally glued to the Coalition parties. Why should the Labor Party mollycoddle them?

We were in a strong position at the conference. We had been at the crease by then for some time and had been stacking up runs at a good rate; I was able to point to the scoreboard with pride. We won the day on foreign banks. Prior to my Government a change to the party platform on this question had been almost unthinkable. Neville Wran, President of the party and Labor Premier of New South Wales at the time, described the feat as 'equivalent to stealing the holy water from the church'. But we brought the party along, as we did on other controversial issues at that conference: financial deregulation generally, the mining of uranium at Roxby Downs, and the hosting of the joint US–Australia facilities.

Graham Freudenberg has often reflected that it was my Government's great good fortune that Labor was in office during a sea change in social democratic thinking taking place right across the Western world. The necessary attitudinal and philosophical changes we had to make in party thinking were made while we were an effective government. Had we not been in power there is little doubt that we would have been doomed to a continued irrelevance. The British Labour Party, for example, had to make its agonising reappraisal while in Opposition. And while the Australian Labor Party led the way in bold deregulatory reforms from 1983 onwards, it was not until the February 1993 conference of the British Labour Party, held not long after another crushing defeat, that it changed its platform to resemble something like that of a modern, relevant party.

Having wrought the changes to the platform, the Government pressed on with its agenda. In September we sought applications for bank licences, approving the prospective entry of sixteen foreign banks during 1985. Fifteen eventually set up business in Australia. In the meantime we introduced further measures to ginger up Australia's banking system. Other financial institutions besides banks were authorised to deal in foreign exchange. Maturity controls were lifted from bank deposits. Banks could pay interest on overnight deposits and on cheque accounts. A moratorium on the application of foreign investment policy to merchant banks was announced. This brought further competition into the financial system.

An unintended but perhaps inevitable consequence of our deregulatory moves was a fierce battle for market share. With breath-taking recklessness, the banks threw caution to the wind in out-bidding each other for a larger slice of the market. Entrepreneurs who thought that asset values were going to rise indefinitely found ready financial accommodation in this scramble. This was an important part of the story of the late eighties in Australia and of the recession which bit so hard at the end of the decade.[43] Financial deregulation was a necessary part of freeing up the economy and there is no question as to the correctness of the policy decision we made in 1984. Unfortunately, the fact that many financial operators were slow to adapt their prudential requirements to the new environment exaggerated the boom and exacerbated the downturn which followed.

In the election campaign we had promised to create half a million new jobs within three years. Already, there were 234 000 more jobs. Unemployment had fallen from 10.3 per cent at the time of the April summit to 8.9 per cent. Investment was up by 5 per cent. Housing activity and car sales were up. Interest rates were down.

After a nervous start Paul Keating was settling in and I allowed him more of the strike. On foreign bank entry he cracked a sizzling boundary. In 1984 he was named *EuroMoney* magazine's Finance Minister of the Year. The magazine's managing director, Sir Patrick Sergeant, praised him as 'bold, brilliant and, above all, brave'. On accepting his engraved silver plate in Washington, Paul raised his bat to the partnership: 'I have the privilege of serving with a very enlightened Prime Minister and a very enlightened Cabinet.'

IV

DIPLOMACY AND ECONOMICS:
AUSTRALIA COMES OF AGE
UNDER LABOR

SEVENTEEN

From 'Finance Minister of the Year', I quickly moved to dub Paul Keating 'the World's Best Treasurer' in what many of us, somewhat more modestly, were starting to think of as one of the world's best governments. From March 1983 through 1984 our fortunes soared, as did those of the country.

We had come into office with Australia in the gravest economic crisis since the Great Depression fifty years earlier. Improvement did not come overnight. In the first week I called for all economic statistics and indicators – 'anything you've got' – to be handed direct to me every day. I told my personal staff to alert me to the least sign of movement in the economy, however small. But I teased the bureaucrats and staff: 'I'll know earlier than any of you when we start to move out of the recession.'

They weren't deeply into deference, even at that early stage, and demanded to know how. 'I will be talking to my friend, Sir Peter Abeles,' I said. Peter was Managing Director of Australia's largest transport company, Thomas Nationwide Transport (TNT). 'If anybody will know, he will. The biggest transport mover in the country is going to be the first to know when we're coming out of recession

– because of changes in the movement of both inputs and finished products.'

I quizzed Peter regularly. 'Anything? Any sign?' I would ask him. He knew exactly what I was looking for. 'No,' he answered, time after time. And then one beautiful day he replied, 'Yes, it looks as if things are changing.' From that day in May 1983, weeks ahead of the official statistics, my confidence was on the rise. Before long the official figures rolled in confirming the end of the recession. By the time the September Quarter national accounts figures came out, growth in Australia's gross domestic product had hit 4.4 per cent, the highest rate ever recorded. When the December Quarter figures were released on 29th March 1984 that figure was revised upwards to 5 per cent. Private sector growth had made its first positive contribution in six quarters. Retail and motor vehicle sales were also on the rise. Inflation had been all but cut in half, down now to about 6 per cent. Company profits for 1983 had rocketed by 39 per cent over the year, the highest since 1973. Everything, it seemed, was rising – save for inflation and unemployment which, thankfully, were plunging.

In March and April of 1984 my own approval rating in the opinion polls was around 75 per cent. Those who ribbed Paul with 'World's Best Treasurer' were also ribbing me with the tag 'Mr Seventy-Five Per Cent'. Wearing that title, however transient I knew it must be, was not the hardest thing in the world at the time.

The Government was riding high, and we needed to be. Although we had overcome most of the obstacles left by the outgoing Government, Fraser had left one last hurdle that we would soon have to jump. It was the need for an early election. His rush to the polls the previous March had thrown out of kilter the House of Representatives elections (every three years) and the half-Senate elections (where, normally, half of the Senators at the expiry of a six-year term are elected at the same time as the House of Representatives). His double dissolution on

3rd February 1983 put half of the Senate put up for re-election before 30th June 1985.

From the outset Labor had little real choice but to bring on a House of Representatives election early; either that or send the country to the polls twice within a year (a half-Senate followed by a House of Representatives election) with all the expense, waste of energy, and uncertainty which that would have entailed. That was never a serious option. So the first Hawke Government was always likely to be a short run thing – a sprint, even. We could possibly have spun it out until June 1985, but history and tradition were on the side of a pre-Christmas poll.

Politics, of course, played its part in any decision to go to an election early. Prime Ministers call elections when they think they have the best chance of winning.[44] In this instance Labor had its eye not merely on winning the next election but on increasing its majority to such an extent that it would, in effect, win two elections at once. Our majority was now twenty-five seats in the House of Representatives. Towards the second half of 1984 we faced the prospect of pushing that majority higher.

A 'Wranslide' – the term used to describe Premier Neville Wran's smashing electoral victory in NSW in October 1978 – was in the offing. His victory had made it impossible for the Liberal Party in that State to overhaul his lead in just one election. Everything was moving in our favour – even the drought had broken for us soon after we had been elected. But we still had to concentrate on the fundamentals and we faced a tricky August Budget. The Budget had to be as attractive as we could responsibly make it; we offered tax cuts as a reward for wage restraint, while at the same time applying the fiscal stick. The Budget deficit for 1983–84 finally came in at $7961 million, down from the estimated deficit in the 1983 Budget speech of $8361 million. In the 1984–85 Budget we lopped the deficit further to $6.7 billion.

The fiscal engine was still being co-driven from my office. 'The progress of the economy and the economic policy over the past year gives us an opportunity to establish a base this year for a long period of economic growth for many terms in government,' Ross Garnaut wrote to me in a memorandum on 24th June 1984. He warned about the dangers of 'a soft-on-outlays budget', saying that if this eventuated it was likely, despite the good start, that our attempts to entrench community, union and business acceptance of greater international orientation for Australian industry would fail.

Even as we brought in the Budget at a 6.1 per cent real growth in outlays, to Ross and other advisers this was still on the high side. More discipline was needed; and so in the aftermath of the Budget I struck the Government's famous trilogy commitment. This was a promise to the Australian people that there would be no increase in taxation as a proportion of gross domestic product (GDP), no increase in public expenditure as a proportion of GDP, and no increase in the deficit as a proportion of GDP. Indeed I committed the Government to a reduction of the deficit in absolute terms.

The trilogy commitment was startling in its novelty but it did succeed in conveying in a structured, cohesive form the essence of our approach to economic management. There was a nonsensical suggestion at the time that I had somehow foisted the trilogy on the Government. The formulation certainly came from me but I discussed it with the Treasurer; and it later emerged as a statement of the Government's position which was adopted by the Cabinet, the ministry and the Caucus. In essence the trilogy merely spelled out our economic goals as a government from the time we took office. It sharpened those goals into a three-pronged commitment which we placed at our own back. From then on we could only move forward. Naturally we were taunted by the usual cynics. The Shadow Treasurer and Deputy Leader of the Opposition, John Howard, said, as did other commentators, that the trilogy would not and could not work. As usual they were proved wrong.

Everything seemed to be going smoothly but the wind was soon knocked right out of my sails. For the first time in my life I was caught adrift in a vast and lonely sea which threatened to engulf me. On 9th August 1984 Hazel took the unusual step of ringing my Principal Private Secretary, Graham Evans, from Melbourne and insisting on an appointment with me the moment she arrived in Canberra later that day. It was the immediate pre-Budget period with all that entailed in preparing for the resumption of Parliament, but Graham could tell that she would not be deterred. She came straight to my office from the airport.

On 1st August our younger daughter, Rosslyn, had given birth to her second child, Paul. The birth had been by Caesarean section and as the doctor cut into Ros's waif-like frame – a mere 38 kilograms – he saw a body ravaged by heroin addiction. Her muscle tissue was degenerating and she was literally wasting away. She was twenty-four years old and was likely to die if she continued to take heroin.

Hazel had decided it was time for radical action; I could not be shielded from knowing the full extent of our daughter's condition. I was devastated and overwhelmed by sorrow for this beautiful girl, who as a youngster had always been able to get me to spoil her, but with whom I had spent too little time when she became a teenager.

Until this moment I think I had subconsciously drawn up a mental balance-sheet of myself as a family man. I was well aware of the entries on the liability side of the ledger: the relative lack of time spent with Hazel and the children compared with the generous giving of myself to the public and pursuit of career, and my infidelities. Against that, on the assets side, I guess I had entered the material security, if not lavish lifestyle, I had always provided, the sense of excitement and broadened horizons my life had generated for them and the knowledge that, in my own unconventional way, I loved them deeply.

This comfortable construct was now in ruins. I was shattered by the bombshell of Hazel's full disclosure. Rosslyn had left home when she was fifteen; I felt numb with guilt now as I wondered whether she would have exposed herself to the dangers of the drug culture if I had been more available.

The destabilising effect upon my work was immediate. I had to go straight from my meeting with Hazel into official talks with the Malaysian Prime Minister, Dr Mahathir. I had met Mahathir earlier that year in Kuala Lumpur while bureaucrats and other observers looked on apprehensively, waiting for the sparks to fly. Instead, the electric antagonism that had flared between Mahathir and my pre decessor, Malcolm Fraser, gave way to a reasonable rapport. There was more to the rapport than diplomatic gloss. On that earlier occasion I had intervened with Mahathir on behalf of the Australian construction company, Leighton, pressing its claims for a large hospital building contract over those of a competitive French tenderer. The French were, in fact, in town that day to clinch the deal, but Leighton got the job.

Perhaps it was because Mahathir and I are both direct characters that we seemed to get on well. Now, the very rapport we had established made any pretence of normality impossible. The Prime Minister, a medical practitioner, immediately sensed that something was wrong. I was so shattered by what Hazel had told me that I found it difficult to talk or think sensibly during the meeting with my counterpart. In the end I broke down and told him what had happened. I apologised for not being able to treat him the way I would have wanted but explained that I found concentration almost impossible. Mahathir, for all his tough-guy image, which I was later to come to know well, was gently understanding; in those strange circumstances we soldiered on as best we could through the program, including a formal dinner that night.

There was a lot more soldiering on to be done. The Budget was only twelve days away. Other issues, national and international, were exploding all around me. I had just returned that day, 9th August, from three days in Port Moresby where much to everyone's relief Commonwealth Heads of Government of the South-East Asian and Pacific Region read the last rites over Malcolm Fraser's CHOGRMs (Commonwealth Heads of Government Regional Meetings). Malcolm's CHOGRMs were largely a wasteful duplication of the South Pacific Forum meetings. They diluted the value of the broader CHOGM forum and ran the risk of factionalising that body. While in PNG I met the new Prime Minister of New Zealand, David Lange. Since his election in July his Labor Government had taken aim at the ANZUS alliance by barring US naval ship visits to New Zealand ports, unless the ships were declared to be nuclear-free. I was unimpressed with the policy, and with Lange.[45]

At the same time my own Foreign Minister, Bill Hayden, was making waves for the ANZUS alliance from Geneva. When I arrived back in Australia, to Hazel and Mahathir, I had to deal with Bill's implied threats to close the joint facilities if America did not enter into serious discussion with the Soviet Union about arms control. I did not need this now, or at any time.

I understood and entirely supported Bill's commitment to spur the United States into serious discussion on the issue. But putting the joint facilities on the table as a bargaining chip was never on; not on this, or any other issue. I regarded it as intellectually unacceptable and morally indefensible. If Australia's interests and the broader strategic interests of the West were best served by hosting the joint facilities on Australian soil then those interests could not be compromised. The joint facilities could not go up for grabs with every argument or disagreement Australia had with the United States, whether it be about arms control, wheat or some other matter of importance to us. Following my intervention Bill cleared the table of the bases as quickly as he had put them on it.

In the run-up to the Budget on 21st August I also had to deal with the trauma and controversy surrounding two Labor icons. From early January 1984 Mr Justice Lionel Murphy of the High Court of Australia, a former Attorney-General in the Whitlam Government, had been at the centre of a vicious media campaign suggesting that he had links with organised crime. A Senate inquiry was established to examine the so-called '*Age* Tapes'. These were a tape, transcripts and summaries of telephone conversations illegally taped by New South Wales police and allegedly involving Murphy as a party to some conversations. The contents of the illegal phone taps had been leaked to the Melbourne *Age*.

At the same time Mick Young was also in trouble. Having returned to Cabinet early in 1984, he was now in strife for an alleged breach of Customs law. He had failed to declare gifts, including a toy Paddington Bear, on his return from a recent overseas visit. He had always maintained, and I accepted, that he did not know the gifts were in his bags. On 17th August an inquiry found him innocent of any impropriety.

In the midst of the Mick Young trauma, on 15th August, a mere six days before the Budget, Treasury Secretary John Stone made his contribution to the feeling of vulnerability in the air with his Veuve Cliquot news to Paul Keating of his resignation. We were not unhappy with the news itself but the timing, from our point of view, left a little to be desired.

Then on 21st August came the Budget. No sooner was that over than on 25th August I headed for a three-day meeting of the South Pacific Forum at Tuvalu, followed by a two-day visit to Fiji. As was usual Australia played the lead role and I was appointed media spokesperson for the group. The Tuvalu agenda was loaded with important global and regional political issues: nuclear disarmament, nuclear testing and the dumping of nuclear waste. Australia's initiative for a South Pacific nuclear-free zone was dealt with at length. We discussed the decolonisation of New Caledonia and issues of functional co-operation among the thirteen member countries in trade, shipping and fisheries.

This hectic program had done nothing to dull the pain of my feelings about Rosslyn. When I returned from Fiji this private agony and the pressure of unfolding political events made an almost unbearable burden. I arrived home to further controversy centering on Lionel Murphy. A Senate-appointed committee of inquiry had reported its findings on 26th August. The committee of six Senators was to inquire into the authenticity of the tapes and transcripts generated by the New South Wales police phone taps. If they found them to be authentic, they had then to consider whether the material revealed misbehaviour on Murphy's part such that he could be removed under the terms of the Australian Constitution.

The committee of six Senators could make no finding on the authenticity of the tapes and transcripts. In any event this was of little consequence because the committee found that, even if the material was complete and unaltered, it did not constitute any misbehaviour by Murphy. However the committee's report was overwhelmed by a fresh sensation. During the course of the Senators' inquiry, the New South Wales Chief Magistrate, Clarrie Briese, stepped forward and recalled incidents which, he said, led him to believe that Justice Murphy had improperly attempted to influence him about the conduct of committal proceedings against one of Murphy's friends.

This triggered a tragedy which engulfed many good people. It ended after a second judicial trial (the verdict of the first trial having been set aside by the High Court) in which Murphy was found not guilty of having attempted to pervert the course of justice. Fresh allegations then surfaced but by this time Murphy was diagnosed as having incurable cancer. He returned to the High Court Bench for one brief sitting on 21st October 1986. Just one hour after his last two judgments were handed down, he died.

Not long before his death we had Lionel and his wife Ingrid – who was a tower of strength to him throughout his ordeal – to dinner at the Lodge. Afterwards, while Ingrid and Hazel talked in the sitting room, Lionel and I reminisced alone in my study. I could hardly believe and will never forget his gentleness towards his accusers and tormentors, and those of his High Court and other judicial brethren from whom he had hoped for greater understanding. His great monuments of legal reform, more efficient use of Senate resources and enlightened constitutional interpretation will endure. But for me what will always remain is the memory of the sad, warm eyes of a charitable man at peace with himself.

Lionel Murphy's trials and tribulations had become part of a lurid atmosphere where organised crime was projected as an issue in a media and political campaign that assumed McCarthyist proportions. A desperate Opposition, languishing in the opinion polls, grabbed at the issue. For Opposition Leader, Andrew Peacock, the opportunity arrived with the Government's decision to wind up the Costigan Royal Commission into the activities of the Federated Ship Painters' and Dockers' Union, leaving any of its unfinished work to the newly created National Crime Authority (NCA). The Opposition contended that the Government had sought to thwart Mr Frank Costigan QC's activities and to frustrate the fight against organised crime.

In an extraordinary outburst as I was leaving the Chamber on 13th September 1984, Andrew went for broke. He flung at my departing back some words which I did not hear at the time. He said, 'This little crook ... a perverter of the law ... one who associates with criminals and takes his orders from those who direct those criminals.' I don't know what got into him. Such behaviour was not, in my experience, a true reflection of Andrew's nature. Later he wholeheartedly withdrew the allegations and apologised. But, for now, the accusation had been made and was on the Hansard record.

The outburst had appalled both sides of the House. A few days earlier I had tabled in the Parliament the full correspondence between the Government and Costigan about the establishment of the NCA and the transition to it of his commission's activities. The Government had always regarded the Royal Commission model as an unsuitable long-term body for fighting organised crime. Nonetheless, at each step, the Government remained solicitous of Costigan's views, extending the life of his commission and increasing its funding. This was reflected in correspondence between us in October and November 1983. In particular, Costigan wrote to me again on 5th March 1984: 'I am anxious both that the new Crime Authority commence operation as soon as possible and that I hand over to it in an efficient manner the investigations I am now conducting ... Your government's determination to establish the body is welcome to me and in the public interest.'

However it was obvious from the correspondence I tabled that the Government and Costigan had differing views about the timetable which should apply to the winding up of the Royal Commission. But, neither the Government nor Mr Costigan ever impugned the other's motives. If there was a dispute it remained a rather confined argument about means, not ends.

Knowing all this, the Leader of the Opposition had launched out into no-man's-land. We were unforgiving. In a no-confidence motion on 2nd October 1984 we attacked Peacock on the floor of the Parliament. His claims were wilful and reckless and, to his certain knowledge, without foundation. I pointed out that we had doubled the

funding of the Costigan Royal Commission in our first year of government from $2.9 million to $5.9 million. In the last two financial years
we had boosted spending on the Australian Federal Police by 20 per
cent and increased AFP staff by 13.7 per cent. We had established the
office of Director of Public Prosecutions, insulating the prosecutorial
function from political interference. We had established the National
Crime Authority. I questioned Peacock's sincerity on this issue by
pointing out that he had not even bothered to speak in the House on
the Bill establishing the NCA.

Andrew Peacock may have wished that he had not spoken in this
day's debate either. Having come to the end of a truly awful speech, he
blamed the clock for not being able to deliver some of his most damaging material. With more time he could have said much more, he
claimed. We immediately moved for an extension of time. He floun-
dered hopelessly, to his own acute embarrassment and that of those
sitting grim-faced behind him.

However Peacock's appalling accusations cut deeper than he knew.
When he first made his frustrated outburst he had no way of knowing
about Rosslyn and the trauma in our family life. By linking me with
organised crime – for which, read drug-trafficking – Andrew was
rubbing salt into the deepest wound of my life. Of course he did not
know this. But the story would soon break publicly.

A public demonstration of my anguish about Ros' condition came at
a press conference in Canberra on 20th September, when I was asked a
question not about Ros but about my elder daughter, Susan. Two years
earlier to the day, Susan's conviction for the use and cultivation of
marijuana had been set aside by a New South Wales District Court
judge. In August a scrappy report about the case had appeared in the
now defunct *National Times*, a paper which, more than any other, was
wallowing in the unfounded innuendoes of that period. The question
about Susan and drugs touched my private pain: 'You don't cease to be

a husband, you don't cease to be a father and my children and my wife have a right to be protected in this matter. But I trust it will not be necessary,' I said. Tears were streaming down my face.

Naturally the media was full of it – 'the Prime Minister breaks down' – but the reason for the tears was still unclear. The public were left in no doubt about where I stood on the drug trade. At the press conference I described it as 'an abomination and a threat to the stability of our society'. But there was genuine perplexity about the cause of my emotions on that day. With Ros's agreement we decided to set the record straight and make a public statement about the family predicament. As Hazel described it in her book, 'We wanted to put a stop to the innuendo that was not only unfair, but which also interfered with appropriate treatment for Ros and her own family.'[46]

We decided that Hazel would appear as spokesperson for the family on Terry Willisee's national television program on 24th September. With a calm and wholly admirable dignity she revealed what had caused me to break down and cry in front of a national audience.

By this time Hazel had already established a position as a widely respected person in her own right. She had an easy, natural charm which endeared her to all sections of society. Her genuine interest in the underprivileged was often reflected in a busy schedule which took her around the country. Arising from our son Stephen's long continuing commitment to work with Aboriginal people, she had developed her own interest in coming to know their special problems and needs; she devoted much of her time to their cause. Hazel continued to be an enormous support for the whole of my time in office. She took the opportunity offered by the Willesee interview to ask the media to respect the privacy of Ros and her husband Matt (also an addict), while they set about trying to rebuild their lives.

The interview had a positive side for Hazel. She sought to open up public discussion about drug abuse, a subject that was all too often taboo.

The occasion also offered her an opportunity to broach another taboo subject – men crying in public. 'I would rather a man who can show what is a natural expression of grief, rather than suppress tears in order to be manly,' she wrote later. 'Bob has, over the years, demonstrated an outstanding capacity to return to strength after grief or defeat, and perhaps it is because he *can* cry.'[47]

But for the moment that resilience was far away. I remained inconsolable and deeply depressed. I seriously contemplated resignation. I recall one night, in particular, stewing on my dilemma. 'My God!' I thought. 'What's the point of it all? Give it up and concentrate on the family.'

Not even Hazel, I think, knew the full extent of my despair and just how close I came to relinquishing the prime ministership in 1984. I had dreamed for a long time of becoming Prime Minister and I had prepared myself assiduously for the task, but with my daughter's life and my family's happiness now called into the balance, the price seemed too high.

Eventually I was able to put things back into perspective and see the present tragedy more philosophically. I could not repair the damage, for which I felt such guilt, by leaving my post. If I resigned I would be throwing over my wider responsibilities to the Australian community and to the great political party that I led. As to the family, the healing had already begun and, strangely enough, was progressing precisely because I was Prime Minister. I had given up drinking to become Prime Minister. The pain caused in the past by my drinking could never be exactly compensated, but we were now spending more time together than ever before.

At the time, however, I was taking it hard. Friends and colleagues were magnificent in the way they rallied around. The flood of support coming from all parts of Australia and overseas was truly extraordinary. It came from many quarters and on all levels – spiritual, practical, psychological, and from across the political spectrum.

At that stage the Left's Senator Nick Bolkus probably thought of me more as a factional enemy than as his Prime Minister. We would later become close, but back then his antagonism was set aside when he heard of Ros's condition. 'If your family is interested in the response of Chinese medicine to heroin addiction (one which has had some success), then I have some contacts which may be useful,' he wrote to me.

Conventional medicine was also on tap. Senator Don Grimes, my Minister for Social Security, was the only medical doctor in the ministry and had also spent years on the Senate's committee on drugs. Don and I had never been particularly close but he, too, comforted me generously from the basis of his training and experience.

Mail came from across the political divide. I recall, in particular, one letter from former Liberal Party minister and, at that time, Opposition frontbencher Ian McPhee, Federal Member for Balaclava: 'Apart from Scobie [Ian's son], I have never known a more adorable child than Rosslyn. You may recall I even sent her a 5th birthday card from the US,' he wrote, adding words of comfort to Hazel and me. John Dawkins, Minister for Finance, and not always my greatest fan, wrote to me in late September: 'To have one's very soul exposed to friends and enemies alike is a gruelling experience, particularly for politicians engaged as we are in such an unforgiving pastime.' He then painted the bigger picture, helping me to put my private grief into perspective: 'My respect for you and your gift for leadership have grown continuously since we set out on this great venture – the cause and course of which remains absolutely correct.' John also had some words about our political opponents: 'The main disappointment is the failure of this puny Opposition to make a real match of it without resort, perhaps not surprisingly, to these contemptible and self-defeating antics.'

Presumably he was referring to Andrew Peacock's earlier stunt in the Parliament. By now Andrew's accusation against me was rebounding savagely upon him. His approval rating sank to a record low, just 25 per cent, in the immediate aftermath of his 'little crook' smear. My own rating remained solid, still at 66 per cent. As preferred Prime Minister, I was favoured by 73 per cent of electors surveyed, compared with 15 per cent who felt that Peacock would make the better Prime Minister.[48]

Moving into October all the polls, public and private, were showing Labor miles in front, with a landslide victory in the offing. The pressure for an election, which had to be held anyway, was irresistible. In the words of party strategist and New South Wales numbers man, Graham Richardson, 'it was just obvious that you had to go, so we went!'[49] On 8th October 1984 I announced a 1st December poll. It was the start of a long, seven-week, nightmarish election campaign.

The timing was propitious, everything was showing up for Labor, with all the economic statistics and the evidence of public opinion pointing our way. There were signs everywhere that we were headed for a long stretch of government with our already sizeable majority about to receive a healthy boost. But the person most responsible for making this all possible in the first place was now at a low ebb and running virtually on empty. This time around I just didn't possess the verve and élan that had so transformed the fortunes of the party early in 1983. I couldn't focus and give to the task my customary single-minded concentration.

A metaphor for the whole campaign came early. While I was batting for the Prime Minister's XI in a cricket match against our friends of the Canberra press gallery I attempted a hookshot but the ball smashed into my face, splintering my glasses. I was raced to hospital where several slivers of glass were removed from my eye. The doctors told me that if the glass had penetrated a fraction further I would have lost the sight in that eye. My eye was very painful for some time but, fortunately, there was no permanent damage. This was true of the campaign too. I went to the crease determined to give it my best shot but I wasn't seeing the ball as clearly as I would have hoped – and my footwork and stroke play were not up to the standard I, and others, had come to expect.

When the election finally came around it went the same way as my eye – it was painful, but there was no permanent damage. There was no Wranslide. In its place, a small swing against the Government of 1.4 per cent narrowed our majority to sixteen seats.

Unquestionably, Labor would have fared better with me at the top of my form. But my lacklustre performance did not altogether explain the result. We had established the Australian Electoral Commission in November 1983 and introduced sweeping electoral reforms. House and Senate membership was enlarged. We introduced public funding of election campaigns and political parties had now to disclose the source of campaign donations. In other moves aimed at fairness, cost efficiency and simplicity, we abolished the system of candidates' names appearing on the ballot paper in alphabetical order, bumped up nominee deposits to discourage frivolous candidates, shortened voting hours and simplified Senate polling. Formerly, ballot papers could only be validly marked by placing a number in the square beside each candidate. But in recent times Senate ballot papers carried a multitude of names and had grown unwieldy. The complexity and requirements of the ballot paper meant that the informal vote had rocketed. Under our reforms all that was necessary now was a single mark to indicate the party preference.

It worked, but not exactly as we anticipated. In the 1984 election the informal vote for the Senate dropped from just under 10 per cent to under 5 per cent. But the rub came in the voting for the House of Representatives. Attracted to the simplicity of the Senate ballot, a number of voters thought they could mark their Lower House ballot in exactly the same way. Unfortunately for both them and us the informal vote for the House of Representatives swelled from 2 per cent to nearly 7 per cent. On the best surmise the bulk of the informals were Labor votes.

ALP National Secretary Bob McMullan noted in his campaign director's report on the 1984 federal election: 'Scrutineering information as is reliably available, together with ANOP[50] research indicates that after taking account of the informal vote factor, the 1984 election may be judged as approximately a re-run of 1983, i.e. a virtual no-swing situation.'

There were other factors in the 1984 poll not purely to do with my lacklustre campaigning performance. The formal campaign was the longest in federal electoral history. It was universally disparaged as too long and indeed it was. McMullan makes this point in his report but then he spells out the dilemma confronting me as Prime Minister: 'The widespread expectation, if not certainty, that the Government would call an election no later than February–March 1985 and almost certainly in December had created a pre-election climate which would have dominated Australian politics irrespective of the timing of the announcement.' The timing was also partly dictated by the need to allow plenty of time for voter enrolment.

In other respects Labor suffered for its own fair play. I was trenchantly criticised by some of my colleagues for my decision to allow the Opposition Leader, Andrew Peacock, a nationally televised debate in the lead-up to the election. But having challenged Fraser in 1983 to such a debate – a challenge he refused – I did not see that I could, with integrity, refuse Peacock's identical challenge. The well-known British commentator on Australian elections, David Butler, made the point using soccer language: 'The other own goal was the great debate.' He noted: 'An honourable Bob Hawke felt bound by a promise made when he was unsuccessfully challenging Prime Minister Fraser to a televised confrontation in 1983 ... Mr Hawke gave Mr Peacock ninety minutes of television time before a huge captive audience, that saw him as being treated as equal with the Prime Minister and demonstrating comparable authority and articulacy.'

I performed well below my capacity and Peacock won the debate. It was, however, the first and last time Andrew ever got onto any sort of equal footing with me. I faced a different opponent, John Howard, in the 1987 election. But Andrew kept going around on the Liberal leadership hurdy-gurdy, and popped up again as Leader of the Opposition for the 1990 election. Observers who had seen him in the 1984 campaign raised the spectre that he would do well again. It was tiresome at times, but I frequently had to caution people not to make the mistake of thinking that 1990 would be a repeat of 1984. Those who persisted with that mistake were corrected by history. By universal assessment – including that of the Liberal Party – Peacock was thrashed in 1990, both in the debate, which was the campaign highlight, and in the campaign generally. That 1990 campaign was, for me, the best measure of how emotionally debilitated I had been during the earlier contest.

In 1984 the extent to which commentators, party officials and colleagues were talking of a landslide was, in large measure, due to the success of my prime ministership throughout 1983 and 1984. Fit and on top, I had raised that expectation. But family tragedy had brought me and Labor's hopes back a little nearer to the field.

I remained below par for quite some time. Although I steeled myself to perform the duties of being Prime Minister, I did not cease to feel a father's devastation. Meanwhile Ros showed enormous courage and commitment. In January, when she was still in a frightful state, she had flown to America for treatment. Frank Lowy, head of Westfield and a friend of many years, very generously rearranged his own travel schedule so he could accompany her on the flight and see her safely installed at a clinic in California. Ros was determined to rehabilitate herself and live to be a good mother to her sons, whom she adores. It was only after she returned from the USA in April of 1985, got settled after a couple of months and was working again, that I felt fully restored myself.

Years later, when I was no longer Prime Minister, detractors sought to rewrite the history of the Hawke Government by drawing out the period during which I was affected by Ros's illness. That interpretation is absurd. In the punishing, competitive, intensely ambitious and high-stakes world of national and international politics, you cannot perform below par for a protracted period and expect to remain Prime Minister – certainly not for another seven years, winning two more elections in the process. Ultimately the electorate is the toughest judge in these matters.

EIGHTEEN

I did not expect any lessening of the load of prime ministerial responsibility in the post-election period. The pressure of events, abroad and at home, put any such thought out of the question.

In the international context two crises dominated this period and their resolution largely depended upon a cordial rapport with the United States leadership – something peculiarly in my province. There was the crisis in ANZUS caused by the New Zealand Labor Government's nuclear ships policy, and the MX missile crisis of February 1985.

David Lange had won the New Zealand election on 14th July 1984. As it happened the United States Secretary of State, George Shultz, was in Canberra that night and was my guest at the Lodge. After some trouble in tracking Lange to a hall in Mangere, a suburb of Auckland, George and I rang him to congratulate him. Obviously we were aware of New Zealand Labor's nuclear-free policy and the possible implications of that to the ANZUS alliance. George was on his way to Wellington for an ANZUS Council meeting and would then talk to David about the implications face to face. Representatives of my Government (the Foreign Minister, Bill Hayden, and Defence

279

Minister, Gordon Scholes) were also due in New Zealand the following day and they, too, would be meeting with David about the implications of New Zealand Labor's policy for ANZUS. Right now, George
and I had but one purpose in ringing David and that was to congratulate him on a thumping election victory. But Lange would see in this
sincere gesture a conspiratorial, bully-boy tactic aimed at heavying
New Zealand into a change of policy. According to him, we cut into his
victory celebrations, lending them an ominous edge and, thereafter, 'a
frisson of apprehension prevented me from enjoying the rest of the
evening'.[51]

His gloss on this and later events, suggesting that Australia and the
United States ganged up to pressure New Zealand to abandon its
nuclear ships policy, is extraordinary in view of what actually
happened. The only conspiring I did with the Americans over New
Zealand was to cool down the hotter heads in the United States administration who wished to deal with our trans-Tasman friends in a far
rougher way.

I had initially met David, Prime Minister to Prime Minister, in Port
Moresby shortly before Hazel's shock news about Rosslyn. We were
both attending the opening of the new Papua New Guinea Parliament
House and the CHOGRM.[52] David came by arrangement to my room
at the Travelodge Hotel for an early breakfast meeting. We only had an
hour so there was no time for beating around the bush. I came directly
to the central issue of ANZUS ship visits to New Zealand ports,
quickly spelling out Australia's position. Innocent assumptions about a
threat-free world were futile, I told him. In the context of a very real
East–West conflict we regarded the ANZUS Treaty as vitally important. I told him it was nonsense to suggest you could have an alliance
relationship but tell your ally that its ships couldn't enter your ports.

I was not belligerent, nor did David regard me as being so, although
he may say otherwise now; but respect for my own country and for his

led me to spell out the implications of his party's no-nuclear ships policy directly and specifically. He listened intently. I then invited him to state his position. As he did so his words seemed to lack all conviction. The more he spoke the more this impression grew. In the end I felt compelled to tell him that it seemed he didn't really believe what he was saying and his government seemed prepared to cop the Left's view in return for a freer hand to run economic policy. He replied without equivocation, 'That's right.' He indicated that the nuclear-free policy had been fashioned by the Left and accepted by the party, and there was virtually nothing he could do about it. I told Lange I was angered by this and couldn't understand how he could possibly conduct foreign policy in the best interests of New Zealand on the basis of such a compact. He shrugged resignedly and said that unfortunately that was the way it was.

Following that exchange on such a vital issue, a level of cynicism infused my thinking about David Lange. My cynicism bordered on contempt when he subsequently floated around the world as the great man of principle on the nuclear-free issue, at one stage mooted as a possible recipient of the Nobel Peace prize. I would have kept my reflections about him to myself, but he has been so uninhibited in his public observations about me that it is appropriate to set the record straight. In doing so I must in fairness point out that on the important issues Australia pursued during our meetings together in the South Pacific Forum, David was supportive.

At the conclusion of our breakfast Ross Garnaut, who had escorted Lange to the meeting, came back into the room. I explained to David that Ross was an economist on my personal staff. Ever on the look out for the funny retort, David said, 'Oh! I've got one of those, I think, but I haven't met him yet.' My God! What sort of a fellow is this? I wondered. I soon discovered that smart asides were characteristic of Lange, for whom continual riposte was a weapon of interruption. He seemed to find sustained sessions of concentration difficult; it was virtually impossible to have a serious conversation with him for any length of time. Just as the exchange of ideas and concepts was beginning to quicken or take on some new significance, he would slip off into light relief. Humour has its place in discourse between leaders but the key to its use is balance. I thought David Lange lacked this entirely.

The crunch for the New Zealand leg of the ANZUS alliance came in February with the intended visit to New Zealand ports of the USS *Buchanan*. The Americans had delayed the visit of any US naval ship to New Zealand for as long as practically possible. In the normal course of the relationship they could have been expected to show up right away. The United States held off, having been led to believe that all David needed was some room to sort through political problems with his party and smooth the way for US naval ship visits. Shultz certainly believed Lange had intended to convey to him during the former's visit to New Zealand in July the impression that the impasse could be worked through, and that US naval ships would still be welcome in New Zealand ports. Australian ministers Hayden and Scholes, having dined with Lange at the Australian High Commissioner's residence at that time, came away with the same impression.

And so Lange had his running room. When the Americans finally signalled a visit they chose the *Buchanan* in deference to New Zealand's sensitivities. They would neither confirm nor deny that the ship was nuclear, the essence of their policy, but they were prepared to live with whatever claims the New Zealand Government might make as to why they did not think the USS *Buchanan* had nuclear weapons on board. For example, the ship was small and unlikely to be nuclear-armed. At around this time the former New Zealand Prime Minister, Bill Rowling, one of the authors of the New Zealand Labor Party's anti-nuclear policy, was on his way to the United States as his country's new ambassador, convinced that the *Buchanan* visit would take place.

But Rowling's successor as leader of the Labor Party did not have the weight to deliver on his assurances, at least as they were understood by both New Zealand's ANZUS partners. Lange's lack of authority within his party and his Government is evident from his own writings on the subject. 'The American ambassador wrote to me with the stark advice that it was the *Buchanan* or nothing. This letter I took to cabinet. The cabinet had not changed its mind: the *Buchanan* was not coming. I wrote back to the ambassador telling him that New Zealand was unable from its own resources to determine if the *Buchanan* conformed with our policy, and for that reason we must decline its visit.'[53]

Turning away the USS *Buchanan* sank Lange's credibility with the Americans. No longer would they do anything based solely on his word, as they understood it. Whatever he had intended he had undoubtedly had the effect of misleading both George Shultz, a man whose diplomacy was based wholly on meaning exactly what he said, and the Americans in general. Henceforth the United States trusted Lange only so far as his words were backed by clear, assertive actions.

The barring of the *Buchanan* had the immediate effect, too, of sinking the trilateral defence arrangement between the United States, Australia and New Zealand. By adhering to the no-ships policy, New Zealand infuriated the United States. For six months or more they waited for the New Zealand Government to get its act together, assured that it would.

The United States feared that New Zealand's attitude to nuclear-powered ships would be relayed around the world. Japan was America's chief consideration. The Japanese had an anti-nuclear constitution which formally, at least, prohibited visits by nuclear-powered or nuclear-armed ships. In practice, however, the Japanese never inquired about the nuclear capability of visiting US naval ships. As a result nuclear ships were virtually never out of Japanese ports and harbours.

Europe was another concern. The last thing the United States wanted was for dominoes to fall among NATO countries. This was the time of Greenham Common and the British Labour Party's unilateral disarmament policy. With good cause, the Americans were worried about the United Kingdom in particular.

As it happened I was in Washington at the time of the USS *Buchanan* incident facing a diplomatic emergency of my own – the MX missile crisis. I was at a low ebb personally, and now had two fires to put out: the United States–New Zealand conflagration and the other, ignited by my own party, racing towards me on another front. But first, New Zealand.

I made it clear from the outset, both to the United States and New Zealand, that their differences were to be resolved between themselves. We would play the honest broker, we would clearly state our position, but beyond that we would not go. We would throw our best efforts into maintaining our defence arrangements with both the United States and New Zealand, and what we could not do trilaterally we would seek to achieve bilaterally. Indeed we told the Americans that far from punishing New Zealand, Australia would increase its defence co-operation so as to compensate New Zealand during their absence from the trilateral relationship.

After *Buchanan* the United States withdrew defence co-operation from New Zealand. They refused to exercise with them, banned reciprocal military placements in either country, withdrew United States port facilities from the New Zealand navy, and curtailed the exchange of military intelligence between the United States and New Zealand. The US anger and desire for retribution was by no means exhausted by these steps. In February 1985 in Washington, there were some in the Administration and many more in Congress who wanted to vent their spleen about the Lange Government's no-ships policy in a way that went far beyond security arrangements. They wanted to impose economic sanctions on New Zealand. There were irate Congressmen, including liberal Democrats, who were badgering the Republican Administration to take a tougher stand.

This was never on as far as I was concerned, and I immediately went in to bat for New Zealand. On this occasion and in subsequent visits to Washington, I argued strongly against any punitive measures by the United States against the Kiwis. To both George Shultz and the Defense Secretary, Caspar Weinberger, who was particularly incensed by the no-ships policy, I repeatedly asserted that the issue had to be quarantined. 'Whatever you may think about Lange, the people of New Zealand should not be damaged by some discriminatory trade war,' I argued. Our Ambassador in Washington, Bob Cotton, was also pressing New Zealand's cause. He said that the United States must understand that the New Zealand Government had the job of running their country in what they perceived to be their people's best interests. 'For our part, we do not agree with it, we think it is wrong-headed, but that is the decision they have made,' Bob pointed out. Cotton had a down to earth way of expressing things that the Americans appreciated. He told them, 'You might think the New Zealanders are mistaken, but they're good people, they're worth having as friends, and if I were you, I'd treat this ships business as lightly as you can.'

In my own discussions with the Americans the State Department headed by George Shultz was always more likely to take the broader view than the Defense Department led by Weinberger. Neither department is monolithic in outlook, but the weight of opinion for bringing New Zealand to book over their no-nuclear-ships policy was greater at Defense than it was at State. Yet although Defense was a harder nut to crack, Australia's argument on this issue prevailed there too.

Cap Weinberger was a man of undoubtedly strong views but he was susceptible to reasoned argument. He accepted that the tough stand the United States took toward New Zealand on defence co-operation should not spill over into economics and trade.

While happy to do battle for New Zealand's cause at that time, I had problems of my own on that Washington visit. Mine were of a lower order of magnitude than those posed by the no-ships policy. Our issue was nonetheless a hot and potentially dangerous one, exposing raw nerves both in Australia and in the United States.

In Australia the question of uranium mining and of nuclear disarmament, though not logically related, had become intertwined. Together they had become the great cause, pushed with considerable impact, particularly among young voters, by the newly formed Nuclear Disarmament Party. The NDP had campaigned on the single issue of nuclear proliferation during the 1984 election. They had a popular and novel leader, Peter Garrett, star of the band, Midnight Oil. The NDP had won considerable notoriety, partly due to the length of the campaign and the changes we had made to the electoral laws. Its showing at the polls stirred the ideologues in my own party and kept alive the dwindling remnants of Labor's anti-Americanism.

Across the Pacific in the United States nerves were raw because of the intensities of the Cold War and the dominoes spectre raised by the stance of the New Zealand Government. In February 1985 I arrived in Washington sandwiched between these conflicting sensitivities. Triggering the problem was an undertaking I had given on an earlier visit to Washington for Australia to provide limited assistance to the United States in the testing of their powerful new MX intercontinental missile. In consultation with the Foreign Minister, Bill Hayden, and the Defence Minister, Gordon Scholes, we agreed to give US aircraft take-off and landing rights at an RAAF airfield. This would assist the Americans to monitor the splashdown of the MX missile in the Tasman Sea to the east of Tasmania.

Our undertaking came after we had inherited an embryonic agreement from the Fraser Government allowing the use of RAAF facilities to monitor the splashdown within Australia's exclusive economic zone which extends 200 nautical miles from Australia's coast. When this earlier agreement was first raised with me by the Americans in June of 1983 I stipulated that the use of Australian facilities would only be contemplated if the splashdown was moved into international waters. This was a significant modification of the Fraser Government agreement. Even then the use of an Australian airfield was only endorsed after American representations asserted that aircraft reconnaissance from Australia was the only feasible way of monitoring the splashdown.

Our co-operation had no necessary connection with the ANZUS Treaty. Nevertheless it was consistent with it and it was clear to me that perfecting the MX delivery system was an important part of the Western alliance's strategic program to catch up with the Soviet Union. The Soviets were at this time testing their own missiles in the Pacific. In these circumstances it seemed more than appropriate to offer the limited use of Australian facilities to our allies. The MX undertaking was a security issue and quite properly kept within the knowledge of this small group of ministers. By and large the Cabinet accepted that security issues were matters properly left to the Prime Minister and members of the Cabinet Security Committee.

The MX story broke in the Australian media during the first week of February 1985 after an enterprising Australian researcher based in the United States unearthed relevant information about the tests from a defence document requested under the Freedom of Information Act. I was on my way to Brussels and by the time I got there on 3rd February, all hell had broken loose in Australia.

News of the 1983 MX agreement set off a bout of residual anti-Americanism and pacifist naïvety within the party. Educating Labor to a mature foreign policy outlook was a gradual process and this episode occurred at a time when we had not entirely emerged from the trough of the past. The issue also raised party sensitivities about the extent of consultation which should flow from the senior levels of government back through the various tiers of the Labor Party: the Cabinet, the broader ministry, the Caucus and the party membership in general. Our first two years in government had seen vast changes in party outlook, both in economic and foreign affairs and for some the movement had been a little too swift. MX was seized upon by those who felt bypassed and unhappy with the pace of change. Here was their chance to say to the upper reaches of the Government: slow down and consult more.

In Brussels I was surprised at the breadth of party reaction against any involvement by Australia in MX missile testing in our region. The harbingers of party feeling on the subject were Senators Graham Richardson and Robert Ray, right-wing numbers men from New South Wales and Victoria respectively. These two heavyweights were touring the provinces of Japan together and returned to their hotel to find that the switchboard had been lit up with calls for them. Taking the bundle of messages back to their rooms, each of them hit the phones. Then they rang me: there was uproar in the Caucus, with heavy opposition coming from Left and Centre Left members.

Although it may have been just possible to get majority support for the decision in the Caucus, opposition would not have stopped there. Pressure was building for a special conference of the Labor Party aimed at overthrowing the MX decision. In that event the issue would no doubt sweep far wider than just MX, enveloping ANZUS and the joint facilities. This presaged the worst of all possible worlds. Having a collateral issue strike at the heart of Australia's alliance with America was dangerous nonsense and I could not allow it. To risk the initiatives we had taken in the international arena and to put in jeopardy the permanent and fundamental features of the Australia–United States alliance seemed to me ridiculous. I had no doubt about the sense and correctness of my original decision. But since it had now become an emotional peg on which to hang the latent dissatisfactions of the disapproving Left and others who felt rather isolated from government decision-making, it made no sense to persist with the original agreement. It was not critical to the functioning of the alliance or to the maintenance of it; if I had believed this to be the case I would have taken my opponents head on.

On that night of 4th February 1985 in Brussels, while I was fielding calls from Richardson and Ray and from the Foreign Minister, Bill Hayden and the Defence Minister, Kim Beazley, Paul Keating rang me. As distinct from those cooler heads, who shared my view, Paul was gung-ho. He recommended a 'take 'em on, we'll beat 'em, don't back down' approach. Understandably, I took no notice because he was not expert in foreign affairs and he had no understanding of the MX issue within the broader framework of maintaining party support for the Australia–United States alliance and the joint facilities. His was a 'crash through or crash' response which is sometimes useful, but on this occasion would have been counterproductive.

Before leaving Brussels for Washington I decided to withdraw our offer to assist the Americans in their testing of the MX missile. Meanwhile the Australian media was full of hyperbole about my undoing; the gist of it was that I was to be browbeaten and otherwise humiliated by the Americans.

Once again they had it wrong. My friend George Shultz visited me on my arrival in Washington to tell me that Australia's help in monitoring the MX splashdown was no longer required. Quite independently of anything I had said on the subject, George Shultz and the Defense Secretary, Caspar Weinberger, had both concluded that to press Australia on a collateral issue of MX missile testing would be to risk unravelling the fundamentals of the alliance. Their advisers had alerted Shultz and Weinberger to the way the issue was developing in Australia. Of course given the annoyance about the New Zealand ships' policy, there were more aggressive voices in the lower echelons of the United States Government urging Shultz and Weinberger to take a tougher line with Australia. But both knew that any harm to the United States alliance with Australia could only come if they took this issue of lesser importance and blew up its significance beyond the alliance itself. Furthermore, the last thing either of them wished was to harm a friend whom they regarded highly.

The following day George hosted a lunch for me, after which he read a joint statement to those who had been so fervent in their speculation about the hammering I was to receive in Washington. He told the press conference in the foyer of the State Department: 'There are a variety of ways to monitor an MX test and the monitoring effort need not involve the provision of Australian support. A decision has been made by the United States to conduct the MX tests without the use of Australian support arrangements.'

I stood beside George as he read the statement: it was not the easiest situation that either of us have ever found ourselves in. The subject had caused me obvious political difficulty and embarrassment, but listening to George I found myself indebted to my friend for the constructive way in which we were able to resolve our problem.

Despite the closeness of my relationship with the United States Administration, I was rather annoyed by one aspect of our discussions on the MX. On my earlier visit to Washington it had been put to me that it would be very difficult and significantly more expensive to test the MX without American aircraft having access to our airfields for the purpose of monitoring splashdown. I was asked to endorse a nascent agreement entered into by my predecessor. But now, in 1985, I was told that with very little difficulty and at no significantly greater expense the monitoring of splashdown could be done by US naval ships. At this point I thought it was a great pity that hadn't been made clear in the first place. I am not saying that I was deliberately misled by the Americans, but they may have pressed their case a little too eagerly at the outset. No matter, I now had to deal with the problem as it existed. I had an unqualified commitment to the alliance and to the maintenance of the joint facilities. I certainly wasn't going to create additional difficulties by questioning the pretext upon which the original agreement was entered into.

Latter-day myth-makers have attempted to paint me in this period as wounded to the point of paralysis. Yet faced with one of the biggest furores of my prime ministership, popularly billed as the 'MX Missile Crisis', with rattled journalists and frazzled staffers running around in a state of high anxiety, I was calm. Why? As was often the case throughout my prime ministership, I was able to lower the temperature and take control, even at a time when I was not at the top of my form. That is why the Defence Minister, Kim Beazley, has since praised my handling of the MX crisis: 'He [Hawke] pulled off what in the circumstances can only be described as a miracle,' Beazley said. '... [W]ithout doing any substantial damage to our standing in the relationship with the United States, he got George Shultz, against all the advice that George Shultz was receiving, to let us off the hook.'[54]

What, in reality, had been prised from the hook were the benefits to both Australia and America of the alliance and the facilities. By removing the MX bait, the disenchanted within the Labor Party ceased circling for tastier morsels. Indeed when I returned to Australia and reported to the Cabinet and the Caucus, the parliamentary party unanimously reaffirmed the importance of ANZUS and the joint facilities. The Caucus resolution was the strongest yet on the very commitments that, by jettisoning the MX agreement, I was trying to protect.

And so, from a brief and awkward minus arose a fundamental plus. In retrospect the MX imbroglio was really the last time that a foreign affairs and defence issue significantly stretched the Government or the party during the period of my prime ministership. There were incidents and arguments as late as the Gulf War in 1991 but they were not of the same order. MX was the watershed. From then on the party came increasingly to understand that the Government was pursuing policies squarely based on Labor philosophy and on the recognition in the party platform of the importance of the alliance with the United States.

NINETEEN

Labor's years of ambitious bidding for government from the Opposition benches followed by the profligacy of the Whitlam years had given it a reputation for financial recklessness. From the beginning we were determined to eradicate this perception. This meant that many of our moves would be unpopular. In 1984 our resolution to clamp down on middle-class welfare caused a furore; this centred on our decision to apply an assets test to pensions and to impose an income test on pensioners over seventy years of age.

We pressed on with this reform despite electoral misgivings in our own ranks, a hypocritical tirade from the Opposition which reached a crescendo during the 1984 election campaign, and relentless attacks from sections of the media led by the Melbourne *Herald*. According to them, this eminently fair decision was going to bring an end to civilisation as we knew it.

Some of my colleagues wanted to abandon the move when the heat was turned up. I refused to budge because it was intrinsically correct; it also had a taxation dimension. I had told Parliament that the absence of an assets test had led to a proliferation of tax avoidance schemes.[55]

We were able to move in this small discrete area of tax reform early, but we did not act without providing the opportunity for wide consultation. We established a broadly-based review panel to advise on the proposed income and assets test. The review panel headed by Professor Fred Gruen of the Australian National University reported in May 1984. In the spirit of the Economic Summit Committee of the previous year, the Gruen Committee consulted widely among pensioner and service organisations. I noted when presenting the Gruen Report to the Parliament on 1st June 1984 that 'it is important that the Government gets community support for tackling the hard and thankless task of expenditure restraint through means testing welfare'.[56]

Australia's entire taxation system was crying out for radical overhaul in much broader ways than this. It was decrepit and rife with opportunities for avoidance. I had flagged tax reform as a central issue from the very outset of government. Rich and corporate Australia was fast developing the view that only the benevolent, or perhaps the foolish, paid tax. Professor Russell Matthews, who headed the Committee of Inquiry into Inflation and Taxation in 1975, had put the position graphically:

> … the essential problem is not to make the rich pay higher rates of tax, or even more tax, than the poor; it is to make the rich pay any income tax at all. There has recently been some discussion about the potential for tax revolt in Australia. It must be recognised that a massive tax revolt has already taken place; but it is a revolt of business taxpayers against wage and salary earners, of the rich against the poor.[57]

The High Court of Australia, led for many years by the former Coalition Government Attorney-General, Sir Garfield Barwick, had not helped. With a fairly monotonous regularity the Barwick presumption for the taxpayer against the Commonwealth seemed to prevail.

By the time my Government was elected, the main burden of the Australian income tax system fell on those who could least afford it. Ordinary wage and salary earners didn't have the financial capacity to hire accountants and lawyers to diminish their tax burden by deductions, capital conversions, income splits, deferral and other means. They paid and with bracket creep – inflation taking their incomes into higher tax brackets – they paid heavily.

At the time 39 per cent of full-time earners in the workforce were paying income tax at the 46 cents marginal rate; the figure was soon expected to jump to well over half of the workforce. Something like three million of Australia's five and a half million full-time earners would be paying tax at the 46 cents rate. The contrast with earlier times was stark. Thirty years before upper income earners paid more than half the personal income tax collected in Australia. In 1985 that figure had been cut to just 20 per cent. Australia's taxation system had ceased to be progressive.

Bracket creep has a disincentive effect. Employees work harder, or show more enterprise, only to have their financial reward significantly diminished by higher marginal tax. The taxation system had clearly ceased to satisfy the fundamentally important criteria of equity, efficiency and appropriate resource allocation.

A central weakness of Australia's income tax system was the absence of a capital gains tax. With good legal and accountancy advice the rich could always find ways of converting otherwise taxable income into capital gains. Income tax avoidance also flourished through the proliferation of untaxed fringe benefits. Medium- and high-income earners were able to shift their receipts from taxable cash income to income in other forms such as luxury cars or school fees for their children – a practice which was proliferating by the month.

The system was also riddled with a myriad of other weaknesses and loopholes. Years of seeking to slant tax concessions to particular vested interests had opened up many opportunities for avoidance.

Dramatising tax avoidance even more than Matthews was Frank Costigan's report of December 1981 to the Fraser Government.[58] 'If ever a cheap political trick blew up in the perpetrator's face, it was the Costigan Royal Commission. No one was more surprised, more embarrassed, more alarmed, than were the members of the previous Government and their friends when Mr Costigan's investigations took him into the territory of the massive tax rackets over which they had presided in their seven years of government,' I told the Parliament on 2nd October 1984. Costigan pinpointed tax avoidance as Australia's fastest growing industry.[59]

By March 1983 any responsible government had to be alarmed about the weaknesses in our income tax system – the opportunities for avoidance, the inequities associated with it, and its ineffectiveness as a revenue raising mechanism. Tax reform had been an issue at the April Economic Summit. The need for such reform was recognised in the Summit Communiqué as an essential part of the long-term task of national reconciliation, recovery and reconstruction. By early October the Economic Planning Advisory Council (EPAC), the body spawned by the summit, was grappling with the subject. EPAC regarded tax reform as a major priority for achieving sustained, non-inflationary growth.

But tax reform was no simple matter. The first task was to understand exactly the nature and weaknesses of the present system. Next, it was necessary to analyse the alternatives. Any reforms had to be philosophically grounded in fairness, equity and efficiency. Also we wished to avoid foisting changes on the community without consultation. Major unilateral changes delivered in that way from above rarely stick.

In my view government for the long haul was about making lasting, effective changes and not making them all at once.

On 30th October 1983 I wrote to the Treasurer calling on him to provide EPAC with a detailed survey of the present tax structure. Involving EPAC, a framework for consultation between constituent community groups – governments, business, unions, the professions, welfare groups – early in the tax reform process was in line with my aspiration to govern inclusively and consensually.

We had made some preliminary moves on tax reform but a complete overhaul of the taxation structure was definitely for our second term in office. We had also pledged in the 1983 campaign not to introduce a capital gains tax and Labor was duty-bound to honour that commitment during our first term.

Initially Paul and I differed on the politics of capital gains. I always thought we could sell a capital gains tax to the public. Indeed at the 1982 National Conference I had made a precipitate boast. '[I]f we can't sell a capital gains tax, we shouldn't be in the bloody business of politics,' I declared.

I still believed that, and it was now a matter of preparing the ground for action. Paul Keating was at first doubtful but came round to my point of view. Because of extensive abuse in this area, sensible tax administration had become impossible without a capital gains tax. As he had grown in confidence, Paul had requested me to transfer tax policy from Dawkins, the Finance Minister, to him. Dawkins resisted vigorously but I agreed because I believed Treasury was the right place for it. Responsible now for administering the ramshackle system Labor had inherited, Paul simply could not ignore the gaping hole left by the absence of a capital gains tax.

But we had to proceed cautiously as we approached the 1984 election. The Opposition, lusting for office, threw out the window their alleged commitment to smaller government and to trimming the public purse. Peacock had begun to hammer away at our assets test on aged pensions. His other tack was to stir up community fear about Labor's likely moves on tax reform. 'As certain as night follows day,' he warned, Labor would introduce a raft of new taxes: capital gains, death and gift duties.

The last thing Labor needed was to be spooked into making glib promises which the Government and the country would live to repent at leisure. Tax had to be killed off as an election issue but in a way which kept tax reform alive after the election. The opportunity came during the campaign, on 19th October 1984, when I was being interviewed on Perth Radio 6PR by talk-back host Bob Maumill. Maumill is a bright, eccentric soul and he began talking to me about the mess Australia's tax system was in, but emphasised his view that people were frightened of change. I agreed. What was needed, I told Maumill, was general community agreement on changes to the tax system.

We then went to a station break. While advertising jingles played in the background, we continued the discussion. I mentioned that there was a new spirit of goodwill and consensus in Australia following our election and the summit of April 1983. I expressed confidence in my ability to persuade the Australian people, through consultation, to agree to reform of the tax system. 'You mean a tax summit?' Maumill asked. 'Yes, why not,' I replied.

With that, Maumill opened the microphones. He again popped the question of a taxation summit. Again I agreed. I could have easily quashed the suggestion if that had been my intention, but I embraced the idea.

A summit made both economic and political sense to me. It stood to reason that the likelihood of community acceptance of change was enhanced if people first had a chance to hear the various arguments for and against particular changes, and to advance their own views through appropriate organisations in a relevant forum. There was also an obvious political bonus in being able to take time to assess community feeling when it came to making fundamental changes in the tax system. So while the summit idea appeared to some as a reaction to a suggestion made on a radio talk-back show during an election campaign, it nonetheless reflected my basic philosophy about how to go about undertaking fundamental reform.

By that stage Paul Keating was firmly wedded to the imposition of a consumption tax. Treasury had convinced him that the direct side of revenue raising in Australia was in such disrepair that the only solution was to broaden the tax base radically. Treasury had been pressing this agenda for some time but to no avail. During the Fraser years the Treasurer, John Howard, was a keen proponent of a consumption tax but his Prime Minister shied away from the idea.

Fraser had reason to be wary, for a new tax is always fraught with political risk. This, for me, was another reason to involve the community and to commit constituent groups, as far as possible, to any proposed changes. Having mooted the summit in Perth, I learned of Keating's reservations about the idea. I did not take them very seriously. His objections were merely an incantation of Treasury's suspicion of anything that was not initiated or controlled by Treasury officials. To Treasury, making tax policy in public was anathema. They preferred the closed doors and closed sessions which had, in fact, produced the shambolic tax régime that a summit aimed to fix.

The summit proposal quarantined a dangerous issue until after the 1984 election. A critical addendum to the summit proposal in the pre-election period was our formulation of nine principles governing tax reform. Of these principles none was more important than the ninth, which was that no taxation reform package would be adopted without broadly-based community support.[60] Another important principle for settling community concern about tax reform was our commitment not to increase the general level of taxation in Australia, a principle enunciated earlier in my trilogy commitment.

With the election out of the way, work on the taxation summit began in earnest. My economics adviser Ross Garnaut joined me at Kirribilli House to thrash out tax reform options between Christmas and New Year. A broadly-based consumption tax was certainly on the agenda but neither Ross nor I shared Treasury's, or the Treasurer's, enthusiasm for it.

My attitude was 'wait and see'. Certainly a consumption tax was attractive on economic grounds. It was efficient, it was certain, and not even the most practised tax avoider could escape paying it. But the tax was just as replete with problems. It was regressive; lower income earners and social welfare recipients would pay a greater percentage of their income on the tax than would wealthier Australians. The tax had costs and immediate consequences for inflation. Unless the union movement was prepared to forego wage increases to offset the inflationary impact of the tax, prices would spiral. We were already testing the goodwill of the trade union movement under the Accord.

The first collapse of the Australian dollar came in early 1985. If the Government was to keep employment growing and to maintain the impetus for structural reform, we had first to stop the depreciation of the Australian dollar flowing into wages through the consequent inflation. We now had to assess whether a consumption tax was consistent with our ability to maintain stable macro-economic management. A consumption tax also posed severe timing issues. Tax changes had to be considered, implemented, and bedded down, all in the space of a three-year Parliament. It was, for example, a timing problem that prevented the Government from opting in the White Paper prepared for the Taxation Summit of 1st July for the most efficient consumption tax. The Government ended up preferring a retail sales tax and not the more efficient value-added tax that, as it turned out, the

Liberal–National Party Coalition promoted in their ill-fated *Fightback!* manifesto of November 1991.

In short, adoption of a consumption tax was not a straightforward issue. The tax had manifold advantages; equally there were clear disadvantages. If the disadvantages could be ironed out, or compensated, then I was for it. But there were many unanswered questions.

The coming months were spent chasing answers to those questions. A combined team of Treasury and Department of Prime Minister and Cabinet officials worked at fever pitch to produce a 280-page White Paper setting out the various reform options. Ross Garnaut worked on the team, as did Eddie Visbord. Meeting after meeting was held in my office arguing and debating tax reform. There was much to talk and argue about for we had embarked upon the largest single tax reform exercise in the country's history and it was not something to be undertaken lightly.

To begin with there was considerable common ground. In order to change the tax system substantially and to reduce marginal income tax rates significantly, we agreed that solid alternative sources of revenue had to be found. We agreed, further, that widening the indirect tax base was the best way to achieve that necessary objective.

From that basic premise we began to formulate a series of options. Option A was common to all approaches. It aimed at garnering revenue by closing off various tax shelters, havens, benefits, allowances and loopholes. It included a capital gains tax and targeted things like the business lunch, entertainment allowances, fringe benefits, the deductions open to the so-called Pitt and Collins Street farmers, and the huge write-offs offered to investors in certain entrepreneurial ventures, including films.

Option B included A but added a limited extension of indirect taxes by enlarging the wholesale tax area. Option C again included A but involved a 12.5 per cent broadly-based consumption tax. With

Option C we entered the territory of the Holy Grail, Treasury's most cherished reform, with the Treasurer now the reform's most impassioned champion.

It was also with Option C that all the trouble started. To begin with, selling a regressive tax to the Labor Party was not easy. The very notion of taxing meat and milk, fruit and vegetables, bread and butter, did not bring the party a warm inner glow. Indeed it was anathema to everything party stalwarts believed that Labor stood for, as my friend Neville Wran expressed it.[61]

It was a difficult sell both within the Cabinet and the Caucus. Within my office opponents were thick on the ground. Ross Garnaut shared my early view; if the problems with the tax could be efficiently and equitably cleared away, then he was for it. But as Ross did the sums and worked his way through the check list of obstacles, he became more and more convinced that, far from being a panacea, the tax would actually damage Australia's long-term goals. Eddie Visbord felt similarly. While Peter Barron was the most consistent and vociferous opponent on my staff, Bob Hogg, Graham Evans and Geoff Walsh were all against it.

Staffers, bureaucrats and colleagues were urging me to cut the consumption tax idea dead, right from the outset. But this was not my way. There are, no doubt, propositions which are so clearly wrong that it is right to spare everyone both the masochism and the excitement of floating them merely for the sake of it. But the consumption tax was not in this category. The tax was intrinsically worth investigating. If the basic regressivity of the tax could be compensated so that the principle of equity was not violated and unbearable strains were not put on the Accord, then it looked like the sort of tax Australia should have. For too long Australia as a nation had been afraid of change. The very conservatism of the country had driven us towards a tax system which rated, on any criterion of economic efficiency or equity, as one of the worst in the developed Western world. New ideas were called for and the consumption tax was properly among them. Exposing the idea to argument and detailed examination took time. It was not an issue about which one could tell staffers, bureaucrats or colleagues to go away and think about it and return with an answer in a day or a week.

Shaping and modelling the White Paper, which was mainly done in Treasury with input from my staff and office, took months in itself. Cabinet debate on the paper, in draft form, was drawn out and restive. The consumption tax contained in Option C was the source of most of the argument. Paul impressed his colleagues by his command of the material. Many in the Cabinet were uneasy but they were no match for the Treasurer when it came to the detail of argument. The Housing Minister, Stewart West, a stalwart of the Left, was implacably opposed to the tax and argued against it with his usual doggedness, but Paul was too nimble for him.

The sternest opposition came from the Finance Minister, Peter Walsh. Peter was one of the most intelligent of my ministers and always came to Cabinet fully briefed. He often had an appalling lack of feel for the political implications of his position, but not on this occasion. However he was a late entry in the consumption debate and this hampered him. As Finance Minister he was deeply involved in the preparation of the Government's May Statement. It was only with that out of the way that he came to the debate with guns blazing. By then we had entered the final Cabinet meeting on the White Paper on 22nd May and time was running out. We had to get the paper finalised and printed in time for the summit on 1st July.

Politically, Peter Walsh smelt disaster. His worst fear was that the tax would cost Labor the 1987 election. He then envisaged the Coalition dismantling the rest of Labor's tax package – capital gains, fringe benefits, the substantiation requirements, and the rest – but leaving the new consumption tax in place, perhaps even increasing it.

This scenario saw Australia living in the worst of all possible tax worlds. We would have embraced a disaster, with all its terrible electoral consequences, and laboured monstrously only to produce a worse outcome.

Peter also feared the inflationary consequences of the tax. Treasury estimated the tax would add a one-off 6.5 per cent to the inflation rate. He argued that without an assurance from the trade union movement that they would not try to recover the cost of living increases as a result of the tax, inflation would zoom to 15 per cent. He was primed and backed by his department head, Ian Castles, who, under the Coalition, had ridden the consumption tax merry-go-round a couple of times before – Castles was strongly opposed to the tax on equity grounds.

That final Cabinet meeting on the White Paper went on for something like two and a half days. Keating's performance equalled his selling of foreign bank entry at the 1984 conference and his arguments won the day. But the sense of unease around the Cabinet table did not seem to lift as he made his points. There was a zealotry about his presentation that worried even those who were prepared to be persuaded.

For my part, putting the uneasiness of colleagues aside, I felt there was enough merit in the consumption tax proposal to allow Paul to argue the case more broadly in the Australian community and to do so with the Government's imprimatur. To date he had done a first-rate job in developing the tax package and in selling it within the Government. And as Prime Minister I had given him an unlimited opportunity to develop the idea within the Caucus and the Cabinet. He had carried the debate with great skill, encouraged by an enthusiastic department. Having come this far it would have been futile and counterproductive to chop off discussion. Thrashing out the various options was, after all, what the summit was all about.

My role was much broader than the Treasurer's. As Prime Minister I had to incorporate in my thinking much more than the purely technical aspects of the tax. I had to be concerned not merely with the economic impact of the tax but with the social impact, the political impact and ultimately with what was best, not just for the Government but for the country.

Following the Cabinet meeting Paul had free rein to win over the community and the summit's constituent groups to the imposition of a new tax. The White Paper went to the Government Printer with Option C earmarked as the Government's preferred option. Whether it remained that way was very much a matter for the summit.

From 22nd May onwards the Treasurer was off on what became tagged his 'tax cart', flogging his consumption tax proposal with near-missionary zeal. He had a little over one month to stitch together enough support to carry the new tax proposal at the summit. With a plane load of journalists, he criss-crossed the country looking for converts. It was a hard sell, dedicated, zealous, and courageous. Paul could talk economics like a Bruce Petty cartoon. He waved his arms and often grabbed hold of words and metaphors which people could readily understand. This was something that Opposition Leader John Hewson never had going for him when he attempted, with equal zealotry, to sell a consumption tax to Australians in the lead-up to the 1993 election. However, in May and June of 1985 Paul's salesmanship could not clinch the deal. People listened to what he said, they generally understood it – something Hewson could not claim – but they didn't want to buy it.

At odd times ALP pollster Rod Cameron gloomily unveiled the fruits of his market research. The results were dismal, with only something like 10 per cent of those polled thinking we should levy the new tax. Paul often gave the impression he could sell ice-cream to Eskimos, but he could not sell this. Undaunted, he would fire up his cart and zoom off again. Cheered on by Treasury, who had found their champion, Keating barnstormed the country. He appeared oblivious to the politics of the exercise; he was now in the grip of a manic optimism that was beginning to worry his colleagues.

For the first time he reminded me of some of the wild-eyed figures of Labor history I had read about in my youth. Affectionately, I saw in Paul glimpses of that famous maverick, Billy Hughes, Labor Prime Minister in 1915–16. Hughes was often struck by epiphanous shafts of wild imagination that caused him to want to flood Lake Eyre in South Australia, or to turn the Queensland rivers inland. Like Hughes, Paul had a sometimes bizarre dimension to his character. And like Hughes, he was not without vision; certainly both Keating and Hughes saw themselves as producers of great national designs.[62]

But while Keating acted the zealot, the party itself was growing increasingly uneasy and opposed. The news from the branches, through various State conference and council meetings held in June, was uniformly bad.

I deliberately decided not to try and stop the public debate by members of the party, including members of the parliamentary party. Stifling debate would have been futile and, indeed, unfair. What we were talking about was something that was fundamental and it was inevitable that people in the party would have strong views. Meanwhile, beyond the party proper, misgivings were mounting in Labor's industrial wing, principally represented by the ACTU. Back in March the ACTU put out its background tax position, 'Tax Reform in 1985', tying their support for indirect taxation measures to adequate compensation arrangements. As the summit date approached the ACTU was divided about the compensatory mechanisms outlined in Option C.

The willingness of the industrial movement to discount those cost of living rises directly tied to the introduction of a consumption tax was fundamental to the viability of Option C. Without union discounting, the proposed new tax promised to be extremely inflationary.

Aside from the union movement, news from the welfare lobby, particularly through the Australian Council of Social Services and the Women's Electoral Lobby (WEL), was far from encouraging. For them, as for the ACTU, the key concern was compensating disadvantaged groups who would be the hardest hit by the regressive nature of a consumption tax.

The National Taxation Summit opened in Canberra on 1st July 1985 with 160 delegates gathered in the House of Representatives' Chamber. They included State Premiers, business and industry leaders, and the representatives of other special-interest groups. I was acutely aware of the sensitivities of labour, welfare and other sectional groups about the compensation issue and in my opening address I sought to allay the fears triggered by Option C.

The Government's preferred option offered a large cut in marginal tax rates and generous compensation arrangements for low-income earners, welfare recipients and families. I was now offering an independent monitoring authority, stretching the bounds of duty in my support of our preferred option. From the outset I was prepared to let the consumption tax proposal run the gauntlet and to help to support it along the way to see if it could not be made to stand on its merits at the end of the summit. But the real test and arbiter of Option C was the summit process itself; there was no escaping the summit's relevance and the community wisdom it represented. We led the summit to the water of Option C, but the representatives of every sectional interest refused to drink.

The opposition started early and continued throughout. First up was the Business Council of Australia, the organisation prodded into existence by the last summit but now, as some were to view it, appearing like an ingrate at a party hosted, partly, in its honour. For years a consumption tax had headed corporate Australia's agenda as a necessary tax reform. What better tax for business than a tax levied on those other than itself, namely consumers?

The Government had presented business with an opening and now was their opportunity to seize the moment. To everyone's astonishment business jumped up to reject the reform they had once cherished with a fervour akin to that of Treasury. After I had completed my opening address the Managing Director of the Westpac Banking Corporation, the Business Council's President, Bob White, took to the rostrum with a curious rope-trick which left him and the Business Council tied up as an irrelevant bundle in the process of achieving tax reform. 'The Business Council does not support approach A, B or C,' White said, drawing a line right through the Government's White Paper on tax reform. 'We are not on the Government's cart,' he added, using the metaphor to destroy the vehicle.

Queensland Premier Joh Bjelke-Petersen took the metaphor further: 'You've heard a lot recently about Mr Keating's so-called tax cart,' Joh thundered. 'Well, I think that is a very appropriate phrase because he has put the cart before the horse.'

Certainly, if after Paul Keating's hard sell on Option C, the Business Council of Australia was still shying away from the Government's tax cart, then Joh's comment was not without merit. Without business support the tax was practically doomed. The other nails in Option C's coffin were not so unexpected. The State Premiers, the churches, ACOSS, WEL, and others all rounded on the new tax proposal. The ACTU, which had earlier indicated a heavily conditional preparedness to look at the tax, or at least a willingness not to rule it out, were now visibly choking on Option C.

Maybe we could live with business opposed to the new tax, sensing that the opposition was more tactical than real, but we could certainly not do so without the unions' acceptance of it or their co-operation in its implementation. To press ahead without them was to invite political carnage.

By Wednesday night, after three days of sustained attack on Option C, it was time to call a halt to the consumption tax cart before it careered out of control. The community had spoken. Australians wanted tax reform but they did not want a 12.5 per cent consumption tax. A good idea, brilliantly pursued by Paul Keating, who championed it and advocated it to the last, had now run into the wall. It was time to call it quits and get on with making tax reforms which were achievable, not pie in the sky or carts without wheels.

That night I attended a reception at the Institute of Sport. Afterwards it was agreed that I should call in at the Canberra International Hotel where Bill Kelty and Simon Crean were staying. Before seeing the ACTU leadership, I tried to contact Paul so that he could be in on the talks, but by that time he had left Parliament House. He had been meeting continuously with Crean and Kelty and knew how their thinking was developing.

Most of the negotiating room the Government may have had with the ACTU on Option C had already been removed by the Treasurer's own doing. Earlier he and I had met with Bill Kelty who had indicated support for the consumption tax if food could be exempted from it and if housing could be made revenue-neutral by Government-supported incentive schemes. Paul, however, would not wear that.

When I arrived at the hotel that night I asked Bill Kelty to restate the ACTU's position for me. Bill did not mince words. The ACTU would not accept Option C, nor would the other participants at the summit. With that, the consumption tax was dead and buried, probably never again to be revived within the counsels of the Labor Party. With the defeat of the Coalition at the 1993 poll, largely as a result of their own advocacy of a goods and services tax, it is unlikely that either of the major parties will flirt with such a tax again.

On Thursday morning, 4th July, Paul and I met the Labor Premiers (Neville Wran, NSW; John Cain, Victoria; Brian Burke, WA; and John Bannon, SA) in my office. They unanimously reiterated that they could not and would not support Option C. When the summit resumed after lunch, I formally announced the death of Option C. The ninth principle of our taxation reform objectives, broad community support, had not been satisfied.

Later, when closing the summit, I paid tribute to the indefatigable effort Paul Keating had made to lift the level of community debate about tax reform both before and during the summit. 'I want to say, personally, that in the process we have gone through from the beginning of this exercise and up to and including the summit itself, no Prime Minister could have asked for better, closer, more effective co-operation than I have enjoyed with Paul Keating. Thank you, Paul!'

He reached across and touched my arm in a moment of affection between us. At a joint press conference after the summit, Paul paid a formal tribute to me:

> No Treasurer, with the best intentions in the world, can get a reform proposal like this through a Cabinet without the support of the Prime Minister. I'm pleased to say, in the time I've been Treasurer, that support has been unqualified and I appreciate it very much. And I'd like to take this public opportunity, in front of you people who have written so much about our relationship and this issue, just to say that the support's always been there and I've always appreciated it.

He met with me that Thursday afternoon in my office and repeated in private what he had told the press. In an emotional meeting, with just the two of us present, he said that no Prime Minister could have given him greater support and a greater opportunity to press Option C than I had given him, both prior to the summit and during it.

But this was not the whole story of his reaction to the dumping of Option C. Paul Keating is a complex character with many personae, and a richly-tiered appreciation of history and of his own place in it. Publicly, and to me, he was the grateful party, thankful to his Prime Minister. But more often than not, in private to others, he played the injured party whose pride of authorship had been spiked by a Prime Minister who had abandoned his most cherished reform. In this mode he saw himself as the knight on the white charger leading the brave assault, only to be let down by weak-kneed troops who refused to press the fight. When playing out this fantasy, he relegated his Prime Minister to the minion status of fighting the Treasurer's battles. And should this minion fail to play his fantasy role, Paul was only too ready to apply the tag of 'old jelly-back'. It is difficult to gauge how far Paul, trapped in this persona, actually believed his own rhetoric, or the extent to which it was merely a political tactic to rescue his standing in circumstances which could otherwise be seen as a terrible failure.

Whether Keating was being cynical, or Machiavellian, or seriously self-deluded when denigrating me for facing up to the political realities of Option C, the simple fact is that as Prime Minister I not only had the right but the responsibility to exercise that judgment. It was his job to develop the tax, and he did his job and did it brilliantly. But it was my job to make the overall political assessment and to give leadership in the face of the clear danger signals that his zealotry prevented him from acknowledging.

In more recent times Paul has slipped from the persona of injured party, dumped and abandoned by his Prime Minister during the 1985 Tax Summit, and taken on the role of psychotherapist. When interviewed in 1991 he denied that I had betrayed him over the consumption tax proposal: 'Bob was in debilitated psychic circum-stances through 1985,'[63] – and that, in his view, is why I dropped the consumption tax.

Certainly I had other pressures on my mind at the time, but they did not prevent me from making the necessary judgment about Option C. As is often the case, Paul Keating's ability to fashion the dramatic phrase has a mesmeric effect on him. As the words dance before him he often does not see the reality shrouded by those words. On this matter his words hid the blanket opposition of the business community, the trade union movement, the churches and the whole social welfare community. Were they, too, suffering from debilitated psychic circumstances?

Paul's great attraction to grand acts of leadership where one rushes headlong into a fiery furnace made for colourful pyrotechnics but bad politics. No better demonstration of such bad politics could have been given than in the 1993 election when Opposition Leader John Hewson marched to the brink of hell with a GST (Goods and Services Tax), and jumped. Making sure he jumped was Paul Keating, pushing and prodding by exposing the evils of the very sort of tax he had so zealously championed.

With Option C out of the way, most of the Cabinet and the Caucus heaved a collective sigh of relief. The Treasurer responded in a complex manner, but, to his great credit, he drew a line under Option C and threw himself into the task of bringing before the Cabinet, as I requested, a range of alternative tax reform proposals which were essentially based on Option A.

As a result Labor brought in the most far reaching tax reforms in the history of the Commonwealth. We subsequently enacted a capital gains tax, struck at fringe benefits, cracked down on other tax shelters, dropped marginal tax rates – pulling the top rate down from 60 cents in the dollar to 49 cents – and ceased taxing dividends paid to shareholders. By dropping what was in effect a double taxation on dividends, we now had room to raise the top corporate taxation rate from 46 cents to 49 cents. After an independent review we also implemented the Option A proposal for a tax on gold.

Many of these changes would have been impossible to achieve without the Taxation Summit. The political analysts and journalists at the time wrote off the summit as a disaster and a failure. Throughout my time in politics I never ceased to be amazed at the blindness of professional analysts to the actual chemistry of politics in Australia. As with so many of their assessments and prognostications, they were simply wrong.

The summit created the necessary degree of community consensus for tax reform. All the available options for reform were prepared, set out, discussed and debated, so that the community became much more fully apprised of the gross inadequacies of the taxation structure Labor had inherited, and of the means to reform it. Further, in trying and failing on Option C, the Government's resolve to press ahead in other areas of tax reform was stiffened. Had the community not set its face against a consumption tax and closed off that avenue, then some of our colleagues may not have had quite the same amount of courage to push so hard for the imposition of taxes on capital gains and fringe benefits.

Given my time over again I would not have handled the extraordinarily complex business of tax reform in Australia any differently. Suggestions have been made that I somehow lost interest in tax reform after the Tax Summit.[64] This rewriting of history ignores the fact that after the summit I encouraged the Treasurer to press ahead with alternative approaches. I not only gave him every encouragement and personal support but ensured that all the resources of my department and of my economists were available and involved in helping to draw up and flesh out such proposals.

Part of the criticism is that I involved the entire ministry in approving the reform proposals. Factionalism through this period had run riot. To some extent I had encouraged this by refusing to stymie debate. But with the summit over it was time to close ranks and pull together. To present a unified face, for the good of the Government and, in a sense, for the good of the Treasurer, it was necessary to invite all strands of the party into the Government's internal counsels. By involving the party, by involving the ministry in tax reform, we were able to assess exactly the level of support for each proposal and to press ahead with reform with maximum party unity. Here again the facts speak for themselves. After the Tax Summit factionalism within the party settled down and Labor's electoral stocks immediately lifted.

There is one simple and indisputable fact in all of this and it is, arguably, the single most important fact in the history of Australian politics in the last two decades of this century. If I had not dumped Option C in 1985 Labor would have lost the 1987 election. Labor would not have been continuously in power for thirteen years by 1996, and there would have been no prime ministerial mantle for Paul Keating to seize in 1991.

TWENTY

Shortly after Cabinet approved our massive tax reforms, I went to Bathurst to address the inaugural 'Light on the Hill' dinner in honour of former Labor Prime Minister, Ben Chifley. In his famous speech to fifteen hundred delegates at the Annual Conference of the New South Wales branch of the Australian Labor Party, on 12th June 1949, Chifley had said, 'I try to think of the labour movement, not as putting an extra sixpence in somebody's pocket, or making somebody Prime Minister or Premier, but as a movement bringing something better to the people, better standards of living, greater happiness to the mass of the people.'

I related our program of domestic reform, including the tax changes, to Chifley's vision and then emphasised the universality of Labor's mandate as Chifley put it in the crucial sentence of his famous speech: 'We have a great objective – the light on the hill – which we aim to reach by working for the betterment of mankind, not only here, but *anywhere* we may give a helping hand.'

From the beginning of my prime ministership I used the Commonwealth Heads of Government Meetings (CHOGM) as an instrument to give effect to Chifley's philosophy of Labor's universal mandate.

In our early days it was the fashion in some quarters to regard the Commonwealth as passé. I had a different view, based not on sentiment but on a stringent assessment of the evidence.

It was the Commonwealth, for example, which had ensured the transition of the rogue, white-minority-ruled Rhodesia into the black-majority-ruled Zimbabwe, and in a more peaceful fashion than would otherwise have been possible.

That was a significant achievement and one in which my predecessor, Malcolm Fraser, played an important role. At the opening of the 1979 CHOGM in Lusaka which effected this transition Fraser had said, 'All oppression is repugnant, but there is an obscenity about oppression based on no more than the colour of a person's skin.' Over the ensuing days Fraser was instrumental, with others, in getting the newly elected British Prime Minister, Margaret Thatcher, to sign the CHOGM communiqué on Zimbabwe on 5th August. The communiqué confirmed that the heads of government 'were wholly committed to genuine black majority rule for the people of Zimbabwe', and set out the processes for achieving that result. Margaret left Lusaka furious with Fraser after he leaked the substance of the communiqué to the media ahead of its formal signing. It was the beginning of a deep and continuing bitterness on her part. In politics nothing gives rise to more calculated venom than when the Conservatives or the Left fall out among themselves.

In any event the Zimbabwe initiative made it clear to me that the Commonwealth was far more than the mere talk-shop depicted by sceptics. Used properly it could be an instrument for achieving peaceable transformation in areas of dangerous conflict – of giving a glimpse of 'the light on the hill' to the oppressed in many parts of the world.

It was a unique body embracing a cross-section of the world's independent states. Relatively rich countries like Canada, the United Kingdom and Australia were members. The poorest of the poor countries, like Bangladesh, were represented. There were black, white, European, Asian, African and Caribbean members, nations at every stage of the spectrum of economic development. There were countries ranging in size from the eight hundred million of India to the micro-states of the Pacific and Indian Oceans.

Their politics ranged from the conservatism of Margaret Thatcher to those who had been Marxist bedfellows. Yet in a mysterious way, the bonds forged by a common heritage of British imperialism had survived the act of decolonisation; they remained vibrant thanks to a Commonwealth Secretariat, programs of training and assistance to those in greatest need, and the biennial Commonwealth Heads of Government Meetings.

My faith in the Commonwealth was repaid throughout the period of my prime ministership. During this time CHOGM became the powerful, leading force in mobilising world opinion against apartheid and, through the application of sanctions, in bringing to an end that evil system.

In October 1985, not long after the Cabinet decided on the radical tax reforms, I attended my second CHOGM meeting, at Nassau in the Bahamas. The dominant issue was South Africa, and I had worked through my basic position with both the Foreign Minister, Bill Hayden, and the Cabinet. The Commonwealth had to debate seriously the application of sanctions to South Africa. Yet sanctions or any other measures were, in my judgment, but a means to an end – the creation of a free and democratic South Africa from which discrimination based on colour had been eliminated.

Our preference was for dialogue not sanctions. If the peaceful estab-lishment of a non-racial, democratic and representative government in South Africa could be brought about without sanctions then so much the better; as Bill Hayden eloquently put it: 'We want to bring them to their senses, not to their knees.'

This logic underpinned my personal initiative for establishing the Eminent Persons Group (EPG) to try to achieve negotiation and peaceful reform in South Africa. The strategy, refined and elaborated at Nassau, involved the definition of clear benchmarks against which to judge the South African Government's willingness or otherwise to initiate change. A graduated approach was envisaged where, through a first and second set of sanctions, and then further measures if these failed, increasing pressure would be applied to the minority régime.

Having discussed my approach with colleagues, and equipped with the unanimous mandate of both Cabinet and party, I arrived at the Bahamas seeking to find a peaceful means of abolishing the apartheid system in South Africa. In Nassau I was one of five heads of government invited to speak at the opening ceremony on Wednesday afternoon, 16th October 1985. My staff had given me a draft on Tuesday but I did not think it captured the occasion, so I sat up quite late that night and wrote out a new speech. In it I tried to unlock the secret of the Commonwealth's strength. The essence of that strength was in understanding the limits of power, which in turn was crucial for the work of the conference in tackling the question of South Africa. The régime of that country had to be made to understand the truth that whatever coercive apparatus it assembled, apartheid would not, in the end, survive. If the régime could not be persuaded by the moral argument then it would have to face the impact of harsher international sanctions.

The audience reaction showing that the speech had hit the mark was confirmed by Sir Shridath (Sonny) Ramphal, then Secretary-General of the Commonwealth, who told me that it was, to his mind, one of the best speeches delivered at a CHOGM.[65] It set the framework for an inevitably detailed and tortuous debate, which was first joined at the full plenary session of CHOGM with all the officials present.

But the hard, grinding work of attempting to shape an actual agreement had to await the weekend retreat. There is a CHOGM tradition, whereby the leaders go off to a secluded venue accompanied only by their spouses and one staff member each. The Bahamas retreat was some distance away from Nassau at Lyford Cay, a millionaire's playground country club set in a beautiful golf course. I had not touched a putter since my thirties but Kenneth Kaunda, President of Zambia, who had the benefit of his own private course, inveigled me to play. His victory was comprehensive. This stimulated me to take up a game that was to give me much pleasure and considerable frustration – the fate of all golfers. I played frequently at sun-up at the magnificent Royal Canberra course, which was just minutes from the Lodge, walking briskly around 18 holes in two and a half hours. By the time I left office my handicap was down to 16. Golf became a useful part of my personal diplomacy – for example, George Shultz and I tossed around many subjects of importance as we competed fiercely against each other on courses in Australia and the USA. I played with President Bush and Prime Ministers Harry Lee of Singapore and his successor, Goh Chok Tong. With another Asian Prime Minister the reserve he exhibited in my office gave way to a genial rapport once we got the clubs in our hands.

On Saturday afternoon at Lyford Cay the forty-nine Commonwealth heads met without officials. The meeting followed a plenary session that morning where heated argument had erupted over Margaret Thatcher's lone opposition to sanctions. Debate was at times bitter and the atmosphere spilled over into the afternoon. Margaret was implacable as she fought back against attacks by a number of the speakers. She had a terribly rough time and although I repudiated her stance, I sympathised with her for the enormous physical and emotional strain she was under.

The afternoon session delegated to a committee of seven (Prime Minister Lyndon Pindling of the Bahamas, Margaret Thatcher, Rajiv Gandhi, Brian Mulroney and myself, with Presidents Robert Mugabe of Zimbabwe and Kenneth Kaunda of Zambia) the Herculean task of trying to reach some common ground on the sanctions issue. The seven of us met that evening, with Robert and Kenneth preferring, literally, to sit on the sidelines. We were to witness a vintage Thatcher performance, Margaret at her best and worst.

Margaret Thatcher was the hardest working head of government I ever met. Her application was prodigious and she was always extraordinarily well briefed for every meeting. Whatever the subject, she could press her sometimes jarring and belligerent viewpoints with great authority, and for that I deeply respected her. But while she had first-class application, she did not always display a first-class mind. In argument she often seemed to be playing catch-up. She sought to buy time while exchanging views so that she could more easily absorb contrary positions and give herself room to marshal her thoughts and responses.

In my experience she had two techniques for stalling debate. First, she was an inveterate interrupter. I never dealt with a leader who interrupted other speakers so often. It was a cause for irritation among many of those with whom she dealt. Her other technique for slowing the pace of discussion was what I called her delay-by-parenthesis approach. If a leader was unwise enough to attach a parenthetical observation to the main thrust of his argument, Margaret was away. She would grab hold of the parenthesis like a terrier with a bone, tearing into it and worrying it to a degree that often made her interlocutor and the rest of us wild with impatience.

A bizarre example of this technique surfaced in the Lyford Cay committee meeting. We were discussing the Eminent Persons Group and the stage-by-stage concept of sanctions. Brian Mulroney was developing his main argument in support of Rajiv's and my attempt to persuade Margaret to come in behind the idea. Brian was unwise enough to refer to an aside she had made during the afternoon's discussions: 'Margaret, when you said that, I thought that the fat was really in the fire.'

At that her eyes blazed and she pulled herself erect in the chair. 'What do you mean the fat was really in the fire? Just what do you mean? What fat? What fire?' she asked imperiously. 'Brian, I was brought up to mean what I say, and to say what I mean. What do you mean, *the fat was really in the fire*?'

'My God!' I thought. I couldn't refrain from jumping in: 'Margaret! For Christ's sake! Forget the bloody fat and the bloody fire, it's got nothing to do with anything. Just listen to what Brian's saying, will you.' Margaret looked at me in some astonishment but, to her great credit, she copped it. Then I turned to my friend Mulroney and said: 'Brian, get on with it, and leave the fat out of the fire.'

Margaret could also, I thought, be a little less than straightforward at times. There was one occasion when she seemed to me to almost deliberately misunderstand a proposition. One of the proposed sanctions included the proposition that governments would agree not to enter into contracts with majority-owned South African companies. In our private discussion Margaret said she couldn't agree to that because in South Africa there were so many companies with whom Britain had to deal. 'Margaret, we're not talking about in South Africa, we're talking about in our countries. The Australian Government won't have a contract with a majority-owned South African company, you there in the United Kingdom shouldn't deal with such a majority-owned company,' I explained to her. 'Oh, I see,' she replied.

But the very next day she did not see and in our discussion she went off on the same thing again. I thought she was being a little slippery. I do not intend these comments to disguise the fact that I have a certain

admiration for Margaret Thatcher. There is so much of her philosophical approach to domestic and international politics that I cannot
share, but she is a formidable and remarkable person – applied,
committed, dogged, dogmatic, determined and certainly courageous.

As for the Bahamas CHOGM, Brian, Rajiv and I managed to get the
fat out of the fire and bend Margaret to signing her name to the
Nassau communiqué, which embraced the Australian initiative. The
Accord on Southern Africa, contained in the communiqué, authorised
the formation of 'a small group of eminent Commonwealth persons to
encourage ... political dialogue' directed at achieving a non-racial
representative government in South Africa.

I'll deal with the Nassau Accord and the fate of the Eminent Persons
Group in greater detail but, since I've offered a brief sketch of
Margaret Thatcher, let me add an appreciation, too, of Brian
Mulroney and the late Rajiv Gandhi, two Commonwealth leaders with
whom I formed very close bonds.

In one way and another, sometimes inadvertently, Brian Mulroney,
the Conservative Party Prime Minister of Canada from 1985 to 1993,
has been extremely kind to the Australian Labor Party and certainly to
me. My relationship with him was cemented by a flying visit to Canada
in March 1985 when I delivered the keynote speech at Canada's
National Economic Conference. Brian took the idea from the 1983
summit and so I arrived in Canada to a fully primed and receptive audience. Australia, after all, had a good story to tell.

Interestingly, the ideas I put forward at the Canadian summit were
not too dissimilar from what Brian and I were arguing for at the
Bahamas CHOGM. Enlightened self-interest was the central concept.
In the case of both the Australian and the Canadian summits, the goal
was to demonstrate that the self-interest of each group – government,
capital, labour, and welfare – was best served by 'co-operation to create
the most favourable conditions for high levels of real economic

growth'. At CHOGM we were thrashing out a strategy aimed at bringing the South African régime to its senses by waking it to its own self-interest and that of all the citizens of South Africa.

Brian and I were ostensibly on opposite sides of the political fence but perhaps our shared background in labour law and industrial relations brought us closer together than one would at first have thought likely. Although on the conservative side of Canadian politics, Brian was a liberal-minded man. He was not an industrial antagonist and he was utterly committed to the concept of consensus and co-operation. Within the Commonwealth he was my strongest ally in the fight against apartheid and, as with the Bahamas CHOGM, he was always shoulder to shoulder with me in the initiatives I undertook.

He was also a pragmatist. He did not pretend to intellectualise the political stands he took, but his instincts were unerringly correct. When it came to fundamental issues of human rights and what was the best way of getting a society to co-operate, Brian had an innate sense of the right course of action. Personally he was warm and loyal, and we got on famously. His friendship, once won, was real and permanent. At the end of 1991 when the pressures on my leadership were mounting and a second challenge seemed imminent, he rang me and then wrote with an invitation to visit Canada and address the Canadian Parliament. He thought that perhaps such an address could be helpful to me in meeting the challenge ahead. His gesture reflected the depth of the friendship that we had built up over the years and, although I declined the invitation, I appreciated it enormously.

Brian's departure from the leadership was a substantial, albeit unintentional, gift to the Australian Labor Party. He announced his intended resignation from the Canadian prime ministership on 25th February 1993 in the midst of a hard-fought election campaign in Australia. Paul Keating, contesting his first election as Prime Minister, seized on Mulroney's announcement, which enabled him to pin Brian's misfortune on the goods and services tax he had introduced in Canada in 1989. Paul Keating declared: 'The Canadians have given Australians a valuable lesson at a key time in our economic history. What the Canadians are saying is "don't do it, don't make our mistake".' Whatever the reality behind Paul's gloss, Brian's announcement undoubtedly gave the ALP a mighty boost at the right psychological moment.

If Brian and I made something of an odd couple, coming as we did from different sides of the political fence, Rajiv Gandhi and I were an odd couple for a different reason. Rajiv's mother, Indira Gandhi, chaired the first CHOGM meeting I attended, in November 1983, and it was marked by a number of very bitter exchanges between Mrs Gandhi and me. I faulted her consistency in being prepared to criticise some governments for human rights abuses but not others – Israel, but not the Soviet Union. It seemed to me that ideology drove her judgment, not conscience.

On 31st October 1984 the world was horrified by the news of Mrs Gandhi's assassination. This was a double tragedy for the Gandhi family, as her youngest son, Sanjay, had died in an air accident in June 1980. Rajiv was reluctantly pressed into service as India's Prime Minister and it was Rajiv who represented his country at this next CHOGM conference. As with the Kennedys of Massachusetts, the blood of the Gandhis was so mixed into the soil of their country that there was a sense in which the Gandhis and India were mystically intertwined. Rajiv, too, would die in the service of his nation.

Before the 1985 CHOGM Australian officials worried that there would be some residual negative reaction on Rajiv's part arising from the antagonism between his mother and me, but from the beginning our relationship was one of exceptional warmth.

Duty rather than ambition had impelled him into the prime ministership and so he came to the job untrained for high office in politics.

He was, however, a man of such geniality and warmth he immediately endeared himself to CHOGM leaders across the whole spectrum of the organisation's membership.

Rajiv was an important force in the Commonwealth on the South African issue. There was no doubting his passion and conviction; apartheid deeply offended his sense of justice. But his opposition to apartheid was more than a reflection of his non-whiteness. He brought to CHOGM meetings a compassion, understanding and sincerity that made his voice a very effective supplement to the natural indignation of the black African members of the Commonwealth when they spoke upon the subject.

I was honoured and privileged to win Rajiv's friendship during the Bahamas CHOGM. He came to Australia at my invitation in October 1986 and I visited India in February 1989 at his. Hazel and I had dinner with Rajiv and Sonia at their modest home on our last night in New Delhi before returning to Australia. That night was unforgettable in itself, but it became more so in retrospect. At dinner Rajiv contemplated death with a compelling serenity. His life was permanently threatened and he wore a bullet-proof jacket at all times, or at least he was supposed to. 'I'm very naughty, Bob,' he said, 'it is so uncomfortable, sometimes I refuse to wear it. My security chaps get awfully cross with me.' The jacket was the subject of laughter and a sort of macabre mirth over dinner. Although he was entirely fatalistic about his own life, Rajiv worried for his family, particularly the children. He was concerned to secure them a safe education. They could not go with confidence to a university in India or, he reasoned, to one in America. He thought the safest place for them would probably be Moscow, but he had no wish to send them there.

In Australia I had shaped my political career on links to ordinary Australians and my ability to mingle freely with them. My career and fame certainly had carried costs for my family, but fear for the physical safety of my children was not a normal part of our existence. Nor did I feel that I was likely to be a victim of violence. Yet here I was talking with a dear friend who I am sure believed he would die a violent death. As Rajiv and Sonia discussed their children's limited options, Hazel and I were deeply moved. I was so touched by the anguish of the Gandhis that I said, 'Well, what about Australia? Why don't you think about sending your children to be educated in our country?'

I knew my offer would raise some security problems for us and some expense, but under the circumstances this was an offer I felt Australia should make. Rajiv was the leader of an important country, the second most populous in the world. But more relevant than that was his innate goodness and the terrible spectre he faced. He resolved to think about my offer and to stay in touch on the subject, but I heard nothing more from him. On 12th May 1991 he was assassinated by a bomb blast against which his bullet-proof vest was useless.

When Mrs Gandhi was struck down I was appalled. I felt a sense of tragedy for Indira, for her family and for her country. I knew her and respected many of her achievements, but I could not claim to have lost a friend. When Rajiv was killed, that prophetic evening we had spent with him and Sonia in New Delhi came flooding back and I felt an acute sense of personal loss.

But there were happier times in 1985 in Nassau. The Gandhi–Mulroney–Hawke triumvirate was then in full sway. Margaret was at first intractable but, as a trio, we talked her around. Eventually, she signed the communiqué which reflected the Australian initiative of an Eminent Persons Group and a stage by stage application of sanctions – with the emphasis on dialogue rather than sanctions.

From there events moved quickly. The EPG was co-chaired by my predecessor, Malcolm Fraser, whom I nominated for the position, and General Olusegun Obasanjo of Nigeria. Fraser threw himself enthusiastically into the work of the EPG. The group travelled extensively in

South Africa and battled to establish the necessary pre-conditions for dialogue between the South African Government and opponents of the apartheid régime, pre-eminently the African National Congress (ANC). But despite their best efforts the EPG hit a brick wall with the South African Government, which remained wedded to race classification and group rights, not individual rights, and to the retention of the so-called independent homelands. A political system based on 'one person, one vote' in a unitary system was flatly ruled out.

By the time the heads of government of Australia, the Bahamas, Britain, Canada, India, Zambia and Zimbabwe (the Lyford Cay committee) met in London in August 1986 to receive and review the EPG's report, not one of the specified benchmarks in the Nassau Accord had been reached by the South African Government. Margaret, on home ground, was more stubborn and intractable than in the Bahamas. Her iciness at the Marlborough House meeting towards Mulroney, and Fraser in particular, descended into a rude hostility. The only redeeming aspect of the British participation was the surreptitious exchange of notes and a cartoon lampooning his Prime Minister between me and Margaret's Foreign Minister, Geoffrey Howe. Geoffrey, for whom I developed considerable affection, was in a hopeless position; he was appalled by Margaret's views and behaviour, but had to maintain the appearance of support.

I had no doubt what we should do, indeed what we were required to do under the mandate given to us by the 1985 CHOGM communiqué. Rajiv and Brian endorsed my view, as did the other three. In our London communiqué we registered our concern and regret at Britain's unwillingness to adopt fully the eight measures comprising the second tranche in the Nassau Accord; we then confirmed the Commonwealth's intention to proceed with those measures: a ban on air links with South Africa; a ban on new investment or re-investment of profits earned in South Africa; a ban on the import of agricultural products;

the termination of double taxation agreements with South Africa; the termination of all government assistance to, investment in, and trade with South Africa; a ban on all government procurement in South Africa; a ban on government contracts with majority-owned South African companies; and a ban on the promotion of tourism to South Africa.

We also decided on three additional measures which were included in the communiqué: a ban on all new bank loans to South Africa; a ban on the import of uranium, coal, iron and steel from South Africa; and the withdrawal of all consular facilities in South Africa except for our own nationals and the nationals of those countries to whom we rendered consular services.

I reported to the Parliament on my return to Australia:[66]

> Specific and meaningful action has not been taken to dismantle apartheid. A new State of Emergency has been introduced. Nelson Mandela and other detainees are still in jail. Political freedom does not exist and the bans on the African National Congress and other political parties have not been lifted. No process of dialogue for non-racial and representative government is underway ... I wanted us if possible to be united, but above all I wanted us to be credible and effective. Better that those of us ready to act should do so than that we should settle for some transparently ineffectual compromise. We can thank the willingness of the six to adopt strong measures for the fact that the Commonwealth and its international leadership role on Southern African issues have been preserved.

The willingness to move more swiftly than anticipated at Nassau mirrored an emerging international consensus. Other crucial countries and institutions took a lead from the Commonwealth's initiatives. On

15th August 1986 the United States Senate voted eighty-four to fourteen in favour of strong measures against South Africa. The European Community was also considering sanctions, and Japan, too, had shown some preparedness to join the move towards tougher measures.

By the time of the Vancouver meeting in October 1987 it was clear that sanctions were biting deeply into both the economy and, to some extent, the conscience of South Africa.

Meanwhile, in May and September of 1987 Colonel Rabuka of Fiji had staged coups to block Fijians of Indian descent forming the government of that country. These events were obviously going to be an important issue at the Vancouver CHOGM. It was a crisis which produced an amusing excess of enthusiasm from two of my closest colleagues, Kim Beazley, the Minister for Defence, and Gareth Evans, acting as Foreign Minister in the absence overseas of Bill Hayden. To my amazement, they suggested that we should consider using a RAN helicopter to fly in, pluck the deposed Prime Minister, Timoci Bavadra, from the New Zealand High Commission and have him whisked away to safety in Western Fiji. I thought they had been watching too many Rambo movies but said I was a reasonable man and would call in the Chief of the General Staff. When General Gration arrived I outlined their scheme: the look on his face said it all. I didn't hear any more about helicopters from the Two Rambos but we often laughed later when I ribbed them about their vivid imaginations.

I had made it clear beforehand that CHOGM was duty-bound to deal with the Fiji situation decisively and not act as though nothing had happened (which was the inclination of some participants) and I said I believed the Queen would have the same view. The story by political commentator, Michelle Grattan, led to blazing headlines in the *Age*: 'Royal Gaffe by Hawke over Fiji'.

I ignored Grattan's stupidity and went to my scheduled meeting with Her Majesty. Before speaking with the Queen I had talked to her private secretary, Sir William Hezeltine, one of my contemporaries at the University of Western Australia, and said that it was obvious that the Queen's representative, the Governor-General of Fiji, Sir Peanaia Ganilau, should be contacted and told that the events in Fiji constituted a break with the Commonwealth. I said the Queen could not be put in a position where the organisation of which she was head was pretending that this breach had not happened.

Hezeltine agreed, told the Queen, then asked me to repeat my analysis to her. I did so and she expressed her agreement. She immediately made arrangements for the Governor-General to be informed accordingly; CHOGM embraced my position in its decision and communiqué. At a subsequent press conference I dealt with Grattan, whose attitude to me from then on was one of barely disguised hostility.

On 15th October of that year South Africa's Finance Minister, Barend du Plessis, publicly identified the adverse effect of sanctions at the ruling National Party's Natal congress. He spoke of the accumulated billions of dollars worth of non-productive assets, such as oil, which lay stockpiled because of sanctions. He painted a picture of burgeoning infrastructure development if only South Africa could cash in on its reserves of oil and other strategic commodities.

The Finance Minister's speech destroyed at a blow the first leg of the ambivalent argument advanced by Margaret Thatcher and other opponents of the sanctions – that they wouldn't work, but if they did, it would be the blacks who would suffer most.

South Africa itself held the key to its imprisoned economy; it had only to unlock apartheid and open the political process to all South Africans for the sanctions to be removed. The very purpose of sanctions was precisely to bring home to the South African Government that its repressive defence of the status quo carried its own costs and that a change of course would bring benefits. The London communiqué was crystal clear on the point – if Pretoria pursued dialogue and met the benchmarks we had established, then the Commonwealth stood ready to rescind sanctions.

If anything conditions had worsened in South Africa since London. At the Vancouver CHOGM we noted the increased violence and instability in South Africa and the heightened intransigence of the Pretoria régime. Against this background I conceived an initiative which, when accepted and implemented, finally broke apartheid.

Although current sanctions were hurting South Africa, the system still lingered. But, as I told the forty-four other Commonwealth leaders gathered in Vancouver for CHOGM, in the end Pretoria could find ways to evade the full impact of many of the sanctions. I realised, however, that if the international investment community stopped financing the South African régime, it would surely crumble.

From Vancouver I rang Jim Wolfensohn in New York. Jim is an expatriate Australian investment banker of international repute and a man of outstanding quality. I outlined my thinking to him, he accepted its logic and within hours was on a plane to Vancouver to discuss the concept in detail with us. I arranged for him to meet with Rajiv Gandhi, Kenneth Kaunda, Robert Mugabe, and me together with Sonny Ramphal and Chief Anyaoku from the Commonwealth Secretariat. My colleagues were totally enthusiastic about my strategy and Jim's endorsement of its possibilities. Fortified by these talks, I pressed the proposal to mobilise the international investment community to stop providing funds to South Africa. As a result of this initiative an expert study group was established to analyse the sources of South Africa's international investment support. Due largely to the work of that committee and the pressure generated out of it, the sources of investment to South Africa increasingly dried up; the régime and the business community in that country had to face more squarely than ever before the complete untenability of persisting with policies so unacceptable to the international community.[67]

Again Britain was very much the odd country out and Margaret Thatcher and I were once more scrapping over the subject of sanctions when CHOGM met in Kuala Lumpur in October 1989. This was the fortieth anniversary meeting of the modern day Commonwealth and the Kuala Lumpur statement on South Africa showed just how much the organisation had matured. While Britain continued to argue against sanctions, the rest of us agreed to maintain existing sanctions and to tighten financial sanctions further.

The statement called on all relevant banks and financial institutions to impose tougher conditions on day-to-day trade financing, specifically through reducing the maximum credit terms to 90 days. The Commonwealth Heads of Government also pressed ahead with the establishment of an independent agency to review and report on South Africa's international financial links. In addition we agreed to ask the International Monetary Fund (IMF) and other appropriate institutions to examine how international funding and resources might be channelled to South Africa once there was evidence in that country of clear and irreversible change.

Rather than representing a retreat from sanctions, the approach to the IMF underlined the purpose of sanctions – to bring South Africa to its senses. The assistance package, conditional on a palpable change in South Africa, went to the heart of the Commonwealth's desire to see a peaceful end to apartheid.

In Kuala Lumpur, Britain had gone from ruling the waves to waiving the rules. During the conference retreat, held at Langkawi Island, we sent the officials off to provide us with a draft on South Africa to include in the CHOGM communiqué. I asked Foreign Minister Gareth Evans to be as accommodating as he could to Britain's concerns without sacrificing any point of principle. When we met alone as heads of government to consider the draft I was pleasantly surprised when Margaret said she was prepared to accept it. Robert

Mugabe followed her, also indicating his delight, but then said there was just one small point he would like to see amended. Margaret exploded and said that if there were to be any changes at all the whole deal was off. I looked daggers at Robert, as did Dr Mahathir from the Chair. He got the message and left well alone. The draft was endorsed with acclamation.

I took Margaret aside and thanked her sincerely for her agreement to the document which we were now merely to confirm in plenary session in Kuala Lumpur. She was very gracious and said that while it did not represent all she would have liked, she was pleased that we had been able to get an agreed outcome.

But by the time I got back to Kuala Lumpur all hell had broken loose. Margaret had reneged. The press had been informed that she was disassociating herself from the Langkawi Accord. It was decided that we should call a press conference, with me as spokesperson, flanked by Rajiv, Kenneth Kaunda and Robert Mugabe. I revealed Margaret's duplicity, leaving no-one in any doubt as to the enormity of her action.

Perhaps the best measure of the depth of feeling among Commonwealth leaders was the reaction of Singapore's Lee Kuan Yew. Although, of course, strongly opposed to apartheid and supportive of the decisions on sanctions, Harry was nevertheless always extremely cautious, and polite, in his comments about Margaret. On this occasion he was furious, and precise in his condemnation to me of what she had done.

By late 1989 the sanctions were biting still deeper into South Africa's pocket and conscience. The wrong-headedness of Margaret Thatcher's opposition to sanctions was being exposed by a discernible mood change in Pretoria. The abhorrent apartheid system remained, but President F. W. de Klerk, who had taken over from P. W. Botha in February 1989 and was elected in his own right in September on a reformist platform, was beginning to talk reform, however vaguely. He had recently released eight prominent political leaders from prison. However the most famous of the detainees, ANC leader Nelson Mandela, gaoled since 1963, was still a incarcerated.

But not for long. The wall was breached and the possibility of a new South Africa was beginning to emerge. The great advance came on 2nd February 1990 with President de Klerk's historic speech that saw the freeing of Nelson Mandela, the legitimation of the ANC, and the preparedness of the Government to negotiate. A year later, on 1st February 1991, de Klerk announced the death of apartheid in South Africa and also unveiled a 'manifesto for a new South Africa'.

By the time CHOGM members assembled again in October 1991 in Zimbabwe, the processes of negotiation were well and truly underway, the very result the Commonwealth had been pursuing. Australia's lead role in bringing South Africa to its senses through sanctions took on a very special meaning when Nelson Mandela, freed from prison after twenty-seven years, visited Australia in October 1990. I was always convinced that our strategy would bear fruit, yet I never quite conceived of the day I would be able to welcome in my parliamentary office this great symbol of white South Africa's oppression of black Africans. Nelson Mandela is a remarkable man, one of the most remarkable leaders I met during my prime ministership. There is a charisma and a greatness about him, a beautiful mixture of gentleness and compassion, but also an unmistakable toughness. Mandela radiated physical energy; it came as no surprise to learn that he had been, in his youth, a boxer of some note. He obviously kept himself in good condition and moved with an easy grace that carried an air of confident authority. He gave the impression of enjoying, even relishing, the role of leadership; not as a form of personal aggrandisement but because he knew that he now had the instrument and the circumstances for achieving his life's ambition for his people. His physical presence was enhanced by an obvious strength of moral character. I knew immediately that I was in the presence of a great human being.

Nelson Mandela's generosity of spirit was quickly evident as we settled down in my office. He said, 'I want you to know, Bob, that I am here today, at this time, because of you.' He then thanked me for my leadership and initiatives in CHOGM which, he said, had accelerated his release and the collapse of apartheid.

I was deeply moved, both for myself and my country; we were entitled to feel great pride in these more than generous words from this great man. I was encouraged to move straight into the subject I most wanted to discuss with him: the challenges of post-apartheid South Africa. But first I asked him about President de Klerk and here, again, his generosity shone through. I asked, 'Do you believe in de Klerk's integrity?'

'Yes I do,' he answered. 'I believe he is an honest man and he is committed to change.' He indicated, however, that there were other forces in South Africa with a quite different view and so it was important that the ANC adopt a positive and constructive approach to sustain de Klerk. If not, these other conservative forces could prevail.

Mandela realised de Klerk had been dragged to the conference table by the force of world opinion and sanctions. But he also believed that de Klerk, as a matter of intellectual conviction, had come to the view that apartheid was wrong and had to be dismantled.

Mandela's years of prison, rather than crushing his spirit, had obviously enlarged him. He had used the time to think and to plan for the future. It was his vision for the future, not hatred of his gaolers, which radiated from him. He hated the system of apartheid but he was without hatred for individuals. From this attitude sprang his ability to enter into sensible negotiation with the South African régime and his generous comments about de Klerk. Here was a man who had suffered beyond measure at the hands of the apartheid régime, but such was his greatness that he knew his responsibility was not to live in hate but to respond positively in hope and constructive action. Mandela, more than any other political leader I've met, embodies the ideal of the brotherhood of man.

I said to him that if you look at the great continent of Africa, you can only come to the conclusion that it is the tragic continent. If you look at what happened in the postwar period with the ending of colonialism and the granting of political freedom, the enormous tragedy was that with this freedom there emerged economic anarchy, the abuses of nepotism, greed, tribalism, and the application of counterproductive economic doctrines. A continent that could be a net exporter of food had, in fact, become a continent where five million people die each year from malnutrition and starvation. The newly independent countries of Africa – and those providing assistance to them – too often got their priorities tragically wrong.

I continued, saying that it would be absolutely essential that those mistakes not be repeated when democracy came to South Africa. The new Government must take the people into its confidence and tell them, honestly and straightforwardly, that while a large hurdle had been cleared, enormous hurdles still remained to be overcome before real freedom, economic freedom and the satisfaction of the people's material aspirations, could be achieved.

It was critically important, in my assessment, that those in South Africa, the whites with capital, with the experience and the know-how, be made to feel welcome, to understand that they were part of the new South Africa. It would be a tragedy if political freedom arrived but there was such an attitude of hostility to these people that they left or were less than full participants with blacks in sharing the economic challenges and the opportunities facing the country. Inevitably, in those circumstances, South Africa would be the poorer. The capacity to meet these legitimate aspirations of the black people would be diminished, and all that we would be seeing again would be a replay of the disaster of most of the rest of Africa. I expressed the hope to Nelson Mandela that this would be his view too; that when the political changes were made there would be a total commitment to maximising economic growth with the co-operation and involvement of the whites.

In a detailed response he said he was absolutely committed to that view and his organisation would be committed to it also. We moved from our one-on-one meeting in the Prime Minister's office into the Cabinet room where my ministers and his people were gathered. I wanted to raise this subject again so that I could see the response of Mandela's entourage. He spoke with the same fervour, repeating the views he had put to me privately. But it was instructive to watch his party. There were those who clearly agreed with what he was saying but others among his large group seemed sceptical, suggesting, at least, a difference of emphasis.

Mandela's boldness increased his stature in my eyes. It reflected his courage in being willing to speak out, so unequivocally, in front of those of his companions who disagreed with him.

It was immensely reassuring to know that this man would be leading the ANC through what were going to be extremely difficult negotiations. Mandela understood that while black South Africa was engaged in leaping over that first enormous hurdle of moving to political democracy, that was but the beginning. The next task, in this highly competitive world, was to shape a political and economic administration and philosophy capable of meeting the needs of his people.

For me, the challenge at all times when we were conducting the fight against apartheid, in the Commonwealth and elsewhere, was to kindle the knowledge that getting rid of apartheid was but the first step. The bigger challenges were ahead. It was heartening in listening to Nelson Mandela to know that in this great and critically important leader we had a kindred spirit.

I had the privilege of visiting South Africa in February 1994 at the invitation of the United Cricket Board of South Africa to be guest of honour and speaker at a banquet to welcome the first Australian cricket side to tour that country since the lifting of sanctions. I was deeply moved when at a large gathering of businessmen who met with me, one of them said, 'Mr Hawke, we used to hate you. But you were right. The tragedy is that we didn't recognise that sooner.'

The important thing is that change has come and it has now come with much goodwill. In de Klerk's case, what was first a conviction of the mind has become, I believe, a conviction of the heart as well.

One of the most satisfying twenty-four hours of my life involved meeting with Nelson Mandela on 9th May 1994 on the eve of his inauguration as President, and then, the next day, being part of a moment of destiny as this enlightened hero assumed the leadership of the new South Africa.

TWENTY-ONE

If the world leaders I met did not always become 'kindred spirits', my capacity to establish warm relations quickly with most of them was a matter of comment by Foreign Affairs professionals. When we travelled I was able, in nearly all cases, to strike up a rapport and friendship. This sprang largely from my direct 'let's get on with it' style.

Trips abroad were often very pleasurable for those in the entourage with time to spare, but for me the work schedule rarely allowed this luxury. Our trips were usually flying visits packed with high-level official engagements. In such circumstances there was little time for idling with diplomatic niceties over cups of tea. This involved no disrespect, but the reverse: a desire not to waste the time of other busy people. My style was to dispense with ceremony and go straight to the real matters on the agenda. I found that this 'going to work fast' approach was appreciated.

As the Prime Minister dealing with foreign affairs, it helped, too, that I made sure I was always thoroughly on top of the relevant details and concepts; my capacity for devouring and assimilating massive briefs had been developed through long years of advocacy with the

ACTU. I could combine rapport with a detailed knowledge of the issues to be covered in every meeting. For me, each overseas journey I made, each visit to Australia by a foreign leader to whom I devoted time, was part of the pursuit of the broad foreign policy objectives we had set down from the first days of government.

As I pursued this strategy and Australia's competence and integrity in the international arena were recognised, I was sometimes used as a conduit by leaders of the world powers and in countries in regions where international stability was potentially endangered. Labor came to power in 1983 when the Soviet Union was accurately characterised by Reagan as the 'evil empire'; when I left office in December 1991 it had disappeared. Radical transformation, or at least its beginnings, had also occurred elsewhere: in South Africa, in China, in Indo-China, in Korea and in the Middle East.

We had played the major role in South Africa. In other instances of momentous change it was my privilege to have been not just an eye-witness but to have had, at times, a part in these processes which dramatically transformed the course of history. Developments in China and the Soviet Union were pivotal to the changes which swept the world in the 1980s.

In a very real sense it was the economic reformation and modernisa-tion program in China that spilled across its borders into the Soviet Union and indirectly helped to spur political agitation and renewal which brought about the collapse of the Soviet Union and its satellite states.

My predecessors, Whitlam and Fraser, were well regarded in China. Gough Whitlam showed great foresight when he visited China as Opposition Leader and recognised the People's Republic as the 'sole legal government of China' in one of the first acts of his incoming Labor Government in 1972. During Malcolm Fraser's prime minister-ship Australia was the first country to strike a bilateral aid agreement with China. Indeed it was at Malcolm's invitation that Zhao Ziyang, the Chinese Premier, visited Australia during April 1983, just a month after Labor reclaimed office.

The groundwork of Whitlam and Fraser smoothed the way for me, but the times were propitious for other reasons. China's open policy was still in its infancy. Deng Xiaoping had only acquired the power to pursue this approach in December 1978 and the path was strewn with obstacles. While relations across the border with the Soviet Union were in fact tense and suspicious, elements within the United States military and defence establishment still harboured illusions about a covert alliance between the two great communist powers.

A well of ancient prejudice stemming from war and ideological antagonism existed between China and Japan. China had no diplomatic relations with Indonesia, Singapore or South Korea and other countries in the region which could be important to China given its new economic philosophy. Israel and the Jewish community were out of China's diplomatic orbit, as was the Catholic Church.

So Australia in 1983 was available to act as a conduit for China to those countries with whom it wished to develop more constructive relationships. We were not a threat and it was understood that while we were in alliance with the United States, mine was a government that had an independent and positive stance towards the countries of the region and beyond which were going to be of importance to China as it embarked on its policy of opening to the rest of the world. In particular, taking a global view, it was much more likely that in any dispute involving the intrinsic economic interests of the Asia–Pacific communities and Europe, Australia under the Hawke Government was much more likely to side with the former than the latter.

There was also an economic complementarity between Australia and China. In developing a market economy and opening up China to the rest of the world, the Chinese leadership had in mind the experience of

Japan and the Asian 'tigers'. As it had been in the growth of Japan and Korea, Australia was recognised by China as an important future supplier of raw materials.

Subsequent events have reconfigured China's diplomacy of the early to mid-eighties. China now has good relations with all the ASEAN countries, intimate economic ties with Taiwan, Korea and Hong Kong, and much closer relations with Japan than with most Western countries. But it was quite a different picture in 1983. Australia then presented a non-threatening opportunity to help in the acceleration of opening to the rest of the world and as a source of assistance to China in its program of rapid industrialisation.

From the first weeks of my prime ministership I began to establish an unusually close relationship with those driving the reform program in China under the control of Deng Xiaoping: the Chinese Premier, Zhao Ziyang, the Party Secretary, Hu Yaobang, Hu's right-hand man, Hu Qili and Vice-Premier Wan Li. These men, with the endorsement and authority of Deng Xiaoping – then, and still, the most powerful figure in China – were directly responsible for implementing the massive program of reform in that vast nation, home to one fifth of the human race. The sheer magnitude of the task facing the leader of a country of more than one billion people spread over an enormous land mass of divergent physical characteristics and resources almost beggars the imagination. The complexities involved in understanding and administering a country of those dimensions, judging the implications of decisions for each part of it, and assessing the impact of those decisions for your own people and on the region and beyond require a rare mixture of skills. In Zhao Ziyang I encountered a person who measured up to these challenges; it was no surprise to me that Deng Xiaoping had entrusted such awesome responsibility to this man.

Zhao's prescience and breadth of outlook was obvious during my first meetings with him in April 1983. He was not naturally a gregarious, extrovert personality. One got to know him more through the intimacy of dialogue and I was fortunate enough to enjoy this experience over many hours in formal and informal contexts. He had considerable intelligence and wisdom and he was rapidly making up for the lack of international experience he brought to the premiership from his position as Governor of Sichuan Province.

By the time I met him he had travelled extensively. For example, from 20th December 1982 to 18th January 1983 Zhao visited eleven African countries, the first visit to Africa by a Chinese Premier since Zhou Enlai in 1964. His travels abroad, to Africa and elsewhere, defined China's opening to the rest of the world. This force-fed internationalism equipped Zhao to talk with authority across the whole gamut of world issues.

There was only one hitch to his productive six-day Australian visit in 1983. We had not yet elected the new Speaker and Bill Snedden, who held that position under the Fraser Government, was therefore seated on Zhao's right at the parliamentary lunch in his honour. I had been speaking with Zhao for some time through his interpreter, sitting opposite, and indicated to Bill that he might like to talk with our guest. He did so for a while and then leant across Zhao and, to my horror, said to me, 'Prime Minister, I think we should congratulate the Premier on his use of the knife and fork.' I watched the eyes of the normally impassive interpreter momentarily widen with shock. She was equal to the occasion, however, and must have covered Bill's *faux pas* with some innocuous translation. I monopolised Zhao's attention for the rest of the meal.

His visit was a forerunner to my own trip to China in 1984. The following year Hu Yaobang, accompanied by Hu Qili, came to Australia. In 1986 I was back in China again. It was acknowledged in diplomatic circles that no other national leader had spent so many hours in direct, intimate discussion with the Chinese leadership. The relationship produced advantages for both countries and was also used for broader purposes.

In pursuing these bilateral opportunities I learned early during my 1984 visit how necessary it was sometimes to be prepared to ignore the conventional niceties of the formal processes beloved by diplomats. Before our meeting with Zhao I met in our embassy with the Ambassador, his officials and my own people. I told them I wanted to raise directly with the Premier what I saw as the opportunities for specific co-operation between Australia and China in the iron and steel sector. The Ambassador was aghast – this was not the way to operate, Prime Minister. He asserted that there must be preparatory discussions at the official level, otherwise our hosts could feel that they were being ambushed.

I thought this was a serious misreading of Zhao and said so forcefully. After the meeting I took Ross Garnaut aside, repeated my scepticism about the Ambassador's advice and said I was convinced I should raise the proposition directly with Zhao. Ross agreed. When I went to it the next day Zhao embraced the concept with fervour. Our concurrence was reflected in our joint communiqué and a short time after that a deal was struck for a Sino-Australian joint venture in a mine in Western Australia with production feeding into the expanding Chinese steel industry.

The following year when Hu Yaobang and Hu Qili visited Australia, I met them in Perth and we travelled together to Mount Channar in the Pilbara in Western Australia, now the site of this very successful and profitable joint venture. The Mount Channar iron-ore mine was China's first investment of this type. This development and China's 10 per cent investment in the Portland Aluminium Smelter in Victoria are China's largest overseas investments.

From Mount Channar, while en route to Canberra, we called in at Whyalla to visit the BHP steel mill. China later became Whyalla's main market for steel, taking around 40 per cent of production during a time of depressed demand in Australia. Indeed the Chinese market helped keep Whyalla going until the domestic market improved.

I have vivid memories of the hours I spent with Hu Yaobang in Australia. He was a remarkable man and a much loved figure in China, for good reason. One could not help but like him. He was like a chirpy little sparrow, tiny, with sparkling eyes, and a complete extrovert. He revelled in the openness of Australian society.

In Whyalla virtually the whole town turned out to greet us. It was at a time when my popularity in Australia was high and people were waving and seeking to attract my attention. But all of this was lost on Hu: the people of Whyalla had turned out en masse for one reason only – to see him! Hu was waving back and smiling, believing that the whole event had been staged for his benefit. His exuberance was wonderful to see.

I was able to get my own back later. Visiting Nanjing in China during May of the following year, crowds of people gathered around us, delighted to see the General Secretary of the Chinese Communist Party. They rushed up to Hu and touched him, in a scene reminiscent of Whyalla the year before. But I rose to the occasion, behaving as if the whole of Nanjing had turned out for me.

Hu was forever underlining the significance of our relationship and I was never in any doubt about the importance he assigned to it. On my first visit to China in 1984 I was scheduled to meet him during a stopover at Nanjing while en route to Shanghai from Beijing but a storm made the Nanjing landing impossible. Undaunted, Hu made a special trip to Shanghai to talk with me.

At that time Indo-China headed our agenda. Australia was by now a significant player in the search for a settlement in Cambodia and China was restive about the impact of our intervention on Vietnam. The Chinese were anxious to contain Vietnam's influence in Indo-China and Hu sought reassurance that Australia's position would not result in benefiting Vietnam at China's expense. In China's view the time was not yet ripe for a settlement in Indo-China. Rather, China wished to exhaust her historic enemy through political and economic isolation and by the cost to Vietnam of fighting both in Cambodia and on its border with China.

We understood the Chinese argument but did not share it. With Soviet help Vietnam could maintain its military presence in Cambodia, despite the costs imposed. In the meantime the Cambodian people continued to suffer and the Soviets dug themselves more solidly into Vietnam. Our goal, therefore, was to end the current impasse in Cambodia rather than encourage its continuation. Despite our agreement to differ on this matter, the discussions confirmed and deepened the respect between us.

The Chinese leaders welcomed my real interest in their country and in the new direction they were pursuing. Zhao and I spoke for hours about the economic and political implications of those changes. Given the commitment to a more open market economy, with all that must entail for an internationally compatible pricing mechanism and increasing wage and salary differentials, I asked Zhao how real it was to keep talking about China as a socialist society. Zhao smiled: 'The language is significant for us but it is not the most important thing. What matters is that our people understand that there is no longer one big pot from which everything comes. They have to understand that there will be thousands and thousands of smaller pots which must be efficient and competitive.'

I smiled in return at his eloquent encapsulation of the beginnings of an economic approach which, in my judgment, was going to constitute the most important revolution in China in the twentieth century – one that would not only transform his country at some time in the first half of the next century into the largest economy in the world, but would in the process change the global economic and political balance of power.

With a prescience of which I was not then aware, I said that I believed these economic changes would inevitably unleash pressures for political change. Zhao agreed. Neither of us were to know that before the decade was out the truth of my observation would lead to his demise.

Given this close relationship and my understanding of the new realities in China, Hu and Zhao often asked me to act as their intermediary in Washington and other places. For example, when Hu met me in Shanghai he asked me to reassure the United States that China's uneasy relationship with the Soviet Union was not some elaborate cover for a grand Sino–Soviet alliance. The United States, he said, need not fear a hidden agenda involving an ideological and military rapprochement between China and the Soviet Union.

I was happy to play a role in augmenting international understanding about China and I readily conveyed the message to Washington and other Western capitals. Certainly, on this particular issue, there remained within sections of the United States Administration and the American establishment some residual apprehension that the flashes of tension between China and the Soviet Union was all part of a gigantic hoax. This thesis had it that during a crisis, when the chips were down, this hoax would be revealed for what it was as the two communist giants joined forces against the West.

This idea of a resumption of a pre-1959 alliance between the Soviet Union and China was absolute nonsense. I had witnessed at first hand the enormous apprehension and, in some quarters, hatred that China had for the Soviet Union. I was only too happy to act as China's emissary on this score and help to demolish a thesis which was counterproductive to the formulation of sensible policy. It was in the interests of the United States and of us all that the changes taking place in China should be nurtured. Not to do so was to encourage the very recidivism that the hoax-proponents feared.

When I returned to China in 1986 I had the opportunity for more extensive discussions about the Soviet Union. In a remarkable gesture of friendship Hu Yaobang spent days travelling with me to the outer provinces. After dinner with the Governor of the western province of Sichuan, in the capital Chengdu, Hu and I talked late into the night. During the conversation I spoke of the value to China of re-establishing relations with the Catholic Church. I had been to Rome just a month before and in a long audience with His Holiness, Pope John Paul II, had talked at length with him about China and had agreed to raise the question of the normalisation of China's relations with Rome. I told Hu that formal recognition of Rome would be an important statement about the attitude of the Chinese authorities to religious freedom in China; recognition of the institutional importance of the Pope and the Church in the Christian world was a reasonable part of the entry price for fully fledged international citizenship.

Hu Yaobang readily acknowledged the points I was making. However, he pointed out the obvious difficulty that China had as long as Rome continued to recognise Taiwan as the legitimate government of the whole of China.

At that point Hu seized on the discussion about the Catholic Church to make a deft and humorous deflection across to a subject that more fully engaged him: 'Talking about the Pope brings me to my next topic of conversation – the Soviet Union, which thinks it's the Pope of the communist world.'

He went on to discuss the Soviet Union's role in world communism and China's continuing scepticism about the extent to which the Soviet Union was in fact changing. It should be remembered that Mikhail Gorbachev had only just come to power in March 1985 and no-one then realised the magnitude of the changes that would sweep the Soviet Union before the close of the decade. At that point Hu still harboured – as did Deng Xiaoping in my discussions with him – China's great fear of

Soviet communism as an overbearing, hegemonic power. It was Hu's view that something had gone seriously wrong with Soviet communism, enhancing a predilection for enlargement. Like the Danish Queen and her lover in *Hamlet*, its appetite grew by what it fed on; it was as if the Soviet state needed to expand continuously in order to survive.

Hu instanced the Soviet-inspired invasion of Cambodia by Vietnam and its invasion of Afghanistan. He pointed to the continuing weight of Soviet military strength on the Chinese border since the 1960s. Since Mao the Chinese had gone through a period of paranoia about the Soviets' willingness to use nuclear weapons against them. Hu had left that particular nightmare behind and, at his most optimistic, was alive to the changes that Gorbachev's rise to power could bring. But a deep caution and suspicion remained and the thrust of Hu's outlook was very much: 'Let us wait and see. It's too early to say what Gorbachev means; let us not lower our guard at this stage.'

Apprehension about the Soviet Union permeated all discussions with the Chinese leadership. However Zhao Ziyang seemed able to peer deeper into the future than anyone else. In particular he was attuned to the likely impact upon the Soviet Union of China's reforms. Zhao and I often talked about the Sino–Soviet relationship. One night, during the course of several hours of discussion, I said to Zhao that one of the most significant aspects of the revolution currently taking place in the Chinese rural economy was what it would mean for the Soviet Union. Certainly the consequences for China were profound but those changes must inevitably have an effect upon the Soviets. The two countries were contiguous and China was getting a massive growth in agricultural output and very significant income increases for its peasants. Surely knowledge of this would feed through into the Soviet Union, at least in the border regions.

We were sitting alongside each other with an interpreter behind us. 'Of course you're right, Bob,' Zhao said. 'Every day, thousands and thousands of Soviet citizens cross our borders. They come in and they see what we're doing, what's happening on our farms, what's happening to the increase in output, what's happening to the incomes of our farmers. Then they return to the Soviet Union where they broadcast the changes. That will inevitably have its impact within the Soviet Union. It is, indeed, part of the change we are beginning to see now.'

If the economic revolution had not occurred in China after 1978, the massive changes that later swept the Soviet Union would have been delayed, perhaps for several years.

The foresight displayed by Zhao and Hu Yaobang was no guarantee of their own survival. In particular, one always had some apprehension for Hu. After he left us in Guangzhou in 1986 I felt close enough to his protégé and possible successor, Hu Qili (a relatively young man then in his mid-fifties who spoke excellent English), to ask him a direct question.

'When you sit down in a meeting with Hu Yaobang and he is leading your delegation, he has a brief in front of him. Now, you all have the same brief and you know exactly where the meeting is heading,' I commented. 'Yes, that is right,' Hu Qili said, nodding inquisitively. 'What is your feeling when Hu Yaobang departs from the brief, closes it up and just goes off on his own?' I asked. By this stage, Hu Qili was laughing. 'It petrifies us,' he said.

One of Hu Yaobang's most interesting departures occurred during our long conversation in Sichuan. He said that socialism had been discredited by the Khmer Rouge in Cambodia, so the government after the withdrawal of the Vietnamese would not be socialist and that Sihanouk, the only leader with national standing, would have to be part of the post-Vietnamese leadership. Closely anticipating the eventual outcome, he said that the United Nations would need to hold the ring, pending elections.

The beginning of the end for Hu Yaobang came shortly after his visit to Australia in 1985, when he went on to New Zealand. He announced there, quite off the cuff, that China's People's Liberation Army (PLA) would be cut by a million troops. While the decision to reduce the size of the PLA had been taken back in China, it remained a secret until Hu disclosed it in faraway New Zealand.

The full story of Hu Yaobang's, and later Zhao's, demise and its tragic ramifications, is a complex one. Their deep belief that economic and political liberation were inextricably connected was not shared by some others in the leadership, most importantly Deng himself. Deng is a man of enormous courage and resilience who, against all the odds, survived Mao's purges and was resurrected from the political grave to become China's paramount leader. Deng had a clear perception of the need for fundamental economic reform if China was to maximise its opportunities for growth. And he understood that if the necessary moves towards a market economy were to succeed, then China had to open up to the rest of the world, both to obtain the required capital and technology and to have access to markets which could absorb China's expanded productive capacity.

He was prepared to fight hard to achieve this program against his conservative opponents in the leadership hierarchy who were steeped in an increasingly irrelevant ideological past and were terrified of change. Deng was the pragmatic strategist. He believed that this was the fight, above all others, which had to be fought and won; and he was prepared to fight it with no holds barred. But he neither believed in, nor thought he could carry, a fight on two fronts – the fight against the conservatives for political liberalisation as well as for economic reform.

Those who were opposed to Deng's economic reform program had Hu in their sights. His New Zealand indiscretion was later compounded in their eyes by what they regarded as his benign handling of the vexed question of possible visits to China by United States warships. In December 1986 widespread protests by students occurred at a number of Chinese universities. Hu was blamed and removed from office in January 1987 but his influence on the course of Chinese history was far from over.

On 15th April 1989 Hu Yaobang died from a heart attack. His death sparked the student demonstrations that led to the tragic events in Tiananmen Square from 3rd to 5th June. We were kept informed from our embassy in Beijing of the dramatic developments during May, including the disclosure on 24th that Zhao, who had been attempting to negotiate with the students, had been stripped of office.

I was disturbed for my friend and desolated by the tragedy of Tiananmen where in 1984, with Zhao, I had reviewed troops of the PLA. Immediately before I spoke on Friday, 9th June at a memorial service in Parliament House commemorating the victims of Tiananmen Square, I had received the latest cable from Beijing setting out in graphic detail the circumstances of the death of many of these victims. I was both sickened and sick at heart. My well-reported tears as I spoke at the service were for those young people and for China itself, for I knew that China and its people, with whom I had developed such close relations and for whom I had such affection, would inevitably suffer from the world's reaction to this brutal repression.

I condemned what had happened, immediately extended the visas of Chinese students in Australia and took steps to suspend projected interchanges with China, including the cancellation of my visit there scheduled for the following October.

I did not then, nor do I now, share the simplistic view that we could expect the immediate transformation of China into some sort of Western-style democracy. I maintain the position that political reform will be the inevitable consequence of continuing economic liberalisation and the increasing incentives for individual enterprise. My hope, amidst all the despair of June 1989, was that these processes of economic reform would not be reversed by the conservative forces who might believe they now had the running with Deng. For this would have been the greatest tragedy – a return to the economic lunacy of the past, with all the danger of permanent closure to the rest of the world and even more limited opportunity for political dissent.

Fortunately, my hope has been realised. Deng has not only not deviated from, but has accelerated, his commitment to the economic reform processes. After an appropriate period of diminished contacts, the rest of the world, including Australia, has resumed full economic relations with a China which, I believe, will never repeat the tragedy of 1989. I base this belief on an assessment of what has happened in the party structures and on my own recent experience. At the 14th Party Congress in 1992 Deng was able to institutionalise the commitment to economic reform, not only in a formal sense but also by securing the election of a younger and supportive leadership in the relevant party organs.[68]

My contact with the Chinese leadership lapsed for three years. In late 1992 after I had left office an approach was made to see whether I would be prepared to visit China in 1993. I accepted the invitation and was welcomed in Beijing by President Jiang Zemin who is also Party Secretary and Chairman of the Military Commission.

I had, of course, wondered how the chemistry would work – what the leadership attitude would be towards the early friend who had so strongly condemned the events of 1989. Jiang Zemin could not have been warmer or more gracious in his greeting. With him, and all those I met, there was an understanding and acceptance of the past including, I think, their knowledge that I had refused several invitations to visit China until the changes of 1978. I had a continuity of contact with the process of economic reform in their country. I had said and done what, in conscience, I had to in 1989.

The processes of economic reform in China are irreversible. Deng has ensured that will be the case beyond his own departure from the scene. The PLA is directly involved in the reforms through a range of its own economic enterprises that cover manufacturing, tourism and development. There is no locus of power and sentiment with a will to revert to an unproductive past.

The rest of the world has a vested interest in being associated with and assisting these reforms. China will become in the lifetime of our children the largest economy in the world. I believe, as well, that with appropriately co-operative reactions from the rest of the world (including an accelerated acceptance of its application to join the GATT) China will become a valuable, constructive and vitally important member of the community of nations.

Across the Sino–Soviet border another paradox was unfolding. China had forged ahead with economic change and the Soviet Union, influenced to some extent by what was happening there, was beginning to move also – but not nearly so fast. What was unnerving to the Chinese authorities was the speed of political change in the USSR and its implications for China. The tension was evident when Mikhail Gorbachev visited China in the middle of 1989. His visit was a critical rallying point for pro-democracy demonstrators and, along with Hu's death, was part of the tumultuous prelude to Tiananmen Square. Since Gorbachev's rise to power in early 1985, his *perestroika* and *glasnost* policies had riveted the attention of the world. The Soviet Union had gone from being the 'evil empire' to one with which even President Ronald Reagan, the author of this epithet, was prepared to deal, albeit cautiously.

My own attitude towards the Soviets had softened considerably after Gorbachev's ascent to power. In 1979 I had been the victim of vicious duplicity by Soviet authorities on the subject of exit visas for Soviet

Jewry.[69] Other instances of barbarism by Soviet authorities, including the shooting down of Korean passenger airliner Flight KAL 007 on 1st September 1983 with the loss of 269 lives, further jaundiced my view.

Ordinary people the world over were materially and psychologically worse off as a result of the Soviet régime. It bred international insecurity and led to a huge expenditure on armaments which would have been better spent on meeting the needs of these people. Within the USSR itself, the evil inflicted by the Soviet régime went beyond the suffering imposed on dissidents. The facts, speaking louder and louder as time went on, revealed a system monumentally unable to provide even the basic requirements of its citizens.

By the time I visited Leningrad and Moscow, from 29th November to 2nd December 1987, my fifth visit to the Soviet Union, policies of *perestroika* and *glasnost* were being pursued by Soviet leaders who were of a very different ilk to their predecessors. Naturally, I had followed Soviet developments through the cable traffic and the international community, including, of course, those world figures who had met with the new Soviet leader. Margaret Thatcher, for example, had met Mikhail Gorbachev. She both trusted him and praised his bold initiatives. Ronald Reagan was now of the same opinion. Australian businessmen with dealings in the Soviet Union also carried favourable reports of developments there.

In March 1987 the Soviet Foreign Minister, Eduard Shevardnadze, Gorbachev's friend and confidante, visited Australia. His liberalism and fundamental decency were evident; meeting with him mellowed my attitude towards the Soviets still further.

My trip to the Soviet Union was only the second time an Australian Prime Minister had visited the USSR. As I was accompanied by the Foreign Affairs Minister, Bill Hayden, my visit was in fact the most senior exchange between the two countries. During more than eight hours of formal talks I held with the Chairman of the Soviet Council of

Ministers, Nikolai Ryzhkov, and other ministers, together with a further three and a quarter hours I spent with the General Secretary, Mikhail Gorbachev, it became obvious to me that what I had heard from Reagan, Thatcher and others was correct. A sea change was sweeping the Soviet Union and with it, the entire world.

These were still early days and it was not a time for giddiness or naïve optimism (perhaps of the sort that I had displayed in 1979 when I believed that Brezhnev's Moscow was as good as its word). But despite a 'once bitten, twice shy' reserve on my part, I found the atmosphere in Moscow distinctly different this time around. Nor was this a merely superficial change. One could sense a depth and urgency in their conversation. Ryzhkov stressed to me during one of our discussions that he and Gorbachev, who had been friends for many years, had long talked about the crisis building in the Soviet Union.

Ryzhkov was not underestimating the obstacles in their path. Opposition took many forms. The brute, ideological reaction from the communist hardliners was the easiest to pinpoint. But more pervasive was the inertia and resistance to change coming from those fearful of taking a step forward.

Ryzhkov said that he had just been chairing a meeting of the Council of Ministers. He complained the problem was one of mindset, of opposition to new ideas. I told him he didn't have this problem on his own; the paradox was that those who label themselves as radicals so often prove to be the most conservative of all.

In welcoming me to Moscow on 30th November 1987, Ryzhkov went so far as to compare Soviet restructuring with the revolutionary changes that Labor had made to the Australian economy. He saw our two countries united 'under the flag of *perestroika*'.

I responded in the spirit of the occasion. I observed that in Australia, too, we were living in a time of rapid and dramatic change. Coping with change involved questioning the assumptions of the past. This inevitably created problems, and any government preaching the doctrine of change and adaptation often found itself in a politically uncomfortable position.

But this was as far as I could draw the long bow before Ryzhkov's comparison snapped. In the years before the Hawke Government the Australian economy had been mismanaged and neglected but the restructuring facing us was of a different order entirely to that confronting the Soviet Union. As Ryzhkov ticked off the list of glaring inadequacies in the Soviet command system I was struck by excitement and anxiety simultaneously. The excitement of being present at the birth of a new society was one thing; imagining the infant's long and hazardous road to maturity was another.

These sentiments reached full pitch when I met Mikhail Gorbachev. Even with all that has happened since, I still look back on that meeting as one of the most important, and certainly most fascinating, of my prime ministership. It was the first time I could assess this man, of whom I had heard and read so much, face to face, unfiltered by the viewpoints of intermediaries.

We met in a splendidly ornate room in the Kremlin. There was one other person present, Gorbachev's interpreter, a man close to him and an obviously brilliant exponent of his craft. He was so alive to idiom and humour that the conversation flowed like quicksilver, as near to being a direct *tête-à-tête* as was possible in the circumstances. We seemed to click immediately and a meeting that was scheduled to last for around twenty minutes went on for more than three and a quarter hours. Gorbachev was quick to smile and his famous charm was evident from the outset. However, we both felt there was little time to waste on social pleasantries. Gorbachev's high intelligence and warm personality gave him a lightness of touch, no matter what the subject, but he was always deadly serious in the thrust of his conversation.

We were both very well briefed and could talk readily on the basis of a shared knowledge of the subjects we were discussing. In that way we covered the field. We looked at bilateral issues, the reform agenda within the Soviet Union, relations between the USSR and the United States, relations with China, the politics of the Middle East, Africa and Indo-China.

Gorbachev's whole presence inspired trust. But I could not leave it at that. 'We will judge the Soviet Union's intentions not by their words but by their actions,' I told him. In particular I instanced Afghanistan and Indo-China.

On Afghanistan, Gorbachev foreshadowed the Soviet withdrawal. In regard to Cambodia he recited the formula that Vietnam was a sovereign, independent nation. It was a formula rendered inadequate by the Soviets' looming presence in the region and, in particular, by their large naval base at Cam Ranh Bay. I told Gorbachev that the USSR ought to use its influence with Vietnam which, with Laos and Cambodia, was an island of stagnation in the East Asian sea of growth. Indo-China was imposing an enormous financial burden on the Soviets, whose interests, as well as those of their client states and the region itself, would be best served by ending the current imbroglio.

Gorbachev was responsive and gave me the impression that Soviet influence would be brought to bear in a search for a solution to the Cambodian tragedy. When we discussed superpower rivalry directly, the extent to which the Soviet mood had shifted from belligerence to reasoned respect became abundantly clear. Gorbachev spoke of the easy working relationship he enjoyed with Ronald Reagan and George Shultz. Not all traces of Cold War hostility were gone, however, and he was still apprehensive about reactionary opinion within the United States which opposed accommodation with the Soviet Union. This was a subject I raised with Reagan in my letter to him of 4th December 1987:

> You, of course, know Mr Gorbachev well. I found him to be intelligent, astute, quick, charming but liberally endowed with scepticism about the West. I hasten to add that he respects the integrity of yourself and George Shultz but professes to express his apprehension about the motives, and to some extent, the influence of the more extreme "forces of the right"

My five-page account to the United States head of state about my meeting with Gorbachev is an example of the way conversations between leaders wash through the capitals of the world, helping to shape ideas and attitudes. It is a useful and routine part of international dialogue.

Australia's membership of the Western Alliance was a given whenever I was abroad, whether in Beijing, Moscow or other foreign capitals. It was part of the sub-structure of all strategic discussions I had with the Chinese and the Russians. There was nothing underhand about it; Australia's alliance with the United States was always presented as central to Australia's interests.

Mikhail Gorbachev certainly understood this as we spoke, and as he sounded off about the American Right he was seeking, through me, to get an echo of what he was saying heard in Washington. In his view, the influence of the Right was slowing the pace of arms negotiations. The Soviet Union and the United States had just reached agreement on intermediate range nuclear forces. The historic INF treaty represented the first time the superpowers had agreed actually to cut their nuclear arsenals rather than simply slow their rate of growth. But Gorbachev was looking beyond INF to the reduction of strategic and chemical weapons. He indicated that Soviet willingness to negotiate was becoming entangled in the paranoia of the American Right.

That I should be the message-bearer for reconnaissance on arms negotiations and other strategic concerns was an indicator of the personal chemistry that developed between us. Just as importantly, it reflected Australia's growing importance as a middle power and, frequently, as an opinion leader in international and multilateral forums. My closeness to the Chinese leadership helped, too, and Gorbachev and I spoke at length about developments in China. The leading role Australia was playing in the debate about sanctions against South Africa explained why Gorbachev wanted to spend time talking with me about developments in Africa. At each point in the lattice-work of international politics there seemed to be an intersection of interests between Australia and the Soviet Union.

Other factors pushed the Soviet leadership into putting so much time and effort into the Australian visit. The Australia–United States alliance was taken for granted, but that did not make us ideologically blinkered, and the Soviets understood that. As with the Chinese, Australia was seen as a country with whom one could safely do some reality-testing. Suggestions made in good faith could be usefully explored, without prejudice, and bad ideas killed off without international embarrassment.

Australia also provided some insights for the internal renovation of the Soviet system. While not a first-rank economic power, we are nonetheless a developed economy with experience and expertise which were of interest to the Soviets. In meetings with leading economic ministers I was accompanied by a delegation of eleven Australian businessmen. This allowed them to make direct contact with the top echelons of the Soviet leadership and to express their views about how to expand trade and other forms of economic co-operation between our two countries.

Gorbachev's acute awareness of the grotesque inadequacies of the Marxist–Leninist command system of economic management, then collapsing under its own inertia, provided the backdrop to our entire conversation. His euphemism to describe the Soviet economy – 'we are in a pre-crisis condition' – was, in reality, a thin disguise for the massive failure of the Soviet system. As we moved across the range of global issues, everything, in a sense, was secondary to Gorbachev's perception of the need to concentrate the country's energies and resources into revitalising and reshaping the economy.

The Soviet command economy employed eighteen million bureaucrats. In a world where the whole dynamics of production were being revolutionised by new technologies in computers and telecommunications, these po-faced comrades with comfortable security of tenure sat at their desks making literally hundreds of thousands of individual wholesale and retail pricing decisions across a vast range of products. And while the Soviet dinosaur encumbered itself with that particular form of lunacy it lumbered, as well, under the burden of some 20 per cent of its gross domestic product being directed to armaments and defence.

This was the system which according to Gorbachev's predecessors was going to bury the West. The Soviet leader I met in Moscow knew this was a load of codswallop. For Gorbachev, it was not a question of conquering the rest of the world, but one of whether the Soviets were going to be able to save their own. But here was his dilemma and, in the end, his undoing. He recognised the problem, but he could neither formulate and implement the solutions nor give that task the necessary priority it demanded over his program for political reform. His priorities were precisely the opposite of the Chinese leadership, and that is why we can be certain that China will make a successful transition to a market economy, with political liberalisation inevitably following at some later stage, while we must live in hope that Russia, and the rest of what was the Soviet Union, will be able to achieve and sustain reform in either field.

Gorbachev used the language of economics but did not understand its implications. He repeated to me several times the proposition that the Soviet Union must become 'organically a part of the international division of labour'. I agreed but pointed out that this necessarily meant establishing within the country an internationally compatible pricing system and, therefore, dismantling the vast, hugely expensive network of state subsidies which distorted the allocation of economic resources.

Gorbachev accepted this but never brought his Government to making these basic decisions. Rather he employed a scatter-gun approach which aimed at the edges rather than the core of their economic problem. His major energies were directed at creating more political 'openness' but, as admirable as this was, his failure to deliver on the material expectations of his people eroded his authority and, ultimately, made him vulnerable to his opponents.

Gorbachev understood that the provision of Western technology and expertise, which he desperately needed, would be conditional upon an improvement in human rights in the Soviet Union. Australia was particularly concerned about restrictions on family reunion, the right of Soviet Jews to emigrate, the right of entry and exit for visits, and the plight of prisoners of conscience in the Soviet Union. We had been negotiating with the Soviets for some time on a human contacts agreement aimed at liberalising Soviet policy in these areas.

I raised all these matters with Gorbachev and, given my long association with the cause of Jewish refuseniks,[70] I argued that the attitude of the Soviet Union towards Soviet Jewry was untenable; it was a terrible violation of their human rights. I urged him to change his policy in this area so that those wishing to could leave the Soviet Union. Without that, I said, we couldn't have the fully rounded relationship that we both wanted. I didn't raise the subject belligerently and Gorbachev responded in kind as we spoke at length about Soviet Jewry.

He conceded the incorrectness of past decisions and his preparedness to look at changes both in the law and in administrative practices. I then handed him a list of six refusenik cases, typical of a larger group of twenty-eight cases of which we were aware. I told Gorbachev that I wanted these people released. This was the one point in our conversation where he toughened his demeanour. He became a little aggressive, not towards me personally, but in the strength of his presentation.

'We invest all this money in training and educating these people and then they are seduced away. We can't allow that,' he said. 'I can understand that,' I responded. 'Don't think you have this problem on your own. It happens all the time in my country.'

'Mr Prime Minister, you might be prepared to put up with that, we are not!' he said, gesturing for emphasis. Gorbachev was not just being obstinate. The brain-drain was a real problem which assumed a larger significance for him as he envisioned a new, growing and more liberal Soviet Union. I remembered Shelepin's plaintive defence to me in 1971 that while Jews were less than 2 per cent of the population, they constituted at least 15 per cent of scientists and those with access to state secrets regarded as essential to national security. And it was not difficult to imagine what compelling incentives there would be for these people to leave behind the constraints of the Soviet system and accept lucrative offers to live and work in a free society. So in talking to Gorbachev I had no wish to skate lightly over the realities that were concerning him. But whatever those realities, he had to give way.

We spent a good deal of time discussing the Middle East. I shaped my observations, in large part, around what the Soviet Union should see as its own self-interests. There was no advantage for them, I argued, in the Soviets continuing to support those Arab states and the PLO who were still committed to the destruction of Israel. This was an objectionable absurdity which the world would not and should not tolerate. Maintaining it would simply mean declining influence for the Soviets in the region.

The essential conditions for a settlement, I said, were twofold: first, the PLO and the Arab states must unequivocally recognise Israel's right to exist behind secure and recognised borders; and second, Israel in turn should be required to recognise the PLO and enter into negotiations for an overall settlement including the rights of the Palestinians.

Gorbachev did not dispute this analysis. I then urged him to use his influence with the PLO to this effect and said that for my part I would use my influence with the Israelis and the United States to the same end. I knew I would have a receptive ear in the United States because I had already discussed this approach with George Shultz and had his total agreement.

Gorbachev agreed to do this but I shall never forget his whimsical observation: 'Bob, you must remember that the PLO doesn't always do what we ask them.' Nevertheless, he was true to his word and it was no accident that within twelve months Arafat had publicly embraced this position.

It is almost impossible to capture the full flavour and impact of my long session with Mikhail Gorbachev. The timing and extent of our discussions, the rapid-fire way in which we were able to exchange opinions and information, the parity of views we held on so many important issues, made for a totally exhilarating experience. This short, compact man with the bright, brown eyes and the birth mark standing out vividly on his balding, intelligent head radiated energy; it was impossible not to be engaged by him. I came out of the meeting completely fired up. It was one of the rare occasions since I had given up drinking that I actually felt like a drink. I resisted, but my staff were willing surrogates. The occasion called for champagne.

As it turned out there was much to celebrate. On the morning of my departure from Moscow Gorbachev's interpreter came to see me with a message directly from the Secretary-General. It concerned the list I had given Gorbachev. 'These people are being released,' he said. It was not everything I had asked for, but it was the substantial fulfilment of a long-held dream. And it helped to erase the nightmare of 1979.

We left the Soviet Union with the feeling of a job well done. I knew that in Gorbachev I had been with a man of destiny. Even if his plans for internal reform came unstuck, even if he did not retain the leadership of this nation in transition, history would surely record his contribution as indispensable to the close of the Cold War and, ultimately, the end of communism.

The international responsibilities of office were obviously stimulating and enjoyable, and no visit gave me more pleasure than the quick trip to Ireland in 1987 after the Vancouver CHOGM. The Irish overflowed with warm and genuine goodwill from the moment the Taoiseach (Prime Minister) Charles Haughey greeted us at the airport. I quickly became mates with this shrewd and genial man. Everyone we met seemed to have a relation or dear friend living in Australia. This was not surprising given that almost one-third of Australians claim Irish ancestry; half of my ministry was of Irish descent. The closeness between our two countries was evident when I had the rare honour of addressing the Dail (Parliament) – only the third foreign leader, after Presidents Kennedy and Reagan, to do so. The response was overwhelming, as though one of their own had returned home.

At the other end of the spectrum to the exhilaration of the Irish sojourn was the visit to Australia in 1988 of the Romanian President, Ceausescu, and his wife. We had been landed with this abominable pair as a result of an invitation extended earlier by the West Australian Premier, Brian Burke. Both the Governor-General and the Prime Minister receive a detailed intelligence run-down on visiting heads of state. Sir Ninian had read the briefing which laid out Ceausescu's terrible record, including his deliberate decimation of Romania's elderly people by transporting them to the country side to die in harsh winters without heating. The report referred to Ceausescu's extravagance (he wore his suits only once then threw them away), obsessive suspiciousness and mistreatment of everyone, including his closest colleagues. This extended to installing hidden TV cameras in the hotel bedrooms of his ministers. As we waited at the cold, windswept RAAF base for Ceausescu to arrive Sir Ninian asked me whether I'd considered doing the same thing with my ministers. 'There wouldn't be enough film, Ninian,' I replied, in what was the only light moment of a depressing two days.

Ceausescu and his wife looked like what they were – evil incarnate. Paranoia, the normal companion to wickedness, abounded. They examined in minute detail their suite at Government House – the one used by the Queen – and refused to settle in until the soap in the bathroom had been replaced with cakes which had not been unwrapped; their preoccupation with the possibility of assassination made them fear that someone might have impregnated the soap with poison. Looking over the settings in the dining room for the next evening's state dinner, they indicated they would refuse to attend unless the President was given a chair with armrests to match that of the Governor-General. These were the minor manifestations of a larger depravity of character; as chilling as it was, it came as no surprise when they were murdered by their own people in the uprising of 1989.

Their murders were a dramatic episode in a wider demise – the death of the communist system.

TWENTY-TWO

It was neither possible nor desirable when travelling overseas to divorce oneself from what was happening at home and I kept in touch by phone, fax and cable, making whatever decisions or suggestions were necessary. I always felt confident leaving the ship in the hands of the acting captain, Lionel Bowen. Lionel was unflappable and he was loyalty personified. We had developed a close friendship which was only ever put in jeopardy by excessive clouds of my cigar smoke wafting over him in the Cabinet room where he sat next to me. As in all things, Lionel was good-natured about this, but I think no-one was more relieved than he when we banned smoking in Cabinet in 1988 not long after we moved to the new Parliament House.

This sense of confidence was suddenly shattered during my visit to Japan and China in 1986. I was in Japan from 14th to 16th May renewing the close relationship I had forged with Prime Minister Yasu Nakasone during my first visit in 1984. Much to the surprise of the guests assembled at a dinner in my honour, Nakasone had then revealed the intimacy of this rapport by referring to me in his speech as 'my good friend Bob' – very unJapanese – and I, of course, reciprocated with 'Yasu'.

The timing of this visit to Japan was important for Australia. Nakasone had just chaired the Tokyo economic summit of the Group of Seven and he was able to assure me that the leaders – as I had requested in individual letters to them – had addressed agriculture in a thorough and positive way for the first time. Japanese leaders confirmed their support for our position that agriculture be given a prominent place in the upcoming Uruguay Round of multilateral trade negotiations. Japan, they said, stood ready to work with Australia to achieve this. I welcomed these assurances.

Japan expected decisive progress at the September 1986 ministerial meeting of the General Agreement on Tariffs and Trade to launch the new round. Meanwhile both Japan and Australia agreed that work done in the Organisation for Economic Co-operation and Development should serve as useful preparation for these negotiations. I emphasised Australia's willingness to participate in the discussion on agriculture in the OECD but stressed that such discussion should not divert attention from the need to have agricultural trade issues fully addressed as part of the agenda in the multilateral trade negotiations. Japanese leaders also agreed with me on the value of further consultation among Asia–Pacific regional countries before the September meeting.

Japan is Australia's major trading partner and much of the credit for this should be given to the solid and far-sighted work done by Sir John McEwen – with great help from Sir John Crawford. My discussions with Nakasone on bilateral issues were cordial and productive. I emphasised that the concept of Australia as quarry and farm to Japan, with Japan acting reciprocally as a supplier of value-added manufactures was a tired equation which, from our point of view, cried out for rethinking. The Japanese market for our traditional exports of raw materials – particularly iron ore and coal – and agricultural products remained fundamentally important, and we wanted to see this trade expand; to this end I stressed Australia's reliability and international competitiveness in that area. As part of the exposition I was proud to be able to underline our success in radically reducing the historically high levels of industrial disputation in Australia. But I told Nakasone and other Japanese leaders that as a result of our gradual restructuring of the Australian economy we would increasingly have the capacity to become competitive and attractive suppliers of manufactured goods and services, including tourism, where I welcomed investment by Japanese interests in Australia. It is a matter of real satisfaction that the composition of our exports to Japan has come to reflect the trends I foreshadowed in 1984.[71]

But back in Australia the significance of my visit and the important issues raised by it were largely obscured by Treasurer Paul Keating's infamous remark about Australia becoming 'a banana republic'. His outburst came on 14th May 1986 while talking to Sydney radio personality John Laws. Within hours 3 cents had been sliced from the Australian dollar, which toppled below 70 cents.

Keating had fallen victim to his own rhetoric. 'If in the final analysis, Australia is so undisciplined, so disinterested in its salvation and its economic well-being, that it doesn't deal with these fundamental problems, then the fallback solution is inevitable because you can't fund $12 billion a year in perpetuity every year, and then the interest on the year before that, and the interest on the year before that, the only thing to do is to slow to a canter. Once you slow growth under 3 per cent, unemployment starts to rise again,' he told Laws. Laws: 'And then you have really induced depression.' Keating: 'Then you have gone. You know, you are a banana republic.'

His remarks followed the disastrous trade figures for April which had been released by the Australian Bureau of Statistics the day before. Australia's current account deficit leapt to $1.48 billion, a bad figure in anyone's language, but made worse still by Paul's language.

Before leaving for Tokyo I had had a chance to discuss the figures with him and the rest of our Cabinet colleagues. They were certainly no cause for celebration, but we were determined to deal with them without panic. All agreed on the need for belt-tightening, particularly when it came to cutting back on funds available to the States. We expected some flak but we decided to press ahead with the case for these cuts at the forthcoming Premiers Conference. That was where I had left things when Paul burst onto the stage with prognostications of a banana republic.

Being in Tokyo in the midst of a busy program before flying to China, I could do little about the remark. I was intensely annoyed because when I left Australia the Government was perceived to be in control of the economy. With Paul's sinister flourish, that perception, invaluable for maintaining stability in the markets and buying time for grappling with the underlying problems of the economy, had been, at least temporarily, overturned.

To be fair to the Treasurer, he did not say that Australia had become a banana republic but that we were in danger of becoming one if we did not take remedial action. We had a fundamental balance of payments problem, and our current account deficit was of such magnitude that if we continued to go on spending very much more than we were earning we ran the risk of ending up in that condition.

His remark had been blurted out in the kitchen of a reception centre in the semi-rural electorate of Burke, held by Neil O'Keefe. Neil was an outstanding local Member and talented worker who was to become one of my most loyal supporters in the later challenges by Keating to my leadership. Meanwhile Paul had created a disaster for the Government, as he acknowledged later himself.[72] His timing could not have been worse. I was overseas; there had been a dramatic deterioration in Australia's terms of trade, which was something beyond the Government's control; prices for our major export commodities had crashed to historically low levels; and this was coupled with a falling dollar – since February 1985 the Australian dollar had lost 40 per cent of its value. Australia's current account deficit had climbed dramatically to about 6 per cent of our gross domestic product. In addition, we had started the long drawn-out Budget-making process. The detailed, painstaking preparation of the Budget, not due until the third week of August, is always a period of comparative hiatus as far as Government economic decision-making is concerned. The Prime Minister and Treasurer are tied up for months on end developing the economic strategy for the Budget.

I was concerned that Keating's statement could set off an unwarranted panic, something I had been careful to avoid when talking about the economy in the preceding months. Before going overseas I had publicly acknowledged Australia's deteriorating economic position, but it was not a subject for glib comment or the use of hyperbole. In the talks Paul and I had earlier we were at one about the problems posed for the Australian economy by the shock of external forces. These were not something new; they had been evident since the previous year. Our only difference was his extravagant use of language.

When I learned in Tokyo of Keating's indulgence I was shocked, but unlike my staff, I did not see it as an attempt by him to hijack policy. I saw it, rather, as buckling to some extent under the enormous pressure he had been experiencing. Paul does not have a particularly robust constitution and he had been working for a long time under this pressure. By May 1986 he was in bad shape. He had been exhausted by the Tax Summit and by the preparation for it and then the Budget which immediately followed. At the same time he had the enormous responsibility for the Government's new tax legislation.

In Parliament he was not his usual self. He had allowed Opposition needling over a breach of promise lawsuit brought against him in the early seventies to get under his skin. His reaction to their goading was understandable but bordered on the hysterical at times: 'You stupid foul-mouthed grub ... you piece of criminal garbage,' he exploded at Coalition frontbencher, Wilson Tuckey, after that unsavoury performer had made a particularly odious insinuation.

The Government was then hit with the awful decline in the terms of trade. All the good work we had done in turning the economy round since 1983 – record expansion, record employment growth and a halving of inflation – had foundered in this decline which was producing a high and unsustainable external deficit.

I am sure that if Paul had not been so dispirited he would not have made the banana republic comment. There was another element to his outburst. In line with previous practice, the Treasurer declined to comment on the April figures. This set the media baying that Keating was hiding from them. With the Government shipping water, Paul decided to go public. Against this background, he fell into overstatement which a frustrated media hammered for all it was worth – and it was worth a great deal.

The charitable explanation for Paul's remark is that it was a desperate attempt to focus public attention on the very significant problems confronting Australia. There is no doubt he regretted the banana republic expression. He saw the way his words were turned against both the Government and the country. When I talked to him about it subsequently he wished he had chosen another form of words. But you cannot unsay things, and we had to try to make a virtue out of his dire remarks. His metaphor, though unfortunate, added a dramatic edge to what I had been saying myself. The Australian public had to concentrate its mind on the fundamental problems imposed on us by the stark turn around in the terms of trade.

Meanwhile I pushed on with my program in Japan. But even before I had flown on to Beijing, Paul had sped from linguistic overdrive into policy improvisation or, as my staff were warning, hijack. On

16th May, at a long-planned meeting of the Advisory Council on Prices and Incomes (ACPI), where business, unions and government consulted about aspects of the Accord, Paul Keating seized on the occasion to announce another unscheduled meeting of ACPI to discuss all aspects of the economy. 'Everything is up for discussion as it relates to economic policy, the economic outlook,' Paul told the media, which quickly tagged the proposed meeting (with no demurrer from the Treasurer) a mini-summit.

It was breathtaking stuff, particularly in the light of Keating's earlier hostility to summits as a policy instrument. His lack of consultation was galling to me and to the Cabinet. No-one had given him, or any minister, a licence to change government policy on the run. He seemed to be reeling under the pressure generated by his statement and grasping at some sort of diversion. In trying to retrieve his position, and with his back to the wall, he felt he had to offer some positive initiative to overcome the negative reactions to the banana republic spectre which was now dominating the airwaves.

It was time to act. Certainly my staff were more annoyed than I, in the initial stages, by what was happening. But after the mini-summit brainstorm, I did not need any persuasion to bring matters back under prime ministerial control. There would be no summit. By definition, ACPI, given its constitution, was not a body to undertake such broad economic considerations.

A hurried summit conjured visions of panic. What's more, talk of a summit would create expectations which could not be met. The circumstances were damaging enough for me to do something unusual: I gave a background briefing to the media. There was no secret about the fact of the briefing. Paul was certainly aware of it.

From Tokyo I had requested the Deputy Prime Minister, Lionel Bowen, to take charge of events. I also arranged with him to gather senior ministers in my office in Parliament House so I could talk to them by conference phone at an appointed time from Beijing. Paul Keating, the Industrial Relations Minister, Ralph Willis, and Community Services Minister, Don Grimes, were among those attending.

I made it clear in the conference call that there would not be a mini-summit nor would ACPI be enlarged to include the States, welfare or consumer groups. To the extent that there was going to be any meeting at all, it was to listen to what business and labour had to say. As for handling these processes, the Deputy Prime Minister, Lionel Bowen, was to be in charge and other ministers or groups wanting to make an input should do so via the Acting Prime Minister. In this way the Government would be clearly identified as controlling the situation, rather than some other institution, the expanded ACPI, that Paul had dreamed up. It was important to emphasise that there were not two sources of policy-making. It was also important to play down any false expectations the summit idea might have fuelled. Rather than a summit we would handle the processes in the normal way through the Cabinet upon my return. In the meantime Lionel Bowen was in charge.

Looking back over some of the cuttings from the period. I read references to Paul doing a table-thumping routine during the conference call. I couldn't see Paul – maybe he was putting on an act at his end – but as far as I was aware, from his language and tone of voice, the conversation via telephone hook-up was fundamentally amicable. He did express concern that I had 'shafted' him in the background briefing. I assured him that I had done no such thing. Indeed when I was leaving the briefing my staff said to me, 'You weren't tough on Paul, considering the damage and embarrassment he's caused.'

My main concern was *not* to be tough on Paul. I had one overriding purpose: to settle things down and to stop the Treasurer taking the Government down a dangerous side-track. There were those who were quick to interpret my intervention as slapping Keating down after he had shot to prominence with his banana republic statement. And there were those in the media wanting to paint the events as some sort of virility contest between Paul and myself, having more to do with machismo than policy. These are the sort of sensational ideas beloved of the media but they have little to do with reality. There was, of course, some tension between us as a result of my intervention from Beijing but that soon settled. The day I arrived back in Australia, Paul came straight up to my office, shook my hand and we sat down and talked about the issues. I assured him of my continued regard for him and of my personal affection, and we then got down to the business of working on the Budget together.

I had decided to make a 'state of the nation' address as soon as possible. It was scheduled for 11th June. The speech was designed to take the Australian public into our confidence and to educate the nation about the essential realities confronting it. Paul's remarks had traumatised both the public and the markets – a form of shock treatment gone wrong. I wanted the speech to be an intimate exercise aimed at producing comprehension rather than inducing panic.

Essentially, I wanted to tell the Australian people about the extent of the difficulties and challenges facing the country. The drama of the banana republic statement, Keating going it alone in Australia while I was overseas, the talk about a summit, had all conveyed the impression that the Government had run off the rails, and this perception had to be dispelled.

The Government had not lost its way, far from it. But the Government and the nation faced tough choices and tough decisions. So I spelled out the problems. The reality was that the world was paying us less – international commodity prices had sunk to an appallingly low level. This was brought about by a sharp decline in oil prices due to problems within OPEC, combined more generally with rapidly growing commodity supplies outpacing demand – all exacerbated by the subsidy war between Europe and the US in agricultural products. My message was simple: we couldn't live beyond our means. Australia's destiny as a competitive trading nation was in our own hands and we all had to be prepared to make sacrifices. In the longer term, there was reason for confidence in ourselves and our ability to meet the challenges.

We had to be prepared to adjust and reconstruct our economy and our attitudes. This would involve pain and restraint but, as I put it, it must be 'restraint with equity', as we moved to broaden our export base. Mineral and agricultural exports would always be basically important to the Australian economy but the goal was to make them less so. As to restraint, I wanted the public to be left in no doubt about the Government's and my own resolve: 'I will not shirk the hard decisions that are necessary to ensure a bright future for us and our children.'

To make these hard decisions effective it was necessary to get the union movement to temper its wage demands, indeed to get the union movement to accept what amounted to a cut in real wages. In the run-up to my address on 11th June I had been pushing the cause of wage restraint through discounting the full amount of price increases, on the ACTU wages committee. With the national income having been slashed over the previous year by 3 per cent and with inflation running at close to 9 per cent, compared to around 3 per cent for the rest of the world, there was simply no way that wage earners could be compensated fully for increases in the Consumer Price Index. On top of that the Federal Government had to show restraint by cutting Government spending.

I had confidence in the Australian people, in their capacity to face the facts and make an extra effort to meet and overcome challenges which they understood. We could take on and match the best in the world. To a nation that cherished its sporting and cultural heroes, I cited Joan Sutherland and the examples of John Bertrand and Ben Lexcen who, against the odds, had won the America's Cup for Australia.

Despite my opinion that Australia would eventually win out, there was no doubt that the country was in for an exceptionally harsh period. Pressure on the Government was enormous. Keating's banana republic statement and the events which flowed from it had momentarily weakened an essential mainstay of Labor's term in office. For one of the Government's undoubted strengths was the Hawke–Keating axis, the combination of a Prime Minister and a Treasurer competently astride the complicated processes of running the economy. We were recognised as the economic drivers and decision-makers within the Government, the shapers of policy. Paul's statement had given the appearance of a rift in the partnership and this had its effect on electoral and market perceptions, coinciding as it did with such adverse external circumstances.

The political environment, to say the least, was uncongenial. The Budget Cabinet was locked up and the only news of what we were doing was all negative. The talk was of slashing, cutting and belt-tightening. This was made worse by the fact that no actual decisions had been announced and, of necessity, no detailed strategy unveiled. The decisions and the strategy awaited the Budget and they could not be released ahead of time.

Then, just as we were finally putting the Budget to bed, the Australian dollar took its worst fall yet, plummeting by 10 per cent in a matter of twenty-four hours. Who in the Government could forget that calamitous Monday, 28th July 1986? Certainly not the Expenditure Review Committee. We were sitting in the Cabinet room in the old Parliament House concluding our third weary, punishing month of Budget deliberations when the dollar started to tumble.

There was depression in the room as Paul Keating sombrely called from his portable Reuters screen the drop of the dollar, like a boxing referee going through the count. The dollar started at about 63 cents. As it plunged into what the more pessimistic Members thought was a free-fall, Paul called the dollar's descent through the 60 cent mark and down through the high 50s until it finally bottomed at 57.15 cents.

For those present – myself, Treasurer Keating, the Finance Minister, Senator Peter Walsh, the Trade Minister, John Dawkins, the Industrial Relations Minister, Ralph Willis, and Senator John Button – the mood swing was as sharp as the downward slide of the currency. Peter Walsh captured our sinking feeling when he later said: 'I was closer to despair than I'd ever been in politics, because I thought we had been a good Government ... and yet we'd been hit with this, and we didn't really deserve it, and how the hell were we ever going to get out of it.'[73]

These were dire times indeed. But, as with the currency crisis which had struck in our first days of office and, again, in December 1983 when the Australian dollar was floated, it was no time for panic; it was time to think our way through what had happened and to act.

We immediately reopened our Budget deliberations and began to slash and burn Government spending in a fashion called for by the crisis confronting us. We determined that the 1986 Budget should contain no real growth in Government outlays. It was a radical decision and one which we knew would be extremely difficult for the Labor Party to absorb and accept. Philosophically, the party had been brought up on the notion of Government playing an expansionary role, opening the public purse to spend on health, education, welfare and other traditional objectives. To declare, suddenly, that there would be no real increases overall in these areas would, we knew, cause much discomfort in the party.

Having elaborated the general principle upon which we intended to act, the ERC set about making the cuts and achieving the savings.

Where we had thought to bring in a Budget deficit of about $5 billion, we set to work on reducing this to $3.5 billion. The extra $1.5 billion in savings was achieved during a frantic two-week period when, as John Dawkins has pointed out, 'some previously unthinkable things, became thinkable'.[74]

One decision, in particular, caused uproar – the decision to lift a ban on uranium sales to France at a saving of $70 million. It was a fight which ideally would have been left to cooler times but the present exigencies did not allow us that luxury. The savings may appear small but Budget targets are met by many such small savings; there are always special arguments not to make any of them. In any event I had committed the Government to taking hard decisions and this was one of them. I was personally buttressed by my long-standing opposition to the party's uranium policy, which I regarded as wrong-headed and illogical.

Caucus groaned when the issue came before it but the decision of the ERC was validated in the vote and another of the party's sacred cows was culled from the herd. If continuing the ban on sales of uranium to France had been able to achieve any worthwhile political objective, then that would have been a valid consideration. But our policy was in fact a benefit to France, since the spot price for uranium had fallen. Instead of having to buy uranium from Queensland Mines at a fixed contract price, France was purchasing uranium elsewhere at a lower spot price, leaving the Australian Government to compensate Queensland Mines for the cost of the ban. In consequence, Labor's policy was imposing a penalty upon the Australian people. Indeed as I later argued, we were asking the poor in Australia to subsidise a prejudice which was serving no purpose.

Reopening the 1986 Budget and carving a further $1.5 billion off the deficit was the highwater mark of the ERC's importance as an instrument of government. There were hard choices to be made, particularly the lifting of the uranium ban, but at the same time we were all party loyalists conscious of the aspirations of Labor in government. We aimed to make Australia a better country – fairer, more equitable, more competitive, more aware of the international context, more able to provide more people with a better quality of life. But this aim could not be realised without pain and an astringent questioning of priorities.

During this time the ERC drove the economic reform package. It became a very tight, technically proficient, well-disciplined group, small enough to get a lot of work done, and quickly. There was no dead weight on the ERC; everyone had a significant contribution to make. Peter Walsh may have been useless as a political barometer, as I think he would gruffly concede, but he was brilliant as a logician and analyst. There was much of John Stone in him. Like Stone, Peter came from the wheat-belt of Western Australia. Originally a farmer himself, he had acquired an Economics degree from the University of Western Australia. His style was dour and often caustic; there were no beg-your-pardons with Walsh. He would look at an issue and say, 'There must be this amount of savings, and we can do it this way; that portfolio should make this contribution, and even if there's some political pain, that's what's got to happen.' He was rigorous and tough, with a mastery of his brief. More than most, he enjoyed an evening drink or three, but you could be certain that he was across any issue that came before the ERC in Cabinet. Peter would have read everything about it and forgotten very little of its detail.

John Dawkins, another West Australian, was similar in some ways. As a political guide he was about as reliable as Peter Walsh. But as a lateral thinker with a good mind and a capacity for hard work, Dawkins was first-rate. He did not have Walsh's strong logical streak and he would often go haring off on some unrewarding tangent. Even so, it was always worth listening to him and a number of the more creative suggestions for dealing with the 1986 Budget crisis came in fact from John – lifting the ban on uranium sales to France and levying fees on tertiary students on a capacity-to-pay basis, for example.

No member of the ERC worked more diligently than Ralph Willis. He brought to the meetings a good mind, professional expertise, and a profound compassion tempered by his increasingly firm understanding of the constraints imposed by the economic context in which we were working. Whenever he spoke, Ralph was listened to with respect.

Paul Keating was, obviously, always a significant contributor to ERC meetings although he wasn't quite as assiduous in his attendance and timing as the other members of the committee. These were extremely trying times for Paul personally. His earlier personal pressures continued to dog him, compounded by some bad management on his part. Annita, his wife, was in poor health during this period and in fact delayed going into hospital until after Paul's Budget speech on 19th August 1986. With Annita unwell, Paul Keating the parent was under greater pressure. More than any other politician I have known, Paul took the role of father as a serious duty. At that time, too, the now defunct *National Times* was practising its characteristic bastardry by snooping around his friendship with property developer Warren Anderson. The paper sent Keating a list of questions about Anderson's business interests and tax affairs. Quite understandably, Paul would have no part of the *National Times'* sleazy paranoia; he had nothing to fear either from his friendship with Anderson or anyone else. Nevertheless, the innuendo surrounding the investigation of Anderson and Paul's friendship with him created an atmosphere of rumour and speculation which deeply offended and unsettled Paul. The article on Anderson was published just days before the August Budget and it was a pressure he could have done without.

A self-inflicted injury made 1986 even worse for him. It became public knowledge that he was being pursued by the Deputy

Commissioner of Taxation for his failure to file his 1985 tax return on time. Paul publicly admitted the mistake but it was an embarrassing moment for both the Treasurer and the Government. His biographer Edna Carew wrote:

> The revelation provoked considerable resentment: here was the country's Treasurer, who had waged a relentless campaign for tax reform and, in the name of economic rationalism, introduced measures that carried some pain as well as some pleasure, ignoring his duty as a taxpayer. Keating's oversight provided his critics with a fresh supply of ammunition; they declared that his action smacked of the arrogance of someone who felt above the common throng. Talk-back radio programmes buzzed with indignant callers, ready and eager to bucket the Treasurer.[75]

It was a stupid mistake, as distinct from the totally unfair attack to which he was subjected in regard to his claim for living away from home accommodation and travelling costs even though he now lived in Canberra. The latter was a perfectly legal claim with solid precedent on the other side of politics, but this did not deter the Opposition. It became another burden in what I imagine Paul himself would designate as his 'annus horribilis'.

Despite all this I still regarded him as my logical successor. Nonetheless, I had doubts about him and I noted them on some tapes I dictated at the time. The relevant entry reads: 'He is exceedingly unpopular in the Caucus, very unpopular, unfairly so in my judgment, quite unfairly so, but he is. And one of the things I've found … going around the country, [is that] he's on the nose out there in the electorate. Paul is going to have to cultivate the Caucus and, in a sense, cultivate the electorate … He just is not an electoral leader at the moment and is not seen as such, and this is unfortunate. He's just got to get closer to the Caucus and closer to the people. It's put to me now by his friends, that if there were a ballot now for the deputy leadership, if something happened to Lionel, Paul couldn't win it.'

Politically the Government was taking a hammering throughout 1986 and Paul's problems added to them. Even our heroic effort in the ERC, scraping and clawing the deficit back to the $3.5 billion announced in the Budget, was viewed cynically in both the media and the markets. The accuracy of our projected deficit was doubted although the actual deficit for the year turned out lower than we had predicted, eventually coming in at $2.7 billion.

The August Budget went further than massive deficit reduction. We also announced that the Government would support only a 50 per cent indexation of union wage claims at the next two national wage cases. The move, in effect, spelled the end of wage indexation as an article of faith in the labour movement. In December the move away from indexation was complete. Under the new 'two-tiered' wages system workers' pay would be tied to productivity gains. The approach was formalised at the March 1987 National Wage Case. We had embarked upon a major structural reform of Australia's labour market, pushing it towards decentralisation, a step which few would have previously thought possible.

Yet while we were embarked on these significant reforms, bad news kept flooding in on us. The United States credit rating agency, Moody's Investor Services, downgraded Australia's rating from AAA to AA+, and our current account deficit continued to balloon, exceeding even the appalling April figure. Government morale sank like mercury at an approaching storm. Another election, due by early 1988 at the latest, was approaching rapidly. My goal of a long-term Labor govern-ment accustomed to winning, with Labor recognised as a natural party of government, seemed destined in the eyes of most observers to be running into the sands of Labor's historical assumption that its destiny was to grab power rarely, and to govern gloriously but briefly before returning to that barren wilderness on the left of the Speaker's chair.

As far as I was concerned, to borrow the Australian idiom – Bugger that for a joke! But convincing the troops that modern Labor was about winning, not about licking its wounds in Opposition, was not easy at this time. Often I was viewed as the naïve optimist, or worse, as Senator Robert Ray has recently attested: 'Every Caucus meeting, Hawke would stand up in his address to them (Caucus colleagues) and affirm the fact that we were going to win the next election. At first this was greeted with a degree of silence, then a degree of sarcasm.'[76]

The year 1986 was indeed a bleak one for the Government. The polls showed Labor trailing the Coalition and the mood among most in our party was calculated to rocket us into Opposition. My own popularity was high, certainly above that of the main Coalition protagonists, Andrew Peacock and John Howard, as preferred Prime Minister, but I felt more and more isolated in my belief that Labor could win a third term.

The recidivists and pessimists among our ranks had been able to throw off the shackles of the past when Labor was on the up. The euphoria of growth in 1983 through to 1985 when employment was growing at a staggering rate, when we almost halved the rate of unemployment, had given way to a self-defeating gloom. Inflation, interest rates, unemployment, all were worsening with our declining terms of trade and cheaper dollar. Justifiable pride in what we had been able to achieve in health, education, housing and welfare, legislating and implementing policies which were right at the heart of Labor philosophy, had given way to doubt.

In contrast, I remained convinced we would win. It was not a stance that I adopted simply for the sake of rallying the troops. Rather it was founded on my belief that the Australian electorate was becoming increasingly sophisticated and economically literate. If the Government was prepared to trust the people with the facts, then the people would respond, no matter how much they were hurting, by voting for the interests of the country ahead of perceived self-interest, however cynically the Opposition appealed to those instincts. This was the strategy I adopted as I moved from 1986 into 1987.

TWENTY-THREE

The 1986 Budget reflected the crisis of the times. But coming into 1987 it was obvious that further measures had to be taken well ahead of that year's Budget. Proper macro-economic policy and the associated need to reassure both the domestic and international markets that we were continuing to address Australia's changed circumstances demanded that we produce a further economic statement – nothing less than a mini-Budget.

The job of finding substantial expenditure cuts to be announced in a May statement fell, as usual, to the Expenditure Review Committee. As ERC chairman I had always been assiduous in my attendance. This time, however, I told my ERC colleagues it was going to be different; for a lot of the time I wouldn't be there. Rather, I intended to be out moving around the country telling the story that Australia had lost about $9 billion in national income because of the dramatic fall in the prices we received for many of our exports. I would be spreading the message that we could not expect the world to sustain our living standards; instead we would have to make tough decisions and get used to new realities.

This was no time to be bogged down in Canberra in a morass of gloom and depression about our electoral prospects. I believed that, given the facts, the Australian people would make the right decision. Indeed I have always maintained that, with the possible exception of 1980, Australians have made the right decision in every election since 1949 – when the country, weary of the restrictions of war and the immediate postwar period, rejected Labor's Ben Chifley for the redoubtable R.G. Menzies.

While taking the Government's message to the Australian people, I left behind Steve Sedgwick, Ross Garnaut's successor as my economic adviser, as my surrogate on the Expenditure Review Committee. His brief was to keep me informed of the ERC's daily deliberations on the understanding that no binding decisions would be taken by the committee on any sensitive issue without my intervention, either to endorse a tentative position or to overrule it.

As the Government knuckled down to the task of directing Australia onto a new course, a bizarre melodrama was being played out on the conservative side of politics. The rock-solid Coalition which Menzies had founded was being riven and thrown into turmoil by the junior Coalition partner. Significant sections of the National Party had acquiesced in a death wish for the party to go its own way. The ageing but ambitious National Party Premier of Queensland, Sir Joh Bjelke-Petersen, was precipitating this crisis with a bid to make his eccentric brand of flat-earth, flat-tax politics an Australia-wide phenomenon.

'Joh for Canberra' might have been one man's delusion of grandeur but for the fact that there were others far smarter than Joh (former Treasury Secretary, John Oswald Stone, and the National Farmers' Federation President, Ian McLachlan, for example) who were prepared to take the Queenslander seriously. These and others like them supplied the ultimately fatal ingredient to the Joh push and added some light touches for Labor at a gloomy time. In the 1950s and 60s Labor had been kept from government largely through its own disunity and disarray. Now in government, it was always a source of amused satisfaction to me when the Conservatives took to each other with greater gusto than they did to us.

Disunity was not just a problem between the Coalition partners; within the Liberal Party itself Andrew Peacock continued to face off against John Howard, who had been Opposition Leader since 5th September 1985, when the Liberal leadership had been handed to him in a farce of Andrew's own making.

On 23rd March 1987 Howard sacked Peacock from the front bench for disloyalty. At this time too, ideological warfare was being waged within the Liberal Party. Liberal 'wets' were falling like ninepins as Howard sought to make his party drier than a bone. Peacock was fired, Senator Peter Baume, unable to stomach his party's opposition to the Government's affirmative action proposals, quit the front bench, and Ian McPhee was also in trouble. He finally fell in April.

With the Coalition racked with conflict, several of my closest advisers (Bob Sorby, who had succeeded Peter Barron, Graham Freudenberg, my speech writer, and Richard Farmer, part-time party consultant) sensed an opportunity and began pushing strongly for an early election. Indeed Farmer was urging me to go to the polls as early as March, and the others were not far behind him. But their pitch was hitched entirely to Opposition negatives and the election was viewed not as a contest of strengths but a vote on the respective weaknesses of the parties.

It was savvy advice but, I thought, too limited. The weight of Cabinet and party officialdom was certainly against an early poll and continued to be so. But that cut less ice with me than the economic imperatives of governing Australia out of the crisis into which the country had been thrown by crashing commodity prices. Our first priority was the economic statement we were in the throes of preparing, together with educating Australians about the dire nature of our predicament and the remedial steps that had to be taken.

On 1st April I ruled out the prospect of an early election with words which, in retrospect, were too categorical. I flagged the election for the latter part of the year or early in 1988. Colleagues breathed a sigh of relief but Freudenberg, for one, was most upset and shot off a memo the next day: 'I must place on record my deepest anger about the manner, timing and content of the announcement yesterday'. He did acknowledge, however, that the decision as to when to call an election is probably the most difficult a Prime Minister has to make. Governments live or die by it and a wrong call is irreversible and irredeemable. It is the one decision where the buck stops at your desk and nowhere else.

With an election temporarily off the agenda, the ERC pressed ahead with preparing the May Statement. But before I took off around the country, I made a decision which basically changed the chemistry of the ERC by appointing the Left's Brian Howe, Minister for Social Security, to the committee. When the Treasurer heard of this he came bounding up the stairs in a state of near apoplexy; he complained that Howe was not equipped for the task and that the meetings would drag on endlessly as Brian attempted to pursue an unrealistic Left agenda. I told Keating he was wrong and that the decision would not be changed. I believed it important as we moved further into sensitive areas of expenditure restraint to have a senior representative of the Left on the ERC. Brian, for whom I had developed a growing respect, would help to secure the broad support we would need in the party in the difficult months ahead.

Keating, brought up in the unforgiving school of the NSW Right, thought this was crazy stuff and said that I would regret the decision and to remember that he had warned me. I was so confident in my reasoning, I responded that he would come to see the decision as a master-stroke. And so it was, as he was gracious enough later, under a little prompting, to concede.

Some of the ERC's most difficult decisions were in the social welfare area. The May Statement contained expenditure cuts of $2.6 billion, involving a further dramatic shift towards needs-based welfare. When it came to subjects like assets testing, unemployment and sickness benefits, Brian Howe's role was invaluable. He brought to the ERC's deliberations his detailed knowledge of the social security portfolio and a deep understanding of the welfare constituency.

Brian showed in his contributions on the ERC just how far the Left had come from the early days of government. In place of knee-jerk reactions there was a cool-headed, mature assessment of the best way to spend limited resources. Most of these expenditure cuts caused Brian some ideological pain, for this was a constituency the Left had claimed as its own. And for Brian it was more than ideology. He had been a Methodist minister in the poor inner suburbs of Melbourne; his life had been one of dedication to the underprivileged. But he was able, while maintaining his loyalties and commitments, to start talking the language of priorities with the rest of us. That meant making careful cuts now or facing the prospect of further indiscriminate reductions in the living standards of all Australians as our current account deficit deteriorated still further.

Already we were $1500 per Australian family poorer as a consequence of the world paying drastically lower prices for many of our exports. Now was the chance to arrest that slide and determine a new course for the country and Brian Howe threw himself wholeheartedly into that endeavour.

I cannot speak too highly of his contribution to the ERC process, which was not confined to the parameters of his own portfolio but was important to the general debate. The May Economic Statement contained a billion dollars of asset sales. Many of these were uncontentious – for example, a partial sale of our embassy site in Tokyo and other land sales – but they presaged the broader privatisation debate ahead. When it came to privatisation, Brian was able to argue from his ERC experience that one dollar simply could not do two jobs. Putting a dollar of equity into the running of an airline was paid at the expense of programs for the unemployed or the single mother. In those circumstances, Brian understood acutely what the priorities of a true Labor government were.

Perhaps the most interesting feature of Brian Howe's inclusion on the ERC was the interaction between him and the initially antagonistic Treasurer. Their mutual wariness gradually gave way to a constructive combination which would before long help to craft one of Labor's most admirable and enduring initiatives, the Family Allowance Supplement.

But the news of the hour was the mini-Budget, unveiled on 13th May 1987. The May Economic Statement produced savings of $4 billion, a remarkable 2 per cent real cut in outlays. It had been a hard exercise in which we had garnered savings from the largest policy areas. Social security, education, community services, health, defence and Commonwealth–State relations had all been comprehensively reviewed. We had been running a very tight monetary policy which, naturally enough, had resulted in high interest rates. The May Statement decisively recast that policy, shifting the emphasis from monetary to fiscal discipline. And by starting the job ahead of the normal August Budget we ensured that the benefits of the spending cuts would be reflected in the full financial year 1987–88.

Political and economic benefits flowed simultaneously and quickly from the May Statement. The Labor Party was certainly pleased with the outcome. They could see in the ERC's handiwork that the Government was indeed implementing the principle of 'restraint with equity' I had promised the previous year. The media and the markets were generally surprised at the extent of our pruning and responded positively; indeed the reception by the financial markets was better than we had expected.

By this point the political scene was changing rapidly. I had previously ruled out an early election. I did not intend to dodge the tough decisions and simply take advantage of the increasing disarray in the Opposition ranks. But now the hard decisions had been taken and they had been well received. The education program I had undertaken had worked well with both the party and the people. The Coalition had formally broken down and the schism within their ranks had deteriorated further since my statement of 1st April. Our legislative program was being blocked in the Senate. The Australia Card Bill, integral at that stage to the Government's tax reform package, had twice been repudiated in the Senate. The Senate was also thwarting our legislation to extend equal access to television services to five million Australians living in country areas.

Many factors, therefore, but not all opinions, were pointing in one direction. Sorby was still keen on going to the polls early and Freudenburg and Farmer had lost none of their enthusiasm. The Treasurer was now keen on going early. But Cabinet and party opinion generally were against a mid-year poll, especially since the Government could run into 1988 for which Treasury was prophesying much better economic conditions. Indeed there were plenty of doom-sayers who thought if I went early I would be committing political suicide and taking the Government with me.

I appreciated better than anybody these dangers. To truncate the life of a government is an awful responsibility for a Prime Minister to bear, as Malcolm Fraser found when he went early in March 1983. I would be running against all the normal assumptions by going early, in the aftermath of a harsh Budget and May Statement and in the middle of winter. The easy course was to let the Parliament run its term.

I felt very lonely and a little frightened, but a combination of instinct, polling research, and my own political judgment strengthened my conviction that it was time to move. After assessing our performance, the people's understanding of what we were doing, and looking at the condition of the Opposition I concluded that we could win. It would not be easy, the campaign would probably determine everything. Nonetheless, I thought we could do it.

On 27th May I called an election for 11th July 1987. In announcing the date I said that Australia's greatest need was for certainty, stability and continuity, but these qualities were not only relevant in an economic context. Appropriate management of the economy was fundamental but quality of life issues, concern for the national heritage, resource management and environmental protection were high on our agenda and had been from the very beginning.

On coming to office in 1983 we had immediately stopped the proposed building of the Gordon-below-Franklin dam in Tasmania. At that time another of Australia's heritage treasures, the magnificent Great Barrier Reef, was mostly unprotected – only 14.5 per cent of the Reef region was incorporated in the Great Barrier Reef Marine Park. By 1987, thanks to the diligent work of Barry Cohen, my first Environment Minister,[77] the total reef area was protected in the park.

In another historic heritage decision, Uluru, the world's largest rock and the symbolic heart of Australia, was handed back to its original owners and later given heritage protection. In 1986 we nominated Stage II of the Northern Territory's spectacular Kakadu National Park for World Heritage listing. Kakadu is famous for wetlands and galleries of well-preserved Aboriginal rock paintings; we implemented a multi-million dollar scheme, as we had done with the Uluru national park (now the Uluru Kata-Tjuta National Park), to develop Kakadu into a national wilderness park of world renown. In December 1986 Cabinet took an in-principle decision to nominate Stage III of the park, but as we moved into the 1987 election campaign that decision lay in abeyance.

Labor's credentials as a green party were well established by this time. Nonetheless, the election campaign provided us with a perfect opportunity to differentiate ourselves further from our Coalition opponents on environmental issues. Perhaps no-one saw this better than Graham Richardson, the Senator from the New South Wales Right who had made his reputation to date as a party strategist, organiser, numbers man and pragmatist *par excellence*, but certainly not as a greenie.

Richardson, paunchy, urbanised and sedentary, was a hard-nosed materialist not readily associated with philosophical intangibles. It came as a great surprise to Graham's friends and opponents when he started to emerge as a champion of green causes. Opportunism was the quick and easy explanation given by many of them. But when he first started talking to me about the environment in early 1987 I sensed, even then, something more in Graham's conversation than a sharp political mind glimpsing an electoral opportunity. He dates his conversion to sitting on the shores of Lake Sydney in Tasmania eating a picnic lunch with leading environmentalist Dr Bob Brown. The ambience of the mountain lake and Brown's passionate communication of his environmental creed produced an epiphany for Graham which led him to fight for green causes. Other factors had also prepared the way for this new committment; dinner-time discussion with his environment-conscious children had certainly influenced him, and his reading on the subject began to reflect their concerns. Logging practices in Australian forests, air and water pollution, and land degradation all became the standard fare of Graham's discourse.

But the old Richardson was mixed in there too, the superb political operative quick to sense electoral opportunity. He discerned in the Australian constituency a mirroring of his own increasing environmental awareness. In fact there was something of an insatiable appetite for environmental issues out there and Graham stressed that the party would do best to recognise this. Saving the Franklin was one thing, as were Labor's other initiatives, but there were new and fresh challenges in which Labor had continually to renew its green credentials.

I agreed with Richardson on both the intrinsic and the electoral worth of environmentalism. I had been reasonably green long before Graham but his conversion kept me sensitive to and abreast of the movement, a movement now aided by a powerful and skilful ally. His recruitment to the green cause would have its greatest influence after the 1987 election when I made him Environment Minister and upgraded the portfolio to Cabinet status. But as a backbencher in the 1987 election campaign, Graham was certainly influential in steps then taken to protect the environment and shore up the environmental vote.

He was particularly keen that we should try to prevent logging in the wet tropics of north-east Queensland. The immediate threat there came from the State Government's decision to plough a road through this wilderness area, including the magnificent Daintree rainforest.

Having called the election for 11th July, one of my first moves was to announce the Government's intention to have the northern rain-forests included on the World Heritage List. We also moved to gazette Stage III of the Kakadu National Park. Of course electoral considera-tions were involved but there were purer motives as well. I feared that, should Labor lose the election, an incoming Coalition government would simply leave Stage III unlisted. Proclamation would protect Kakadu from the Opposition's 'let her rip' mentality.

My capacity to deal effectively with the environmental lobby was enhanced by having recruited Dr Craig Emerson, a very bright young economist, to my personal staff in June 1986. Craig had worked for Peter Walsh – the bane of the greenies – and had then become an

Assistant Secretary in the Department of Prime Minister and Cabinet. I was attracted by his intelligence and vivacious integrity; there was a boyish enthusiasm about everything he did. Craig came to me as a specialist in the micro-economic area and, after sitting in on 12th June 1986, when Graham Richardson brought Dr Bob Brown to meet me, he also became my indispensable adviser on the environment. That meeting set the scene for the subsequent establishment of the Helsham Inquiry and our nomination of substantial areas of Tasmanian forests for World Heritage listing.

I detailed Emerson to work closely with the lobby – particularly the Australian Conservation Foundation (ACF) and the Wilderness Society – in the lead-up to the election. I told him there was to be no 'elastic agenda', for some of the environmentalists were unrealistic and never-ending in their demands. As a result of Craig's good work, the specific areas of commitment were limited to Tasmanian forests, Kakadu, the Wet Tropics rainforests and Shelbourne Bay in Queensland.

I was prepared to be receptive to their concerns but not to be the captive of the greens. Apart from specific agreements, there was no holy writ. Often decisions were made after rough exchanges in which environmentalists together with miners, developers, farmers, loggers or other interested parties were called upon to argue their case. And within the Government there were ministers consumed by development to the virtual exclusion of environmental considerations. This made for several tense, protracted struggles, and occasional exchanges of pleasantries, throughout the life of the Government, with the Cabinet always prepared in the end to accept my call on the outcome.

It was a style of government which assured to all interests an open and fair hearing. It contrasted with the methods of the Opposition who often adopted a punitive attitude; they had a closed door and a closed mind on the subject of the environment and entered the 1987 election threatening to eliminate the Department of Arts, Heritage and the Environment and to abolish Government funding of the ACF.

It was little wonder that the ACF abandoned its long-standing policy of not endorsing particular political parties and recommended that its members vote for the Labor Party in the House of Represent-atives. The Wilderness Society ran television advertisements saying that Bob Hawke would protect Tasmanian forests and the Opposition would not. This was a first preference strategy, a voluntary call by the green movement itself for environmentalists to give Labor their primary vote. It was the forerunner of a much subtler garnering of the green vote – the second preference strategy – which was developed by the Labor Party itself and was to prove so important in the 1990 election.

Labor was clearly seen as a better manager of the environment and this proved crucial in a number of marginal seats. But economic management was more important to the bulk of electors. Labor could point to a strong performance after four years in government: record employment growth, lowered inflation and a complete overhaul of Australia's financial system. But these significant achievements had been obscured to some extent by the massive turnaround in the terms of trade which had sent a tremor through the country and shaken voter confidence.

Labor's re-election strategy was simple: to educate a shell-shocked public about the crisis that had befallen Australia and to call for courage in confronting that crisis. Labor had a plan, and we had unveiled the details in the Budget and mini-Budget; it was now up to the country to hold its nerve and see that plan through.

While we offered belt-tightening 'restraint with equity', the Coalition offered the nation reckless abandon – a massive, unfunded tax cut. Here was the critical danger and test for me and for Labor –

who was reading the Australian people right? Our message was stirring but solemn. There was always the temptation for voters to turn from that to the thrill of an extravaganza – $7.3 billion worth of tax cuts tied to hot-air balloons.

The Government's realism and sound economic policies provided Labor's basic insurance for re-election but I also took out some extra cover. Our sombre message did require salesmanship and razzamatazz. I insisted, in the teeth of considerable opposition, that John Singleton Advertising be appointed Labor's agency for the election, replacing Forbes McPhee Hansen, which had done the job for the past thirteen years.

Forbes McPhee Hansen was a committed, professional agency, but in this campaign we would need to be able to react quickly – and John Singleton seemed to be the right man to help us win decisively. Whatever Singleton lacked, it wasn't flair. He had also demonstrated the speed of response in translating ideas into advertising product that I was looking for. This immediacy and imagination had come together for me in August 1986 with the 'Australian Made' campaign. The Government called for tenders and submissions from advertising agencies and Singleton's 'true blue' theme and approach was shown by market testing to be far and away the best we received. He captured the essence of the campaign in a simple, easily communicable form which, as the research showed, struck home to the Australian public.

I was impressed by the professionalism of Singleton's agency and with the success of the campaign. But Singleton had a past to live down, a history of anti-Laborism symbolised by his creation of earlier times – the ineptly named Workers' Party. For many of my colleagues this offspring was a black mark against him. They remembered as well the work he had done for the likes of former New South Wales Liberal Premier, Sir Robin Askin, and for Queensland National Party Premier, Sir Joh Bjelke-Petersen.

Labor Party campaign director Bob McMullan, particularly, feared party reaction should Labor switch its account to Singleton. Upsetting the party in this way, he reasoned, would detract from running the most effective campaign. In addition, he worried at the new agency's capacity to organise the necessary media outlets in the same way as our existing agency, with whom he had an easy and well-established relationship.

These were legitimate concerns on Bob's part but I had a totally contrary instinct. This, together with personal knowledge of Singleton, made me insist upon the change. During a lengthy sabbatical from advertising, Singleton had been hired by Barrie Unsworth, then running the Labor-owned radio station 2KY in New South Wales, to boost the station's ratings, which he had done. Whenever I was interviewed by him Singo always gave me a fair go and he was never unreasoning or rabid. His Workers' Party aberration was an unfortunate interlude, no doubt, but one which, in my estimation, he had now supplanted with a total and exuberant commitment to the Hawke Labor Government. As a last test of loyalty, I suppose, I remember questioning Singleton before finally giving him the account. It was at a dinner and the language was direct: 'If we go with you, are you with us all the way?' I asked. 'To the death, mate,' Singo replied, better, even, than a blood oath.

In the event, booking John Singleton Advertising was generally acknowledged to have been a stroke of brilliant lunacy. The best proof, of course, is that John was used again in 1990 and 1993. Bob Hogg, who was vehemently opposed to my choice of Singo, now works with him; I have told them both that I expect them to equal my record of four victories in 1996.

Party reaction to the choice, as I expected, was not a continuing problem. Vindication of the choice came early. During an inspired weekend of work at his agency in Hunters Hill, Singleton and songwriter Terry Hannigan composed the classic battle hymn of Labor's campaign – 'Together: Let's Stick Together, Let's See it Through'. When they performed it one night in the Cabinet room of the old Parliament House some time prior to its release on 9th June 1987, with Terry playing the guitar and the pair of them having a go at the words, it was clear to all of us present that here was something special to rally the faithful and to send a tingle up the spine of the nation:

> We're on our way;
> We're on the right track;
> Australians have always been good at fighting back.
> With a little more strength and patience we'll see Australia
>   right;
> Nothing worth having ever happens overnight.
>
> We gotta keep on holding tight;
> To that great Australian dream;
> Nobody ever got anywhere;
> Changing horses in mid-stream.

In between verses ran the recurring chorus, 'Together: let's stick together, let's see it through.'

Singo described this anthem as a fluke, but it is the kind of fluke that can only happen after years of experience and with plenty of God-given ability. The words were right, the music was right, the refrain was right, the mood was right, the voices were right – everything blended together perfectly. 'Let's stick together' was certainly a turning point in party morale as the doubters, of whom there were many, caught a scent of victory.

But there was still a long way to go until 11th July. Tax policy was always going to be a major issue during the election campaign. The Opposition was committed to repealing most of our far-reaching income tax reforms aimed at broadening the tax base and putting an end to rorting. Under the Coalition capital gains would not be taxed, fringe-benefits tax would be emasculated, and runaway tax avoidance of the sort that typified the late seventies and early eighties was again in the offing.

Against Labor's reforms it was difficult to discern precisely what the Coalition was proposing, as Opposition Leader Howard refused, right up until a fortnight into the campaign, to release his party's tax policy. And while Howard held back the crazies on the Conservative side of politics took up the slack. Bjelke-Petersen, for example, advocated a 25 per cent flat tax – 'voodoo economics' had taken over.

It didn't take much imagination for Singleton to characterise John Howard as a top-hatted magician tricking up paper money from a collapsible table. But nothing conjured by our advertisers in the early part of the campaign could match the real thing: John Howard's launch of the Liberal's long-awaited tax policy on 10th June 1987. It was then that Howard unveiled his $7.3 billion worth of tax cuts in an attempt to buy his way into office. The attempt was reminiscent of the 1977 election campaign when Prime Minister Malcolm Fraser, with John Howard as his Treasurer, held out a 'fistful of dollars' inducement to voters. We didn't intend to give Howard a second opportunity to renege on the promise, as they had done after winning that election.

Like 1977, the hip-pocket move was seductive, our party research showed, but it failed to appreciate the increasing sophistication and economic literacy of the Australian electorate under Labor. 'Whingeing' Wendy Woods, John Singleton's sidekick from his radio days, was now helping out with the Labor Party advertisements.

Wendy's grammar may not have been too good but she voiced the question on most Australians' lips: where's the money coming from? 'Whingeing' Wendy was not just an advertising creation, she was a real Australian and she could not only ask the question but debate it as well. Indeed she did debate the question, intelligently and articulately, against some very bright opponents. 'She's only a Rex Harrison away from being Prime Minister herself,' Singo ribbed me.

We disputed the general arithmetic of Howard's tax policy from the outset. Keating and I both attacked the profligacy of the program and the prospect of a massive blow-out in the Budget deficit. But officials had alerted the Treasurer to the real time-bomb waiting to be exploded in Howard's face. They pointed out that the Opposition had been guilty in their calculation of a double-counting error of approximately $1.6 billion. On 18th June Paul was able to produce a detailed statement proving conclusively that Howard's figures did not add up. He savaged the Opposition remorselessly on this point, and Howard, to his acute embarrassment, had to admit to the double-counting error, which he said was only $540 million. By then a lot of people had stopped counting for John.

The allure of tax cuts was fast vanishing as a selling point for the Opposition. Swinging voters were more concerned about how the tax cuts would be paid for than the attraction of the cuts themselves. This point was not lost on State Premiers, especially the four Labor Premiers, who condemned Howard's tax proposals. They were well aware of the totally devastating effect the cuts in federal payments for community services would have on the welfare of their citizens.

We did not want a bidding war with the Opposition but we were extremely aware of hardship in the community, particularly among low-income families with children. Since coming to government we had done much to help those most in need; but latterly, evidence had been accumulating of child poverty concentrated among poorer families.

We were governing for hard times and any new initiatives had to be targeted on areas of greatest need. To us there was no greater need than the children of relatively poor families.

This was the genesis of the greatest social reform of my Government, and perhaps of all Labor governments: the Family Allowance Supplement. The $400 million per annum allocation, adding to existing social security child payments and integrating them into one system, was the centrepiece of my 23rd June policy speech at the Opera House in Sydney. The launch was organised to extract maximum value from the allocated thirty minutes of free television time. But more rousing than anything on that day, than Roger Woodward at the piano, Julie Anthony singing the National Anthem, or Peter Faiman's stage craft, was the announcement of, and reaction to, this historic new program.

It came in an electric phrase which rang through the Opera House: 'By 1990, no Australian child will be living in poverty.' This sentence was to encapsulate the most hurtful paradox of my whole political life. It launched what the welfare organisations have acknowledged as the single greatest child-support decision in federal history;[78] the scheme has been more effective in dealing with the problems of child poverty than anything that has ever been done and billions of dollars have now been paid through the program to families with children in need.

But I had stupidly let pass an abbreviation that has diverted attention from this great achievement and allowed my opponents to pillory me for promising the impossible. The printed attachment to my speech, distributed to the media, made the meaning crystal-clear; it spelled out the intention of the reform that in the future there 'would be no financial need for any child to live in poverty'. I have no-one to blame but myself for allowing the literally unfulfillable shorthand version of 'no child living in poverty' to remain in the speech. We were not a dictatorship with storm-troopers ensuring that parents in every household would spend the family allowance supplement on their children. Inevitably there would be instances of the money intended for meeting the needs of children being dissipated in other ways. Nor could any government ensure that kids would not run away from homes that they found uncongenial and take up life on the streets.

The critics' jibes hurt me deeply but what has sustained me as I have moved around Australia are the hundreds of mothers who have come forward unsolicited, with children in their arms, in strollers, or walking beside them, and saying something similar to the young woman in the western suburbs of Sydney: 'Thank you Mr Hawke, for what you've done! This has made the difference between just existing and being able to do something for our kids.' She had tears in her eyes.

In the end it's the unprompted gratitude of mums and their kids that is more important and lasting than the cheap shots of people trying to score a political point. These mothers provided some of the warmest moments in politics for me and I was proud to have delivered on the essential promise. Labor had ensured that by 1990 there would be no *financial need* for any child to live in poverty.

Launching our new campaign and our new child welfare measure was an emotional moment for all of us. Two days later, on 25th June, I faced another emotion-charged occasion while attending a fund-raising dinner in the federal electorate of Oxley, which Bill Hayden had represented since 1961. This was Hayden territory and, as many of the local stalwarts saw it, Bill would now be Prime Minister but for me.

Much had changed since 3rd February 1983, that extraordinary day when Bill Hayden stood down as Leader of the Labor Party in my favour, and Malcolm Fraser called a general election. We had now been a highly successful Labor government for more than four years, with Bill as my distinguished Foreign Minister. He was generally a solid support to me in Cabinet deliberations and we had worked well together as Prime Minister and Foreign Minister. I recognised his capacities and gave him a free reign in his portfolio. At the same time Bill recognised that foreign affairs was an area in which the Prime Minister had a direct and continuing concern and involvement. On this basis we worked constructively together from the outset.

Nevertheless, the wound of 3rd February 1983 had never been publicly salved and the occasion now arose to do just that. Before I called the 1987 election, Bill had asked me to speak at a fund-raising dinner for him in Ipswich, his hometown in Queensland; but he well understood the demands upon a party leader during an election campaign, and after the poll date was announced he graciously offered to withdraw the request. I told him that it was something I wanted to do and we would keep it in the program.

We arrived at the Amberley RAAF base in the late afternoon and I went immediately to a quiet room which had been set aside for me. In a reflective mood, with a cup of tea and a cigar, I began to jot down my thoughts.

I knew it would be Bill's last election, as we had already spoken of the governor-generalship. He had come to see me one evening in early 1987 to discuss some portfolio matters but it was clear that he wanted to talk more generally. He spoke generously of the job I had done as Prime Minister, and then began to reflect on the past and the scar left by the events of February 1983: 'That scar will always be there, but I have learned to live with it and have no problem with it,' Bill said. He then moved on to discuss his family and their feeling that, somehow, Bill Hayden had been adjudged as not fit for the highest office. 'There is one thing, though, that would eliminate that feeling on the part of my family,' Bill continued, 'and that is if I became Governor-General.'

I was very moved by this and thought: Damn it! Why shouldn't Bill Hayden be Governor-General? He had the character, range of experience and diplomatic skills developed through four years as Foreign Minister to fit him for the office. There was an exact precedent on the other side of politics: Liberal Prime Minister John Gorton had appointed Paul Hasluck Governor-General in 1969 after Hasluck had served five years as Foreign Minister. I told Bill that if he wanted the governor-generalship I was happy to offer it to him. I indicated it would not be available until the beginning of 1989 because I intended to extend Sir Ninian Stephen's normal five-year term to cover the 1988 Bicentennial Year.

This was an emotional moment between two men who had moved past antagonism without yet achieving the bonding that normally comes from being protagonists together in great causes. We both had tears in our eyes – something unusual for Bill – but through those tears we saw each other more clearly than ever before. He had steeled himself not to expect compassion and warmth in political life but he saw me extending these qualities to him. And I saw a man courageous enough to expose the most sensitive nerve-ends of his personal life and seek solace, not simply for himself, but for the family he loved.

Now, as I jotted down my notes at the RAAF base, I wanted to share with the public the sense of our private reconciliation. The setting was ideal for making some important statements about the Government, built around the relationship between Bill Hayden and myself, and the great contribution he had made to the Australian Labor Party and to the Government. It was time for a clear public statement of all the things that were in my mind about Bill Hayden. It was important for Bill, it was important for me, and it was important for the party.

As I sat alone the thoughts flowed quickly, and within half an hour I had the outlines of what many regarded the finest speech of the campaign. The Booral Bowlers' Club was packed when I rose to speak. 'There was no engagement in this campaign to which I have been looking forward more than this,' I opened. 'This is not because I think a visit by me is necessary to make Oxley safe for democracy. Bill

Hayden has done that. My sense of commitment and excitement about coming here is simply because it is a meeting with and for Bill Hayden'. I then went deeper than people were expecting. 'I am not going to ignore or be hypocritical about the past, because I know that I have at one period caused Bill more pain and, perhaps, more sorrow than anyone else ever caused him,' I said, speaking now in a hushed atmosphere, as if everyone present felt that they were witnesses to an important moment in Labor history.

'It is ... a measure of the greatness of Bill Hayden, a measure of his unqualified commitment to this great Australian Labor Party ... to the ordinary people of Australia that he has submerged his own personal feelings to the pursuit of the interests of that party and to the interests of those people ... For it would have been easy for Bill to carry the wounds that had been inflicted, in a destructive way. Yet he chose not to, becoming a very constructive member of the Government. No minister has done more in the discharge of his portfolio responsibilities to advance within this country and internationally the interests of Australia. In particular, no-one has done more to advance the interests of all mankind in the cause of peace and disarmament.'

I emphasised our co-operation. 'I doubt that there has ever been a more effective co-operation of talent and commitment in the conduct of this nation's international relationships between a Foreign Minister and a Prime Minister than there has been between Bill Hayden and myself.'

I then took the audience on a quick global tour, outlining the ways in which Bill Hayden had pressed Australia's claims, and the deep concerns of others, across the countries and continents of the world; the United States, the Soviet Union, China, Asia generally, the South Pacific, the Middle East, Africa and South Africa in particular, and the Commonwealth were all mentioned in this fly-past of Bill's contributions as Foreign Minister.

I built up to the paramount issue of peace and disarmament: 'There is no greater imperative in this age upon any government than the pursuit of peace. The pursuit of peace is not something which is easily achieved by the simple method of waving your banners, shouting your slogans. I cast no aspersions upon those who do those things. I simply make the point that in relations between nations, the pursuit of peace and disarmament is a hard, undramatic, grinding, unremitting task involving hundreds and hundreds of hours of work and of bilateral discussions with others either of a like-mind or of a mind which you believe is capable of persuasion to something like your own point of view. And, in that task, in that undramatic but necessary task, Bill Hayden has played an absolutely outstanding role.'

I then referred to Australia's work in the field of reducing intermediate-range nuclear forces, seeking to achieve a comprehensive test-ban treaty and a new convention to ban chemical weapons, and concluded at that point: 'When the history books are written, Bill Hayden will go down as one of the greatest, if not the greatest, Foreign Minister of Australia in the twentieth century.'

After the speech Dallas and I embraced, Bill squeezed my hand and said thank you, although he didn't need to say a lot. Their eyes said it all – it was something that passed between Bill and Dallas and myself. To complete this very special moment, Bill was direct and generous when he spoke. 'What happened in early 1983 did have its pain. In no circumstances have I sought to deny that. It would not be either convincing to the public or truthful ... but you have been a good leader, a greater leader when the going's been rough for the team, you've never hesitated to put your head down and go into the ruck.'

The Ipswich speech gave me the opportunity not only to reconcile publicly with Bill Hayden but to draw attention to the Government's foreign policy successes. The following day, 26th June 1987, I spoke on another subject of fundamental importance to the Government: Labor's policy for women. My own commitment to equal opportunity had been evident from the outset of government. At an early stage I appointed Dr Anne Summers to head the newly-renamed Office of the Status of Women, making that office part of my own Department of Prime Minister and Cabinet and giving Dr Summers ready access to me and to the Cabinet.

My first Government acted quickly to ratify the United Nations convention on the elimination of all forms of discrimination against women and to pass the Sex Discrimination Act to accord with its terms. In 1984 we championed affirmative action, which we believed was both morally right and economically sensible.

Through the mid-eighties the Government oversaw a massive burgeoning of women's participation in the workforce and was responsible for a rapid increase in child care facilities and assistance. Completion of secondary education by females in Australia had increased dramatically during Labor's time in office, jumping from 44 per cent in 1983 to nearly 70 per cent during 1987. The early introduction of the Government's Women's Budget Program, with its full-scale assessment of the impact on women of the Federal Budget, was unparalleled in the world.

On 28th November 1985, almost at the end of the United Nations decade for women, I outlined the Government's national agenda for women, specifying Federal Government objectives for women in the spheres of education, employment, child care, aged care and health. 'We want to give women a choice. We want to give women a say. And we want to give women a fair go,' I told the Parliament.

By 26th July 1987 my message was much the same – 'a fair go, a fair say and a fair choice'. Our opponents, on the other hand, offered no such thing. The Liberal Party, incredibly, opposed our equal opportunity legislation. This was too much for 'small "l"' Liberal Senator Peter Baume from New South Wales, who resigned from the Opposition front bench in disgust.

If equal opportunity wasn't a strong hand for the Liberal Party, neither was micro-economic reform: streamlining, trimming and modernising the Australian economy to make it more efficient, productive and competitive. The Government had already been responsible for sweeping micro-economic reforms, although they were reforms of such magnitude that the term mirco-economic was often not associated with them. The dollar float, the abolition of exchange controls, financial deregulation, the whittling down of obstacles to foreign investment, tax reform are all properly classified, however, as micro-economic reforms.

The 1987 election campaign marked a new phase in the Government's aspiration to achieve far-reaching micro-economic reform of the Australian economy. A speech to the Ballarat Businessmen's Club on 6th July 1987 was the watershed, definitive statement of the Government's micro-economic reform objectives for our third term in office and beyond. I began by promising sweeping reform of the nation's transport infrastructure. I promised to deregulate crude-oil marketing in Australia and to aim at trebling the size of Australia's high-technology computer and communications industry. I promised to encourage the gradual amalgamation of trade unions, to continue steadily to eliminate unnecessary business regulation and to take further steps to help Australian firms tap export markets. I promised a continued refining of Australia's research and development skills. The elimination of outdated work and management practices was also specified as a goal: 'We will promote the further enmeshment of the Australian economy with our dynamic regional neighbours, including China.' And lastly, I promised the further development of the tourism industry.

Micro-economic reform wasn't exactly a sexy subject. Nevertheless, it was intrinsically important to Australia's future and the election was not simply about being re-elected but gaining a mandate to institute the Government's future program. I put this blueprint into a broader perspective: 'It is the process of national reconstruction – of restructuring our economy and restructuring our view of Australia's place in the world.' The program would sharpen the focus we had started to bring to 'transforming the nation from the complacent Lucky Country to the productive country, the innovative and hard-working country'.

All that, however, was in jeopardy if Labor failed on 13th July. We had come a very long way since September 1986 when Labor, ten points behind in the polls, was being written off as a prospect for retaining office. For eight months until the calling of the 1987 election we had steadily improved our vote.

Everything, really, depended on the campaign, when, as we had hoped, the intense pressure highlighted the difference between Labor and the Opposition. The Government's professionalism, competence, discipline, unity, teamwork, restraint, strong and determined leadership, and clear sense of the way ahead was consistently displayed. The Opposition's lack of these qualities was just as obvious. Where Labor campaigned flawlessly, the Liberal campaign was full of embarrassing gaffes. Where we were unified, they were disunited. Where we offered 'restraint with equity', they offered profligacy.

In the final week of the campaign Labor's emphasis was almost exclusively on highlighting the contrast between the Government and the Opposition on the issues of economic management, leadership and unity. Leadership, in particular, was a key campaign issue. 'Probably more than [in] any other election for which I have been national campaign director, the stark contrast in leadership was a decisive factor,' Labor's National Secretary, Bob McMullan, wrote in his campaign director's report after the 1987 election. 'This leadership question intermingled with related issues of unity and the leadership team. In the mind of voters the issue of unity and disunity is correlated with the issue of weak leadership, i.e. how can a leader who cannot control his party run the country?'

This was perhaps a little too harsh on John Howard. Former Prime Minister Billy Hughes once said of Robert Menzies that 'he can't lead and won't follow'. Howard's misfortune was to have behind him an entire Coalition fitting that description. In the face of adversity he campaigned with courage and determination. Unlike Andrew Peacock, the man he replaced as leader, who was more the amiable dilettante, Howard was a hard-working, fully professional politician – his double-counting gaffe aside.

Despite Howard's pertinacity, disappointment lay ahead. On 11th July 1987 Labor recorded its historic third successive election victory, pushing our majority in the House of Representatives from sixteen to twenty-four seats. This stunning triumph was one to be shared and savoured by all on our side. Party professionals on both sides could not recall a more professional campaign than that run by Labor. 'This was the most researched and the best researched election campaign the party has ever conducted,' McMullan wrote in his report. 'Co-operation and discipline of the ministers in this campaign was probably the best of any with which I have been associated.'

The ministry, my loyal and brilliant personal staff, Labor's new advertising agency, party workers – there were many to thank. I knew it was the result of a great deal of work from a great many people and that Labor's superior teamwork and overall competence had played a decisive part. I was confident, too, that my own leadership and party management over more than four years had been an important factor in the victory. Indeed a study by the Australian National University put it this way: 'If Hawke had been no more popular than his party; if the Liberal and National leaders had been at least as popular as theirs; and if nothing else had changed, then Labor would probably have lost the election by at least four seats.'[79]

TWENTY-FOUR

The party was euphoric at achieving what had never been done before in its history. I was determined to seize the added authority of this third successive term to push through changes that had been too difficult to manage in the earlier context.

Reform of the public service and the structure of Government departments was high on the agenda. My increased interest in this area had been stimulated by changes at the head of my own department. I had inherited Sir Geoffrey Yeend, who had held the position of department head since 1976. This made him suspect in the eyes of the more paranoid of our Caucus members who also blackmarked him for the sin of having been Bob Menzies' private secretary between 1952 and 1955. I rejected suggestions from these quarters that I should dispense with Sir Geoffrey's services, adopting my general rule of assuming commitment to the incoming Government. Geoff never let me down and his loyalty to me developed beyond the bounds required by his office. He accepted the agenda of the new Government and did his best to assist in its implementation. His awareness of, and adherence to, appropriate procedures and protocol were often the butt of jests by the less reverential of my staff, particularly Peter Barron. At a

South Pacific Forum conference in the Cook Islands, Barron told
the head waiter of the officials' dining room that a notorious con-
man, using the name Sir Geoffrey Yeend, would probably try to get
himself a table at dinner by pretending he was an adviser to the
Australian Prime Minister. Whatever happened, this shyster must
not be allowed a seat. Yeend was duly barred, but he took it in good
part and his suave ability to handle the wild boys earned him their
respect.

With his retirement I appointed Mike Codd on 10th February 1986
to head my department. Codd's career had not flourished under our
Government. He had been shifted from Secretary of Employment and
Industrial Relations to chair the Industries Assistance Commission
and then back to head the Department of Community Services, but I
liked what little I had seen and heard of him in this period. It was,
however, Geoff Yeend's high assessment of Codd that caused me to put
him on the short list. My interview with him quickly confirmed Yeend's
judgment and I acquired, as department head, one of the most
outstanding public servants with whom I've ever dealt.

Codd – a fellow son-of-the-manse – combined acute intelligence
and toughness with a marvellous capacity to get the best out of those
who worked with and under him. He is a big, lumbering fellow, a
former Australian Rules footballer whose eccentric taste in shirts and
ties was a constant source of wonderment to those of us accustomed to
the conservative habits of his peers and predecessors. I liked his
appetite for hard work, his preparedness to question the status quo
and, with all this, a wonderfully quizzical sense of humour.

Mike and I had talked during 1986 of significantly reducing the
number of Government departments. The concept was sound but it
was seen as such a strike against empire by so many ministers and
bureaucrats that, given the circumstances of the time, in my political
judgment it was not then worth pursuing.

The times were now propitious and I didn't waste an hour in moving towards a massive restructuring of the Public Service. I was not going to allow reform to be bogged down and ultimately disappear in a round of endless interdepartmental committees. Codd and my own people were instructed to finalise the earlier plans and to do it quickly.

Just three days after the election, on 14th July 1987, I announced sweeping changes to the structure of the Commonwealth administration, reducing the number of Government departments from twenty-seven to sixteen and the number of public servants by three thousand. Although not the driving consideration behind the restructure, savings were nonetheless an important factor and were calculated at $96 million in the coming financial year.

The purpose of the reforms was to achieve better policy co-ordination, administrative efficiencies and improved budget processes. The changes sought to enhance ministerial control of departments by moving to a two-tiered ministerial structure. Each of the sixteen Cabinet ministers was responsible for one of the large portfolios. They were supported, in most cases, by one or more non-Cabinet ministers responsible for specific parts of the Cabinet minister's portfolio, or by ministers assisting across the full spread of the ministry.

The changes made for an improved Cabinet process since all portfolios were now within the Cabinet. The reforms also permitted a greater focus on the main priorities of government, freeing Cabinet ministers from some areas of routine administration.

Some government departments (Defence and Social Security, for instance) remained substantially unaltered. Generally, however, departments were amalgamated or added to in some way; the formula for amalgamations and add-ons was, as far as possible, the natural linkages and logical relationships between policy areas.

The Department of Community Services and Health is a good example of how it was possible to shrink the number of government departments and the Public Service while at the same time slightly increasing the number of ministers – from twenty-seven to thirty. I would have baulked at simply expanding the ministry and, in fact, had done so when it was first suggested to me by Left, Centre Left and Right faction convenors prior to the election. Three more ministries would make their post-election task easier but this was not, of itself, persuasive.

After the election, however, I saw this request for a further three places in the ministry as a means of getting a quick, no-nonsense approval from the factions for the sweeping changes I proposed to the Public Service. The appointment of three additional ministers could be justified on the grounds of the workload of existing ministers and the cost was minuscule against the massive savings effected by the restructuring.

On the Monday morning following the election, Paul Keating, Robert Ray, Graham Richardson and Gareth Evans, all of the Right faction, came to see me. 'We've got to have thirty spots in the ministry,' they told me. 'All the factions agree with an increase of three.' 'I'll do it on one condition,' I replied. As I outlined my intended reforms there was some surprise, including from Gareth, who'd had ideas about a reduction to twenty-two departments, but there was little demur.

I gave undertakings that the junior ministers and those coming into the three new slots would not be called assistant ministers or parliamentary secretaries, but would have the full status and entitlements of ministers. I regarded the arrangement as a reasonable *quid pro quo* if I could get unanimous factional support for my reforms of the Public Service. It had the added advantage in helping assuage a political problem which had arisen, oddly enough, from our having won the 1987 election so handsomely. The win pushed the size of our majority from sixteen to twenty-four seats, enlarging a back bench already stacked with substantial talent. It made good political sense to open up further opportunities for the back bench by adding ministries which could be justified in their own right.

Having made this agreement with me, Keating, Ray, Richardson and Evans went off to discuss the plan with the Left and Centre Left. When I checked with these factions, they, too, had agreed to the plan. I was then in the happy position of making the radical changes I wanted with the agreement of the party across the spectrum.

Discussions then turned to the make-up of the ministry. As a rule I did not lobby for anyone to be included in the ministry and accepted the individuals who emerged from the Caucus processes. But on this occasion I was adamant that the ministry include more women; it was absolutely unacceptable to me that, in the light of what we had been saying about affirmative action and increased female participation in all spheres, we were not aiming to increase the representation of women in the ministry.

Although Gary Punch from NSW appeared to have the numbers ahead of Ros Kelly from the ACT, I insisted on her getting the nod. She was not inferior to him on merit and was therefore, on affirmative action principles, entitled to be promoted. In the meantime I learned that the Left had not included a woman in their group of ministers and, equally incredible, the Centre Left had met and decided on dumping the only Tasmanian in the ministry, Senator Michael Tate. And none of the factions had provided for an additional Queenslander.

In those circumstances, I met with faction representatives on Tuesday, 21st July 1987. Richardson and Ray fronted for the Right; Bill Hayden, Mick Young (SA), and Senators Peter Cook (WA) and Rosemary Crowley (SA) for the Centre Left; and Gerry Hand and Brian Howe (Vic.) with Senator Bruce Childs (NSW) for the Left. I didn't beat around the bush. 'I am making the position absolutely clear,' I said, addressing the Centre Left. 'Tate has to be reinstated. It is up to you how you do it, but quite clearly, you, Peter Cook, are the one who is in the firing line – there is nothing personal in what I am saying.' As to the Left, I said, 'There has to be a woman. But I just don't want any woman, I want Margaret Reynolds because I want a Queenslander as well.'

The Centre Left and the Left both responded with a litany of the enormous difficulties associated with my demands. Nonetheless, they accepted the logic of my position and went away to see how they could work it out. As the faction representatives filed out Peter Cook stayed behind. He indicated his willingness to consider standing aside for Michael Tate but sought further time to think about it.

Over the coming days the Centre Left and the Left went to and fro but, at the end of the day, Tate and Reynolds both got up. Peter Cook was the Centre Left's sacrificial offering and on the Left, Nick Bolkus stepped aside for Reynolds. Both Senators accepted their fate with grace and were generous in their comments about my handling of this matter. At an early stage Nick had somehow got the idea that I had blackbanned him from the ministry. When he learned this was not so, and when I later insisted on his right to fill the next appropriate vacancy, his attitude changed. He became a valued Cabinet minister and a close friend and confidante.

The selection of the ministry following the 1987 election was a case study in the mature and effective way the factions had come to work together in the broader interests of the party. But the broad-mindedness of the factions didn't always extend to disappointed ministers whose perception of their own merits, I found, tended to differ from that formed by their colleagues. Dumping by the Caucus or the withholding of a cherished portfolio created fertile ground for ill-will towards the Prime Minister. I learned to regard this as an occupational hazard. I had, for instance, been close to Barry Cohen and occasionally played golf with him, usually to his financial advantage. His faction the Right, insisted that he had only survived after the 1984 election because of the factional agreement that there would be no changes to the ministry, and were now adamant about his exclusion from their ticket. I spoke on his behalf but my new authority didn't extend that far. Although Barry didn't think well of me, his displeasure was nothing compared with the later venom of three failed ministers – Gary Punch, Peter Duncan and Stewart West – at the time of the Keating challenges.

Negative reactions by disappointed individuals could not, however, divert our attention from the broad thrust of restructuring the economy and positioning Australia to play a prominent role in the negotiations for a more liberalised international trading system. Reform of the Public Service was relevant to these objectives in two ways.

The Government was not in a strong position to challenge the private sector to restructure and make itself more efficient if, as the largest employer in the country, we hadn't started to put our own house in order. It was generally conceded that we had already done more in this area than any previous government, with particularly wide-ranging changes being made to the traditional public service environment in 1986; bureaucrats faced tougher disciplinary action, the centralised power of the Public Service Board was curtailed, and the merit principle governing promotion was strengthened.

We brought in further changes with the massive departmental restructuring after the 1987 election. These changes, and indeed very much of our thinking on public service reform, owed a great deal to David Block, whom I had recruited in 1986 to head up an Efficiency Scrutiny Unit. Block was an ex-South African, a former banker with a wide range of senior executive experience in business, a man of first-rate intellect with a most direct and engaging personality. One of his major strengths was an ability to capture the confidence of both the chiefs and indians in the bureaucracy, who well knew that some of their comfortable and cherished practices could fall foul of his astringent, probing mind. On the basis of Block's recommendations, we abolished the Public Service Board and replaced it with a Public Service Commission with independent statutory responsibilities for policies on recruitment, promotion, mobility, discipline and retirement.

The second way in which the 1987 public service structural reform was directly relevant to these broader Government objectives was in the creation of the Foreign Affairs and Trade Department. Increasingly, foreign policy *is* trade policy, and trade policy *is* foreign policy, as the strands of international political and economic relations become further intertwined. In Australia's case, as a large trading nation rich in minerals and agricultural products and with a gradually diversifying export base (and in a dangerous environment of growing protectionist sentiment), our interests were best served by recognising this interdependence and pulling the two formerly distinct portfolios together.

As Foreign Minister, Bill Hayden represented the department in Cabinet and I appointed Michael Duffy as the Minister for Trade Negotiations. This was a totally new area for Michael but I knew that his warm, affable manner, dry wit and capacity for detailed work would provide the right ingredients to build on the progress we had already made.

The work I had begun in the 1983 Bangkok Speech[80] had been continued with an outstanding contribution from John Dawkins as Minister for Trade between 1984 and 1987. The GATT ministerial meeting to launch the new Multilateral Trade Negotiations round was scheduled for September 1986 at Punta del Este. By 25th August 1986, thanks to John's indefatigable efforts assisted by Australia's Ambassador to GATT, Allan Oxley, Australia had assembled what became known as the Cairns Group of agricultural fair-traders.

On that date the group of fourteen fair-trading nations gathered for the first time in Palm Cove, just north of Cairns, determined to seek for their agricultural exports the same régime of international trading rules as the major industrial countries had for decades applied to trade in industrial products. As it happened, the group which assembled in Cairns went beyond the Western Pacific region I had first envisaged.[81] Collectively they accounted for nearly one-quarter of world agricultural exports and for the overwhelming bulk of non-United States and non-European Community food exports. What brought these fourteen nations to Cairns was the crisis in world agricultural trade which had been building for several years. The level of consumer transfers and subsidies to European farmers had been escalating for well over a decade and by 1986 the distortion of the world's agricultural production and trading systems had reached ludicrous proportions.

In welcoming the fair-traders to Cairns I emphasised the high cost of protectionism for fair-traders and subsidisers alike. The Europeans were channelling $US100 billion a year into agriculture in direct subsidies and consumer transfers. Resultant surpluses were being dumped on world markets with the aid of large export subventions. They were hurting fair-traders and damaging their own cost, price and employment structure. The United States' massive retaliation against the Europeans was replicating this insanity.

The efficient agricultural producers meeting with us in Cairns had become, together with the poorer developing nations, the innocent victims of this trans-Atlantic trade war; the subsidising and restrictive market-access policies of other major industrialised countries, including Japan, were further damaging us and them. World Bank figures demonstrated the staggering dimension of this insanity: the costs of distortions of grains, livestock and sugar markets amounted to $US36 billion a year (in 1980 prices). The direct cost to farmers in developing countries was then almost $US28 billion a year; the world was witnessing the absurdity of the rich developed nations directly slashing the income of the developing world, thus denying it the capacity to service the debt it was incurring to alleviate, amongst other things, rural poverty.

In Australia's case I indicated that the Common Agricultural Policy of the European Community had been costing us a billion dollars a year in lost markets and reduced prices, while the United States Export Enhancement Program would cost our wheat farmers alone more than $600 million in the coming year.

And so the Cairns Group was born as a third force in what was to become the seven-year-long struggle of the Uruguay Round. Individually, the countries making up the group would have had virtually no influence on the round. Collectively, however, they formed what has generally been recognised as an extraordinarily persuasive lobby in the cause of freer trade.

It was no accident that Australia assembled and then chaired this group throughout the whole period. My Government recognised the important issues and principles early and, at the political and bureaucratic level, provided the intellectual and administrative horsepower to transform a good idea into an effective negotiating instrument. Our capacity to take this leadership role also came from the fact that we were able to come to the table with clean hands. In an opening address to the World Economic Forum in Davos, Switzerland in January 1989, I could put the challenge to the international community on behalf of Australia, and be listened to with respect, by proudly stating our record: 'We are restructuring our domestic economy, and we are opening ourselves up to free and fair international trade.'

No-one could, or did, argue with the facts. I noted the steady reduction in assistance to Australia's car manufacturers and to our textile, clothing and footwear industries. Tariffs on chemicals and plastics were to be reduced. Our steel and heavy engineering industries were being revitalised through sectoral plans aimed at encouraging them to look outwards to compete in the world's markets. I emphasised that Australia's barrier protection was generally by way of tariffs, which we were committed to reducing. Tariffs are a transparent form of assistance which cannot be placed in the same category as the non-tariff protection provided to agriculture and, in some cases, industrial production in Europe, North American and Japan. Tariffs allow significant market access to imports and they do not weaken our trading partners' access to traditional markets through the dumping and other export subsidisation which characterises so much of the policies of those economic powers.

These were the strong domestic and international foundations upon which Michael Duffy, as I expected, was able in his own unspectacular but effective way to consolidate Australia's leading role in the protracted struggle for a more liberalised international trading system in general, and for agriculture in particular. Michael had been a reluctant and very infrequent international traveller before assuming this portfolio and it was interesting to see him gradually coming to terms with the new demands. He sometimes reduced us to tears of laughter as he informed us in his droll, deadpan manner of the exigencies faced by the world traveller. One evening in the Cabinet anteroom he described his agonies in Islamabad when struck down with the dreaded tummy-bug, but he got no sympathy from Paul Keating, who had not yet discovered Asia: 'Serves you right,' said Paul, 'they're the places you fly over on your way to Europe.'

One place we certainly didn't fly over in these years was Washington, for we found ourselves in constant conflict with successive United States' administrations on trade policy. Except for 1984 and 1987, I was there arguing Australia's case each year from 1983 through to 1989. Our arguments were not at the level of the principles which should govern the conduct of international trade; both Reagan and

Bush were philosophically committed free-traders and they were both very supportive of Australia's work in establishing and leading the Cairns Group.

Rather our fight with the Americans centred on the adverse impact on us of their retaliation against the Europeans. The United States had lost world markets for agricultural products under the onslaught of the Europeans' subsidised export of the huge surpluses resulting from their Common Agricultural Policy. The United States emerged as a stock-holder of unprecedented proportions and the trouble really started for Australia when the US Congress enacted the 1985 Farm Bill. Our farmers were caught in the cross-fire of subsidy and counter subsidy as the treasuries of the United States and Europe waged an irrational battle with each other, using their own taxpayers' and consumers' money.

The dispute was replete with paradox in terms of both international and domestic politics. Ronald Reagan and George Bush were embar-rassed by the economic damage being inflicted on Australia at a time when our personal rapport had brought political and security relations between our two countries to what they declared was their best-ever level. They did not seek with any fervour to defend the indefensible. They were prepared to justify their own trade-distorting measures as an attempt to bring the Europeans to their senses, but they conceded that this objective was no defence to the direct argument I kept firing at them: 'If you get shot in the head, it doesn't hurt any the less that the bullet wasn't intended for you but for someone else.'

My hammering of Presidents, Cabinet members and Congressional committees was broadened to the widest audience when I was extended the rare privilege of addressing the Joint Session of the United States Congress on 23rd June 1988. In a wide-ranging speech I went to the heart of the issue:

It would be wrong of me, here in Congress, to pretend that within our otherwise excellent relationship trade is not an area of very real concern to us ... Australia's primary producers are unsubsidised and are among the most efficient in the world, and yet we are finding ourselves squeezed out of markets by practices which distort prices and levels of production. In agriculture, we find ourselves caught in the cross-fire of a destructive and counterproductive trans-Atlantic subsidies war. The costs of this subsidies war cannot be reckoned purely in economics ... There is also an impact, a damaging impact, upon the perceptions which Australians have of the major trading powers, the United States included ... Australians must not be given reason to believe that while we are first-class allies, we are, in trade, second-class friends. Trade issues must not be allowed to fester, or to erode our wider friendships or alliance.

This was not merely rhetoric. In Australia the issue was standing traditional alignments on their head. Having secured the broad acquiescence of the Left to my policy on the Australia–US alliance and the joint facilities, I asked the Administration to understand that something significant was happening when my office received calls from the most conservative farmers' groups saying they wanted to mobilise a thousand farmers to march on Pine Gap.

I was not prepared to use the joint facilities as a bargaining chip[82] but I wanted to convey to the Americans that if they showed no understanding of our problem then the basis of support in Australia for the alliance could be undermined. Both Ronald Reagan and George Bush did show this understanding, but George did not seem to have got the message across to the albatross he had draped around his neck as Vice-President – Dan Quayle.

Quayle visited Australia in April 1989 and quickly endeared himself to everyone by declaring that United States farm polices did not harm Australia. Michael Duffy, as usual, did not mince matters and called the Vice-President 'a fool if he didn't see Australia's viewpoint'. Nor did I spare Quayle in private discussions. He has a very low golf handicap, but he certainly wasn't up to scratch intellectually or as a practical politician with a grasp of the realities of international life. Meeting with him was a constant strain for he had neither the mental capacity, nor a store of relevant knowledge, to which he could resort to make any discussion valuable.

I confronted the Vice-President with the facts about what had happened to wheat during the course of their Export Enhancement Program; America's share of the world wheat market jumped from 29 to 43 per cent, Europe's share fell from 17 to 14 per cent but Australia's share slumped from 20 to 12 per cent. This was met with that bemused and empty grin which, in retrospect, makes me glad that I didn't ask him to spell 'wheat'. Some staffer had put it into his head that Australia hadn't been hurt by his country's trading practices. He wouldn't – but even more pathetically, couldn't – budge. Dan Quayle's wife, Marilyn, was a strong argument, in their household, for affirmative action – she was icier than Dan but a much tougher and more competent operator. I found it offensive that this man was a heartbeat away from the Presidency of the United States.

Perhaps I felt this all the more strongly because during my 1988 visit to Washington George Bush had involved me intimately in his strategy for election as President. George and Barbara gave us a dinner with a few friends and officials at the Vice-Presidential residence, knowing that at about 10.30 I was to go to the Australian Ambassador's home to meet Michael Dukakis, his Democrat opponent.

After a genial meal George rose, made some complimentary remarks and said he was taking me off to another room for a conversation just between the two of us. He was straightforward when we were alone. He was then a long way behind in the polls and he said, 'Bob, you're the master – you've shown you know how to do it by winning three elections. What do you think is the right strategy from here on in?' While I was far removed from Bush on a range of social issues, I was certain he would be stronger than the Democrats in pushing for a more liberalised international trading régime in the GATT round, and as far as I was concerned this was of paramount importance for Australia. I also liked the man very much; as Vice-President, he had always been charming and helpful to me.

I said that the basic elements of a successful election strategy are to emphasise your own strengths and the weaknesses of your opponents. George had a good story to tell about economic and employment growth under Reagan's Republican Administration, although in my judgment this growth had not been equitably distributed. On the international front, the United States had moved from humiliation at the hands of Iran and the debilitation and danger of the Cold War to a point where the threat of Soviet communism had all but been eliminated. In all these facts lay his strengths and the weaknesses of his opponent, and I told him I believed he would win if he concentrated on this story. This made sense to George as it obviously did to the many others who were advising him, for it became the basis of the strategy that saw him come from well behind to victory in November. He added some rough personal stuff about Dukakis on the campaign trail but his basic decency came through when he said to me, 'Bob, I will fight like hell to win and I think I'll make it. I'll be saying some rough things about my opponent but I want you to know, if I do lose, that he is not a bad man. He will regard the relationship between our two countries as important and it will stay in good shape under him.'

This generosity of spirit was not evident when I met Dukakis later in the evening. He had nothing positive to say about Bush. He seemed a tense individual with a large set of stock phrases but lacking enough

For The Right Honorable
Robert Hawke
With best wishes, Ronald Reagan

28. Meeting Ronald Reagan.

29.*(above left)*
My first US visit established an
effective working relationship
with Reagan.

30.*(below left)*
With Paul Keating.

31.*(above)*
Jubilant at Australia's win
of the America's Cup in 1983.

32.*(left)*
On a flight on the VIP aircraft,
1987.

33. *(above left)*
With pupils from
Patoonga School,
Kakadu, at
Parliament House,
September 1985.

34.*(below left)*
With Ros, Hazel,
Sue and husband, Jan,
election night 1990.
I'm holding their
second child, Ben.

35.*(above)*
Election night,
5th March 1983.

36.*(left)*
In Papua New Guinea,
1990.

37.*(right)*
With George Bush in
Washington in 1988.

38.*(below)*
Addressing the Joint
Session of the US Congress
on 23rd June 1988.

39. *(above)*
At a dinner given by
George and Barbara Bush
in our honour,
Washington 1988.

40. *(left)*
John Button and I at a
dinner at 10 Downing
Street with Margaret
Thatcher, 1989.

41.*(above)*
A press conference held by myself and (*left to right*) Rajiv Gandhi, Kenneth Kaunda, and Robert Mugabe, at CHOGM, Vancouver, 1987.

42.(*right*)
With my friend Rajiv Gandhi in New Delhi, 1989.

43.(*right*)
Reviewing the Chinese
People's Liberation Army
troops with Party Secretary,
Zhao Ziyang, in 1984 in
Tiananmen Square.

44.(*below right*)
My meeting with
Mikhail Gorbachev in
December 1987 was one
of the most fascinating of
my prime ministership.

45.*(above)*
The Queen carried out her duties
with her customary dignity and
efficiency during her visit in our
Bicentennial year.

46.*(right)*
The opening of the new Parliament House
had a special significance — exactly 61
years before, the Queen's father had
opened the first 'temporary' Parliament
House.

47.*(above right)*
Playing golf with Greg Norman
in 1988.

48.*(far right)*
With Allan Border, Australian
Cricket Captain, at Lords in 1989.

49.*(above left)*
With my new Green friend,
Senator Graham Richardson, 1989.

50.*(below left)*
Jacques Cousteau and I joined forces in
1989 to have Antarctica declared
'A Nature Reserve — Land of Science'.

51.*(above)*
Welcoming Nelson Mandela to
Parliament House in Canberra, 1990.

52.*(above left)*
(*left to right*) John Kerin, myself, Bill Hayden, Kim
Beazley and Ralph Willis. John Kerin, Kim Beazley
and Ralph Willis were sworn into the ministry by
Governor-General Bill Hayden on 9th December 1991.
Ten days later Paul Keating won the leadership and
appointed a new Cabinet.

53.*(below left)*
My relationship with the Australian people,
a source of great joy.

54.*(above)*
Three successive Prime Ministers —
Gough Whitlam, Malcolm Fraser and I — gave
our different perspectives on government in 1992.

55. My last official duty as Prime Minister was to accept for permanent display in Parliament House the Barunga Statement painted by Aboriginal artists to commemorate the commitment made to them in 1988.

confidence to engage in a substantial free-flowing discussion. He did have a real interest in Australia and Bush was right in his assessment that Dukakis regarded the relationship with us as important. I finished that evening with the strong belief that Bush would be the next President of the United States.

As close as I was to successive Presidents, and as effectively as my ministers worked with their counterparts – Dawkins with Clayton Yeutter, Duffy and then Blewett with the US chief trade negotiator, Carla Hills, and John Kerin with his opposite numbers in Agriculture – I readily concede that we were never really able to get a satisfactory outcome from the Americans with our continuing arguments and protestations. They were unfailingly courteous and gave us every opportunity to put our case. But, in a way, they were caught like us in a wider, more intractable problem which could only be addressed, over time, in a broad, multilateral setting.

We had already made an important contribution to strengthening these multilateral processes by the creation of the Cairns Group. I wanted now to bring together my two fundamental and interrelated themes of a freer international trading environment and Australia's greater enmeshment with the region. There had been talk over many years about the need for some form of structured consultation among countries of the Asia–Pacific region. My friends from each side of the Pacific, former Japanese Prime Minister Nakasone and George Shultz, had floated ideas for a forum to encourage co-operation in specific sectors. United States Senator Bill Bradley had proposed a Pacific coalition on trade and economic development designed to reinforce the Uruguay Round and remove barriers to economic growth in the region. But nothing substantial had ever come of all this talk. By the latter part of 1988 I was convinced that the circumstances were propitious to act decisively to give effect to the clear perception I had expressed as early as 6th February 1984. Speaking in Seoul I said, 'For

Australia the idea of a more economically integrated Asia–Pacific region is becoming increasingly real. We see advantage in seeking to maximise the benefits of the economic interdependence between the countries of the region. There can be little doubt that, looking not too far ahead, the Asia–Pacific region must be accepted as a major catalyst for stronger world-wide economic performance.'

Our diplomatic missions in the region were instructed to assess reactions to a push for greater regional co-operation. The reactions were not unfavourable and on 31st January 1989 in Seoul I launched my concept of Asia Pacific Economic Co-operation (APEC).

I told a luncheon of Korean business associations that the time had come for us to increase our efforts towards building regional co-operation. I said we wanted to assess the region's attitudes towards the possibility of creating a more formal intergovernmental vehicle of regional co-operation capable of analysis and consultation on economic and social issues, not as an academic exercise but to help inform policy development by our respective governments.

I had strengthened the draft speech we had prepared, and was able to speak with more confidence as a result of discussions the previous day with President Roh Tae Woo. Roh was the leader of a major regional economy whose involvement would be critical to the success of any new regional institution.

Roh gave immediate and effusive support to APEC, going out of his way to make it clear that he wanted to be seen to be identified with it. The fact that I had warm and friendly relations with President Roh was significant. We liked and trusted one another. Hazel and I had been invited to his home and had played tennis there with Roh and his wife. When I outlined the APEC concept to Roh it was to a man who was prepared out of friendship and trust to discuss seriously any proposal I raised with him. It was yet another example of the importance of personal relations in the conduct of international affairs.

What I had in mind for APEC when I first discussed it with President Roh and later pursued it with others was a framework of effective regional co-operation which could improve the Uruguay Round's chance of success. In addition, APEC could provide a forum for openly discussing obstacles to trade within our own region. In Korea, for example, reforms of the sort that are envisaged for the region had already begun to have an impact in the form of lower tariffs, liberalised imports and reduced restrictions on foreign traders. Recommendations of the Presidential Commission on Economic Restructuring showed further progress towards a more open Korean market.

I was able to speak from a position of strength. We had floated the Australian dollar, deregulated our financial markets, liberalised our foreign investment policy, cut the rate of company taxation, reduced by a third the level of tariff protection afforded to Australian manufacturing industry, and made our primary industries more responsive to changes in the international market place.

The third area in which APEC could benefit the region was by identifying the broad economic interests which countries of the Asia–Pacific region had in common. This speech came to be recognised as one of seminal importance.

There has been some suggestion that in launching APEC I was so irritated with the United States' attitude to bilateral trade issues that I was inclined to leave the Americans out of the new regional group. This was never in my mind. There were some in the Association of South East Asian Nations, most particularly Malaysia, who had a well-developed antipathy towards the United States, and Malaysia certainly would have preferred to exclude the Americans. But, on any rational examination, a regional group seeking to maximise the chances of economic co-operation in the Asia–Pacific could not seriously contemplate leaving out the major economic power, the United States.

That would have been a nonsense. Looked at from another perspective, the last thing one wanted was to encourage a future in which the United States withdrew into economic isolationism. We did not want a USA, unable to come to terms with Europe, unable to find a solution to its continuing trade war with that continent within the Uruguay Round, moving to create a dollar bloc. Indeed the worst-case scenario at that time was the emergence of three major trading blocs based on the dollar, the yen, and the deutschmark.

The fundamental basis of the APEC initiative was freer international trade. The creation of a more formal vehicle for regional co-operation was not sleight of hand for the institution of a Pacific trading bloc. On the contrary, as I spelled out in Seoul, Australia's support for non-discriminatory multilateral trading solutions in the GATT framework was clear, long-standing and unambiguous. Australia had been working with the Cairns Group of nations since 1986. Cairns established Australia as an intelligent, relevant, hard-working nation whose views on the free-trade issue were well known and understood. APEC had the same intellectual thrust as Cairns, although it was broader in aspiration. The concept at the heart of both Cairns and APEC was the optimisation of each country's economic opportunities by the creation of the greatest possible freedom in international trade. Efficient producers would have the best chance of selling their products on the international market.

APEC's passage from conception to birth as a significant international institution involved, by historical standards, a remarkably short gestation period. I launched the APEC initiative at the end of January 1989 and, following excellent and extensive work by the able Dick Woolcott, Secretary of the Department of Foreign Affairs and Trade, we had our first formal meeting in November of that year in Canberra. Ministers from Australia, New Zealand, the Republic of Korea, Japan, the United States, and the six ASEAN countries all attended. Later, the People's Republic of China, Taiwan, and Hong Kong joined. For the first time, ministerial representatives of both China and Taiwan sat down together at the table of an intergovernmental organisation.

ASEAN members were initially cautious about a too rapid development of APEC. ASEAN, a defensive organisation established to counter the threat of communist expansionism and subversion in the region, had achieved a stature beyond the expectations of its creators in 1967. But it was essentially a political grouping and, as such, it had created virtually no organisation or structure for enhancing economic co-operation and growth in the region. The phenomenal growth which did occur within ASEAN and its neighbours was the result·of individual countries pursuing policies of market liberalisation, competition and the creative use of high savings for investment in economic development. APEC effectively filled this void. Australia was, however, conscious of ASEAN members' pride in their organisation and we used our good relations with them and acceptance by them, both bilaterally and in the post-ASEAN ministerial dialogues, to give them confidence in the important role APEC could play in the future.

Since APEC's foundation in November 1989, it has built a detailed co-operative work program covering a wide range of issues calculated to enhance effective economic co-operation between member countries.[83] It has a full-time Secretariat. In November 1993 APEC took the logical next step from ministerial meetings to a heads of government gathering. Hosted by the United States' President, Bill Clinton, leaders of fourteen APEC nations met in Seattle in 1993 and said in their communiqué: 'Our meeting reflects the emergence of a new voice for the Asia Pacific in world affairs ... We believe our dynamic region, representing 40 per cent of the world's population and 50 per cent of its GNP, will play an important role in the global economy, leading the way on economic growth and trade expansion.'

Paul Keating, my successor as Prime Minister, was a late convert to the significance of Asia and the importance of fostering co-operation in the region – a conversion which I wholeheartedly welcome as I do his initiative in promoting the Seattle meeting. His reluctance to recognise my foundational role in the establishment of APEC was put in perspective by the acknowledgment from President Clinton in Seattle: 'I want to salute those who had the vision to establish it, such as former Australian Prime Minister, Robert Hawke ...'

My reward has been in the fact of APEC's growth and its acceptance by the international community as an important new force for liberal-ised economic co-operation in the region and beyond. And this profound pleasure has been intensified by the knowledge that Australia, under my leadership, can claim to have played a part far beyond our numerical status in the final successful outcome, in December 1993, of the long, seven-year negotiations of the Uruguay Round.

Meanwhile, I had not allowed this focus on the international environ-ment to distract the Government's attention from a domestic issue which was close to my heart: the needs of Australia's Aborigines. In our first period of government Clyde Holding had worked with commit-ment to lift the profile of Aboriginal affairs and to increase, in real terms, the resources allocated to the needs of the Aboriginal people. With the appointment of Gerry Hand to the portfolio after the 1987 election, we moved to an historic new stage. Gerry conceived the idea of involving the Aboriginal people more directly in decisions affecting their welfare. He and I discussed the concept at length. Out of this came the establishment of the Aboriginal and Torres Strait Islander Commission (ATSIC) which replaced the Department of Aboriginal Affairs and the Aboriginal Development Commission. With the creation of sixty elected regional councils and a board of twenty Aboriginal commissioners under the leadership of that devoted representative of her people, Lois O'Donoghue, Aborigines were for the first time given an effective role in making decisions about the programs which affect their lives.

In June 1988 Gerry Hand and I went to an Aboriginal festival at Barunga in the Northern Territory, to which thousands of Aborigines had come from Arnhem Land, the Central Desert, Western Australia, South Australia, Queensland and New South Wales. I threw spears with them and saw Pitjantjatjara and Yolngu people dance together; we were told it was the first time they had done this. There was a gift-giving ceremony and then, as we sat on the ground amid the eucalypts, the Aboriginal elders spelled out to us their hopes for the future.

In response I pledged the Government to achieve a reconciliation of black and white Australia:

> I hope that the Government will be able to make it possible for Aboriginal and non-Aboriginal Australians to reach a proper and lasting reconciliation through a pact or treaty ... I have never been hung up about the precise word we use to describe this ... What is important is the process: that we work towards some form of agreement under which reconciliation can take place.

The dedication of Gerry Hand's successor, Robert Tickner, and the support of the Opposition led to the creation of the Council for Aboriginal Reconciliation, made up of fourteen Aboriginal and Torres Strait Islander representatives, including the Chairperson, and eleven non-Aboriginal representatives. It is a matter of great joy to me that my Barunga concept, ridiculed by much of the media and others at the time, is now being worked through in practical, co-operative terms with a view to achieving a treaty of reconciliation, or its equivalent, by the beginning of the new century. Nothing could have given me more pride and satisfaction than that my final act as Prime Minister, on the morning of 20th December 1991 in Parliament House, was to receive for permanent display the Barunga Statement, painted by Aboriginal artists to commemorate our meeting and the commitment made in 1988, that day we sat down together on the red Australian earth, with gum trees and sky surrounding us. In accepting the Statement I said:

> I don't take this time to recount all the achievements of the Hawke Government in regard to Aboriginal people because while I have enormous pride in what we have achieved no-one talking of a problem of these dimensions could believe that you have gone anywhere near far enough ...[84] what we've got to understand is that, if you're really serious in this country as you come to the end of this century, the first century of our existence as a nation, and you want proudly to take Australia into the 21st Century there is no chance that you're going to be able to do that unless you do have a reconciliation. Personally I would like to see that embodied in a document. I think it is infinitely more preferable that we have the courage to do that. But it is also true that the document itself, in one sense, is not the important thing. The important thing is what's in our minds and in our hearts.

TWENTY-FIVE

The 1987 election victory brought with it an historic third term but it also marked a watershed in my relations with Paul Keating. With the 1987 poll the time had come in Paul's mind for Labor's most successful leader ever to begin clearing the way for his successor, and the sooner the better. His ambition became the prism through which all events of the past and present were viewed.

At the Caucus meeting after Labor's victory, I enthusiastically thanked my entire ministry for the magnificent job they had done during the campaign and all Members for the remarkable discipline they had shown. Ministers and Members thanked me for what they said were generous comments, given the importance of my own role in the victory. In this context it came as a surprise to me to be given a report that Keating was riled and sulking because, in paying tribute to all, I had failed to lavish special praise on him. Nothing was further from my mind than offending him. He had done a marvellous job in the run-up to the poll, as had the entire Labor team. Inadvertently, however, I had put a marble under his mattress and he was restless with resentment. Two strands of thought dominated Paul's mind to produce this attitude and to lead him to create his edifice of disruptive expectations.

First, he deliberately transformed a non-committal conversation with me in 1980 in the Boulevard Hotel, Sydney, into a binding undertaking to stand down in his favour after two terms should I become Prime Minister. I had accepted a suggestion that I meet Keating, since he was President of the NSW Branch which had indicated its support of my move to the Federal Parliament. This made sense and in a meeting in Sydney we talked about the party's federal prospects. I made no secret of my hope to lead the party and at some point in our discussion observed that in about two terms as Prime Minister we should have gone a long way in laying the basis for the reforms we sought to achieve. In a sense I was outlining a loose chronology against which Paul could measure his own obvious leadership aspirations. Certainly no hard and fast timetable was proposed, and at no point did I give any unequivocal undertaking to Paul or to anyone else – not that anyone else was seeking it – that two terms was the contract, and then I would hand over to him. It suited Paul, however, to put this gloss on the conversation and it seemed the further we got from the Boulevard in 1980 and the further we went into government, the more fixed did that gloss become in his mind.

The facts surrounding my succession to the leadership of the Labor Party do not sustain Keating's interpretation of what took place in 1980. His tardiness in switching his allegiance from Bill Hayden to me in July 1982 did not suggest a belief that he had a gold-plated guarantee of succession. And of course in 1982 any talk of a two-term transitional period would have been met with derision by those working on my behalf.

Second, Paul Keating had a sense of urgency because he believed Labor's time was running out. He had doubted we could win in 1987 and now believed we were in our last term before being thrown back into Opposition. So here he was in 1987, driven by a flawed interpretation of the past and a mistaken analysis of the future, focusing more and more of his attention on replacing me as Leader. It was a focus which, founded as it was in error, came to distort his analysis of the historical record. Before long, the version according to Paul was that, single-handedly, he had floated the dollar, deregulated the financial sector of the economy, run the Expenditure Review Committee, powered the Government and won the elections – he was the prime mover and, in all but name, the Prime Minister.

Against these distortions which built up after 1987, it is perhaps useful to reflect on the working relationship which had developed between Paul Keating and me in government. After his nervous start as Treasurer, when much of the responsibility for the Government's economic policy fell on me and my office, Keating and I went on to become, along with Curtin and Chifley, the most powerful political combination in Australian history.

Paul's confidence soared and, in keeping with the way I ran Cabinet and the ministry, I was keen for him to have his head and to assume fully those responsibilities which were properly his. Very occasionally, as in the case of his giddy and potentially suicidal commitment to a consumption tax in 1985, I moved to cut off his oxygen supply, but I was generally more than happy to let him run his own race. We were fellow travellers – he was heading where I was going, and I was going where he was heading.

I worked inordinately long hours as Prime Minister and in this way I was able to be a backstop and support to any ministers, including Keating, when they sought assistance or when the broader interests of government required my intervention.

With Paul I developed a particularly effective and easy working relationship in the area of economic policy as he mastered the concepts and detail of his complex portfolio. In the regular discussions we had together, I confirmed the big judgments on domestic economic policy which were, rightly, his prerogative to initiate. We had the confidence of the coterie of senior ministers who constituted the ERC and I cannot recall an instance where our combined judgment was ever set aside by them or the Cabinet.

I appreciated the fact that when I did have a particular interest which did not coincide with his own, and which required extra Government expenditure or the foregoing of revenue, he was always supportive. This happened particularly in the areas of tourism and sport. We were fortunate in having John Brown as the relevant minister in the early years of government. John understood from the beginning the vast potential of tourism and sought funding for an expanded promotion campaign, using the services of Paul Hogan in particular. The sceptics were thick on the ground and were led by Peter Walsh, who lacked all vision on this matter. I supported Brown absolutely and, while the Treasurer had some doubts, he backed us in our demands. The Government gave the tourism industry unprecedented support, which has paid off by providing Australia with one of its great and growing export earners. In the year before we came to office, Australia received just under one million tourists from overseas. That figure is now about 2.75 million and it is estimated that by the year 2000 it will be of the order of seven million.

Similarly, we invested substantial and unprecedented funds in sports development. Funding was aimed at achieving a level of international excellence, particularly through our outstanding Australian Institute of Sport, and at encouraging wider participation at the grass roots level. We paid particular attention to the relatively neglected area of women's sport.

After Brown had left the ministry – with a deserved reputation as the best-ever minister in these areas – I decided we should support the Australian horse-breeding industry which was haemorrhaging to New Zealand because of the more attractive depreciation provisions available in that country. I insisted that we should more than match those provisions; as a result, our industry, certainly on a per capita basis, stands comparison with any in the world.[85] On all of these decisions, although he has no basic interest in sport, Paul stood behind me against the philistines in the ERC and the Cabinet. I was more than happy to reciprocate when some of our colleagues were doubtful about his imaginative decision to provide federal financial assistance by way of grants to deserving talents in the arts. All of these decisions had the great virtue of being intrinsically worthwhile and electorally attractive.

Although we were vastly different characters, both temperamentally and in our interests and hobbies, Keating and I made a fair fist of getting along together. Since childhood I had been passionately interested in most sports, which attracted him not at all, and I still played cricket, tennis, golf and snooker. Paul never turned up for any of the Prime Minister's cricket matches against touring sides; I had established these on coming to office to give promising young Sheffield Shield players an opportunity to play against international cricketers. I am pleased, however, that he has continued this admirable practice just as I think it has been appropriate for him – despite the cynics – to have developed an interest in Australian Rules football through his association with the great Collingwood Football Club.

My penchant for horseracing and punting used to fascinate Paul, mainly, I think, because this was so foreign to him. In a perverse way, he seemed to respect the total relaxation I found in analysing a form guide as if it were a Cabinet submission – and usually making a profit in the process. French Empire clocks were his fascination; he had an absolute passion for them, perhaps not unrelated to his visceral republicanism and his tardiness at keeping appointments. On a couple of occasions he had me over to his house to explain in loving detail the esoterics of his numerous clocks. They were handsome objects to be sure, but I must say I could think of better ways of filling in my time than polishing them and taking them to pieces and putting them together again. However I respected his deep knowledge of the subject and the disciplined way in which he had built his collection.

One hilarious incident involving his elegant acquisitions occurred in our first year in the Lodge. Paul had acquired an antique English silver tea-set which was his pride and joy at the time. He had polished it to within an inch of its life and then sealed each piece in a plastic bag. He was going away to the snow for the weekend and decided that he couldn't risk the cherished tea-set being stolen while he was away. Apparently he had turned up at the Lodge and deposited it in a large box for safe-keeping with Tony Duffy, the butler. Tony put it away in a safe place. He later told Hazel and me that the Treasurer had left us a lovely present. When Paul turned up on Sunday evening on his return from the snow I suggested a cup of tea. Tony thought it appropriate to produce the beautiful present from the thoughtful Treasurer, and tea was served in the immaculate antique silver set, now carefully removed from its plastic bags. Paul, close to apoplexy, grabbed the pieces, went to the kitchen, wrapped them up, took them home and repeated the loving process of polishing and wrapping. All of us later, except Tony, had a good laugh, but we were never asked again to be custodians of the Keating treasures.

Our relationship remained warm. Paul and his family often came to the Lodge for a weekend meal with us and Rosslyn and her two boys. The nature of our relationship can be judged from the fact that, even in later years, Hazel, who had the use of the Lodge grand piano, lent her own piano to Annita for the use of her children.

The fact is that despite some tensions over the years and some resentment which Paul felt over the dumping of the consumption tax proposal and in the aftermath of his banana republic outburst, by 1987 the Hawke–Keating relationship was one of the Government's great strengths, and would remain so for some time to come. But the 1987 election victory had triggered Paul's leadership fantasy, and this was now the treasured object he began to polish with fervour.

In the meantime the wheels of government kept turning. Our disciplined decision-making since 1986 had put us in a good position by August 1988 to bring down a Budget with a huge surplus. But, before that date, Australia would experience the excitement of the Bicentenary celebrations; in commemorating two hundred years of European settlement I had insisted that we should recognise throughout the year the unique contribution of the preceding forty thousand years of Aboriginal civilisation. The Bicentennial organisational structure we inherited from the Fraser Government proved less than adequate. Jim Kirk, a retired oil company executive, came in at a late stage; by virtue of a truly dynamic performance and with the help of Wendy McCarthy and others, he ensured not only that we spent a successful and enjoyable year of celebration around the country but also that there was substantial investment in bicentennial projects of enduring benefit.

A feature of the year was the opening on 9th May of the new Parliament House by the Queen. A great deal of maudlin nonsense was written at the time about leaving the old premises, which were dated, dysfunctional and overcrowded, with many staff and support services working in appalling conditions. The media conjured up stories about how much more difficult it was going to be for them to have contact with ministers. This was always self-serving rubbish and one can only wonder what evidence there is to support the proposition today.

There is a delightful ambivalence in the Australian public's opinion of the new Parliament House; they knock its Members unmercifully as a matter of course, but they are tremendously proud of the building. From the very beginning of construction the managers made provision for the public to visit the site and view the work in progress;

hundreds of thousands of Australians became involved with the project. Now some 1.4 million people a year visit the building and show their pride in having a Parliament House of such striking architectural qualities and symbolic importance.

Internal strife in the Fraser Government has left me a permanent place in the new Parliament House. Bill Snedden, who had become Speaker after being replaced as leader by Fraser, carried on the feud by insisting that as Speaker he should lay the foundation stone of the new building, while Fraser argued that he should have the honour as Prime Minister. They had not resolved the matter by the time of the 1983 election. To me there was nothing to argue about. I wasn't prepared to imagine that Harry Jenkins, our Speaker, would have any Snedden-like pretensions and so, thanks to Malcolm and Bill, I have the honour to be there as Labor Prime Minister on the foundation stone of this magnificent building.

The opening of the new Parliament House had a special significance for the Queen. Exactly sixty-one years before to the day, her father, then Duke of York and later King George VI, had opened the first, 'temporary' Parliament House in Canberra. As usual Her Majesty carried out her duties with the dignity and efficiency which have become her hallmark; and as usual we also found time among the serious matters of state to have our customary exchange about her horses and the rising stars of the Australian turf. On the Sunday the Queen had a chance to see one of these stars, Beau Zam, fight out a thrilling finish with Bonecrusher, the New Zealand champion, in the feature race of the special Bicentennial meeting staged by the ACT Racing Club. A newspaper photograph showing me jumping up with excitement next to the sedately seated monarch elicited some disapproving comments from the narks. I took great pleasure in pointing a little later to a photo of the Queen showing similar exultation when one of her horses won in England.

The Queen, who clearly enjoyed this day in Australia, must have one of the most unenviable jobs in the world. Head of state but servant of the Government, her capacity to influence events within her own country is minimal. She is required to attend the most boring functions and on occasions to meet civilly people to whom, by most reasonable standards, you wouldn't give the time of day. Far from the relatively cosseted treatment accorded to her predecessors by the media, her life and particularly that of her family are constantly subject to investigation and exposure by an insatiable and lurid press. An abundance of creature comforts is no recompense for such obligations and intrusions. Yet through all this she displays dignity and, as I found to my pleasure, a delightful sense of humour. Propriety forbids disclosure of our personal conversations but some of her heads of government, at home and in the Commonwealth, would have withered at her witty and incisive pricking of pomposity. Her knowledge of Commonwealth countries – their politics, economics and culture – is profound and I always found her company thoroughly enjoyable.

Our first Budget in the new House, brought down on the 23rd August, was a proud day for the Government. The fiscal discipline of the past was rewarded when we announced a massive $5.5 billion surplus, the biggest in the nation's history. 'Unquestionably, a dramatically better state of affairs now exists than when I warned in 1986 of the threat of Australia degenerating to the status of a banana republic,' the Treasurer told the House. 'In ten budgetary statements stretching back to 1983, we have painstakingly sifted through Commonwealth outlays, attacking waste, setting priorities and making quality changes with long-term beneficial effects.'

In 1987 the Government had promised a balanced Budget. 'In the event, our sound fiscal management delivered a much better result – a surplus of $2 billion, the very first in the thirty-five years for which comparable records have been kept,' the Treasurer continued. But the

Budget surplus announced on this night was almost three times that size, a massive turnaround from the prospective deficit we inherited from Fraser in 1983.

In short, the Budget promised lower inflation, high economic growth and a stabilisation of Australia's foreign debt. It was pitched in the context of a wage–tax trade-off, pledging significant tax cuts from the following July and so removing the pressure for substantial wage claims. We were getting the Budget to pay the costs which would otherwise have been imposed upon employers by higher money wage claims. This marked a further instalment in the development of what was the essence of the Accord.

As was his custom Paul had shown me the draft Budget speech and, as ever, he was receptive to suggestions I made. These were nearly always stylistic because by that stage an enormous amount of work had been done to reflect the substance of our decisions accurately. I thought the tone and content of the final product was just right – justifiably proud but not over the top. Unfortunately, in the euphoria of his press conference Paul went further and used a phrase that was later to be thrown back at him. Speaking of the Budget he said, 'This is the one that brings home the bacon.' Pigs seem to have loomed large in Keating's life in these last six years but the real trouble was that a central part of the bacon that Paul wanted was the leadership.

He had been chipping away since he came to talk to me about it in January. I told him then that I intended to continue and almost immediately stories canvassing a leadership change – stories obviously inspired by Paul – started appearing in the press. It was his way of keeping the pressure on, as was the increasing reference to the 'Paris option', the oft-expressed Keating predilection to get out of politics and Australia altogether and live in Paris. I took most of this with a grain of salt but it was said often enough to make me give some thought to what would happen if he did decide to go.

The day after the Budget I was interviewed on national television. Given that Paul had been seeding the gallery with talk of the Paris option, it was not surprising that I was asked about his intentions and what would happen if he decided to leave. 'We would miss him,' I replied. 'He has been an outstanding Treasurer, not just by Australian standards but by international standards and we would miss him.'

Pressed further by the ABC's Paul Lyneham, I responded, 'I don't think there is a danger [of Keating's leaving the Government], I suppose you've got to say there was a possibility. I certainly hope, and I expect, that Paul will stay ... Now I certainly don't discount that he could go. I certainly don't want him to go, I want him to stay, I think he will. But being hypothetical about it, if he were to go, there are people of very considerable talent in the ministry, and the position would be filled,' I concluded.

I have repeated my exact words here because they make their own point. If plain English has any meaning, it is clear I was bending over backwards to contain a particular line of questioning which owed its origin to Paul Keating himself. When, finally, I allowed the slim possibility that Paul might leave politics, what was I to say? That the Government would be ruined? That a team which included the likes of Gareth Evans, Kim Beazley, Ralph Willis, John Button, John Kerin, Robert Ray, Graham Richardson, Peter Walsh, John Dawkins, not to mention myself, couldn't continue as a government? This was nonsense. But nonsense was the order of the day, as the media, driven by Keating's incipient campaign, whipped from innocent words the very opposite of their intended meaning. 'PM takes shot at Keating', the headlines blared. 'Clear message Keating not indispensable', they yelled as all hell broke loose.

This created the setting for a confrontation between Keating and me which essentially spelled the end of our friendship, although not the end of our working relationship. Paul came to see me in high dudgeon, seething with self-righteous indignation. Everything had to be weighed, it seemed, according to his sensitivities and I had committed the cardinal sin of daring, in response to pointed questioning, to put the Government ahead of Paul Keating himself.

My words to Lyneham were interpreted by Keating as deliberate knockout blows directed at him. From a man who fashions his own discourse after the manner of a sledge-hammer this was a bit rich. I had called him an 'outstanding Treasurer' but this somehow made me an ingrate. He understood my words as spelling an end to the Hawke–Keating partnership. He was the one who had fuelled the Paris option but I was now the one responsible for putting the Concorde on the tarmac.

Keating used some pretty flash language during our conversation that day but nothing quite as lurid as the version he later gave to the producers of the ABC's 'Labor in Power'.[86] Paul is a revisionist, applying to his recollection of events and conversations the same loving care with which he seeks to restore his French Empire clocks to what he hopes was an original beauty of form and style. His reaction was in fact hysterical and, to my mind, illogical and self-deluding. I knew that his taut, emotional state was partly due to sheer exhaustion. Everybody who knows Paul knows that working long hours for weeks at a stretch does not come easily to him; the Budget preparations had placed him under considerable pressure and strain. And as a totally committed family man, his youngest daughter's year of prolonged ill-health had imposed an additional burden.

Understanding all this I refused to respond at his emotional level. I explained that he was being stupid in his interpretation and that I thought he would come to see things differently. I told him he was being immature and to grow up. Apart from fatigue, Paul's outburst was also a measure of how consumed he was by ambition to displace me. He had spent much of 1988 denigrating me behind my back, arguing that the Government was running out of steam and that a change was needed. Stories of Keating's behaviour invariably got back to me. One of my staff asked me at the time, Why don't you hate the bastard? I felt sorry for him more than anything. At the time my political stocks were on the rise. People remarked that they had not seen me in better form, and I felt that way.

As he got the loud and clear political message from the party that it wanted me to stay, his frustration level rose commensurately and his frustration was reflected in his poor arithmetic. He claimed a majority of Cabinet supported him and that he would have forty-four votes in Caucus. This was self-delusion writ large. His only dedicated supporter in Cabinet was Employment, Education and Training Minister, John Dawkins, and John was not an entirely disinterested observer, for he dearly wanted to become Treasurer. According to Richardson, Paul might have had five votes in Caucus.

I was relaxed about the leadership but I was disturbed at the degree of instability produced by an apparent rift between the Prime Minister and his Treasurer and the public perception of disunity. So when Richardson suggested I go back on television to clear up any misunderstanding that may have arisen from the Lyneham interview I was prepared to do so. Speaking on Channel Nine's 'A Current Affair' on 25th August 1988 I told Ray Martin, 'It is not accurate to talk about a rift, Ray. Paul Keating has been in politics a. long time and he has a totally legitimate ambition to succeed me as Prime Minister.' In the course of the interview I again said some flattering things about Keating's abilities and his contribution to Australia's national life.

With that, Richardson rang Keating to tell him to cool down, that I had put everything right. But Paul was beyond reason and turned the conversation into a tirade of abuse against me. It was an indulgence made worse by the fact that Richardson was ringing on a car phone. Within hours a transcript of the conversation was out and about. My press secretary, Barrie Cassidy, handed me a copy while I was en route to Sydney for a Labor Party fund-raising dinner at the NSW Parliament House. I read it with mounting anger. If that was the way he wanted it, then I, too, could be a pretty fair exponent of telephone abuse, the difference being that I was prepared to front my interlocutor directly.

I rang Keating from Sydney and blasted him unmercifully. I can't recall his getting a chance to say anything of consequence in reply. Cassidy said afterwards that my language would have emptied the bar of the John Curtin Hotel in my drinking days. Having cleared the air, I then went and raised a considerable amount of money for the party.

Others, particularly some of Paul's colleagues from the NSW Right, helped to calm him down. In the meantime his chief urger, John Dawkins, came to see me on 29th August 1988. Dawkins is a complex character, bright, but in many respects politically immature. And like Keating, Dawkins often finds it difficult to look you in the eye when he is talking to you. This led to a rather embarrassed and sheepish conversation on his part. Generously conceding that I had done a good job, he said we were now reaching a stage where we needed a new jump and this might be easier to take with Paul as leader. Dawkins' embarrassment was not helped by the dismissive way in which I dealt with him. I told him he was wasting his time.

The outbreak was now under control but the atmosphere remained tense. Keating and I agreed to meet and try to sort out our difficulties. It was a friendly enough meeting but there was evidence that he was still living in a dream world. He said something extraordinary which demonstrated to me just how ignorant he was about the demands of being Prime Minister. 'You know, Bob, I think that if I ever do become Prime Minister I will remain Treasurer and do that job as well,' he ruminated. I was prepared to humour him but this was too much. I burst out laughing. 'Paul, you simply have no idea, no idea at all of what's involved in being Prime Minister!' I exclaimed.

He had no realisation, obviously, of the time required to do the job properly. For an intelligent man, he had not thought it through; indeed I doubt whether up to the moment he became Prime Minister he understood what it was all about. Keating did not work consistently long hours. He certainly put the hours in when it was necessary but generally he was a late arriver and an early leaver. He had come to accommodate the job of Treasurer within a congenial time-frame.

By contrast, I knew from experience that being Prime Minister is a seven-day-a-week job. I rarely worked less than sixteen hours a day and very often more. Apart from being across the whole range of domestic issues, I made a point of reading everything of relevance in the international and intelligence areas. Every weekend involved dealing with at least two bulging briefcases of cables, reports and important correspondence.

Apart from the hilarity induced by Paul's concept of combining the Prime Minister's job with that of the Treasurer, the meeting had an ominous note to it. Keating proposed a further meeting with others present at which a transition agreement about the leadership would be struck. In other circumstances I would have dismissed the suggestion out of hand, but the background events made me consider this proposition. Despite the reservations I had about Paul he was my most likely successor. He was not, as I had conceded under questioning, indispensable, but he was an extremely important member of the Government and together, as Prime Minister and Treasurer, we were a deadly combination. His threats to leave politics and the country were becoming more strident, and more believable.

With the 1990 election not that far off, I was basically concerned with maximising Labor's chances of winning the poll. Our position would not be strengthened, in my view, if the Treasurer were to pull up stumps. And so, with considerable reluctance, I entertained Keating's suggestion of an agreement about the leadership.

There was some coming and going between us as to who, precisely, should also be present at the meeting he suggested. Eventually we fixed on two men who were close to both of us, TNT Chief Executive, Sir Peter Abeles, and the ACTU Secretary, Bill Kelty. As intimates of each of us, Peter and Bill already believed that there should be a meeting of friends to resolve the differences between Paul and myself.

We agreed to meet at Kirribilli House in Sydney on 25th November 1988. Against my basic judgment, but because I wanted to contain the relationship and to maximise our chances at the 1990 election, I indicated that after winning that election I would, at some stage thereafter, step down as leader, clearing the way for Paul.

Looking back now, it is easy to characterise the agreement as a mistake, particularly when one considers its personal and political consequences. But what concerned me then was the importance to the party of maintaining an effective relationship between Keating and myself, for I knew that whatever strains arose from his ambitions and despite quirks of behaviour, including contempt for others, the Hawke–Keating combination had to be harnessed for the greater good of the party and the country.

I used the occasion to give him some advice about what leadership entailed. In the course of the Kirribilli discussion I referred to the concerns of Paul's colleagues and we all discussed his unpopularity with the electorate. As this was a talk held in good faith among mutual friends, I told him that leadership involved respect for others: 'If you're going to be a successful leader, you've got to have your people around you feeling that you don't treat them with contempt,' I said. In this context I referred to his notoriously late arrival at Cabinet and ERC meetings. This went to the very heart of my worry about him. I often had to delay scheduled meetings because of unavoidable matters which required my attention, but his habitual lack of punctuality in even being in his office, let alone at a meeting, was a stark example of the way in which people felt that the Treasurer did not treat them with respect.

He has since portrayed this as my behaving like a schoolmaster. It came from the best of motives and expressed not only my concern, but that of others, who consistently complained to me that Keating was contemptuous of them, that their timetables and programs were not important to him, that he was the only one who mattered. This was well-intentioned advice about an impression which Paul could easily have rectified. Instead he chose to parody himself, treating my advice with the very contempt I was warning him against.

We agreed that the meeting and our agreement would remain secret but I finished the Kirribilli session with a sense of foreboding. I thought I had done something that in all the circumstances would be in the immediate interests of the party by ensuring the best possible atmosphere for the next election. But I had reservations about Keating's capacity to remodel himself for leadership. I consoled myself with the hope that he would rise to this challenge and prove himself worthy of the succession I had now entrusted to him.

V

MAKING HISTORY:
LABOR'S FOURTH TERM

TWENTY-SIX

The Kirribilli meeting occurred at the mid-point of our third term. I knew that my capacity to deliver a fourth victory for Labor in 1990 would depend on the simple principle I had outlined to George Bush a few months earlier: that elections are won or lost on the voters' perceptions of how well those in power have governed, and the quality of the Opposition as an alternative government.[87]

I felt confident on both scores and did not share Keating's apprehension that time was running against us. This was the mainspring of his view, unacceptable to me, that it was his turn to occupy the leadership. Believing as I have said that the Australian electorate had got it right on every occasion since 1949, with the possible exception of 1980, I felt the operation of this principle would work in our favour if we kept our heads and continued to provide sound government.

A major test of our capacity and willingness to do this came in 1989 with the pilots' strike which threatened to devastate the Australian economy.

The pilots' union (the Australian Federation of Air Pilots) was an elitist organisation supremely confident of its ability to impose its will upon the airline industry and the Australian travelling public through the monopolistic bargaining position it enjoyed. It had never affiliated with the ACTU and normally remained aloof from any industrial disputes in which other unions in the industry were engaged.

The pilots had good reason for their confidence. Historically their tactic had been to present a log of claims and press it on one of the two major airlines which, under the Two Airlines policy of the Coalition Government, had exclusive rights to the domestic routes between the capital cities. Neither Australian Airlines, the Government-owned operator, nor Ansett, owned jointly by TNT and Rupert Murdoch, were ever prepared to withstand prolonged pressure from the pilots. As a result pilots employed by these two airlines enjoyed conditions which, by international standards, and certainly compared with those of the Australian workforce, were extraordinary. Before the 1989 strike a captain on a 727 received base earnings of $100 936 a year and a first officer $60 561 for flying an average of 36.8 hours *per month*.

But this was not good enough for the Australian Federation of Air Pilots (AFAP). With the rest of the union movement continuing to exercise very considerable wage restraint under the Accord, the pilots lodged a claim for a 30 per cent increase in salaries. This was an outrageous demand in itself but the danger went far beyond the airline industry. We knew (and indeed the ACTU made it quite clear) that if the pilots were allowed to get away with this then all bets were off as far as the Accord was concerned. The unions would use their industrial strength in a growing economy to extract whatever wage increases and improvements in conditions they could. The foundation of our economic policy – wage restraint in return for an improved social wage – which had enabled Australia to enjoy record employment growth and to improve its international competitive position, would be destroyed.

I was not prepared to allow this to happen and personally took control of the Government's resistance to the Federation's claim. My first approach was to appeal to reason and what I hoped would be the enlightened self-interest of the pilots and their union leadership. I told them not to make the mistake of living in the past; the rules were different now and they were the beneficiaries, with the rest of the community, of the new rules. I made it clear that the Government did not want a fight and that we would co-operate in a hearing of their claims in the arbitration tribunal according to the principles which applied to the rest of the workforce. The bottom line was that neither the Government nor the airlines would surrender to industrial action by the pilots in support of their claims.

I was able to speak from strength both because the Government's position had merit and because we had the unqualified support of the two airlines and the ACTU. In handling the crisis it helped that I had close personal relations with each of the airline chiefs and with Bill Kelty, who dealt with the dispute on behalf of the ACTU.

Sir Peter Abeles, the chief executive of TNT and Ansett, had been a friend since 1970 and our friendship had strengthened over the years. Peter is of Hungarian-Jewish origin, outstanding in both intellect and business acumen. After his arrival in Australia in 1949 he progressed from being a door-to-door salesman of knitwear and books to building one of the biggest transport empires in the world, operating in some eighty countries with a total of more than 70 000 employees. Peter is one of the most generous and decent human beings I have met and I know of many instances where his instincts have led him to sustain out of his own pocket people who have fallen on hard times. His fluency in five languages and a broad compassion make him truly a world citizen. He played a prominent role in the 1983 summit and was totally committed to the principles of the Accord. Since his appointment to it by Paul Keating in 1984, he had served with distinction as a member of the Reserve Bank board.

Ted Harris was a friend from my earliest days as ACTU President when, as a senior executive with Ampol, he had been the most constructive force for good sense among employers in the oil industry. He had served governments of both political persuasions at the NSW and federal levels in a number of capacities, including the administration of funds for sporting development. Ted is a fine Australian citizen, a man of strong character and forthright views who had done an excellent job as Chairman of Australian Airlines from the time of his appointment in November 1987. He had a very close personal relationship with Bill Kelty, as did Sir Peter.

The pilots, and some sections of the Opposition and the media, made much of these personal relationships. Lacking any argument of substance as to the merits of the case, they attempted by innuendo to attribute improper motives to the continuous collaboration between the four of us during the dispute. These mischievous efforts did not deter us from doing what we knew was necessary in the national interest. Sir Peter never during my time as President of the ACTU or as Prime Minister asked me to do anything to favour his business activities. In fact I did more to damage his interests – and those of Australian Airlines – than any other politician. The Two Airlines Agreement was a cosy duopolistic arrangement which guaranteed permanent profits to the two operators. When the Government announced in 1989, as part of our continuing program of micro-economic reform, that the agreement would not be renewed once it expired in 1990, Sir Peter accepted that decision, although it was detrimental to Ansett, as being in Australia's best interests.

The President of the pilots' union was Brian McCarthy, a captain with Australian Airlines. McCarthy had limited industrial experience and, with those around him, believed that with perhaps a little more pressure, the tactics of the past would pay off again. I do not remember any significant industrial dispute in which union members were so badly led and indeed, in the end, destroyed by their leadership. Members were instructed to resign from their jobs with the airlines and to take jobs – taxi-driving was suggested in the union letter – to tide them over until the companies and the Government capitulated. It is difficult to imagine more counter-productive advice, for with the resignation of their pilots both companies were left unrestricted to pursue the alternative strategies we devised to keep the airline system going.

These consisted of supplementing the services of the few pilots who had not resigned with recruitment in Australia and overseas, the leasing of aircraft with crew from overseas and the use of aircraft and flying personnel from the Royal Australian Air Force and Royal Australian Navy. These were drastic steps for a Labor government to take. But the broad labour movement had become so committed to the Accord principles, and was sufficiently outraged at the pilots willingness to accept the benefits but not the obligations of the Accord, that we had no difficulty in sustaining the support of our colleagues throughout the dispute. The Government subsidised the airlines to cover the cost of maintaining on the payroll those who would otherwise have had to be stood down for lack of work; the amount of the subsidy was reduced as far as possible by arrangements for staff to take annual and long-service leave.

McCarthy ignored the implications of all this and, most particularly, the strength of our support in the labour movement. The pilots had felt it beneath them in the past to be associated organisationally or in industrial action with the broad trade union movement; their calls now for solidarity from that movement and their condemnation of others as 'scabs' had a hollow ring.

As the pilots came to realise the absolute determination of the Government, the airlines and the ACTU, their tactics became rougher. I could understand the increasing desperation of men who were facing up to the fact that through stupidity they were destroying their own careers. This is why, on 28th November, in my office in Canberra I pleaded unsuccessfully with their representatives to come to their senses for the sake of their members. But understanding their desperation did not mean condoning the contemptible tactics to which some of the pilots resorted; in one case a coffin was sent to the wife of an Ansett pilot who was contemplating returning to work with the company. Death threats were received by airline executives and pilots who remained at work. The intimidation was so fierce that a pilot, describing what had been said to him, broke down in tears in Sir Peter's office.

The dispute did have its lighter moments as the RAAF and RAN aircrews joked with passengers about the luxury conditions of the lumbering Hercules transport aircraft which were pressed into service. Meals were basic and served in cardboard boxes but were delivered with panache by a serviceman in a cummerbund with a white serviette over his arm. Navy aircrews always got a laugh from passengers when they threw out a long plastic chain and anchor when coming to a stop after landing.

While the travelling public accepted the inconveniences of the limited, makeshift schedule that we were gradually able to build upon, the tourist industry was in a state of panic. Many operators suffered badly and much of the industry was crying ruination. They were aided and abetted by an Opposition which took an opportunistic and hypocritical attitude throughout the dispute. The Coalition parties had consistently blamed Australia's economic problems on excessive wage increases generated by 'greedy' trade unions with no concern for the national interest. They knew exactly the general wage and economic implications of caving into the pilots; but Opposition Leader, Andrew Peacock, and the Shadow Tourism spokesman, David Jull, embraced the cause of McCarthy and the pilots and attacked me in particular for the toughness of my stand against their new militant friends. The Coalition position was as execrable as the pilots' was untenable.

After thirty weeks the dispute was over. Ruled against in the arbitration tribunal and in the civil courts where action and counter-action had been taken by the pilots' union and the airlines, the AFAP had no alternative but to capitulate. All the attempts by parts of the media to give McCarthy some sort of hero status and all his public exposure could not make a silk purse out of a sow's ear. A thoroughly unjustifiable claim had been exacerbated by ill-informed leadership and vicious tactics by some disgruntled members.

I never doubted the course the Government had to follow and was increasingly confident that the public would come to understand and support our position. It was a fight I had tried to avoid but, once unavoidable, it had to be won. I got no personal joy from the outcome. What I saw were hundreds of decent but misguided men whose leaders did not understand the fundamental changes which had occurred in Australia over the previous six years. They had been lulled into believing that yesterday's tactics would work today; in the process very many of them destroyed the careers they cherished. I personally intervened with Sir Peter Abeles to ask that Ansett should not pursue action against individual pilots or seek to recover damages awarded to the company against officials of the AFAP. That organisation had self-destructed but I did not want to see any further burden on its members, who had suffered enough from self-inflicted wounds. Being the big-hearted man he is, Sir Peter agreed to my request.

The outcome of the dispute saw a dramatic change in the economics and productivity of the industry and in pilots' income. Before the strike Ansett and the associated EastWest Airlines employed 1046 pilots. After the dispute this figure was reduced to 598. In contrast to the pre-dispute work practices, flying hours virtually doubled to 73 per month; the base earnings of a captain and first officer increased to $135 000 and $78 289 respectively. Pilots working after the dispute in effect got the 30 per cent increase but received it in return for productivity improvements that were never on the table in the original claim.

Environmental matters assumed greater significance in this period. It was said that the Hawke Government developed a green thumb. If this is true it was certainly a well-tended and bitterly contested part of Labor's anatomy. In Graham Richardson the environmentalists had, in the Cabinet, one of the party's most energetic, persistent and astute ministers. They loved him and they were entitled to, for on every major issue on their agenda he listened to their case intently. He was not, as some of his opponents claimed, their cipher; but once convinced of the intrinsic merits of their position he would, without necessarily embracing every aspect of that position, advance it vigorously within the Government.

The very fact that Richardson espoused an environmental cause almost guaranteed a more spirited opposition from some members of the Cabinet and ministry. The Centre Left ministers, particularly Walsh, Dawkins and Cook, harboured a well-developed dislike for Richardson as the personification of the New South Wales Right, whom they regarded as ruthless and opportunistic operators. There was no doubt that Graham could be as hard as anyone in the business of factional politics, which were not always played according to Marquis of Queensberry rules, but their opposition to him on these issues did less than justice to the genuine feelings he had about the environment. For their part, there was no doubting the strength of their convictions about the need to maximise Australia's opportunities for economic growth. In this they had the vociferous support of organised industry groups, particularly in the mining and timber sectors. All this meant that when environmental issues were before the Cabinet we could be sure of a lively debate.

Richardson's persistence was probably best exemplified by the debate over logging in the Tasmanian Lemonthyme and Southern Forests areas. Before the 1987 elections we had set up an inquiry headed by Justice Michael Helsham of the New South Wales Supreme Court to report on the World Heritage value of the forests. There was considerable surprise when the majority report, delivered on 17th May 1988, concluded that most of the forest could be logged.[88] The large environmental lobby was outraged, and Richardson shared their chief concern which was for the region's ancient mountain ash (five hundred years old in some cases and among the tallest trees in the world) and the surrounding habitat.

Richardson, adamant that the report lacked principle and was unacceptable in pragmatic terms, was determined to see it rejected. Peter Cook, then Resources Minister, led the case for accepting it and, despite the lack of congenial chemistry between them, was supported by his senior portfolio minister in the Cabinet, John Kerin, the Minister for Primary Industries and Energy. These two had strong support from Walsh, Dawkins, the Industry Minister, John Button, and Gareth Evans, who was then Minister for Transport and Communications. This formidable line-up took a strong pro-development line linked to the inherent employment problems of Tasmania. Many Tasmanians felt their State had suffered from the Government's emphasis on the environment, going back to our 1983 decision on the Franklin dam. Pro-development ministers accepted their argument that putting these forests substantially off-limits to loggers threatened further hardships to the State. The population of the areas involved was overwhelmingly made up of blue-collar workers already suffering high levels of unemployment. The fact that environmental decisions caused hardship to particular communities made them all the more agonising and finely balanced.

My door was always open to Richardson, as indeed it was to all ministers. He argued his case at length with me and it would have been foolish not to have listened to him. I certainly did. But by coming direct to me he was accused of pre-empting Cabinet. The accusation was fundamentally wrong-headed since every minister had the same opportunity to persuade the Prime Minister to their point of view. Indeed it was standard procedure for virtually all ministers to seek to do so – they wrote, they called in, they phoned. Then they ran their arguments again in Cabinet. In the case of Helsham it was again, and again, and again, for the final decision was the culmination of some fifteen hours of debate spread over six weeks and four separate Cabinet meetings.

Departments, staffers, consultants, loggers, industry groups and environmentalists were actively involved with everyone firing off letters and submissions. Peter Cook brought outside experts – a professor and a Tasmanian forester – into the Cabinet room to support his position. Richardson spoke in response for two hours, which hardly indicated a belief that he had the decision tied up in advance.

Before those long, gruelling Cabinet sessions I had not signalled my hand to Richardson or anyone else, for I was determined there should be an unfettered debate. During the course of just such a debate a number of ministers were won over to Richardson's side. The Minister for Trade Negotiations, Michael Duffy, came Graham's way, as did Defence Minister, Kim Beazley. These were not the types to be won over by arm-twisting; nor were they suckers for soft, 'feel good' causes. They were hard heads who needed real arguments to persuade them. Nor is Paul Keating exactly your warm and cuddly politician. And although Richardson and Keating went back a long way as fellow members of the New South Wales Right, they were not, as is often believed, natural allies on every issue. But Richardson was able to convince Paul of the green cause in relation to Helsham and the Treasurer backed him in Cabinet well before I showed my hand.

As was my style, particularly on highly contentious issues, I gave everyone an extended opportunity to put their case and to respond to the arguments of their opponents. I was by nature sympathetic to the environmental argument without dismissing the legitimacy of the pro-development concerns. It was an excellent, if draining, debate with every element fully canvassed. It was not a case where one could assert dogmatically that one position was absolutely right, but in the end I came down on Richardson's side. The Cabinet, as always, accepted that this concluded the matter.

By our decision we expanded environmental protection from 8 to 70 per cent of the forests in question, about one-third of the total tall forests area of Tasmania. We did not ignore the loggers and added to Peter Cook's compensation and alternative employment package to provide a sum of $50 million for these purposes. Not all the environmentalists were entirely satisfied – they seldom are – and the forest industry didn't like the decision at all. There is no 'exactly right' decision in such matters; I felt, however, that we had got somewhere near that elusive mark.

Whatever doubts I may have had about the Tasmanian forests, I was absolutely certain as to the correct course of action to take on the other major environmental issue that arose in this period. In May 1989 the Cabinet had to decide whether it would sign the 1988 Convention on the Regulation of Antarctic Mineral Resource Activity (CRAMRA). This consensus convention permitted mining and drilling for oil to take place in the Antarctic. Its drafting had taken years of work by officials, work to which Australia had been party. When I looked at the agreement in detail and discussed it with my staff, particularly Craig Emerson, I decided that it was preposterous for Australia to be associated with such a proposal. The world had only recently experienced the disaster of the *Exxon Valdez* oil spill onto the Alaskan coast and it was inconceivable that we should put at risk the one remaining pristine continent. The unpolluted character of this fragile territory was highly important to the conduct of crucial environmental research work, particularly in regard to the threatened depletion of the ozone layer.

Although this was not a local issue with immediate employment and development consequences for Australia, there was still resistance in the Cabinet to my views. Graham Richardson, my alleged conspirator in all things environmental, was vehemently opposed as was Gareth Evans, who was by now Minister for Foreign Affairs and Trade. They pressed their arguments: a no-mining stance would damage Australia's relations with our Antarctic Treaty partners; the convention was a *fait accompli* and we would be ridiculed internationally; rearguard opposition was pointless as the work had already been done; whether we liked it or not, the new treaty had to be ratified for reasons of realpolitik. I refused to accept these arguments and said in effect: No! We are going to try to lead the world on this issue and change the world's thinking on it. This was viewed as a classic piece of unrealistic Hawke optimism but I was convinced it could be done. I believed that my thinking was in tune with a growing anxiety around the world on global environmental issues such as the impact of greenhouse gases and the damage to the ozone layer. The future of the Antarctic fell squarely within these concerns. I felt the general public was years ahead of bureaucrats and governments in such matters, and that we could advance the right case on a rising tide of public opinion which, in the end, the bureaucrats and their political masters would not be able to withstand.

And so, with an amused tolerance and almost total scepticism, the Cabinet let me have my head. We announced that Australia would not sign CRAMRA and that we would seek the agreement of our Antarctic

Treaty partners to replace that convention with a new agreement which would provide for a comprehensive protection of Antarctica as a 'Nature Reserve – Land of Science'.

My first step in what was dubbed 'Mission Impossible' was to enlist the support of France. Australia had been in conflict with France over its nuclear testing in the Pacific; what's more, we were at one with the South Pacific Forum countries in condemning repressive French policy in New Caledonia. An entirely new atmosphere emerged with the election of the Socialist Michel Rocard as Prime Minister in 1988 and the signing soon after of the Matignon Accords. These set out, in agreement with the Melanesian and European communities, the steps towards a referendum in 1998 on the future status of New Caledonia.

This new ambience was important but my main hope centred on the famous underwater explorer, adventurer and environmental champion, Jacques Cousteau. I knew that Cousteau identified with our stance and that he had the ear of President Mitterand and, to a lesser extent, Michel Rocard.

I count my close friendship with Jacques Cousteau as one of the great bonuses of my period as Prime Minister. We met for the first time on Sunday, 18th June 1989, at a working breakfast in Paris at the Hôtel Meurice where I was staying on a quick official visit to France. Some people attract attention because of their fame but make you wonder when you meet them what it would be like to spend several days alone in their company. With Cousteau, however, the man himself is the magnet. Jacques had turned seventy-nine a few days earlier but he exuded the physical and intellectual vitality of a man half his age. His penetrating eyes sparkled behind his glasses, and a constant half-smile played across his strong, tanned face. The mixture of gentleness, enormous strength of character and physical vibrancy gives this small, lean Frenchman a presence that would dominate in any gathering. With his warm and generous character goes a razor-sharp mind which effortlessly recalls statistics and assembles logical, persuasive argument. Jacques Cousteau is a passionate environmentalist; it is a commitment which springs from both mind and heart.

There was a mutual sense of excitement as we joined forces in pledging to take on the world. Cousteau had already spoken to Mitterand and promised to speak to him again before I met the President the next morning; he had also spoken with Rocard. Jacques was enthusiastic about our strategy of mounting the international campaign around the concept of making Antarctica a 'Nature Reserve – Land of Science'. As we discussed in detail how we would shape a joint Australian–French initiative to mobilise world opinion, I was thrilled to realise that in Jacques Cousteau I had made a good friend and found a redoubtable ally.

I met early the next morning with Michel Rocard at the Hôtel Matignon, the official office of the Prime Minister. We had spent several hours together on Saturday at the Paris Air Show and quickly established an easy, first-name rapport. Rocard is a small, lively man with a sharp intelligence, a beautiful sense of humour and a no-nonsense approach. We immediately set to work in our shirtsleeves – it was a hot summer morning – at a table set in the beautiful gardens behind his office. There were only two advisers present. We shaped a joint declaration announcing our intention to work for the overturn of CRAMRA and the achievement of the Australian concept for comprehensive protection of Antarctica. We also agreed to the formation of a working group to pursue environmental matters of common concern.

The release of our communiqué had to await my luncheon meeting at the Palais de l'Elysée with President Mitterand. There was no 'François' and 'Bob' with this austere gentleman; but he was, by his formal standards, warmly enthusiastic in our pre-lunch discussions about the Australian approach and said he had been persuaded by

Cousteau that we should move ahead together. He placed the presidential seal on the work of the two prime ministers and the battle was now under way.

I put the case to Margaret Thatcher in London and George Bush in Washington. Margaret tended to be suspicious of anything sponsored by the French but gave me a polite hearing without any promise of support. The President was equally polite but was locked into the position of his officials, who were among the most unrelenting proponents of CRAMRA. I was encouraged by a meeting with Senator Al Gore, later US Vice-President. Gore believed that public opinion could be mobilised behind the Australian–French proposal and promised his strong support to effect a change in the American attitude. He delivered on this promise with his lobbying to secure the passage of supportive legislation by the US Congress in 1990.

From this point on it was a matter of a concentrated diplomatic campaign to change the mind-set of all the Antarctic Treaty parties who believed the matter had been settled by CRAMRA. We were helped greatly in this campaign by Sir Ninian Stephen, whom I had appointed in 1989 as Ambassador for the Environment. I supported the work of ministers and officials with personal letters to all relevant heads of government. At the same time our friends in the Australian environment lobby were networking with their counterpart organisations to increase pressure on their governments.

Gradually our tactics paid off and the dominoes started to tumble. After successive meetings in Paris in October 1989, in Chile in October 1990, and in Madrid in April and June of 1991, we won the day. Governments signed an Environment Protection Protocol which prohibits mining absolutely in the Antarctic for fifty years. After fifty years, relaxation of the ban can be blocked by one-quarter (seven) of the existing consultative parties. In the international community this is accepted as meaning in practical terms that the Australian concept of Antarctica as a 'Nature Reserve – Land of Science' has been established in perpetuity.

Gareth Evans, who had resisted me so strongly at first but then worked prodigiously in support of my initiative, wrote of our achievement: 'Australia – with France – has the satisfaction of knowing that we have fundamentally changed the terms of the environmental debate about the future of a whole continent.'[89] In more colloquial terms, he said to me: 'You bugger, you were right!' I smiled to myself as I thought back to the amused scepticism around that Cabinet table in May 1989. I was proud but, more than that, I had a deep sense of satisfaction in knowing that, given sufficient determination, good ideas can triumph against the odds.

As we moved through 1989 towards the time for the next election we faced increasing difficulties on the economic front. Like every economist in this country and around the world, we had underestimated the resilience of the market economies in the wake of the stock market crash of October 1987. Everyone was haunted by the memory of the crash of 1929 and the Great Depression which followed and the conventional wisdom, to which we subscribed, was to run an easy monetary policy to avoid a collapse of the economy.

Far from collapsing, the economy started to boom again. We kept fiscal policy tight as we moved to a substantial budgetary surplus while wages policy under the Accord could not have been tighter. As economic activity increased, sucking in higher levels of imports unmatched by corresponding increases in exports, we were running into the fundamental problem of a deteriorating external account and rising debt. In the circumstances our only option was to tighten monetary policy; interest rates were forced up over 20 per cent before the unsustainable boom was finally cracked. With the benefit of hindsight, there is no doubt that we should have tightened monetary policy earlier; the depth and length of the recession would have been less severe. This was the worst mistake of my time in office and I deeply regret the fact that many ordinary Australians paid a heavy economic and social price for it in unemployment, bankruptcy and the personal traumas that accompany these tragedies.

However we didn't have hindsight to help us as we came to the end of 1989. We had an electorate resentful at some eighteen months of rising interest rates and fearful of an end to employment growth. The high-rollers of the eighties had come unstuck; their assumption of continuously rising asset values had exploded and the spectre of corporate collapses cast a pall over business confidence.

But the scenario was not one of unrelieved gloom. Despite the concern about interest rates, we were widely perceived as sound economic managers by a public now more sophisticated in its under-standing of Australia's problems and challenges; our performance in creating one and a half million jobs at twice the rate of the rest of the OECD was recognised and respected. And we had delivered sub-stantially on our 1987 election promise to advance significant micro-economic reform in this term of government.[90]

As well as our own solid performance, we had the continuing saga of Opposition disunity working for us. Over the years the Liberal Party has been wilfully negligent in its pre-selection of candidates for safe seats. Time after time, nonentities or proven failures had been accommodated only to disappear without trace in a sea of mediocrity. In 1987 the dearth of talent in the federal Coalition ranks had allowed credence to be given to the absurd 'Joh-for-Canberra' push. With Coalition talent unreplenished by that election, the fertile imagina-tions of some Liberal king-makers seriously pursued the idea of bring-ing John Elliott, Elders–IXL chief and Federal President of the Liberal Party, into the Parliament as the saviour of their dilapidated fortunes. Elliott, who had an equal contempt for Howard and Peacock, had no doubts about his capacity for the job but was not prepared in the end to sacrifice his substantial business interests to take on the uncertainties of two political fights: winning the leadership of the parliamentary Liberal Party and defeating me at the polls.

And so the same old hurdy-gurdy continued to whirl in Canberra as Peacock intensified his campaign against Howard in the early months of 1989. Sir Peter Abeles had a 'deep throat' within the Liberal caucus who must have known that whatever was told to Sir Peter would be passed on to me. On the basis of their information I was able to taunt Howard in the House on 13th April that the knives were out and that Peacock was gathering the numbers to oust him.[91] Howard scoffed and seemed genuinely unaware of what was happening. Less than four weeks later, on 9th May, Peacock toppled Howard by forty-four votes to twenty-seven. Peacock–Howard–Peacock: barring further insurrections Andrew Peacock would once again be my opponent in a federal election.

Leadership challenges are never clean and tidy affairs but in this case the distaste of many Liberals for what occurred extended to the wider public when the main Peacock plotters, including Wilson Tuckey, went on national television and, with incredible stupidity, boasted of lying and scheming to secure Howard's downfall. Peacock's leadership was tarnished from the outset.

The inherent instability created by the circumstances of Peacock's resurrection was fuelled by the contradictory positions projected by the Opposition on our most vulnerable issue – interest rates. John Stone had wondrously reinvented himself as a National Party Senator from Queensland – one of the more remarkable metamorphoses in Australian political history. He was now the Coalition's Finance spokesman and in that capacity was giving tacit approval to the Government's high interest rate settings. He was supported by John Howard, who did not seem unduly inhibited by any problems this might cause for Peacock. While in the final stages of 1989 Stone and Howard were prophesying relatively high interest rates from a putative Coalition government, Andrew, still unburdened by any economic expertise despite a stint as Shadow Treasurer, was going around the country promising massive cuts in interest rates should he become Prime Minister. In politics one is always thankful for small mercies but the Coalition chaos around this sensitive subject ranked quite high on the mercy scale.

The Opposition's sheer incompetence on interest rates paled into insignificance, however, against their performance on one of the most critically important areas of modern government – health policy. Before we came to power in 1983 two million Australians did not have medical and hospital insurance. For many lower-income families the prospect of ill-health and hospitalisation was a financial nightmare. In 1984 we fulfilled our election pledge by introducing Medicare, a health insurance system which was characterised by universality and equity. All Australians were covered and equity was guaranteed by a common levy on taxable income so that the greatest contribution to the funding of the scheme was made by those with the greatest capacity to pay.[92] Medicare consistently grew in popularity and by 1990 was supported by well over two-thirds of the population.[93]

Despite the obvious public acceptance of Medicare, the Opposition was driven by an ideological obsession which derived from a greater commitment to the medical profession and the private health funds than to the sick. They had been working on an alternative health scheme which promised a return to the worst features of pre-Medicare days. But despite repeated promises of the imminent release of a detailed and costed health policy, promises which stretched back to May 1989, by the beginning of 1990 the Coalition had yet to unveil its plans. The Minister for Health, Neal Blewett, who had deftly run the gauntlet of the States and the medical profession when introducing

Medicare, was now reaping his reward by making savage attacks upon the Opposition. The policy had been long promised. Where was it? he asked.

The Opposition had, in fact, decided to go quiet on health policy, ditching the scheme authored by their Shadow Minister, Peter Shack, one of the early plotters for Peacock's return as Leader. Peacock was back and now they each had to share the consequences of their mutual flirtation. Shack's press conference of 25th January 1990 put me in a mood to enjoy the coming Australia Day holiday. I liked his opening gambit: 'Now, I want to say to you, with all of the frankness that I can muster, the Liberal and National Parties do not have a particularly good track record in health and you don't need me to remind you of our last period in government.' But he improved: 'We have laboured under a misapprehension that there was a billion dollars to be got out of Medicare. There is not!'

It was not just Shack but the entire Coalition outfit, now headed by Peacock, that was responsible for this shambles. If the Coalition was so maladroit on this fundamental area of public policy, what hope did Australia have that it could handle any of the others?

The Coalition's ineptitude explained in large part why our party research was showing that whatever disaffection there was with the Government, people were not prepared to vote for the Opposition. Electors showed a willingness to defect to minor parties: the Democrats, Greens and Independents. We had to be realistic about this and devise electoral strategies designed to win these voters back to Labor.

The research showed Labor enjoying an advantage over the Opposition among this bloc of voters on the issues of leadership, unity, economic management, industrial relations, health policy and community services generally. We were preferred overwhelmingly on the environment, where the divide between the Government and the

Opposition was starker than on almost any other issue. We had earned this recognition by a consistent commitment to environmental concerns from the first days of government. My launch of the Government's environmental blueprint 'Our Country, Our Future' on 20th July 1990 was accepted as a natural extension of this commitment.

This position reflected a great co-operative effort by a number of departments, particularly Graham Richardson's and my own, with his staffer, Simon Balderstone, and my adviser, Craig Emerson, doing a magnificent job of co-ordination with environmental groups and the National Farmers' Federation.[94] Out of this work there emerged in the statement a comprehensive scheme for protecting and reclaiming the environment,[95] including the One Billion Trees project. This aimed to have a billion more trees planted around Australia by the year 2000. The usual smart alecs in the Opposition and the media dismissed the project as fantastic; by 1994 it was well ahead of target.

It became part of the Government's deliberate strategy as we moved through 1989 and towards the 1990 election to highlight, wherever possible, the difference between the Government and the Opposition on green issues. If environmentally sensitive electors were not going to give us their direct vote, then it was important that they understood the consequences for their cause of awarding their preference vote to the Liberal or National Parties ahead of Labor.

Balderstone and Emerson had been active since the early part of 1989 in devising a strategy for how Labor could best sell its environmental achievements to the electorate. Combining with Senator Graham Richardson and his office, and with my active participation and oversight, they prepared a third-party preference strategy aimed at attracting support for the Government from those not prepared to vote directly for us. They prepared strategy reports, gave party seminars, arranged for the preparation of magazines and colour pamphlets, all aimed at garnering the green vote. This was serious politics about a substantial issue which Labor addressed differently, and better, than the Opposition.

By early 1990 the third-party preference strategy was well advanced. Party polling underlined the environment as the second most important concern behind the economy, and on that Labor was a clear winner.

Other important factors were coming together for the Government. In December, Labor's Wayne Goss stormed to power in Queensland. Goss went on to prove himself an exceptionally capable premier; apart from Neville Wran I have never seen a State leader who reads his electorate better. He had cracked thirty-two years of conservative rule in Queensland. With the National Party decimated and disgraced and the Liberals too weak to fill the void, Labor's stocks in an increasingly important state were on the rise. In Western Australia, where we feared swings against Labor federally due to the unpopular and tarnished State Labor Government, there was also good news. In February the parliamentary party handed its leadership to the refreshing and highly intelligent Dr Carmen Lawrence.

In Victoria, however, Labor was still bleeding, thanks to the profligacy and incompetence of its Labor Government. Against the example our Government was setting federally with tight fiscal discipline, the Victorian Government had pursued a path of big-spending, heavy-borrowing Keynesianism that was inappropriate and unsustainable in the circumstances of the time. The Cain and Kirner Governments, in the best Labor tradition, had done many fine things in the social area but as far as the electorate was concerned these achievements had disappeared in the morass of financial ineptitude.

While Victoria was a nightmare, there were compensating signs on the electoral horizon besides the continuing chaos of the Opposition. We had run a tight interest rate policy for eighteen months as we struggled to take the excess demand out of an overheated economy. By January 1990 we had obviously flattened the boom, and for the first time since the end of 1988 we were able to start lowering interest rates. This was politically helpful, of course, but it was an economic judgment backed by the Reserve Bank, which had the formal responsibility for interest rate settings, and the Treasury.

Running through a checklist of all the positive and negative factors, I decided that Labor could win in what would be a hard-fought campaign and, on 16th February 1990, I called the election for 23rd March. It's almost certainly true that as we went into this election I was virtually the only person left in the Government who believed we would win. Party morale and expectations were perhaps at their lowest ebb. Colleagues good-humouredly played down what they saw as my eternal optimism and, while committed to the fight, resigned themselves to a spell on the Opposition benches.

I would not accept this gloomy attitude and hammered my oft-repeated conviction about the voting record of the Australian people. Arguably, we had been Australia's best Government. Whether judging the Government from 1983 on its economic performance, its social reconstruction, its foreign policy, its creation of greater equity, its targeting of social welfare at those really in need, its policies concerning women – whichever way one looked at it – we had been a good government. By comparison, the Opposition had little, if anything, to offer. 'If the Australian people have got it right since 1949, why are they going to get it wrong in 1990?' I asked the sceptics.

Andrew Peacock, my opponent once again, was full of a false confidence from having beaten me in the 1984 election debate when, as I recounted earlier, I was in poor shape.[96] He had nothing to lose in 1984 for he was never going to win. But he campaigned well, pumped up by his performance in the debate. In 1990 the economic climate made Peacock a real contender for the prime ministership. What lay ahead for him was a true test of his competence and character. He had a lot to lose this time – we both did! But I was determined to win, and confident that I could.

As I saw it, Andrew was the one carrying the lead in the saddle bag and he had been carrying it for too long. He had entered parliamentary politics much too young and he was starved of real-world experience. He was glib, sartorially elegant, capable of charm and, from an early stage, had been cast as heir apparent to Menzies. This 'heir syndrome', in my view, had worked against him. He took Menzies' seat of Kooyong and gained a junior ministry in the Holt Government while still in his twenties. He gave the impression thereafter of a man waiting for the pinnacle to reach him rather than beginning the tough climb to the top. Believing the baton of the prime ministership was his for the taking, an illusion he maintained with the support of many others in the Liberal Party, he found no need to steel himself for consistently hard work. Peacock does have a capacity for genial companionship and he used it well in his stint as Foreign Minister (1975–80) in the Fraser Government. But he expected power and authority to come his way through natural progression and as of right, not as a reward for disciplined application to the unremitting grind of politics.

On 25th February 1990 at the Australian Broadcasting Corporation's Sydney studios, this lack of application was projected into the living rooms of Australia in the 1990 election debate. Andrew lacked the necessary fund of knowledge that comes from constant dedication.

That day I had locked myself away alone in the study at Kirribilli House and prepared for the debate. I prepared for it just as I would for Cabinet, an ERC meeting, parliamentary Question Time, an overseas trip or important visitor. I had been told by my people that according to the agreed rules of the debate neither of us would have any notes. I was well into my preparation when an agitated Geoff Walsh interrupted me with the news that the agreement between the parties did not bar briefing papers and that Peacock intended using them. It was not Geoff's fault but I was not amused. I made an instinctive decision; Andrew could use as many prompts as he wanted, but I would go on without notes of any kind.

When we set ourselves up in the studio Peacock barely had space on the lectern for all his material. His party's election slogan was 'The Liberals have the answers', but it was soon apparent that their Leader did not. Early in the debate he asked me a question about interest rates. I gave him a short history of the boom and told him that soft monetary policy would have wrecked the economy. Interest rates were central to the economic debate, yet Andrew was left floundering when Paul Murphy, the compere, following the rules of the debate, asked him: 'Do you have a quick follow-up question?' 'Not worthwhile after that answer,' Peacock replied. He did not even have the questions, let alone the answers.

With that, I was allowed a question. 'Andrew, you have said, rightly, that if you are going to get a reduction in interest rates, then inflation must come down. Now, I guess, if you're thinking of getting inflation down, you must have some idea, some target in your mind of what wages outcome will be necessary to bring inflation down. What's the target rate for wage increases you have in the first year?' I asked him. He had not even updated his banter and his glibness came straight out of the sixties: 'You love targets because those who like centrally planned economies always like targets and they want people to meet 'em,' he replied.

Not only did he not have a target in mind, which was a recipe for a wages explosion, runaway inflation and rocketing unemployment, but he was talking to a Prime Minister whose Government had deregulated the financial markets, changed the culture of the workplace and industrial relations in this country, and was responsible for more free-market economics than had been dreamt of by any of the Governments in which he had served.

Soon afterwards he got into an argument with panel journalist Alan Ramsey about the Liberals' pledge to abolish capital gains tax. Andrew wanted to scrap the tax, making this change retrospective to 1985 when the tax had been introduced. Ramsey asked, 'Now how do you justify backdating abolition of a policy that gives a five-year windfall of $450 million to 1 per cent of Australian taxpayers, 1 per cent?' The argument which followed ended this way:

PEACOCK: ... The reality is not only are the men and women who are paying capital gains tax, earning only $35,000 ...

RAMSEY: That is not true, Mr Peacock.

PEACOCK: If you look at the latest figures available ...

RAMSEY: I have.

Ramsey had fingered Peacock on a critically important issue. Abolishing capital gains tax was an invitation to return to the unabashed rorting which Labor had cured with introduction of the tax. Under the Liberals' proposal, 'bottom of the harbour' tax avoidance and evasion schemes, or their variants, would have flourished again. Adding insult to injury was the prospect of giving back five years of capital gains receipts.

The approach to capital gains tax was a major difference between the two parties. 'I see social justice in a fair taxation system,' I said in the debate. 'I see social injustice in giving ... literally billions of dollars to less than 1 per cent of the population. In the last year [for which figures were available], 65 000 people, one-third of 1 per cent, paid capital gains.' I pointed out that the money the Opposition Leader wanted to give back was better spent 'on health and education and the welfare of the needy'.

All the scorers – the analysts, pollsters and party professionals (including the Liberals) – chalked it up as a clear win for me and a crucial determinant of the poll's eventual outcome. What seemed to come through to the viewers, they assessed, was Labor's substance against the hollowness of the Opposition.

By this time Geoff Walsh had recovered his composure. For him and others of my staff, the debate was the turning point of the campaign and they celebrated in my hotel suite until the early hours of the morning.

This election campaign was the least strenuous of my career. We travelled the country but the schedule was less crowded than in the past. In campaigning on our record and the weaknesses of the Opposition, I found a positive response everywhere to what I had made the central phrase in the attack on our opponents: 'If you can't govern yourselves, you can't govern the country.' Two aspects of the campaign were disturbing, however. At several places angry pilots and their families confronted Hazel and me in a threatening manner. I had complete confidence in the security arrangements and had no fear for our safety but I was saddened by the pilots' hatred and their refusal to engage in calm and rational discussion with me. As in the airline dispute, their conduct during the campaign was so outrageous they alienated the general public.

The other disturbing factor was racism. Under the pressure of the election the Coalition once again succumbed to the temptation of playing the anti-Asian card. They misrepresented the implications of the proposed establishment of a Multi-Function Polis. This proposal for a joint Australian–Japanese venture to create a hi-tech city of the future was pictured by the Coalition as a Japanese Trojan Horse; in the Sydney electorate of Lowe, especially, voters were inundated with propaganda suggesting large enclaves of Japanese would become part of their landscape. It was a disgusting and unfounded tactic. My reaction was predictable but the greatest damage to the Coalition came from a front-page comment in *The Australian* by political journalist and author, Paul Kelly, who implied that Peacock wasn't fit to be Prime Minister. In a damning indictment Kelly wrote: 'Mr Peacock has stooped to exploit immigration fears and anti-Japanese sentiment in a way which suggests that Australia's national interests are best served by keeping Mr Peacock in opposition.'[97]

Nonetheless, election night 1990 was always going to be a close-run thing. We knew we were going to lose a swag of seats in Victoria. Indeed of the ten seats lost nationally, nine were Victorian. But somewhat to our surprise we picked up seats in New South Wales, snatching Page and Richmond from the National Party. In Queensland the National Party seat of Kennedy fell to us and we took Moreton from the Liberals. In South Australia we lost Hawker to the Liberals but squared that loss by picking up the seat of Adelaide.

As the night wore on the figures started to come in from Western Australia. This was the final test for us. We knew that we would lose Allen Blanchard's seat of Moore because of the redistribution, but then came the real nail-biters. Carolyn Jakobsen survived in Cowan and Ron Edwards hung on in Stirling by some two hundred votes. As I looked at the figures being posted I formed the impression we were safe, although a number of commentators were calling a loss for Labor.

In the event the Hawke Labor Government was re-elected for a fourth term with a majority of eight seats. Given the albatross of Victoria, I was more than happy with this result. If Victoria had reflected the national average, we would have been returned with a virtually unchanged majority.

Our electoral strategy had been spot-on. Party research showed that Labor came from behind in ten seats after trailing, sometimes by large margins, on the primary vote. In Cowan, for example, Labor trailed by 1693 votes but picked up the seat on Democrat and WA Green preferences; similarly in Stirling, where Labor trailed by 2137 primary votes. In both cases the combined Democrat and Green vote totalled more than 14 per cent. Labor received 15 per cent of the Democrat preferences and 85 per cent of the Western Australian Greens.

The people of Australia had got it right once again.

TWENTY-SEVEN

As always, election victory brought with it the same fascinating but difficult task of allocating portfolios in a new ministry. The general consensus of my colleagues, the bureaucracy and the commentators was that I had, in the past, generally managed a good balance in matching the sometimes conflicting demands of aspirations, talents and roles against the expectations of factions and the requirements of geographical representation. On this occasion, although I had the authority of having led the party to an unprecedented fourth term of government and had seven years' experience, I did not display the competence I should have in the discharge of this uniquely personal responsibility. The country did not suffer from this but I think I ultimately paid a very high price myself.

Graham Richardson had two interests to push. One was to drop Ralph Willis from the ministry; but when I said this was an absurdity I would not tolerate under any circumstances, he backed off; the second was to shift from the environment portfolio. He had done a brilliant job and the green lobby passionately wanted him to stay. Phillip Toyne, the Executive Director of the Australian Conservation Foundation, pleaded with me in an urgent letter of 27th March 1990: 'I must express my strongest view that he should be left to continue on with the valuable work that he has done.' But Graham wanted to move on and he had earned that right. His preference was for Transport and Communications; while I had no doubt about his capacity to do that job it did not fit into the overall pattern of reallocation I had in mind. By common consensus, Kim Beazley was future prime ministerial material, and I had set aside that portfolio for him to broaden his experience. Kim was unhappy about losing his beloved Defence cap but accepted the logic of my decision.

In the end it got down to choosing between the two senior portfolios of Defence and Social Security for Richardson and his fellow Senator, Robert Ray, in many ways Richardson's Victorian counterpart.

Robert Ray resembles Albert Monk in his reluctance to encourage intimacy with colleagues. He can be warm but, when he feels it necessary, he becomes as hard and remorseless as anyone I have ever met in politics. The classic example was the way he stared down for a year the orchestrated and venomous campaign directed against him in Victoria to make him renounce to Senator Jean Melzer the safe seat he had won from her in the pre-selection ballot for Labor's 1980 Senate ticket. Robert does not seek out the media but in my opinion has few peers as a political advocate and analyst on television. He is an efficient and uncompromising minister, willing to listen to argument but unswayed by the status of those opposing him. I had no more rigorous or loyal supporter during the Keating challenges, and one of the few regrets I have in looking back on my time in office is that I did not spend more time with this very considerable individual.

I indicated to Ray that he would take Defence and told Graham he would have Social Security. Ray was happy but Richardson made it clear that he was not. I was upset that after our long association and his great work in Environment, Graham now felt hardly done by. I thought about it overnight and wondered whether he might prefer

Defence, not thinking that Robert would have any passionate views one way or the other. I was half right. Richardson sparked up at the prospect of Defence but Robert Ray was adamant both that he was very keen on the Defence portfolio and that Social Security was not his cup of tea. I now had two unhappy ministers instead of one. By my normal standards this had been a sloppy exercise in management and I had no-one to blame but myself.

I stuck to my original decision and Graham became Minister for Social Security. His unhappiness was compounded by a misperception that perhaps I wanted him out of the Government altogether. In a wide-ranging discussion, the possibility of his going to the High Commission in London arose but, certainly as far as I was concerned, only if he wanted to. I had no desire or intention to remove him. On the contrary, I regarded Graham as a very effective Cabinet minister, and not simply in his own portfolio. He had something relevant to say about most issues which came before us and no minister had more acute political antennae. His reputation as a number-cruncher and tough factional operator overshadowed the fact that he was a very hard-working minister. In this case he absorbed the disappointment of not getting the ministry he wanted and proceeded to work diligently and imaginatively in the complex portfolio I had rather clumsily given him. The legacy of his ill-feeling was reflected rather in his diluted commitment to my leadership; I had succeeded in making him more susceptible to the demands of tribal loyalty from the NSW Right.

There has been a tendency by some observers to write down the period from the 1990 election to the end of 1991 as one of a government paralysed by the tensions arising from Paul Keating's leadership aspirations. This was not true, as I will show; but it is true that the task of government was made more difficult by the increasing irascibility of a Treasurer who, with the retirement of Lionel Bowen, was now

Deputy Prime Minister and impatient to claim what he had persuaded himself was his rightful and early inheritance.

Nowhere was this more evident than in the tortuous arguments which preceded one of the great reforms of my Government, the introduction of competition into the Australian telecommunications system. The system itself and the enterprises supplying it constitute a multibillion dollar industry employing some 150 000 people. No industry was experiencing a more continuous and faster rate of technological change and it was vital to maintain the process of reform we had initiated in 1987 and 1988.[98] This was important not only to give industrial and domestic users access to the most efficient services and equipment but also to position Australia to take advantage of a huge export potential. The nations of the Asia–Pacific region contain half the world's population but only 17 per cent of its five hundred million telephone lines. By 1990 the rapid economic growth and rising living standards of these countries were reflected in a burgeoning demand for new and better telecommunications services.

I had flagged my intention in the campaign to review the total structure of telecommunications in the next term but no-one understood the extent of what we had in mind. I moved quickly after the election and wrote to the new minister, Kim Beazley, on 8th April setting out my requirements for action.[99] I and my advisers, Rod Sims and Peter Harris, emphasised in discussions with Beazley that we had three basic objectives: a genuine alternative to Telecom with the capacity to be engaged in all areas of telecommunications if it so chose; freedom for resellers of capacity (these are the real innovators of services) such that they could keep both Telecom and the new carrier honest in the area of business services; and three, not two, operators in mobile telephony, because this was the next-generation growth area for telecommunications and could prevent a cosy duopoly emerging in the long term.

My preferred way of providing competition to Telecom was to privatise OTC (Overseas Telecommunications Corporation). Beazley was convinced that any new network provider would have to be substantially foreign-owned as there was little expertise in Australia outside Telecom. He was worried by the prospect of delivering a dominant position in Australia's overseas telecommunications to such a competitor; further, he was certain that we would not be able to sell the concept to the party. He was obviously correct in this assumption, as it became clear we had a major fight on our hands with the Caucus and the party on two fronts: first, in allowing any competition to Telecom, and second, in strong opposition to our concurrent proposal to privatise the Government-owned airlines, Qantas and Australian. To move in the direction we wanted in telecommunications and with the airlines, we had to hold a Special Party Conference to change the platform and Kim came to the only practical conclusion: if we were to achieve our objectives we would have to combine OTC with Telecom and bring in a competitor through selling AUSSAT, a facility which provided satellite-based domestic business communications links and broadcasting of television to remote areas.

Despite the political reality of Kim's position, Keating embraced the Treasury view that nobody in the telecommunications business would make a bid to become the competitor if the debt-laden AUSSAT ('space junk' according to Paul) was the chosen vehicle as against the very profitable OTC. This was the purist position of the Treasury bureaucrats, which he attempted to dress up with technical expositions of the relative merits of the two approaches, arguing that Beazley's concept could not work efficiently. But when it got down to this area of argument in the numerous discussions in my office, everybody recognised that Kim – as should be expected of the portfolio minister – was better equipped and more persuasive than Paul.

The Treasurer then moved from one proposal to another in the name of 'fuller competition', once contradicting a position put within the previous twenty-four hours. On every occasion, with the debate often being conducted in my office in front of several officials, Kim continued to win both the political and technical arguments. Paul's apparent obsession became a matter of serious concern to his colleagues and Beazley complained that his life was being made almost impossible by the intensely personal way in which Keating was interfering and making telecommunications reform a personal issue between them. Kim had to cope with this while at the same time overseeing the most complex technological subjects to have come before the Government as well as conducting a continuous campaign of debate, discussion and persuasion with the Caucus, and union and party officials to get them up to the barrier of reform. All of this was happening in the context of continuing leaks to the media of confidential material.

However, Beazley was steadily winning the battle on all fronts. His Cabinet colleagues were comforted by his obvious mastery of his brief and his capacity to assure them that what he was proposing would work; and Caucus and party members were reassured that a strong publicly-owned Telecom–OTC would be well placed to survive and prosper in the competitive market which would be provided by a new private competitor. In all of this he was assisted by his own special qualities of intelligence, wit and genial good nature, not to mention the fact that he always managed to make the rest of us look well dressed.

The final showdown came at the Cabinet meeting of 10th September 1990 which endorsed Beazley's proposals. Keating turned on a spectacular tantrum, threw his pencil on the table and stormed out of the Cabinet room describing us all as a lot of 'fucking second-raters'. His mood was not improved by two things. First, Robert Ray, for whom he reserved a special detestation and described as 'the fat Indian', said to him as he departed, 'Go on Paul, take your bat and ball home.' Second, Keating knew that everyone round the Cabinet table understood, as did he, that Beazley's recommendations were the only ones that could get through the Caucus and the Party Conference and that they would, in fact, bring about a revolution in the telecommunications industry in Australia.

After lengthy discussions with him in my office, I had persuaded a reluctant Beazley to strengthen the competitive impact of his proposals in two respects: that there should be three rather than two mobile licences, and open contestability after the first five years of operation by the new carrier rather than simply a commitment to review the position after that time. I believed this concept of giving the new operator a reasonable period to establish itself and then throwing the field open to further competition – a position advocated by my own advisers – was one point Keating had right.

The Special Party Conference at the end of September endorsed the Government's basic position: for a private competitor to a merged Telecom–OTC based on the sale of AUSSAT. We did not need to canvass in that forum the additional and vital changes which made such a difference to the pro-competitive nature of the final package: no restrictions on resellers, three mobile licences, and the requirement that before Telecom could acquire OTC it had to put in place the switches and accept the interconnect changes which would enable the new private entity to compete effectively.

We had done all this – the greatest reform ever in this critically important industry – in seven months, from the date of my letter to Beazley to my statement in Parliament in November setting out the full package of reforms. And we achieved everything we said we would: lower STD prices, better service for domestic and business customers and the certainty of significant employment growth at the innovative end of the market. The reform process culminated in the sale of AUSSAT, debt-free, to Optus Communications Pty Ltd for $800 million at the end of 1991. The processes which we followed and the outcome we achieved have been hailed internationally as the most effective reform of telecommunications undertaken by a national government.[100] Not bad for a government suffering from paralysis.

My own paralysis was not too evident either when I was called in to save the process of negotiating fundamental reforms on the waterfront (the removal of excess labour and the introduction of company-based rather than pool employment) which was on the point of breaking down after several months of difficult discussion. Bob Collins, whom I had insisted should be in the ministry after the 1990 election, was handling the matter in his capacity as Minister for Shipping, with assistance from Peter Cook, the Minister for Industrial Relations. Collins had put his job on the line by telling the Senate he would resign if he had not substantially achieved these objectives within a year. The self-imposed deadline for his resignation was 6th May 1991.

Collins and Cook asked me to become involved and on the evening of Wednesday, 1st May I reverted to President-of-the-ACTU mode. I had spent the day as Prime Minister: I had breakfast with the Greek Deputy Premier, then met the Commonwealth Secretary-General before flying to Sydney where representatives of the stevedoring companies, including the big operator Conaust (owned by P&O), the Waterfront Industry Reform Authority (WIRA), the Waterside Workers' Federation (WWF), and the smaller waterfront unions met with me in my office in Phillip Street. We talked until the evening, when I had to leave to address a dinner at the Regent Hotel, then returned to Phillip Street. The adrenalin kept flowing as I haggled, cajoled, persuaded and laid down the law throughout the night, talking to those present individually, in groups and collectively, until 7 o'clock the next morning. By then I had secured an agreement which provided the basis of the reform which has revolutionised the Australian water-front.

Richard Setchell, the Chairman of Conaust, a hard-line employer regarded as a *bête noire* by the WWF but whom I found to be an honourable man, was positively effusive in his praise and said of the achievement that 'it was a win for the economy and the international competitiveness of Australia'. Cook and Collins were ecstatic in their expression of gratitude, the latter not simply because the need to contemplate his resignation was removed. I returned to Canberra that morning, hosted a lunch for the Australia–Japan Ministerial Committee, in the afternoon had discussions with the Victorian Premier, Joan Kirner, on air links to Taiwan and on Commonwealth–State relations, and that night attended a dinner for the Australian Mining Industry Council, at which I gave a brief speech. I got home at midnight. After forty-two hours without sleep I was ready for a kip.

As this 'paralysed' Government was completing its historic reforms in telecommunications, I was determined in our fourth term to put my stamp on the wider reconstruction of the Australian economy. We had to change from an inward-looking, protected entity either un-concerned with, or incapable of competing in, the export of manu-factured goods and services. We had already brought the country a long way on this road[101] but in a rapidly changing and more intensively competitive world we could not afford to rest on our laurels. Garnaut had provided the signposts and the assumptions in his seminal report, *Australia and the North-East Asian Ascendancy*, presented to us at the end of 1990. I chaired the work of the Structural Adjustment Committee which directed itself to these issues and included a working session with Garnaut.

As a result of these efforts I was able to make a statement – 'Building a Competitive Australia' – to the House on 12th March 1991, setting out the challenge and providing a wide range of decisions, including further substantial cuts in tariffs calculated to achieve my objective. The statement was generally recognised as the most significant of its kind ever presented to the Parliament. Paul Kelly, not famous as my most ardent supporter, described its importance in these terms:

> The major achievement of the Hawke Government in the fourth term was Bob Hawke's March 1991 ... Statement which stands as an historic milestone ... [he] demolished the edifice of Protection, the cornerstone of the post-federation Settlement. It is this decision, providing it sticks, which will guarantee that the direction of the 1990s maintains the course launched in the 1980s.

Kelly quoted Garnaut's comment that the changes were bigger than the end of the British Corn Laws which earned Peel and Cobden a dozen pages in our high school history books, and continued: 'Hawke's announcement effectively terminated Australia's century of Protection ... [it] confirms the transformation in politics and economics which his government launched in the 1980s.'[102]

One of the central elements of the March Statement gave effect to the commitment in my 1990 campaign launch to make Australia 'the clever country', a phrase first used by John Dawkins in January of that year. The most specific and what I believe will be the most enduring embodiment of that commitment was the announcement in the statement of the first fifteen of the Co-operative Research Centres I had promised in 1990. These were the brainchild of Professor Ralph Slatyer, my Chief Scientist, and a friend going back to Modern School days.[103]

The essence of the program was to provide $100 million of Commonwealth funding to bring together academic institutions and business enterprises to undertake collaborative research and education programs in areas of the natural sciences and engineering. These would be directed towards the establishment of internationally competitive industry sectors. The scheme, described by the President of the Australian Academy of Science, Dr David Curtis, as a 'truly remarkable and far-sighted initiative', has been outstandingly successful, with the original target of fifty centres already exceeded.[104]

In the month following my March Statement Keating did a brilliant job in the Parliament turning around an attack on me by the Opposition, who had alleged that I had done a deal over lunch on changes in the tax on gold in return for donations to the Labor Party. Their allegations rested on uncorroborated statements by the failed businessman, Laurie Connell, and were spurious, as was confirmed by the Royal Commission which investigated the ramifications of what was known as WA Inc., the web of business supporters gathered around him by Labor Premier Brian Burke.

I stumbled twice in the Parliament, giving inaccurate information supplied by my staff about dates. My recently appointed Principal Private Secretary, Dennis Richardson, was mortified by the error and offered his resignation. I refused it for, although I had been severely embarrassed by having to return to the House on two occasions to correct earlier answers, Dennis and other staff had made an honest mistake. The point that mattered was that the record of the actual dates – of when I announced the Government's decision to delay the tax on gold and the lunch which was subsequently held in Burke's office – showed that Connell's allegations were false. The Opposition's attacks did me no lasting damage but there is no doubt that Paul, deservedly, lifted his stocks by this performance. Laurie Connell, far from being a mate, resented me because Burke had told him of my concern about his, Connell's, integrity, which a close friend of mine in the racing industry had raised with me. I was worried that Burke's close association with Connell could cause him trouble in the future.

Despite Keating's brilliant defensive performance on this issue, his erratic behaviour was not confined to the telecommunications debate. Senator John Button was on the receiving end of a bitter attack by Paul in May after publicly musing about the appropriateness of economic settings and the tough times ahead. The good Senator was occasionally given to sharing his thoughts with the press, who loved him for it because it made for lively copy; it was also useful for him in reinforcing with industry his reputation as an independent spirit. This may have been good for John but it was inconsistent with the legitimate requirements of Cabinet solidarity. Paul was entitled to be annoyed. Once he had gone public, I supported him, although he was as much at fault as Button, and should have restrained himself and sought to have the matter resolved in discussion between the three of us. In September the Treasurer extended his aggression beyond his colleagues to include the retiring head of the National Australia Bank, Nobby Clark, embroidering a personal attack on Clark with the unwarranted observation that in an earlier period his bank had been 'technically insolvent'. He backed off under pressure but the exercise left everyone wondering about his judgment.

I was therefore not in a particularly receptive frame of mind when Paul came to talk with me in October about the leadership. He said he was frustrated, but his level of frustration was matched by my increasing impatience with his behaviour. I was becoming more and more concerned about his attitude towards his colleagues and their reactions to him. His ambition to succeed me during this term was an increasingly open secret and I had been approached by many ministers and Members for reassurance that I would stay to fight the next election. At that point, however, I still intended to adhere to the Kirribilli agreement. I was contemplating staying on for another year so that I could see through the work I was beginning on the New Federalism[105]; then, finally, I would attend the next CHOGM meeting in Harare to participate in the successful culmination of all our work in bringing to an end the apartheid system in South Africa. I told Paul this and left the discussion there.

There was soon a dramatic change of circumstances. On Friday, 7th December Keating gave a speech at the Press Gallery's Christmas function at the National Press Club. These speeches were, formally, off-the-record but everyone knew from experience that what was said would appear in the media. Paul's performance was vainglorious and arrogant, disloyal and contemptuous of everyone on the political stage but himself. He was as he put it 'the Placido Domingo of Australian Politics'.

Paul, still unable to come to terms with or to understand the rapport I enjoyed with the Australian public, made disparaging references to me, glibly reducing my leadership style to 'tripping over television cables in shopping centres'. I don't pretend that this sort of reference was not hurtful and disappointing. However the further evidence of a persistent campaign of denigration was not my only concern. What upset me just as deeply was his disparagement of early Labor greats as he summarily surveyed Australian history through the distorting prism of his ambition: 'We've never had one leader, not one …' and with this he dismissed Curtin as a 'trier' and Chifley as a 'plodder'.

My Press Secretary, Grant Nihill, rang me on Saturday morning after he had been told the story by journalists who had attended the dinner and warned that it would certainly be leaked. I was furious at Keating's perversion of Labor history and contemporary politics. As I put it to him later, John Curtin was an absolutely outstanding leader and Prime Minister, judged by the criteria of this or any other country.

In 1942 John Curtin turned the Labor Party around on compulsory military service. For anyone familiar with the way conscription had rent the party during the First World War – and remembering, particularly, that Curtin had been the Secretary of Victoria's anti-conscription campaign – this was a remarkable feat. Here was a leader who, recognising the threat to Australia's survival, was prepared to turn himself around and fight to take the party with him. It was Curtin, too, who recalled Australia's troops to our own immediate theatre of war when Winston Churchill sought to divert them to his imperial designs. Churchill angrily demanded that Curtin reconsider, but he refused. And it was Curtin who, when the Japanese landed in New Guinea and advanced towards Port Moresby, forged the historic alliance with the United States.[106] This summary does less than justice to Curtin's greatness.

Keating's remarks were disingenuous, churlish and inaccurate. However it was not entirely the mind of Keating at work. As I said to him afterwards, the mouth was the mouth of Paul Keating but the words were the words of Jack Lang. Lang was the talented but embittered Labor Premier of New South Wales (1925–27 and 1930–32) who had been at war with the Federal Labor Party and who reserved a special hatred for John Curtin. His supporters in the Federal Parliament voted with the Conservatives to bring down the Scullin Labor Government in 1931; Lang's biographer wrote of his 'copious ability to hate'.[107] It was very easy to accept Paul's own assessment that much of his approach to politics had been shaped by Lang in the regular lunchtime sessions he held with the old man before entering Parliament. I was offended to have Lang's protégé bringing the mid-war hatreds, prejudices and contemptuous attitudes of his mentor into the politics of the nineties.

I told him all this, and more, when I called him into my office on Monday afternoon. In further defence of Curtin, I suggested to Keating that instead of being a mouthpiece for Lang's bile in advancing his own ambition, he should read the federal Hansards covering the economic debates at the onset of the Great Depression: he would find that well before the emergence of Keynes' formal exposition of the case for government deficit spending in such circumstances John Curtin had been years ahead of the game in his eloquent plea for this course of action.

I then watched and listened with astonishment to the explanations and responses of this man who just three nights earlier had suggested that he would bring to the prime ministership a greatness lacking in Curtin. He said that he had been in a disconsolate frame of mind because of the sudden death the night before of Chris Higgins, the Treasury Secretary. His speech, he said, was extempore, with a few thoughts just jotted down before he spoke; he hadn't intended to reflect on me or previous leaders. I asked him not to insult my intelligence with such rubbish. The fact that he was deliberately lying to me has since been confirmed by one of his staffers.[108] He added further insult to injury by saying that he had attempted to ring me on Sunday. Again I told him that I simply did not believe him. I had been at the Lodge virtually all day and there had been no call or message.

This whole performance strengthened my belief that he was not ready for the leadership. As far as I was concerned what had been agreed before was now very much in issue, and I made that clear. Paul said he would need to consider his options and we agreed to meet again to discuss the matter before the end of January.

We met on 31st January 1991. Naturally I had thought a great deal about all the issues involved and had become more convinced that I could not, with any confidence, hand over the leadership of the party to Keating. It was not simply anger about the 'Placido Domingo' speech. Rather my concern at what I saw as deficiencies of judgment and character was highlighted by our conversation on the following Monday. These deficiencies went to a deeper issue. Leadership is not just a matter of technical and political competence but requires commitment to a set of values which uphold the worth and interdependence of the whole human family. It requires aggression at times but, always, it demands an ability to put the interests of one's country above all else. All these reflections reinforced my conviction that I was better equipped to lead the party and, certainly, that I had a much better chance of leading it to victory at the next election than Keating.

I was still prepared to meet him but two things he said showed, absolutely, that I had no alternative but to repudiate the Kirribilli agreement. First, the essence of his argument was that Labor had had more than its natural term of government and that there was virtually no chance of winning the next election. If he didn't have his turn now, he would never get it. I disputed his analysis by repeating my well-known thesis about the good sense of the Australian voters; I said that, despite the recession we were entering, given a continuation of strong government, good communication with the electorate and the in-adequacies of the Opposition, we could win again. He repeated his scepticism, talked up his credentials and said that if he was to have any chance at all he needed time to establish his position with the public as Leader. I repeated my own conviction, the belief of others and the evidence of the polls that I had a much better chance of winning for Labor than he and then, looking him straight in the eye, I asked, 'Tell me this, Paul, are you saying that even if you believed I had a better chance of winning the next election than you, I should stand aside for you?' He answered, 'Yes.'

I was horrified that Paul Keating was prepared to place his own interests above those of a Labor victory. As disturbing as this was, worse was still to come. Keating's 'Paris option' was part of political folklore but it was now given its ugliest formulation. The question arose of what he would do if he didn't get his 'turn' as Prime Minister. I said I thought he should stay but he rejoined, 'We'll be off to Europe. We won't be staying here – this is the arse-end of the world.'

It is perhaps not surprising that in the purported verbatim accounts of parts of our conversation Keating has given to one author[109] he has not included this glowing commitment to the country he sought to lead.

All of us, in desperate circumstances, have said things we regret; I certainly have. I can ignore and forget many of the unpleasant comments Keating has made over the years about me and about others I count as friends. But his comment about Australia will always stick in my craw. In the mysterious workings of political osmosis it goes a long way to explain why Australians will not take to a man who thinks so little of them and their country.

I told Keating that all bets were off and he left to ponder his future course of action. It was soon apparent that he and his allies were still active but I did not allow attention to be diverted from the tasks of government until Bob Hogg, my former staffer but now National Secretary of the party, came to my office on 24th May 1991. His main pitch to me was that the Keating forces would not give up and that I should be prepared to step aside because, if I did not, these forces would damage the party by their continuing thrust for the leadership. I rejected this thinking as a prescription for bowing to terrorism, discussed with him my assessment of Paul's inadequacies for the leadership, and made it clear I would not be moving aside for the Treasurer.

Events now moved quickly. On the evening of 29th May Richardson came to see me. Only five days earlier he had been reported in *The Age* as saying there would be no challenge and that the Hawke–Keating team provided the best chance of winning the next election.[110] He told me that he had just been informed by Keating of the Kirribilli agreement. I don't know how elastic Graham's concept of time is and what 'just' meant to him, but I do know that on the previous day Keating had declared in the Parliament that the leadership 'will only be an issue of relevance ... when the Prime Minister deigns it to be'.[111] That deliberate misleading of the House and the public was irrelevant to

Richardson; he professed his dismay that I had made this agreement with Keating, and now used it to justify his switch of loyalty and to indicate that if I did not stand aside the agreement would be made public as part of a Keating challenge.

Strangely enough, I didn't then nor do I now feel any great ill-will towards Richardson on this score. While Kirribilli was a convenient peg on which to hang his move to Keating, I believe the force of tribalism would have prevailed with him. He had no great love for Keating but Paul was one of theirs and I was not. I explained my reasons for believing it was in the best interests of the party that I should remain Leader and the meeting finished on that note.

I was meeting late the next afternoon in my office with the Queensland Premier, Wayne Goss, and Bill Ludwig, the State Secretary of the Australian Workers' Union, one of my dyed-in-the-wool supporters. We were discussing the question of compensation for retrenched timber-workers on Fraser Island. My staff told me that the Treasurer wanted to see me. I said to let him know that I would see him as soon as I had finished with Goss and Ludwig.

Of course, I did not know that the Keating camp had another time-table – the 6.00 p.m. television news. Laurie Oakes, a close mate of Richardson, had been primed to break the story of the Kirribilli agreement. Just before 6.00 p.m. Keating burst into my office and said he had to see me. I told him that I was sorry, I had people with me and would contact him as soon as the meeting was finished. When he returned soon after in response to my call, he made the specious observation that he had once told me that if he ever decided to organise against me, I would be the first to know. He was telling me now – I have no idea how far down I was, in fact, on the list of those informed – that he was going to challenge me for the leadership. I said, 'All right Paul, that's the way it's going to be,' and he departed.

I arranged a Caucus meeting for 8.00 a.m. the following day to 'report on and deal with a matter of importance raised ... by the Deputy Prime Minister'. Then I met with my closest supporters – Ray, Beazley, Evans, and Crean from the Right, Hand, Bolkus, and Staples from the Left, Duffy the independent, and Neil O'Keefe from the non-aligned group, and we all got down to the business of organising the numbers. I went to bed at about 4.00 a.m. in the knowledge that we would have a comfortable majority. Keating had most of the NSW Right and the Centre Left, while the Left with only three exceptions (Frank Walker and the two ex-ministers who had been dumped by the faction, Peter Duncan and Stewart West) and the great majority of the non-NSW Right and non-aligned Members were committed to me.

At the beginning of the meeting on Friday I said that Keating had indicated he wished to challenge me for the leadership and that I had called the Caucus together to give him that opportunity. I then sat down. Keating and those advising him then sought to invoke the precedent of July 1982 when Hayden had declared the position of Leader vacant.[112] This was not a valid analogy, for on that occasion it was Hayden himself, not I, who had initiated the process of a ballot; but now, my opponents who had instigated the challenge did not wish to call for a vote, which would be by show of hands, to declare the position vacant. The Keating camp walked out and the meeting ended in anti-climax.

Back in my office my close colleagues agreed we had been remiss in not being prepared for this manoeuvre. We decided to take steps to call another Caucus meeting immediately in which we would propose a secret ballot without any procedural motions requiring a show of hands. I informed Paul of my intention, but the birds had flown. More precisely, they had been sent winging on their way by the Whip, George Gear, a strong Keating supporter. Despite messages to all members on car phones and at the airport, the reconvened 10.00 a.m. meeting was boycotted by our opponents and was therefore adjourned till Monday morning.

We moved from anti-climax to surrealism. I had to go with Keating straight from the aborted Caucus to present a united Commonwealth front to a Premiers Conference meeting. As professionals, we did the job that had to be done, but no-one present had their mind entirely on the agenda. On the weekend the telephones were worked overtime; the confidence in our camp was confirmed when the numbers went up in my favour in the ballot on Monday morning sixty-six to forty-four. My counters had been just about spot-on; we had probably lost three or four votes through our poor tactics in not having the ballot on Friday.

I now prepared to put the challenge behind me and get on with the work of government. Despite his statement to the media that 'I had only one shot in my locker and I fired it', Keating and his colleagues had other ideas.

They would not have had to wait long for the leadership to become vacant if my view had not prevailed two weeks later in the most intense and bitter Cabinet debate in my whole time in government. The dispute centred on whether to allow mining at Coronation Hill in the Northern Territory's Kakadu National Park. It aroused all the passions which flare when the issue of Aboriginal rights and beliefs is added to the already combustible environment-versus-development confrontation.

Coronation Hill had divided the Cabinet and alienated the mining industry in 1989 when we significantly changed the boundaries and opportunities for exploration and mining in Stage III of the Park, which we had proclaimed prior to the 1987 election. In that 1987 decision we had excluded a large exploration zone (more than 2000 square kilometres) and had agreed, in principle, that BHP could proceed with its plans for a gold, platinum and palladium mine at Coronation Hill within this zone. I had confirmed this by letter to BHP in October 1987.

Kakadu contains wetlands of incomparable beauty and had become something of a national symbol; it was certainly an icon for the environmental lobby who feared that any mining activity in this, the southern area of the Park, could feed contamination into the wetlands to the north. Richardson had been persuaded that we should reduce the exploration zone to a 20-kilometre strip of high potential which included Coronation Hill and the adjacent El Sherana deposits. Although his own department had produced a favourable environmental impact study, Richardson advocated deferring the Coronation Hill project until a more extensive examination had been undertaken. I talked at length with Phillip Toyne, the director of the Australian Conservation Foundation, and was persuaded of the strength of their concerns; I believed that Richardson's proposal made good political sense and was eminently justifiable in the national interest. After a tough debate – which I led off – in the Cabinet, Richardson's proposals were accepted. Despite the well-publicised opposition of the development-at-all-costs ministers and a public campaign by the infuriated mining industry the polls showed that 75 per cent of Australians supported our decision.

The matter was now before us again in the form of two reports, one by Justice Stewart in his capacity as Chairman of the Resources Assessment Commission (RAC), which the Government had established in July 1989 as an independent body to investigate and advise on matters such as this, and another, also by Stewart, whom we had appointed to report as required under the provisions of the *Aboriginal and Torres Strait Islander Heritage Protection Act* 1984.[113] Don Stewart, a well-respected judge who had done a fine job as the first Chairman of the National Crime Authority, was assisted in the RAC inquiry by other independent members with professional expertise. They conducted a lengthy investigation which gave all interest groups – Aborigines, miners and environmentalists – full opportunity to present their views and to be examined on them. The inquiry also took evidence from a wide range of expert witnesses.

The RAC report came as a shock to most people, for while it found that there were no insuperable environmental reasons for not proceeding with mining in the zone, it expressed the strong view that to do so was irreconcilable with the deeply held beliefs of the local Aboriginal group, the Jawoyn. For me this became the crucial factor in the decision we had to make.

For the Jawoyn in the area, some three hundred Aborigines, the proposed mine was in what they called the Sickness Country and the serpent god, Bula, lived there, underground. They believed that mining would disturb Bula and this would produce dire consequences for them. The miners poured scorn on the Aborigines, saying that Bula was a recent invention concocted to stop the mine. This insult was embraced by Dr Hewson, the Leader of the Opposition, who said on 17th May 1991, 'If you know anything about Aboriginal heritage, Bula didn't exist ten years ago. He suddenly emerged as a device to block Coronation Hill.'

This type of prejudice had been dismissed in the RAC report which said, after weighing the submissions of the Jawoyn representatives and evidence of anthropologists, 'The Bula tradition is not a modern invention. The concepts of the Sickness Country and multiple Bula sites occur in the first anthropological records of the area, which date back to the early 1950s.'[114] I had satisfied myself independently, in meetings with Jawoyn leaders in the Cabinet room, of the truth of this and the depth of their feelings. If any proof were needed it was provided by a moving TV interview, broadcast not long before the Cabinet meeting. The interviewer, speaking to Jawoyn families outside

their miserably poor accommodation, emphasised the economic boun-
ties that could flow to them if they agreed to the mine going ahead.
With a simple and compelling dignity they affirmed that their beliefs
were more important to them than new houses or cars; Bula was there
and he should not be disturbed.

My anger at the miners' attitude was increased by their public
campaign of misrepresentation. The Australian Mining Industry
Council (AMIC) ran full-page advertisements on 28th May: 'Can we
afford to let Mr Hawke make a $38 billion mistake?' When one read
the fine print one found that this was AMIC's calculation of the assets
employed by the entire Australian mining industry – as if these were
suddenly going to be irreparably damaged if we did not do as they bid.
The advertisement did not sit easily with the statement made two
weeks earlier by John Quinn, the Chief Executive of the BHP operation: '... we ... have never suggested ... [the mine] ... is other than a
modest scale mining operation'. The advertisement implied that if the
Government took what it regarded as a principled decision on
Coronation Hill, all the hard heads in the mining industry who make
decisions on the basis of whether there is a dollar to be made would
shut up shop or refuse to undertake further investment. This was
blatant, intimidatory nonsense, as subsequent developments in the
industry have proved. AMIC's advertisement finished on this note: 'Mr
Hawke ... Think hard, but act quick.' I did both. I have the notes of my
remarks to the Cabinet and I reproduce them, in abbreviated form, to
convey the intensity of my conviction that I would have resigned if
Cabinet had not supported me.

I told Cabinet that the miners' position involved a miscellany of
misrepresentation, intimidation and thinly veiled white supremacist
discrimination; it was a position which was totally embraced by
Hewson and the Opposition. 'I repudiate and abhor this unlovely
alliance of the AMIC and the Opposition, for it is an alliance which

ultimately is founded in something I will never accept, that is an unstated but nevertheless real discrimination.' I referred to the RAC report – which I had absorbed in detail – where it said that AMIC had criticised the inquiry for not having 'suggested any mechanism for educating the Jawoyn on the fallacy of some of their mythological beliefs'.[115]

I exploded to my colleagues:

> For three hundred blacks – what they express and what they are prepared to suffer for in material terms – these are 'fallacious mythological beliefs'. The monumental hypocrisy of this position is mind-boggling. The same people who denigrate blacks in this way can easily accommodate and embrace the bundle of mysteries which make up their white Christian beliefs: the virgin birth, the Holy Trinity, God in His (?) heaven – *where* is He? This supercilious, supremacist discrimination is abhorrent to everything I hold most important and to what in the end I believe this party stands for. We can argue about some things but surely in the end we are as one against discrimination. The two inquiries are unequivocal in their findings – as the Jawoyn custodians remain in their presentation to your Cabinet ministers today. We would never contemplate repudiating such findings if they were in respect of the white community and its beliefs. But three hundred blacks are different. You don't want to say it really, but *they* are talking bullshit. We won't say so, but if we give the miners another twelve months to put the pressure on them, the poor silly buggers might come to their senses and think like us! Or at least like Hewson and the miners. Well, as far as I'm concerned, I don't want any part of that hypocrisy and I don't want any part of that discrimination.

It was the most passionate speech I ever made in the Cabinet. Its intensity jolted even some of my closest supporters. I did not pretend to comprehend or to share the Jawoyn beliefs, but I did understand and respect the identification of the Aboriginal people with the land and of their gods with the earth.

I did not have the numbers around the Cabinet table but I did have the authority of the prime ministership. My position on mining at Coronation Hill was accepted. This was comfortable for the more bitter of my opponents, who had the luxury of making it known that the decision represented the will of the Prime Minister and not the majority view of the Cabinet.

Because my view prevailed, I did not have to relinquish office then; but my stand on Coronation Hill may well have cost me the leadership a few months later, for a pledge to reverse the decision was used by Keating supporters as a bargaining chip to pick up extra votes. I am proud that the decision still stands and I believe no government of the future will ever reverse it.

TWENTY-EIGHT

Less than nine months after the Berlin Wall had fallen, signalling the end of the Cold War, a decisive new challenge arose. On 2nd August 1990 Saddam Hussein's Iraqi army invaded Kuwait; within a few days a small nation had been conquered and absorbed by its large neighbour. This stark example of national aggression was a frightening indication of what the post-Cold War world might look like if the international community did not respond forcefully and effectively. It showed how the end of the Cold War might lift the lid from simmering regional disputes and make resort to armed force by lesser players easier than it had been in the days of global superpower competition.

From the very beginning of the crisis in the Gulf I believed that Australia had vital interests at stake. Of course oil was important, for if Saddam Hussein was allowed to gobble up Kuwait he would be eyeing off Saudi Arabia next, and the security and price of oil would be in jeopardy. More important however, I was appalled by the thought that such a blatant act of aggression should be allowed to stand. My memories of World War II and my reading of the tragic history of the 1930s had instilled in me the danger of allowing such action to go unchecked. It would not only be disastrous for the

Middle East. Throughout the world Iraq's invasion of Kuwait would encourage unscrupulous strong nations to use force against weaker ones. Instead of moving forward, the world was in danger of going backwards. It would be a scenario profoundly inimical to Australia's future interests.

Fortunately the international community now had available an effective instrument in the United Nations which, freed from the debilitating polarisation of the Cold War, operated throughout the Gulf crisis as its founders had intended. On the very day of the Iraqi invasion the UN Security Council passed Resolution 660 on which all subsequent action was based, and which demanded an immediate and unconditional withdrawal from Kuwait. Four days later it imposed comprehensive sanctions on Iraq.

We responded quickly to support the United Nations. On Monday, 6th August, the day the Security Council imposed sanctions, the Cabinet agreed on measures to implement them in Australia. This was no empty gesture, for Australia's trade with Iraq was significant, especially to our farmers. We then turned our attention to ensuring that the UN sanctions would be effectively enforced and began urgent consultations with like-minded countries. I spoke to my friend Brian Mulroney, Prime Minister of Canada, which, like Australia, traded in wheat with Iraq. I told him we were imposing sanctions and would be providing ships to help enforce them. I urged Brian to make a similar commitment; he indicated that our decision would be helpful in his deliberations. Indeed, Canada quickly followed our lead.

On Thursday, 9th August, I considered our options in discussions with my Defence Minister, Robert Ray, and the Foreign Minister, Gareth Evans. In directing Australia's role I knew I had in them colleagues whose judgment could be trusted on every aspect of the crisis. This group remained the key decision-making body throughout the months which followed.

Robert Ray told us that Defence could provide a task force of three ships – two frigates and a support ship – ready to leave for the Gulf within three days. I was impressed by the Australian Defence Force's capacity to respond so quickly in support of the UN sanctions against Iraq. Early the next morning, from the Lodge, I spoke to President Bush in the first of the many discussions we had during the months that followed. Later that day I announced our commitment at a press conference in Parliament House and the following Monday, 13th August, I farewelled our first deployment of ships from the Navy's fleet base in Sydney.

From the outset I realised it was important to explain to the public and the Parliament my thinking and the Government's policy on the Gulf War. No-one could tell how the crisis would unfold but I felt it would not be resolved easily or quickly. If we were to sustain public support it was vital to build a clear understanding of the Government's reasoning and objectives. The experience of this perhaps most demanding period of my career in public life confirmed for me that the Australian people are steadfast in supporting a government when they understand what is being asked of them and why.

The Parliament had been in recess during these dramatic events. When it reconvened on 21st August for the Budget, I made a statement carefully placing the Government's decisions, including the deployment of our ships, in the broader context of support for the UN and our hopes that the Cold War would be followed by an era of peace rather than anarchy:

> The world has changed a lot since 1945, but I think the lessons of the 1930s, which underpin the UN charter, still hold true today: that international disputes must not be settled by force; that national borders must be respected; and that those who use force must not be permitted to prevail ... These lessons

establish principles which engage our real, tangible interests, not just our sense of right and wrong. The security and prosperity of Australia will depend in the years ahead on the strength of those principles. The strength of those principles in the years ahead depends absolutely on the support we give them today.

I also referred to a sinister new element of the crisis which had emerged since the UN had imposed sanctions – the decision by Iraq's government to prevent foreign nationals from leaving Iraq, and even to use them as 'human shields' at strategic sites which they believed might be targets for attack. There were about 150 Australians stranded in Iraq and Kuwait and concern for their safety became a constant anxiety over the months ahead.

Saddam Hussein's sheer recklessness in taking such an abhorrent step made me deeply pessimistic that the crisis could be resolved quickly through the application of sanctions. Even at that early stage I feared there was a real likelihood that the world would have to fight to get Iraq out of Kuwait.

I did not relish this prospect. My career had been dedicated to resolving conflict and it seemed a betrayal of my own principles to allow this conflict to proceed to a possibly horrifying conclusion without taking some further steps to prevent it. I wondered whether we could not show Saddam that there was a way out of the disaster he had created. There had been a territorial issue between Iraq and Kuwait for decades. If Iraq would only withdraw from Kuwait and release the hostages there was no reason why its case should not be given a fair hearing in a proper international forum. I thought there must be a way to bring home to the President of Iraq the truth that it was in his own interests, as well as those of his country and the world, for him to withdraw now, in return for which his grievance against Kuwait would be put before and heard by an international tribunal.

In the days after my statement to Parliament I searched hard for a way in which this message could be effectively conveyed. We needed to find someone who might be able to bridge the chasm between Iraq and the rest of the world. I thought of discussing the idea with my old friend the Crown Prince of Jordan, a man of remarkable courage and flair, whom I had met during visits to the Middle East. On Friday, 24th August, after talking it over with George Bush, who agreed with my thinking, I talked to the Crown Prince at length. I sought his views on the value of making contact with Saddam to try to persuade the Iraqi leader to consider how much better his interests would be served by withdrawal than by trying to hold on to Kuwait against the united opposition of almost the entire world.

The Crown Prince was very sympathetic to my concerns but he had a gloomy view of the situation in Baghdad. From my discussion with him it became apparent that such a message would not get a hearing in Iraq. There was probably one simple reason for that: Saddam Hussein did not understand that if sanctions failed the world would not shrink from direct military action. Reluctantly, I accepted that negotiation would not work until Saddam recognised that fact. And as it happened, I do not think he ever did accept it until it was too late.

In the months that followed it became clearer that the sanctions were not working. Saddam's defiance of the international community became more and more blatant as he sought to trade his hostages for international acceptance of what he had done. Many people, including some prominent Australians, went to Baghdad to seek the release of hostages. The Iraqi President used them cynically. A few hostages were let go, but many were not; meanwhile, the Iraqi President could take comfort from the legitimacy which these visitors gave him. However pure their motives, those who went to the hostage bazaar deluded themselves. Saddam was never going to let all the hostages go as long as he had a stream of supplicants willing to come and beg for them. The people who came away from Baghdad with a few released hostages only made the situation worse for the ones left behind. It was an obscene and brutal lottery.

This was well understood by the bulk of the Australians who supported the Government's refusal to participate in the hostage market. Even more impressively, it was supported by many of the hostages themselves. I received some remarkable letters during this period from Australians held in Iraq and Kuwait, attesting to their defiance of Saddam's tyranny and their support for my insistence that the only way to solve the hostage problem was to pressure Saddam Hussein to let them all go.

By early November it was clear he was not going to yield to sanctions. He had plundered Kuwait, and his army of occupation was savagely mistreating the Kuwaiti population. He was also building up his forces in Kuwait. With my key ministers and in discussion with President Bush, I began to focus on the circumstances in which we might go beyond sanctions to contemplate the use of force to expel the Iraqi forces from Kuwait. By mid-November my own thinking on the issues of principle, and much of the detail, of an Australian commitment to combat in the Gulf had become quite clear. I had no doubt that an unequivocal warning needed to be given to Baghdad that the coalition supporting the UN was prepared to go to war to undo Iraq's aggression. And I had no doubt at all that if that warning was not heeded, Australia should be prepared to join others to uphold the UN resolution by force. As I said on a number of occasions at this time, 'peace is bought at too high a price if that price is the appeasement of aggression'.

On 29th November 1990 the UN Security Council passed Resolution 678, which gave Saddam Hussein until 15th January to meet its demands; after that, member states were authorised to use 'all necessary means' to reverse the Iraqi invasion of Kuwait and secure Iraq's obedience to the other Security Council resolutions.

I had been watching the build-up to this resolution carefully. On 27th November, having seen the draft resolution in what was almost its final form, I discussed Australia's response with my advisers. I believed that Australia should indicate as soon as practicable that we would be prepared to commit our forces in the Gulf to operations conducted under Resolution 678, and to take steps now to ensure that they could make an effective contribution if and when war came. Our ships had been deployed in August specifically to help enforce sanctions. Since then they had been serving superbly in that role in the Arabian Sea outside the mouth of the Persian Gulf. I decided that we should authorise them to move up into the Gulf itself, to operate and exercise with US ships and other allied ships with which they would have to fight.

At 10.00 a.m. on 29th November, within a few hours of Resolution 678 being passed, I met Robert Ray, Gareth Evans, Paul Keating (as Deputy Prime Minister) and John Button (as Leader of the Government in the Senate) to agree on a position to be put to the Cabinet. None of us had any doubt about the seriousness of the situation; we were contemplating the first commitment of Australian forces to combat since the Vietnam War.

Both Paul Keating and John Button had grave reservations. Button, who had been unhappy about our initial decision to deploy ships to enforce sanctions, was opposed but he volunteered that he would say nothing about his opposition publicly. Paul Keating was opposed on the grounds that we did not owe the US such support. 'What has the US done for us?' he asked. I was quick to point out, as was Gareth, that we were acting to back the UN, not the US. At this Keating subsided into acquiescence.

We discussed the scale of our contribution. Robert Ray said that we could expand our contribution from the three ships we had in place to five. I thought about this but in the end was reluctant, for two reasons. The first was that I thought our current contribution was both substantial and proportionate, and it was one we could sustain for a long time if that was necessary. Second, and more fundamentally, I thought we had enough young Australians at risk. Looking back now, it is easy to forget that when we made our decision to contribute to UN forces in the Gulf we had no reason to expect that the war would be over so quickly and with so few casualties. We had good reason to expect that Iraq's seemingly formidable air forces would pose a serious threat to our ships. I made my decision to commit Australian forces in the knowledge that we might easily suffer heavy casualties. I did not want to send more Australians into harm's way than I thought was warranted by our size and capacity.

On the following Monday, 3rd December, I consulted Caucus leaders on our proposal and received solid support. In the afternoon the Cabinet agreed to the approach I had proposed. In both the Caucus and the Cabinet there was a keen awareness that what we were planning might appear to go against some cherished Labor principles. Not only were we as a party deeply opposed to war as an instrument of international policy, but many in the Government had initially been drawn to Labor in reaction to Australia's entanglement in the tragedy of Vietnam. I understood the deep feelings of some of my Caucus colleagues, mainly from the Left, and I spent long periods with them, explaining the facts into the early hours of the morning, attempting to allay their concerns and, in particular, demolishing the grotesque attempt to equate this crisis with the Vietnam War.

I addressed some of these concerns the next day when I made my second major statement to Parliament on the Gulf crisis. I announced the Government's decision to commit forces to operations against Iraq under Resolution 678 if that became necessary and explained why we were prepared to take this step. I argued that Resolution 678 would send an unmistakable message to Saddam Hussein and offered the best way of persuading him to quit Kuwait without war. But I also argued that if he was not persuaded, he must be forced to leave.

> Labor comes to this issue with a lot of history. For much of its one hundred years the ALP has struggled to ensure that Australia's armed forces are not used to fight other peoples' wars. In the 1930s, that led Labor to turn its back on aggression, as so many others did in so many other parts of the world ... But Labor learned the lessons of that mistake, and did more than its share to correct it. Dr Evatt [Labor Foreign Minister and an architect of the United Nations system] recognised that aggression must be resisted, wherever it occurs, and by armed force if need be. He also recognised that all nations must be prepared to contribute to that task. As he said in 1945, 'It must be made crystal clear that the nations seeking representation in the world organisation must be prepared to contribute their share of physical force to restrain the action of the aggressor'.

While our decision was strongly supported, some argued that we should have given the sanctions longer to work before resorting to force. I responded that if sanctions had had no effect in three months there was less and less reason to expect them to bring Iraq to its senses in the future. Writing now, three years later, with the sanctions still in place and Iraq still defying the UN on key issues relating to the ceasefire, it is easy to see the wisdom of not waiting longer.

As it was, Iraq had six weeks to withdraw before the deadline expired on 15th January. Within a few days Saddam Hussein had released all the hostages, hoping to win extra time. It only showed how little he understood the determination of the international community's reaction to his aggression.

During this period we took care to ensure that we were prepared for what might happen. At home we undertook consultations with representatives of Australia's Arab and Muslim communities, and I took particular trouble in my public comments on the crisis to repudiate any suggestion of alienation from them. Apart from one or two isolated incidents, our multicultural society proved strong enough to withstand the pressures created by events in the Gulf.

In the days before the deadline expired, a number of efforts were made to avert war. The Iraqi Foreign Minister met US Secretary of State, James Baker, in Geneva. Nothing came of that. On 10th January, the day the Geneva talks failed, George Bush telephoned me again. We confirmed our shared view that without an unconditional withdrawal operations under Resolution 678 must proceed swiftly after the deadline expired.

In the last days, UN Secretary-General, Javier Perez de Cuellar, went to Baghdad with a plan which, if accepted, might have offered a way out. It involved withdrawal by both sides and the installation of a 'neutral' force from countries not involved in the coalition. I felt there were difficulties with this plan, but in the event, on 14th January, Saddam shunned Perez de Cuellar and the proposal fell to pieces. It at least demonstrated that the President of Iraq was not interested in any proposals that involved his withdrawal from Kuwait. This made decisions over the next few days easier.

On the same day my key ministers and I were briefed by officials and officers in the Cabinet room on every aspect of Australia's preparations for war. The highlight of the briefing was an outstanding exposition of the military situation in the Gulf by Major-General John Baker, Director of the Defence Intelligence Organisation. He explained the astonishing scale of military force marshalled in the Kuwait theatre of operations and predicted the scale, duration and targets of the coalition air offensive with great accuracy. He went on to predict the scope and direction of the land war with equal accuracy, but he believed that it would probably take four to five weeks to reach Basra and cut off Iraq's forces in Kuwait. I questioned him hard on this, suggesting that after the air offensive it should only take a few days to gather up the shattered remnants of Iraq's army of occupation. He acknowledged that that might be so, but very prudently insisted he could not afford to assume such an optimistic timetable.

The UN deadline expired at 4.00 p.m. on 16th January, Australian Eastern Summer Time. That morning I called a Cabinet meeting and briefed my colleagues on the situation. All avenues for negotiation had been exhausted, I told them, and we must expect to be involved in war within twenty-four hours. They were supportive but many were understandably anxious.

We expected the war to commence at any moment but we had no specific notice of when that might be. As it happened we heard first from our people in the Gulf early on the morning of 17th January that action was to begin later that day. At 9.50 a.m. I received a call from George Bush who told me that the first actions would start within an hour. We exchanged a few words of encouragement and hope. I immediately called the key ministers I wanted to consult – Ray, Evans, Keating, Button and Duffy – and at 10.20 a.m. I telephoned the Chief of the Defence Force, General Peter Gration, to authorise him to signal our forces that they should join operations against Iraq in accordance with Resolution 678.

At 12.25 p.m. I held a press conference. My statement reminded Australians of the reasons for our decision to go to war, and paid tribute to the men and women of the Australian Defence Force (ADF) who were bearing the brunt of that decision. I finished with these words:

> War is full of terrible uncertainty. We cannot foretell what will be demanded of our serving men and women; but we can foretell how they will meet those demands. We are confident of their skills; we are grateful for their devotion. We know they will serve bravely and well, and we hope, above all, that they will return safely home.

The next morning I received the first of what were to become daily briefings from the intelligence agencies and the ADF on the progress of the war. These briefings, attended by other senior ministers, not only kept us fully informed but gave us an opportunity to discuss any issues which arose. I found them extremely interesting and followed the progress of operations in great detail. At the first briefing it became clear that despite the CNN hype of the day before, the first air strikes on Iraq had not done significant strategic damage. In particular, I was worried that Iraq's Scud missiles had not been put out of action. At 11.00 a.m. Iraq launched its first salvo of eight Scuds against Israel. Together with millions of others, I was relieved to find that they were not carrying chemical warheads, as had been threatened by Saddam. Nonetheless, the risk that Israeli retaliation might rupture the coalition by alienating the Arab and Muslim members was a serious fear for some days until it became clear the Israelis would resist this outrageous provocation.

I recalled Parliament on 21st and 22nd January to report on developments and allow a debate on the momentous events then taking place. This special sitting was one of the finest parliamentary occasions I can remember. Speaker after speaker from both sides rose to back the resolution I had moved, expressing support for the UN and for our forces in the Gulf, while regretting the circumstances that had made the resolution necessary. I was especially touched by Gerry Hand who, struggling to reconcile his abhorrence of war with his recognition of the rightness of the cause for which we were fighting, finally broke off his speech choked with an emotion which was more eloquent than anything he or anyone else could have said.

My concerns about the danger to our ships began to ease as it became clear that the Iraqi airforce, which posed the main threat to them, was being forced to stay on the ground by the coalition air campaign; I was further relieved when it appeared that much of Iraq's airforce had flown to Iran to escape the air onslaught. But there were still grave risks, especially from mines; I decided to send a team of mine-clearance divers to join our task force to help protect the coalition fleet. There was some criticism, including a fulminating call from Singapore by WA Senator Michael Beahan of the Centre Left, that this decision amounted to an expansion of our commitment. I was furious with him and responded in equally direct language. I thought it irresponsible not to take a step which would obviously improve the safety of our ships and their crews. The superb professionalism of our divers was recognised by the US and other coalition forces who used them to train their own people. They continued to do valuable work after the liberation, bringing credit to themselves and Australia.

In some ways the most chilling day of the war came on 14th February when a bunker in Baghdad, believed to have been used for military communications but in fact used as a local air-raid shelter, was attacked and destroyed with pinpoint accuracy, killing hundreds of civilians. Such mistakes are essentially unavoidable but they are nonetheless tragic, and the grief-stricken relatives waiting to retrieve the bodies of their loved ones from the wreckage was for me the most moving television footage of the war.

By mid-February it was becoming clear that the air war was coming to an end and that the ground war would soon begin. Most people feared that the land war could be long and bloody so on Friday, 15th February, when Iraq started making ambiguous statements about seeking a resolution, we took notice. Those first hints came to nothing but a week later, on 22nd February, the Soviet Union announced that Iraq had accepted a peace proposal as a basis for discussion, and it became apparent that this proposal would be put to the Security Council over the weekend. A bewildering forty-eight hours followed, as the nature of the proposal, and the attitudes of the various participants towards it, evolved. We consulted closely with a range of our coalition partners and I spoke personally to John Major and Michel Rocard. I was concerned that a situation might arise in which most of the UN Security Council (UNSC) accepted the Soviet proposal as a basis for suspending the land war, while the US and the UK, who had the most at stake in the operations now waiting to be launched, might have wanted to go ahead. I concluded that we would have to accept whatever conclusion the UNSC reached.

On Saturday, 23rd February, I had a long discussion with Brent Scowcroft, Bush's National Security Adviser, and on the Sunday morning I had a call from Bush himself. By the time George called, the UNSC had met and had decided not to pursue the Soviet proposal and he told me that the land operations would be starting soon. I held a press conference on Sunday afternoon, 24th February, at which I made it clear that the Iraqis had been given every chance to withdraw but had chosen not to. I said I had been stressing two things in the consultations over the past few days: first, that we should take every opportunity to allow Iraq to withdraw if it had genuinely decided to do so; but second, that if Iraq was not prepared to withdraw in accordance with UN resolutions we should maintain the momentum of the military operations which were begun on 17th January to force Iraq from Kuwait.

It was all over in one hundred hours. By Tuesday morning we were receiving reports that Iraqi forces were withdrawing and on Thursday, 28th February, at 4.00 p.m., hostilities were halted. As I said that afternoon, it was a moment of relief and hope, pride and sorrow. Sorrow that war had been necessary and that it had inflicted so much damage on Iraq; pride on the part played by Australia and especially our Defence Force; relief that it was over with so few allied casualties, and none to our forces; and hope that the stand of the international community through the UN in resisting Iraq's aggression would lay a strong foundation for a peaceful post-Cold War era.

The next morning George Bush called and we spoke briefly but with some feeling about the path we had pursued since 2nd August. To me his conduct of American policy, carrying with it as it did the leadership of the international response to Iraq, was a model of courage, discipline and responsibility. I was proud to have worked with him through the crisis.

Some people argued that the job was not finished, that the coalition forces should have pushed on to Baghdad and destroyed Saddam Hussein's régime. I never shared that view, for two reasons. First, the UN resolutions did not give us authority to do it and to defy the UN in the moment of victory would have undermined the moral basis of all that we had been fighting for. Second, we had no idea what it would take to topple Saddam and no idea of whom to set up in his place. The UN military action in the Gulf succeeded because it had very clearly defined military objectives. Where the UN has performed less well since, for example in Bosnia, it has been because it has tried to use military forces to achieve essentially political results without clear military objectives.

The story has not finished with the ceasefire and is not finished yet. Still to be resolved are the plight of Iraq's Kurds, the elimination of Iraq's weapons of mass destruction and, of course, the consequences of the war for the rest of the Middle East. With many others, I saw that the victory over Saddam Hussein gave an opportunity for a new start on the age-old problems of that region. I said on 28th February: 'Our hope is that the sense of commitment and co-operation which so many nations in the Middle East and throughout the world have demonstrated in confronting Saddam Hussein will be shown again in meeting the challenges ahead.' That hope was fulfilled. Almost immediately, comprehensive negotiations began which have yielded the agreement between the PLO and Israel, offering the best prospect ever for peace between Israel and its neighbours.

The Gulf War was in many ways the most demanding single challenge I dealt with in my public life. Great issues were at stake and great risks had to be taken – risks to young Australians' lives. Our part in the scheme of things was not large in comparison with the major players, yet it was worthy. We acted at all times promptly, decisively and with great clarity of purpose. Our strength was to identify, at the outset, Australia's interests and the international principles at stake in the crisis, and to steer by those principles through all the vicissitudes which followed. We took pains to explain our position to our people and to the world. In doing so we built wide support for a tragic but necessary war, among a people profoundly averse to and scarred by war. Australians responded magnificently.

This response came in a year when the country had commemorated the seventy-fifth anniversary of its most famous military action – the landing at Gallipoli in 1915, when the youth of this new nation came together for the first time as comrades in arms. Out of that experience of fighting against tremendous odds, of enormous casualties and of defeat, the sense of mateship which had been kindled in the peaceful bush and cities of Australia was forged into a permanent part of the national character.

I travelled with Hazel and John and Carolyn Hewson to join a group of Gallipoli veterans, marvellous old men, virtually all more than ninety years of age. The most touching experience of my time as Prime Minister came at dawn on 25th April as the sun rose over the historic hills above Anzac Cove. The old soldiers and the hundreds of young Australian backpackers who had travelled to join in the service bonded with each other in profound affection. Later in the morning our veterans faced their grizzled Turkish counterparts, hesitated, then embraced. As I looked back nearly a year later, Gallipoli and the Gulf merged in a swell of pride for my country and its people.

TWENTY-NINE

All my experience as Prime Minister had confirmed a long-standing disquiet about the Constitutional division of powers under which the country is governed. I had expressed these concerns in the series of Boyer Lectures in 1979[116] when I advocated the abolition of the States and the strengthening of local government based on a more relevant distribution of regional responsibilities. This was a counsel of perfection which I felt was not achievable in my lifetime.

I was determined, however, to use my fourth term of office to revolutionise the relations between the three levels of government – Federal, State and local – not by referendum but by achieving better co-operation within the framework of the existing Constitution. My goals were to improve our national efficiency and international competitiveness and to improve the delivery and quality of services provided by the different levels of government.

In launching the 'New Federalism' initiative in a speech to the National Press Club on 19th July 1990, I had two immediate objectives. First, to establish in the public mind the urgency of the need to change our absurdly inefficient duplication of regulations and service delivery. Second, to propose processes for change; as I put it, 'sustained and substantial processes to explore and map the areas where co-operation for common objectives is not only desirable but realistically achievable'.

As to the first, I emphasised that we, alone of all the peoples of the world, have a continent to ourselves yet have denied ourselves the advantages that should flow from this by imposing, under the federal system, a burden of different and often conflicting rules, regulations and requirements:

> Schools in different States have different minimum starting ages, and different patterns of schooling at primary and secondary levels, and different curricula, and different ways of assessing Year 12 students – differences that give totally unnecessary headaches not only to students who may move interstate but also to employers and tertiary institutions who look to the schools system to provide meaningful standards for recruitment.
>
> Lawyers and doctors and other professionals may have qualifications from the best universities in Australia or the world; skilled tradesmen may have the finest on-the-job experience – but to work outside their home State they need a licence from a State licensing board.

I stressed the inefficiency of requiring manufacturers to put different labels on different packages of the same products to meet the varying requirements of State regulations and pointed out the economic farce involved in the movement of products by rail:

> A cargo container being sent by rail between Sydney and Perth may be subjected to:
> * 3 non-integrated rail systems,
> * 4 changes of locomotives,

- 5 different safe working systems,
- 6 different sizes of loading gauge,
- 10 different engineering standards of the basic standard gauge rail track,
- 12 or more hours at sidings or junctions for crew changes, refuelling, inspections.

These self-imposed constraints could be best understood, I suggested, by making the comparison with Europe. 'Look ... at the progress the twelve sovereign nations of the European Community are making: there will be less impediment against trade of goods and services between them in 1992 than there is now between the States of Australia ... key areas of our economy remain Balkanised.'

In trying to bring home the price paid in the bureaucratic overlap involved in the delivery of so many social services, I turned to the lives of ordinary Australians:

The battling family on the city fringe; the Aboriginal community in the remote outback; the frail aged at home or in hospital – they don't want to argue the toss about which bureaucracy provides the help to which they are entitled. And their least concern is some academic argument of Commonwealth versus State rights. And the instinct of the people is correct.

The real emphasis – our real concern – should be the rights and needs of citizens, not as, say, Queenslanders or Tasmanians, but as Australians.

I then set out the processes I was initiating to tackle the issues I had put on the agenda: micro-economic reform, program delivery, industrial relations and the environment. A Special Premiers Conference was to be called for 30th–31st October in Brisbane to begin considering the detailed proposals which would come from the work of a Commonwealth–State steering committee. This committee was to co-ordinate and advance the further examination of these issues. I set up a special high-level group in the Department of Prime Minister and Cabinet to provide continuing support. The States and local government welcomed the proposals, with the result that the Brisbane conference was able to register dramatic progress on a wide front, from a uniform vehicle regulation through to an intergovernmental agreement on the environment.[117]

At the end of the meeting State and local government leaders were unanimous in their praise for the new atmosphere which had been created and for the progress achieved. They were looking forward to consolidating that progress in two further Special Conferences scheduled for the middle and end of 1991. Independent observers commented that the process I had initiated and the proposals which emerged were 'the most ambitious attempt at the practical overhaul of intergovernmental arrangements that has ever been attempted in Australia's near-century of federalism'.[118] Nick Greiner, Premier of New South Wales, called it 'the most constructive thing that I've done in two and three-quarter years as Premier', while Joan Kirner, the Victorian Premier, was kind enough to say, 'May I ... Prime Minister, again thank you for having the vision and the leadership and the patience to enable this conference to happen ...'

Tragically, Paul Keating's use of the issue in his campaign to destabilise my leadership denied Australia the benefits which could have come from a full continuation of the New Federalism initiatives. That campaign began immediately after his resignation as Treasurer when his challenge of June 1991 had failed.

Keating and Treasury had been fully involved in preparing our position on the centrally important question of Commonwealth–State financial arrangements in the lead-up to the Brisbane conference. The major concern of the States was what is referred to technically as 'vertical fiscal imbalance' – economists' lingo for describing the gap, or deficit, between the revenue raised by the States in their own right and what they spend. Quite apart from the matter of loan funds, the States have always been anxious to find ways of adding to their revenue base, including the possibility of acquiring or sharing some of the Commonwealth's sources of revenue.

I had addressed this issue in my July 1990 speech to the National Press Club and had stressed the importance of retaining control of macro-economic management at the centre: 'Australia must have one central level of effective economic management. The level and incidence of taxation and public sector borrowing should be primarily determined at a national level.' But as evidence of good faith I had announced that the Commonwealth would respond positively to the Premiers by relinquishing the bank accounts debits tax to the States. This was confirmed at the Brisbane meeting; the communiqué noted that this decision would represent a transfer of revenue raising capacity of $385 million to the States which, while there would be off-setting adjustments in States' financial assistance grants, 'should thereby increase to some degree the flexibility available to State Governments'.

Keating and I, in preparing for Brisbane, were at one in our view that retaining the capacity to conduct macro-economic policy was non-negotiable and that the Commonwealth could never agree to any change in the revenue raising or sharing arrangements which might jeopardise this. But we agreed that all options should be on the table in the substantial review that was to be established.[119]

Keating affirmed his position strongly at the press conference which concluded the Brisbane meeting. In the light of his subsequent protestations that it would be heresy to consider any suggestion of the States getting into the field of income tax, the following interchange is revealing:

JOURNALIST: '… What is your view to the Commonwealth moving somewhat out of the income tax field to give the States some – '

KEATING: 'Well, that's what the inquiry's about. That's what it's about …'

All this was conveniently ignored when he decided to derail the New Federalism as part of his operation to move Caucus votes away from me. He had fertile ground, for a number of our colleagues detested the idea of any increase in the powers of the States, particularly where they could perceive that operating to their own political disadvantage. For instance, the possible shift of more responsibility for roads or home and community care programs to the States could mean less kudos and fewer photo opportunities for them in their electorates; my related suggestion of helping the States' tax revenue position was anathema to them.

The centrality of these issues was emphasised in the communiqué of the highly successful Special Premiers' Conference in Sydney on 30th July 1991:

> Leaders and representatives noted that the decisions to be taken at the special Premiers Conference scheduled for November 1991 would be fundamental to the overall success of the reform agenda. In particular, that meeting will be considering the crucial and inter-related issues of reform of Commonwealth–State financial arrangements, including reviewing the distribution of taxation powers to reduce vertical fiscal imbalance and a clearer definition of the roles and responsibilities of the respective governments in the areas of program and service delivery …

Keating's cleverly targeted campaign of misrepresentation culminated in a speech to the National Press Club on 22nd October 1991. In a speech which was all about chasing 'his turn' and had nothing to do with the national interest, the New Federalism process had become 'one of the gravest dangers we face as a nation ... the dismembering of the national Government which would inevitably follow from surrendering revenue and other national responsibilities to the States'. Warming to this exercise he lamented, 'It would be a sad outcome of a Special Premiers Conference process dedicated to removing Government-imposed obstacles to economic efficiency if its result was to allow the creation of seven income or sales tax systems where there was only one before.'

The first point to make is that Keating had been claiming that for a long time he was the one who really ran the Government. This was, obviously, nonsense. But he can't have it both ways. If he was running the Government how had he allowed this process to get under way and gather such momentum and why was he part of such a dangerous undertaking? The truth is that while the New Federalism was my initiative, we had talked at length and agreed upon the fundamental parameter of it – which was that nothing should be done to prejudice the Federal Government's capacity to discharge its responsibilities to protect the national interest, particularly in the conduct of macroeconomic policy. We would be prepared to allow the joint working committees to examine any proposal the States wished to put on the table but, in the end, would reserve the right to make our decision about proposed changes on the basis of this non-negotiable principle.

A more detailed examination of the record of the joint press conference following the Brisbane meeting confirms all this.[120] In opening that conference I thanked the Treasurer and Deputy Prime Minister for his involvement and co-operation and at two points I specifically emphasised the commitment to our national responsibilities:

what we've done ... is to establish a process with deadlines, with specific time-frames ... with the States accepting in that process the obligation which must be with the Commonwealth to retain the capacity for proper macro-economic management ... The States ... recognise unequivocally the responsibility that the Commonwealth has for macro-economic management ... We've said we'll go into that [vertical fiscal imbalance] with the aim of reducing it, provided that there is an acceptance of the need to have an outcome ... which gives us the assurance that we can discharge our responsibility.

I was asked by a journalist about 'the likelihood of a State income tax twelve months down the track' and replied that Paul and I would be instructing our officials to approach the possibilities with an open mind, and to look at anything the States might want to put forward. I went on to say, 'I think we share [a view of what] the major criterion [should be]: what in the end is going to be best for the citizens of this country?' Paul had already expressed the same position[121] and said later, in similar vein, about our approach to fiscal questions: '... it may be possible to devise a system ... where there is perhaps more control of revenues by the States. Again, as the Prime Minister said, that's something we can look at. That's the point of the study.'

While the Treasurer was doing his somersault in the National Press Club, I was sticking to the bargain he and I had made with the States on this study. Cabinet submissions inevitably referred to States' proposals being examined by the joint working committee and these proposals were leaked and used by Keating as though they had the imprimatur of the Government. As a matter of principle, however, there was no alternative to allowing the work of the committee to proceed. I did this in the knowledge that the Cabinet and the Caucus would ultimately have the opportunity and the right to determine the

Government's final position in regard to the Special Premiers Conference in November. They would be able to do so in the light of an interrelated set of proposals against which they could make a judgment on the critical question of the protection of the national interest. I knew, as did Keating, that the suggestion of a States' income tax power was a red herring – none of the States were pressing for it and they would have been out of their political minds if they had.

One author, Paul Kelly, writing on this period has suggested I was 'inept' in allowing matters to reach this point. For the reasons I have given, I do not believe that, in good conscience, there was any alternative to acting the way I did. Perhaps this is arguable, but there can be no demur from Kelly's observation about the role of the ex-Treasurer: 'Keating was a saboteur, pure and simple ...'[122]

His sabotage was successful. In the atmosphere of bitterness and uncertainty about the Commonwealth's position created by his misrepresentation, the States declined to attend the November conference. The national interest came a very poor second to Paul Keating's perception of his own.

THIRTY

Keating's resignation from the ministry on 3rd June 1991 brought to an end one of the most significant treasurerships since Federation. From a hesitant beginning Paul had grown in confidence, competence, courage, imagination and determination to contribute to the task of creating a more efficient and competitive Australia. We had experienced our differences, but by general consent the Prime Minister–Treasurer relationship – always crucial to the quality of government – of Hawke and Keating was recognised as the most dynamic in Australia's history. I will always remember with pride – and, despite everything, some affection for Paul – those great things we were able to achieve together which helped to transform our country. Indeed, it is those memories which make it unpleasant to have to weave into the record of my final months in office the dishonourable role played by Paul and his more fanatical supporters.

Brian Howe, the Left's most senior minister, was elected by Caucus as Deputy Prime Minister, but in choosing the next Treasurer I had to make a tough choice between Ralph Willis and John Kerin. Both had qualifications in economics although Ralph had longer practical experience in the macro-economic area from his time at the ACTU, his period as Shadow Treasurer and his work on the ERC. If it had been simply a matter of technical capacity and experience, Ralph was in front and I would have dearly loved to reward him with the position he legitimately coveted. I was faced with the real problem that the four senior positions in government were already held by Victorians: Howe and myself, with Button and Evans, Leader and Deputy Leader respectively in the Senate. I thought that selecting Ralph, another Victorian, as Treasurer would tip regional imbalances too far, and therefore appointed Kerin to the job.

I had confidence in his capacity and he brought with him the understanding and high reputation he had acquired in eight years in the Primary Industry portfolio. His detailed knowledge derived from his own years of practical experience as a farmer and, later, as a bureaucrat in the Bureau of Agricultural Economics had won the confidence of a widely diversified industry. John has a genial, open character and a quirky sense of humour which, as it turned out, was going to be sorely tested. I hoped that his self-effacing amiability and genuine interest in dialogue would create a better atmosphere and sense of involvement with our colleagues.

Indeed, this was the immediate dividend. Kerin did not regard Treasury officials as his exclusive preserve and made them, as well as himself, readily available to ministers and backbenchers. Despite this propitious beginning, John's tenure as Treasurer was doomed from the start, not simply because he inherited from his predecessor an economy in recession but because the insidious and incessant campaign waged against him by Keating and his supporters finally destroyed his confidence.

John Kerin's travails should be put in that context. The recession had been announced by Keating on 29th November 1990, after two quarters of negative growth, with his notorious statement: 'this is a recession that Australia had to have'. He later made the claim that he had

had my agreement to use this form of words.[123] This is simply untrue.[124] While that needs to be made clear, it is not relevant to the issue of substance. In a clumsy fashion, Keating was making the valid point that it was virtually impossible to avoid choking back the economy if we were to deal with the imbalance between the level of imports associated with existing growth patterns and our capacity to generate the export income necessary to avoid an unsustainable balance of payments crisis. His mistake was not in exposing the problem but in the apparently uncaring way he did it.

Some of my colleagues wanted me to have his head for this indiscretion but I regarded the suggestion as absurd. Despite Paul's unfounded claims that he and virtually he alone had been the architect of our positive economic achievements, the truth was that just as we were all entitled to claim credit for those, so we all had to share the responsibility for error. I think he was right in implying the recession was unavoidable but, as I have noted,[125] more timely decisions on the variation of monetary policy could have avoided the length and depth of the recession.

We were all deeply concerned at the human suffering involved in rising levels of unemployment. The task of policy in 1991 was to take action which would start to move Australia out of recession but in a way that would not make our longer term economic position more precarious. Keating, commendably, committed himself to proposing such a policy to the Cabinet. In fact one of his last acts as Treasurer was to present to the ERC on 22nd May, on Treasury advice which he had accepted, the framework for formulating the Budget for 1991–92. This was Keating's firm position, delivered with his usual conviction, at a time when he carried the responsibility to his country of being Treasurer. I set it out in some detail to establish the opportunism he displayed after the Budget, when he viewed things in terms of his self-interest instead of the interests of Australia:

... the economy is near the trough of the cycle and is expected to begin a steady recovery in the second half of 1991.

... policy is directed at generating a recovery so as to deal with what is an unacceptable unemployment situation but in the context of not jeopardising our ongoing need to stabilise our balance of payments and reduce inflation.

... Although the upturn will gather speed through the year, it will be more modest than the rapid standards of the past. Given that we must cement home gains on the current account and also inflation, an upturn of this speed seems about right.

... Our policies must therefore ensure we grasp the opportunity of the best annual CPI outcome for over two decades – and the very real economic benefits that will accrue from lower inflation.

... policy needs to continue to bear down further on the current account deficit by lifting our competitiveness and ensuring that there is a continuing contribution from net exports ... The key message for the recovery is that the immediate pick-up in domestic demand will be modest and that will be consistent with the need to sustain the gains in reducing the current account and inflation.

... That does not mean keeping the economy comatosed. But it does mean using fiscal and monetary policies to avoid the excessive domestic demand growth of some recent periods.

... the demand management policy settings for this recovery would appear to be in place. Particularly with the last cut in interest rates, monetary policy has been eased substantially as domestic demand has fallen and, more importantly, inflation and inflationary expectations have been reduced. Cash rates have been cut by 7.5 percentage points since January 1990 but, because of the lagged effects of monetary policy changes, the reductions made at the end of 1990 and in 1991 have yet to have any real impact on the economy and will be felt more in the remainder of this year and next. Similarly some of the earlier easings have yet to have their full impact.

... At the Commonwealth level, having regard to the need to protect the structural integrity of the Budget, and against the background of the subdued outlook for revenue, I propose that as we start out on the 1991 Budget processes we endeavour to offset the effects on outlays in 1991–92 of the decisions taken since the 1990–91 Budget and of any new policy proposals adopted in this year's deliberations.

His submission ended in this way:

Demand management policy settings for recovery would appear to be in place and the economy is expected to begin a steady recovery in the second half of 1991. Recovery should be sufficient to begin cutting unemployment but with something of a lag but it should not be so rapid as to set back our success to date on the current account and on inflation.

... Fiscal policy will remain critical to continuing this progress and I therefore recommend that Cabinet:

(a) note the large size of the potential Budget deficit for 1991–92;

(b) agree that the key objective should be to achieve a structure of the Budget on the outlays side to ensure that a surplus is restored as steady economic growth is achieved; and

(c) to that end, agree that we endeavour to offset the effects on outlays in 1991–92 of decisions taken since the 1990–91 Budget and of any new policy proposals adopted in this year's deliberations.

This advice was accepted and it formed, in fact, the basis on which John Kerin drew up that Budget. The indisputable fact is that the 1991 Kerin Budget incorporated the policy approach that Paul Keating had recommended.

Kerin delivered the Budget on 20th August, but just as Paul Keating's last Budget a year earlier had to share the headlines with our response to the Iraqi invasion of Kuwait, so John had to compete with another world-shattering event – a coup in the Soviet Union during which President Mikhail Gorbachev was placed under house arrest by communist hardliners, news of which we received in Canberra at 2.00 p.m. on Monday 19th. On the basis of my reading of the intelligence reports, I predicted on the ABC's '7.30 Report' on 21st August that the coup would collapse and this prediction was confirmed the next day. I rang Gorbachev just a few hours after his return from the Crimea, where he had been detained, and shortly after Boris Yeltsin's decisive intervention had ended his ordeal. My call got through just before Yeltsin clambered on to the roof of a tank to address the enormous crowd that had gathered in the Moscow streets. I expressed our relief to Gorbachev that he was free and that the coup had been smashed. He was less concerned about his own trauma than he was for the future of his country. He was, nonetheless, confident of the way ahead, although he could not possibly have imagined the speed at which events would unravel from that point. I told him of Australia's commitment to do whatever we could to help – for which he expressed his gratitude – but did not attempt to take more of the time of this man under such pressure. Gorbachev was kind enough to mention my call in his press conference. He might have been a little less ebullient if he had known what Boris Yeltsin had said to me in an earlier call I made to congratulate him on his role in resolving the crisis. Referring to Gorbachev, Yeltsin said, 'He knows who saved him.'

But we had our own problems to contend with, not so much with the general media and market reaction, which was reasonably positive, but with the attacks being mounted from within our own ranks. When added to the provisions in the March 1991 Statement, our increased expenditure on labour market programs had lifted outlays by 50 per cent from 1990–91 to $598 million and this was welcomed. However, all hell broke loose over our decision to introduce a $3.50 Medicare co-payment to help contain rising health costs by putting a break on over-servicing. I had realised there would be criticism but we had made hard decisions before when it was necessary to meet the long-term requirements of fiscal responsibility. There were few areas for off-setting savings left after all our years of dedicated Budget management and the Medicare co-payment decision was precisely in line with what Keating had prescribed in May.

Because of my concerns, I had asked Brian Howe in the pre-Budget deliberations to gauge whether he could sell the proposal to the Left and it was only after his reassurances on this point that we made the decision. But he had misread his faction, which joined with many other Caucus members in demanding a reconsideration. Brian's genuine remorse was moving but irrelevant in a situation which had become untenable, more especially since Keating and his supporters had promised to reverse the co-payment policy if he were to become Leader. Some of those who had supported the proposal during the ERC discussions reneged and, after much sound and fury and a Caucus committee inquiry, a compromise of sorts was reached; the concept of a co-payment was retained but it was dropped to $2.50.

It was in this tense atmosphere that Keating abandoned the economic responsibility, analysis and strategy he had advocated in May and which we had incorporated in the Budget. He had, then, empha-sised caution and patience, saying that the right demand management policies were in place and that the responsible thing was to offset already committed increases in outlays and to wait for the lagged impact of the substantial earlier cuts in interest rates. He now publicly advocated further net expansions in outlays and cuts in interest rates.[126] To have conceded it was his own strategy that was in place, that he had been wrong and that therefore changes needed to be made, would have been one thing. But to argue now that the Kerin Budget and the Government were at fault reached notes on the scale of hypocrisy beyond Placido Domingo at his best.

John Kerin, who is by nature slow to anger, was in turn infuriated and depressed as stories emerged of pro-Keating forces feeding the press gallery with ammunition to attack him. I admired the way he stuck to his task as we monitored the economy and came to the conclusion by November that, consistent with the basic Budget strategy, there was room for a slight fiscal stimulus. As a result of discussions with a Caucus working group, the ACTU and the Economic Planning Advisory Council, I made a statement to the Parliament on 14th November on the economy and employment. The statement announced further expenditure of some $313 million in calendar year 1992 on the labour market and education and training programs, transport infrastructure, science and industry development.

Unemployment had hit 10 per cent in October and we wanted to do what we reasonably could to contain this movement and restore job growth. The requirements of reasonable behaviour dictated that a balance be struck between giving a mild stimulus and not appearing to depart from the fundamental requirements of the Budget strategy to take account of inflation and balance of payment considerations. If the market judged that we had lost our nerve and abandoned these criteria, the prospects for recovery would have been at risk. In the event, the market assessed that we had turned up the fiscal wick to about the right height and the Caucus was reasonably satisfied. I was able to claim with justification that we had brought in measures 'which meet the critical tests of advancing our economic strategy, while maintaining the integrity of the Budget'.

In refuting the argument from some quarters that it was not appropriate for the Government to have consulted with the ACTU before bringing down the statement I expressed a sentiment I felt passionately:

> Not only do I reject that argument, but I go further. The very fact that our strategy is on track – the fact that the great objective of creating a restructured, low inflation, internationally competitive economy is now within our grasp – is in large measure a result of the constructive co-operation and restraint that have been practised by the working men and women of Australia. That is, precisely, a reason to listen to those who represent them.
>
> Their members have experienced unemployment, not only through the recession, but through the process of long-term industrial restructuring we are pursuing. Yet in the representations they have made to us they have not asked for this process to be slowed. They understand, accept and are committed to its continuation, in the knowledge that it is in the long-term interest of their country.

A week after the November Statement, on 21st November, the Liberal Party released its long-awaited policy blueprint, a 600-page document entitled *Fightback!*. Its central plank was a 15 per cent goods and services tax (GST). The *Fightback!* manifesto was the first time the Opposition had forged a co-ordinated and substantial set of policy alternatives. This, of itself, changed the political landscape.

Both community and commentators had grown used to Opposition negativism. They had also witnessed a fair share of Opposition policy turnabouts and collapses, particularly its spectacular performance on health.[127] The existence now of a fat document containing a raft of policies, with some thread of connection between them, was welcome to individual members of the Opposition, to their supporters around the country and, of course, to the media. This was something novel and exciting.

If not in the novel and exciting category, the Liberals at least had a new leader, Dr John Hewson, a former Economics professor and member of John Howard's staff during his time as Treasurer in the Fraser Government. Hewson had been a comparative unknown when elected to Parliament in 1987 and he owed his leadership to the desperation of the Liberal Party as it reeled from the Peacock–Howard merry-go-round. The Liberals had expected to win the 1987 election with John Howard. They were sure of winning in 1990 with the re-cycled Peacock. When he failed, Hewson was the residual choice. Unlike Howard and Peacock, he was not basically a political animal.

Paradoxically, this fact helped lift the Liberals further in the polls. Hewson was new and fresh – like *Fightback!*. But, like *Fightback!*, he would not withstand close examination and, like his new creation, he would wear out his welcome. He was hardworking, with a good mind, but he lacked political nous. Somewhat like Malcolm Fraser, whose legacy he so scorned, he seemed to find it difficult to be at ease with a wide range of people. All these drawbacks would eventually show through, but the blush had not yet worn off him and, for the moment, circumstances had delivered him a dream run.

By now, with the country in the depths of recession, Labor was on the nose in the electorate. For the first time since 1983, the Opposition appeared unified, while Labor's unity, which had been a major strength of the Government, had been cracked by the Keating challenge. These factors provided Hewson with an ideal opportunity to give maximum exposure to the tough new ideological position represented by *Fightback!*.

Fightback!, however, turned into the tool with which he dug himself so deeply into a political hole that he lost the 'unloseable' 1993 election. Paul Keating became the eventual beneficiary of this. I have often laughed to myself since then – I saved Keating from the GST and Hewson saved him with it.

For the moment, however, *Fightback!* was something of a *tour de force* on the political stage, and John Hewson was enjoying its short-run benefits. The document had taken months to produce and, although there are plenty of wiseacres now, it was not susceptible to immediate destruction. It was complex and I knew that a good deal of time would be needed to destroy it. As I told the Caucus, the Opposition would get a significant electoral advantage and a boost in the polls in the immediate term. The community was excited by what appeared to be a sea change in politics – an Opposition with a mission and a program.

I was certain that over time, as the Government worked on it and put to proper use the resources of Treasury and Finance to analyse the assumptions, the arithmetic and the economic implications of *Fightback!*, we could turn the debate around. *Fightback!* would be seen for what it was: a fundamentally regressive attack on the Australian people.

It promoted a significant flattening of the progressive income tax scales. In their place, *Fightback!* proposed raising a regressive goods and services tax. This meant that the rich would pay exactly the same impost as the poorest in the community on the same goods they bought and the same services they used. The government had examined this idea in the lead-up to the Tax Summit of 1985[128] and we knew the difficulties of compensating for a regressive tax. *Fightback!* contained a compensation package, but one which, I was confident, would not achieve the objective of making equitable something that was intrinsically inequitable.

I also knew, as confidently as I knew anything in my time in politics, that *Fightback!* would not survive. I specifically told the Caucus and the Parliament that the Government would not be alone in attacking it and exposing its weaknesses. As time went by, and as the implications of the package became clear, all manner of community interest groups would join the campaign against *Fightback!*. Then the heat would be on the Opposition. But, I emphasised, that would take time. As things turned out, it was only after the March 1993 election campaign was well under way that the Government, under Paul's leadership, was eventually able to puncture the balloon of *Fightback!* and the GST.

In November 1991, in the hothouse of the Keating challenge, any plea for perspective and time was drowned in a blood surge of ambition. The attacks that were made upon *Fightback!* were blunted and undermined by the Keating coterie.

In the critical position of Treasurer, John Kerin was dogged, but he was being overrun. The treatment meted out to him by his colleagues was appalling, especially when one thinks back to Paul's extreme nervousness and the mistakes that he made when he was first Treasurer. There were no allowances made by him and his forces for Kerin who, by comparison, was facing a much more difficult task.

From Paul's viewpoint it was indeed fortuitous that *Fightback!* appeared in November. If my Government had been given the time that Paul himself found he needed to accumulate data and community support against *Fightback!*, then we could have substantiated our case and delivered the fatal blow to it and the GST.

Some of the Keating group criticised me for failing to launch a full-scale political assault on the Opposition's program quickly enough. The criticism is unfounded. On 28th November 1991 I moved to censure the Leader of the Opposition for perpetrating a hoax on the people of Australia. I referred to its 600 pages of fraudulent figuring and contradictory claims:

> The document is called *Fightback!*, but the real question is: if you are going to call it *Fightback!* who does it attack? ... It would certainly hurt ordinary Australian people. It would hurt those people in the Australian community least able to look after themselves, least able to take the pain. That is why it is a hoax ... It pretends to help ordinary Australians. But, instead, it would dramatically and drastically lower the standard of living of ordinary Australians.
>
> It would wreck the fundamental reforms that we have made to the Australian economy. We would return to the high inflation of the bad old days under the economic academic opposite, with all the consequences that high inflation would have for living standards and competitiveness. The consumption tax would lead to the polarisation of the Australian people. It would lead to the re-entrenching of privilege and it would lead to a return to confrontation in the workplace.

Fightback! proposed $10 billion in spending cuts, including a $2.4 billion cut in social welfare, which would strike a devastating blow at those least well-off. These spending cuts would allegedly fund income tax reductions for Australian workers but, as I pointed out, it was the highest paid – those earning over $75 000 – who would be the greatest beneficiaries. The 2 per cent in that category were Dr Hewson's idea of the workers of Australia, and he had no regard for those at the bottom whom the spending cuts would hurt most.

I referred to the Australian classic, *The Magic Pudding*. Its motto was 'cut and come again'. 'That is how Dr Hewson regards lower middle income Australia, as a magic pudding. He thinks he can slash them, cut them and come again, and come again. That is his view – $10 billion in cuts in living standards for those who can least afford it.'

I had laid out the basic conceptual framework which was never departed from in the sixteen months it took to destroy *Fightback!* I had defeated every Liberal leader in turn – Fraser, Peacock, Howard and Peacock again – each one of them a more formidable opponent than Hewson, and I knew I could destroy him and his repugnant ideology. But events were moving quickly to ensure that, despite this record, I would not be given the opportunity.

THIRTY-ONE

On 8th November Paul Keating said on the ABC radio program 'PM': 'I will not be challenging the Prime Minister.' Graham Richardson went out of his way to confirm this statement as representing a genuine end to Paul's campaign for the leadership. He contacted my Special Adviser, Colin Parkes, specifically to give him this message and also rang it round to senior members of the press gallery.

I don't know what motivated Graham. It may be that he believed what he was saying at the time and other forces later overcame him. Certainly from what emerged later his actions infuriated the Keating war room and may explain the residual resentment which some of Paul's more fanatical supporters are said to harbour against him still. I wanted to believe Graham and it is perhaps a measure of a trusting nature that I tended to do so. I was alone among my supporters in this – and, of course, they were right.

There was no halt to the Keating campaign which now adopted the tactic of attacking a surrogate target – the Treasurer, John Kerin. As the days went on, it became increasingly clear that John was buckling under this pressure from the Keating camp and he made some elementary mistakes. His self-deprecating style, rather than reassuring people, was causing them to lose confidence in him. On 5th December the dénouement came at a press conference where he had to deal with the September national account figures showing the longest – but not the deepest – recession in Australia since the Great Depression.[129] He was in a worried, lugubrious frame of mind and got completely lost in dealing with a technical term in the accounts, the Gross Operating Surplus (GOS) which refers to the gross profit position of companies: 'GOS … GOS … What's GOS?' he asked distractedly of an un-forgiving press corps. As he later described it, he simply froze on the 'S'. His mistake had nothing to do with economic literacy or competence; it was, rather, an index of his failing confidence.

I had heard the press conference on radio and caught it again later on television. I could see John was being destroyed and knew that he had to be moved. The high esteem in which I held John Kerin, the man, rose even further when we met the next day in my office. Here was this huge, physically powerful human being, intelligent, gentle, humorous and as decent as any person in the Parliament, reduced to a political corpse by enemies who had now become carrion crows, ready to feed on him. In accepting the decision with grace,[130] he went out of his way to emphasise his continuing loyalty and affection for me and his understanding of my decision to remove him as Treasurer. Kerin is not a man given to hatred but he will carry an abiding contempt for those who sabotaged him when he was doing his best to serve his country by attempting to implement – as he believed was right – the policies of his predecessor.

In his place I appointed Ralph Willis, who finally had the position he had so long wanted, although this time around it would be short-lived, for Keating would soon reward John Dawkins with the job he coveted. At the same time as making Ralph Treasurer I appointed Kim Beazley as the new Finance Minister. Kim's tenure would also be brief, although he would return to the post in 1994 when Willis resumed the treasurership upon the resignation of Dawkins.

John Kerin's removal added to the atmosphere of crisis which was already building. My followers became concerned that the numbers were slipping away from me. On 12th December 1991 Australia's worst unemployment figures for sixty years were announced. The worsening economy was sapping the morale of the Government.

On the night of 11th December six of my closest supporters in the Cabinet – Kim Beazley, Nick Bolkus, Michael Duffy, Gareth Evans, Gerry Hand and Robert Ray – met to discuss the leadership issue and to review the numbers. I was at the Governor-General's residence for a dinner in honour of the visiting Cypriot President, Mr George Vassiliou. Colin Parkes informed me of what was going on and later the group rang to set up a meeting for the following morning.

We met twice on 12th December, once in the morning and again in the afternoon. The essential message was that my support was being eroded and perhaps I would not win a Caucus ballot. They emphasised their own unqualified continuing commitment to me. This was not a number-crunching meeting but a gathering of friends who had my interests, first and foremost, at heart. They all thought those interests might be better served by my resigning.

They worried that even if I won a ballot our opponents would not let up and nothing would be decided. Indeed, one of Paul Keating's most immoderate followers, Gary Punch, openly said in the office of one of my supporters whom they were trying to win over, that they would press on even if it meant taking the Government into Opposition. Such fanaticism has a certain terrifying logic. If you keep tearing away at a government you will eventually ground and kill it. Even close supporters were influenced by the brutality of the stratagem; if we don't give Keating the leadership there will be no government left, some of them reasoned, and voted accordingly. While it did not influence the vote of any of the six senior ministers, that perception permeated the Caucus and eventually cost me victory.

The discussion with my senior ministers was emotional at times but, as they expressed it, they did not want to see my giant contribution rewarded by a Caucus sacking. They tested me on the possibility of a graceful departure to avoid that result: the United States President, George Bush, was due here on New Year's Day to thank Australia for its part in the Gulf War. The visit was symbolic and, the group of six thought, could provide a fitting conclusion to my years in office. I could meet with the President on Australian soil and shortly there-after step down.

I could see how this might be in my interests but not how it could be in the interests of the Government. I appreciated the spirit in which they were talking to me, as friends. But there was no way I could embrace the idea of a staged exit. I had made it clear to them in earlier discussions – individually and collectively – that I was not staying on simply because I could not bear to leave the job. I told them, and they accepted, that it was my profound belief that I had the best chance, certainly better than Paul Keating, of leading the Government to victory at the next election. 'The next election is critically important,' I told them. 'We have an Opposition more dogmatically, ideologically right-wing than anything we have seen in the postwar period. It has to be beaten, and I have the best chance of doing that.'

As to my personal satisfaction, I had been Labor's Prime Minister for a record term. I had nothing to prove about myself and I'd never relished the pomp and circumstance of office. What was driving me was the need for Labor to remain in government at a critical time in our history. I was deeply concerned by Hewson's dangerous prescrip-tion for the nation. My firm belief was that the Australian people, who had on four occasions voted for Labor under my leadership, would respond again if I went to them and explained the issues. We had come from behind in the last two elections. The fact that Labor's primary vote had declined did not distract me. This fall in support for major parties was a feature of politics around the world; we had demonstrated a capacity under the preferential system of voting to secure a mandate to govern.

'If the party believes that there should be a change of leadership, then that is something the party has to decide. I'm not going to make that decision for them, because I believe it's the wrong decision.' In the end, it simply got down to what was the right thing to do:

> The easiest thing in the world for me personally would be to say, All right, I'll cop the easy way out, see George Bush and then give it away. I've got the opportunity to retire comfortably, spend time with my family and my grandchildren, lower my golf handicap and have a relaxed and rewarding life. But it wouldn't be the right decision and if the wrong decision is to be made, the party will have to make it.

The intensity of my position surprised them. They went off and thought about it and came back after lunch. They began the second meeting by making it clear that if I intended to stay they would stick by me and do whatever they could to help me retain the leadership. And they did stick, something I will always appreciate.

News of the meetings with the six ministers leaked to the media which by now was in a frenzy. The meetings were not reported as showing the support of close friends, but as the opposite – that even my best mates were urging me to go. Some of them now regret coming to see me; if they had their time over again they believe it may have been better not to have done so. Perhaps they were naïve in believing the meetings could be kept secret, but in the fevered atmosphere of those final days no-one's judgment was perfect; as I sat there and listened to them I knew they were decent and honourable men. If they had not held the meeting and had only concentrated on winning votes, would the outcome have been different? Possibly. The voting was so tight that if all our efforts had been bent exclusively on gathering support we might have scraped home.

The backdrop to all this was the fanaticism of those opposed to us. Not everyone, of course, fell into that category but there were enough. If we had just got across the line, where would we have been? I cannot believe that Keating and those close to him would have left it at that. This perception had also become a fear in the minds of many of our Caucus colleagues.

I have speculated on what may have happened if the six had adopted different tactics. But I was influenced myself by the 'where will it all end?' syndrome. For the first time in my life I could be accused of not giving my all to a battle. Is there any 'winning'? I wondered – a rare question for me to contemplate. I instinctively felt that winning a ballot would not end the terrorism which would simply begin again. In the past, when I handled industrial disputes or battled policy issues at the ACTU, contests were fought and won, and that was that. In this case there was no end. This did not mean that I didn't fight hard. It's just that something undefinable was held in reserve; something, probably a feeling of depression, prevented me, however slightly, from giving this final contest my best shot.

On 18th December I met with my friends again. By this time Graham Richardson had told Robert Ray that Keating's supporters were organising a petition for a special Caucus meeting to challenge me. With that, we decided to call a party-room meeting for the following evening. As Robert Ray expressed it, this was the clean way of doing things: 'no show-and-tell ballots, no show of hands, no-one needs to sign a petition'.

On 19th December I arrived in my office at 8.35 a.m. and confirmed my intention to proceed in the way we had discussed. At 9.00 a.m. I handed a letter to the Caucus chairwoman, Carolyn Jakobsen, announcing my decision to convene a special Caucus meeting at 6.30 p.m. Keating released a statement at 10.30 a.m. confirming he would stand for the job of Prime Minister. Around this time I called my staff in and told them I believed I'd lose.

Having brought the issue to a head we knuckled down to some last-minute lobbying. We were helped in this effort by Martin Ferguson, the President of the ACTU, who with his brother, Laurie, the Member for Reid, and Daryl Melham, the Member for Banks, worked on those in the Left whom they regarded as doubtful. My key argument was that I was the best equipped to win the election. Many colleagues raised the obvious point: 'Well, okay, you win now, but they'll be at you again next year.' The concern was difficult to parry with conviction, and all I could say was that Graham Richardson had informed me that there would be only two challenges. If Keating lost the second challenge the war of attrition would end. Most of them recalled Keating's earlier 'one shot in the locker' pronouncement and wondered why they should believe him now.

Although we couldn't overcome that obstacle, we had some success in those final hours and I remember with amusement that I even grabbed back a Keating voter as I made my way to the party room.

At 6.30 p.m. I resigned as Labor Leader to enable the challenge to occur by secret ballot and so minimise any recriminations after the vote. It was a traumatic meeting. The Federal Parliamentary Labor Party is a strange, tough beast but this was a wrenching and painful experience for its members. It was made more poignant by their knowledge that this was the ALP's centenary year; there were some cold hearts to the end but the premonition that they may be about to bring down Labor's most successful Leader in those hundred years hung like a pall over the room.

In all the emotion of this moment, I felt deep sadness but an inner calm. I made a very brief statement in which I said that two things were evident. One was that the Labor Party, the countless rank-and-file who made up the party, wanted me to remain as Leader; the other was that the media wanted Hawke to go. In these circumstances, I said, I hoped that the will of the party would prevail. Paul spoke briefly and with that the tension rose as Caucus members retired to mark their ballots.

When the votes came in, the curtain fell for me on nearly nine years as Prime Minister. Paul Keating won by fifty-six votes to fifty-one. Two of my supporters were absent with my full agreement and understanding: Gareth Evans was on duty overseas and Con Sciacca was with his dying son. If they had been there it would have been fifty-six to fifty-three, and a switch of two votes would have made the difference. The fact is interesting as a matter of record, but to me, at this fateful moment, it was irrelevant. I had lost.

I immediately shook Paul's hand, congratulated him and pledged my support to the new Keating Labor Government. He referred to my enormous contribution and 'historic achievements' and said that I had left 'big shoes to fill', a comment which led one of my more devoted supporters to lament later, 'He's too big for his own bloody boots, and not big enough for yours.'

But for me it was not a time for grudges or hatreds. A fundamentally important decision had been taken, the most important decision a Labor Caucus could make. Beyond all the sadness, I still felt that the most crucial issue was to defeat Hewson and *Fightback!* at the next election and I sincerely hoped that, despite my misgivings, Paul could pull that off. I realised that a variety of factors had led to this final vote. Some had an accumulated hatred – failed ministers, for example, who blamed their misfortune on me. Some were hungry with ambition and believed, correctly, that they had a better chance of advancement under Paul. For some it was a simple matter of tribal loyalty. Some, genuinely disappointed with decisions for which I had been responsible, like Coronation Hill and the Medicare co-payment, thought the quality of my leadership had slipped. Some, equally genuinely, thought with Labor well down in the polls and with Hewson and the Opposition enjoying a new surge of popularity, that a new face at the top and Paul's more aggressive parliamentary skills would improve the chances of electoral victory. And critically, at the margins, others simply wanted to end the tension and saw a vote for him as the only way of doing it.

After the vote, two lines formed in the Caucus room as people congratulated Paul and commiserated with me. This was an odd experience, for emotions were confused. I was confronted with devastated loyalists and the sometimes tearful faces of those who had done everything they could to bring me down – John Dawkins, in particular, wept as he thanked me for all I had done.

I realised that this was the beginning of a very testing time and I began to compose myself for what lay immediately ahead. In my office, my family and staff awaited me. In the long walk down the corridor back to the office I was buoyed up by the company of thirty-eight of my closest supporters.

The press were demanding immediate comments but I told them they would have to wait. I had first to see Hazel and my daughters, Sue and Ros, and to greet my staff, friends and supporters. They had clapped me on the way to the ballot and they clapped me upon my return. Leadership battles are very tactile events and a lot of hugging, kissing and crying occurred. I then went into my final press conference as Prime Minister, accompanied by Hazel and the girls who stood nearby, at the front of the room. Even some of the hardened journalists had tears in their eyes before it ended.

Someone asked, 'Mr Hawke, how do you want to be remembered by the people?' I answered,

I guess as a bloke who loved his country, and still does, and loves Australians, and who was not essentially changed by high office. I hope they still will think of me as the Bob Hawke that they got to know, the larrikin trade union leader who perhaps had sufficient commonsense and intelligence to tone down his larrikinism to some extent and behave in a way that a Prime Minister should if he's going to be a proper representative of his people, but who in the end is essentially a dinky-di Australian. I hope that that's the way they'll think of me.

There was a good deal of humour in that last press conference. I laughed but it hurt. I had taken the party to victory four times, and no-one had ever looked like doing that before. According to all the independent evidence I was the one who got the party across the line, certainly on the last two occasions, probably three, and perhaps all four of them.

My final speech to Parliament was also an emotional experience. It was the last day of sittings and I had been scheduled to leave the next day to spend Christmas and the New Year at Kirribilli House, Sydney. Kirribilli now had a new resident and I noticed, with disappointment, his absence from the House when I made my last appearance.

In extending best wishes to Members and my staff I did not forget the Opposition, several of whom reciprocated generously.

In my time here as Prime Minister we have had some good jousts with you mob opposite and I embrace you entirely in [my] remarks ... Finally, as this will be my last speech in this chamber as Prime Minister ... I would sincerely like to thank all my ministerial colleagues and those of my party who have accorded me the privilege of leading this party, this Government and this great country over the last nine years. It is

impossible to tell you what pride I feel that you have given me
that opportunity. I thank you most sincerely.

Hansard records: 'Whereupon honourable members stood and
applauded.'

I was told by officers of the House that this had never happened
before. When I had finished speaking, Members from both sides came
forward to shake my hand and embrace me. I always have a special
affection for my own people but I will never forget the tears in the eyes
of some Opposition Members as they thanked me for the job I had
done. I will remember in particular the words of one of them: 'You
were a Prime Minister for all Australians.'

To have been given the opportunity to lead my country as it
prepares to meet the challenges, and the dangers, of the twenty-first
century has been an honour and a privilege – and, above all else, it has
been a pleasure.

APPENDICES
APPENDIX ONE – SPEECHES

EXTRACT FROM SPEECH TO THE BIENNIAL CONFERENCE OF THE ZIONIST FEDERATION OF AUSTRALIA AND NEW ZEALAND IN SYDNEY ON 26TH JANUARY 1974

... This then is the reality with which we are confronted – eighteen Arab States covering thirteen million square kilometres and Israel, even with the post-1967 lines (90,000 square kilometres) in control of much less than 1 per cent of that figure, threatened constantly with extinction. And in the light of this reality I do not know what language means if we talk of even-handedness. The policy of the party to which I belong is brief, and, I believe, clear in its implications – the full Resolution is: 'The situation in the Middle East remains the greatest threat to the peace of the world. There can be no peace until the Arab States respect and recognise Israel's sovereignty and right to exist. Equally, there can be no peace until Israeli forces have withdrawn from occupied territories to secure and recognised boundaries and a just settlement of the refugee problem is achieved.'

The very crux of that policy is manifestly the requirement of the Arab States to recognise the right of Israel to exist. Without that recognition there can by definition be no 'secure and recognised boundaries' behind which Israeli forces can withdraw. On their part the Arab States by word and action have consistently demonstrated their rejection of this basic premise. The latest Arab demonstration has cost Israel 2,500 dead, the equivalent for Australia of the loss of more than 10,000 of our young men. Israel, on its part, has made it clear that it will withdraw from occupied territories when its right to exist is recognised, and secure and recognised boundaries are established. Equally it has consistently asserted its preparedness to include the refugee problem on the negotiating agenda for the purposes of achieving a just settlement of that problem. There is no way in logic or morality to distil from an amalgam of those facts an even-handedness of judgement.

Oil is a murky substance and it has, I believe, blurred the vision of men of goodwill. I think there is not the slightest doubt that, were there not the huge reserves of that commodity beneath the sands of these countries, the world would have had a clearer view of where the balance lies in this matter. We can and must be even-handed in our compassion for people whatever their race, colour or creed – I have no greater love for Jew than for Arab. We can and must be even-handed in our demand for justice, equity and a fair distribution of resources for ordinary people wherever they reside – Israel cannot claim to have been perfect in everything that it has done and where criticism is warranted it should be made. But we cannot be even-handed in judgement between States, any more than between individuals, where one side is bent upon the physical destruction of the other.

In the 1930s appeasement under threat and blackmail permitted, among other things, the holocaust in which six million of our fellow human beings, who happened to be Jews, were exterminated. All mankind was diminished by those events. I do not speak here for my party or for the industrial movement which I lead. But as an individual Australian, I know that I am not an island and I know that if we allow the bell to be tolled for Israel it will have tolled for me, for us all, and we will all to that extent again have been diminished ...

Speech at opening of CHOGM, Nassau, the Bahamas, 16th October 1985

We Commonwealth leaders assembled here at Nassau are the inheritors of a great tradition. It is the tradition of a Commonwealth emerged from Empire; like most great traditions it is not without flaw or blemish. But the very fact that we are a Commonwealth that has emerged from Empire with a greater measure of common purpose is itself a measure of the strength of this tradition.

Let us at the outset of this Meeting ask ourselves the question – what have been the elements, the secret if you like, of that strength? And let us ask that question seeking to find in the answer a guide in discharging our high responsibilities.

If I could put it in a simple phrase, I believe the essence of that strength has been in an understanding of the limits of power.

Let me be precise. In the immediate post-war period, it would have been possible for Britain to maintain for longer than it did the colonial status of the Indian sub-continent. It had the instruments of power to do so, but it understood the limits of that power. And those limits were understood through a proper perception of the force of other rights and interests which together constituted a countervailing power. These included the right and determination of peoples to be free to determine their different destinies; and it included an enlightened self-interest on the part of a Britain which understood that, in the long term, its own economic, political and strategic concerns would be better protected by accommodating the new realities.

This countervailing power is not so susceptible to measurement as the power that can be accounted in battalions, squadrons and the elements of military and economic weaponry. But all our history as a Commonwealth has shown that it is no less real for that reason. It has an inexorable capacity to grow and ultimately to overcome those who would take refuge in this sterile accounting of conventional power.

Some would argue that, at times, the limits of power have not been understood sufficiently early. It has been argued of Britain. It has been equally argued of Australia, in relation to Papua New Guinea.

But I repeat, we assemble as a unique institution representing a quarter of the world's population, one-third of its sovereign and independent nations, meeting as equals because, however falteringly at times, we have together learned the limits of power. And that learning process has given the Commonwealth a particular capacity to recognise in time the need for change; to discern civilised directions for change; and, at important moments, to be an effective agent for change.

If my answer then to this question – what is the secret of the strength of our Commonwealth tradition – is correct, I believe it can usefully inform our approach to the major issues before us in the coming week.

Without doubt the predominent of these is, and should be, South Africa, an issue of historic concern to the Commonwealth. If ever there was a regime which should have learnt from our experience the lesson of the limits of power it is that in South Africa.

They are the sterile accountants of our day who would measure their capacity to insulate themselves against the pressure of inevitable change by the size of their military arsenal. They are wrong. For the force of that countervailing power is growing, it is inexorable and it is unquenchable. The spirit of men and women yearning to be free, to have that right to determine their own destiny, will not be extinguished. It will not be extinguished, however brutally that arsenal is unleashed upon them.

The world that is witness to events in South Africa is becoming increasingly impatient. I believe it is looking to us to draw upon our tradition, to seek to apply to South Africa the lessons we have learned from our own experience. This will require us to strengthen, by our decisions, the countervailing power that is growing by the day within and outside South Africa. This will require us to examine and to be prepared to implement the option of further effective economic sanctions.

But just as importantly it will require us to sustain the flame of enlightened self-interest that has now been lit in South Africa, and is manifest in the recent talks in Lusaka between representatives of South African business and the ANC. For the fact is that all the economic capacity that has been established in South Africa and which now disproportionately benefits the few, will only endure and be available for the benefit of all if a new, free and just South Africa is created.

Equally, Australia believes that all nations have a duty to encourage the two superpowers to recognise the limits of power. They have the capacity not only to destroy each other a thousand times over but indeed to obliterate the human race from the face of this planet. This threat, and the squandering of resources it entails, is now central to the concerns of mankind.

And so, while repudiating the illusory calls of unilateral disarmament, we from this Commonwealth have the opportunity to bring the pressure of our resolution upon the superpowers to understand and discharge their obligations to all peoples to work for the progressive reduction of nuclear arsenals through balanced and verifiable agreements.

The peoples of the South Pacific have themselves projected this resolve by their recent successful introduction of the South Pacific Nuclear Free Zone Treaty.

Finally, in our deliberations in the economic area we should acknowledge the limits of power. Australia believes that we live in an era in which recognition of the mutual benefits of a multilateral trading system are in danger of disappearing. Increasingly there are those who would embrace the ultimately self-defeating power of protectionism. This is a dangerous outlook, and one which we should seek, by our work together, to dispel.

We have learned from our experience, we reflect in our tradition, that conflict can give way to harmony. We rightly accept as an article of shared faith that the colour of people's skin is as irrelevant as the colour of their eyes to their political, economic and social rights.

Let us by our approach to our task in the coming days, and by the decisions we take, not only confirm this article of faith within the Commonwealth but seek to make it a reality for all those who look to us for help.

'BUILDING A COMPETITIVE AUSTRALIA', PARLIAMENTARY STATEMENT
TO THE HOUSE OF REPRESENTATIVES, 12TH MARCH 1991

... Today I want to speak with my fellow Australians, not in the jargon of economists but in terms that we can all understand. I do this because, while I will be announcing decisions of fundamental economic importance for the future of this country, the securing of that future is in the hands of each one of us.

Government has the responsibility to lead the community by getting the right policy framework – and we will do that. But it is only with the understanding, the commitment, of all Australians – as individuals, and through their representative organisations – that our nation will best meet the challenges ahead.

What are those challenges? The first is for us all to realise that this tough, increasingly competitive world of five and a half billion people does not owe, and will not give, seventeen million Australians an easy prosperity. The days of our being able to hitch a free ride in a world clamouring, and prepared to pay high prices, for our rural and mineral products, are behind us. From this fact flows everything else.

The challenge for the foreseeable future, is to produce more than we spend. The rest of the world will not allow us to continue indefinitely to live beyond our means by borrowing from them. Our rural and mineral products will remain important into the future. But the challenge is to add to them. That is, we must export more manufactured goods and services and substitute more quality Australian production for imports.

The challenge is therefore to make the decisions and adopt the practices and attitudes which will enable this and succeeding generations to achieve those basic goals.

Those are the challenges. How we are prepared together to meet them will determine the standards we can enjoy and the kind of Australia we will pass on to our children. I will today announce a package of substantial new measures directed to the fundamental task facing this nation: improving the productive capacity of an economy that will be more internationally competitive. Highlights of the package are: tariff cuts, reduced wholesale sales taxes for business, substantial business savings through simpler depreciation, retraining assistance, new support for apprentices and further initiatives in education and research to build the 'clever country'.

... All these measures continue and intensify the far-reaching reforms my Government has initiated over the past eight years. Ultimately, they sharpen our ability to reduce the current account deficit and stabilise foreign debt. I emphasise that they share one overriding objective: building a more competitive Australia.

In this statement I will reaffirm for the Australian people the longer-term economic goals to which we aspire, and identify the progress we are making towards them.

And I want all my fellow Australians to understand where the nation is moving and to understand how all of us – workers, employers and government – have complementary roles to play in achieving our common goals. I say it again: in the final analysis the challenges ahead demand the involvement of all Australians.

... The Australian economy is currently at or near the bottom of a downturn that has been sharper, deeper and more prolonged than we anticipated. I acknowledge the recession has hurt many people and cost many jobs, and that is something I regret deeply. Higher unemployment is likely in coming months. Rural Australia in particular is experiencing a very tough period.

There are some important global factors at work. But I do not walk away from my Government's ultimate responsibility to manage the national economy. And we certainly do not resile from having taken the necessary decision to squeeze demand by high interest rates.

Policy makers and commentators, in Australia and around the world, underestimated the strength of resurgent demand in the wake of the 1987 share market crash. But with the benefit of hindsight, it is clear that had we acted sooner to dampen that surge, some of the current hardship could have been avoided.

The question facing us now is not: will we emerge from the recession? For the decisions necessary to end the recession have already been taken: official interest rates have been brought down by 6 percentage points over the last fourteen months; and tax cuts paid on 1 January will also stimulate demand. Business will begin to rebuild stocks, and international confidence will be helped by the successful end of the Gulf war.

There are testing months immediately ahead. But the best estimate is that we will be coming out of the recession in the second half of this year.

So the real question, and the real challenge, facing us is: how can we ensure that when we emerge from the recession we will be best equipped to take up the opportunities for sustained growth? In particular we have the opportunity to secure economic recovery:

- with low inflation
- and hence lower interest rates
- in an increasingly competitive and productive economy.

And this Government is determined to seize that opportunity.

That is what this Statement is really about today. It is not about short term palliatives, but longer term structural change to make us a more competitive nation.

That was what my Government set out, eight years ago, to achieve – through fundamental reform of long established economic institutions and of deeply entrenched attitudes. We still have a long way to go but today we can certainly say that, together, we have made substantial progress: we are more open to the world and we are more efficient at home.

We are becoming more competitive.

1. Tariffs and Australia's trading future

... the most powerful spur to greater competitiveness is further tariff reduction. Tariffs have been one of the abiding features of the Australian economy since Federation. Tariffs protected Australian industry by making foreign goods more expensive here; and the supposed virtues of this protection became deeply embedded in the psyche of the nation.

But what in fact was the result?

- Inefficient industries that could not compete overseas; and
- higher prices for consumers and higher costs for our efficient primary producers.

Worse still, tariffs are a regressive burden – that is, the poorest Australians are hurt more than the richest. The Industry Commission estimates that the burden tariffs imposed on lowest-income Australians is three times heavier than that imposed on those with the highest incomes.

Right from the start, this Government deliberately and determinedly set about pulling down the tariff walls. By 1992 our existing programs will have slashed the nominal rate of assistance to the manufacturing sector by over one-third, from 13 to 8 per cent, and the effective rate from 22 to 12 per cent.

The results, the benefits, have been dramatic. Since 1985, manufacturing output, employment and exports have all expanded at rates faster than the Organisation for Economic Cooperation and Development average. For the Australian consumer and business, prices for many goods are lower than they would otherwise have been.

Tariff cuts presented Australian manufacturers with a major challenge. To their credit, many of them are meeting that challenge. Their endeavours are too rarely appreciated and their success too often underestimated.

... this Government will continue to open up the manufacturing sector and Australian industry generally through lower protection. I now announce:

- the general level of assistance will be reduced from 10 per cent and 15 per cent in 1992 to a general rate of 5 per cent by 1996;
- tariffs on passenger motor vehicles will be phased down from 35 per cent in 1992 in annual steps of 2.5 per cent to 15 per cent in the year 2000.

This change can be expected to result in an average real reduction of $2000 to $3000 in the price of a $20 000 car, in today's dollars, over the next decade.

I also announce:

- tariff reductions on textile, clothing and footwear will be accelerated so that the maximum tariff will be 25 per cent by the year 2000 and the termination of quotas will be brought forward two years to 1 March 1993; and

- general agricultural assistance will be reduced in line with the pace of tariff reform in manufacturing.

The dimension of what we have achieved is demonstrated by the fact that these changes will bring the average nominal rate of assistance down to 3 per cent, and the average effective rate down to 5 per cent, by the end of the decade.

All these changes will help keep inflation, and therefore interest rates, down. They will also make our exporters and our import competing sector more competitive by lowering the cost of their inputs. The overall impact of the reforms will be a net gain in employment, although jobs will be lost in declining industries.

Throughout my public life it has been my firm conviction that if the community believes that change is necessary in the interests of the community as a whole, then that belief carries with it a necessary corollary – that the community must not leave those individuals or groups who are adversely affected to bear the whole burden of change. It must itself be prepared to share that burden of change, as well as reaping the benefits of change. Accordingly, we will establish labour adjustment programs to assist displaced workers in our car and textiles, clothing and footwear industries with relocation, training, and wages subsidies for redeployment to other jobs. This will cost at least $90 million over the life of the programs … [W]ith these tariff cuts, we demonstrate once again our commitment to liberalising international trade.

The Government has been fortified in this approach by a number of recent reports, not least Dr Ross Garnaut's report *Australia and the North-East Asian Ascendancy*. We have rejected the views of the so-called 'new protectionists' because they are simply proposing, in effect, the same discredited policies that had isolated our national economy from the rest of the world and caused the great damage we are all working to repair.

However much our competitors might bend or break the principles of fair trade, our own self-interest is served by a steadfast refusal to return to the days of protectionism. But I do not for a minute seek to excuse those nations who do flout the rules of international trade, especially those who have caused so much damage to our farm trade.

The problem lies in the inadequacy of the rules on agriculture under the General Agreement on Tariffs and Trade. GATT has been an outstanding success in substantially reducing manufacturing protection around the world. As a result, world trade in manufactures has boomed. But at the same time, agricultural trade has been absolutely corrupted – particularly by the European Community and to a lesser extent by the United States and Japan.

Recently, their combined farm subsidies have averaged more than $300 billion a year, not aggregated over a period of time, but they have averaged $300 billion a year. This is for a sector which produces only about 3 per cent of their GDP. This has imposed a heavy burden on our farmers; despite consistent large productivity gains, they exported the same volume of goods in 1989–90 as they did 10 years earlier. While world trade thrived, agriculture, one of our most important, competitive and significant sectors, has marked time.

So what further steps can we take to improve our trading position?

First, we will maintain our vigorous international campaign to achieve equal treatment for agriculture under the GATT umbrella. The Europeans already accept, due in no small way to the efforts of the Cairns Group, led by Australia, that there can be no result in the Uruguay Round negotiations without substantial reform of agricultural trade. We will keep pushing them as hard as we possibly can.

Members on both sides of this Parliament have recently visited

Washington, and will travel to Europe in coming months, to urge both sides to avoid the chaos and insanity of a trade war. This international campaign by Australia depends for its credibility and impact on one thing: on our general willingness to practise at home what we preach abroad.

Second, the Minister for Primary Industries and Energy (Mr Kerin) will announce a rural adjustment package in April to ensure that those farmers most in need during the current rural crisis receive appropriate assistance.

Third, we will help our farmers and manufacturers take effective action against foreign producers who seek to dump their products on the Australian market at unfair prices. We will strengthen anti-dumping procedures, including by cutting 40 days off the time taken to process complaints.

Fourth, the preferential tariff arrangements for Singapore, Taiwan, Hong Kong and the Republic of Korea will be phased out from 1 July 1992.

Fifth, we will provide $2 million to continue the 'Australian-made' campaign, since reducing our reliance on imports is totally complementary, in economic terms, to expanding our performance in exports.

Sixth, we will upgrade the services available to Australian exporters. In particular:

- We will boost the capital base and range of services provided by the Export Finance Insurance Corporation by making available a $200 million callable capital base to supplement EFIC's existing reserves.
- A new $50 million facility will be made available by EFIC, to enable Australian exporters to meet demands for performance bonds without using their own reserves.
- We will create a new program of fellowships so that Australian business men and women, and recent graduates, can get direct working experience in the Asia–Pacific region.
- We will implement the McKinsey report recommendations including refocusing Austrade's efforts on the Asia–Pacific region.
- We will transfer responsibility for Austrade to the Minister for Trade and Overseas Development from 1 September.

2. Greater efficiency and competition within Australia
... with further tariff cuts, we are dismantling the barriers to competitiveness and efficiency that stand at the borders of Australia.

This Government is also set on dismantling the barriers that exist within Australia. We have pioneered the concept, and the delivery, of microeconomic reform – seen by industry, rightly, as an essential means towards higher productivity and efficiency.

We are freeing up our transport systems; we have revolutionised our taxation system; we are creating more efficient workplaces; we are injecting competition where for too long Australian firms and public sector enterprises have been content with the quiet life. And we are reforming the processes of Government itself through the Special Premiers' Conferences.

In all this, perhaps no issue has achieved the prominence of the waterfront – essential to our export performance.

It is particularly satisfying to be able to report to the House on the achievement, just last week, of a new agreement that will deliver breakthroughs in waterfront productivity. The agreement between the Waterside Workers' Federation and Conaust Ltd, following an earlier agreement with National Terminals (Australia) Ltd, now means waterfront employees and the two largest waterfront employers are committed to a total restructuring of their industry.

In describing the significance of this latest agreement ... I can do no better than to quote the words of Mr Richard Setchell, the Chairman of Conaust, who said it was 'a win for the economy and the international competitiveness of Australia'. By year's end, the national waterfront labour force will have been cut by over 1,500 – in anyone's language, a major gain in efficiency. In all, the agreements provide for productivity gains of up to 60 per cent; in smaller ports and in grain handling, 70 per cent.

What appeared an ambitious program when we commenced these reforms, is now proceeding on schedule, and without major industrial disputes.

In shipping, we are ahead of schedule in delivering smaller, more efficient crews on existing vessels and the introduction of new ships crewed at manning levels equal to or better than those of our major trading partners.

In telecommunications, in aviation, in road and rail transport, in removing through national uniform regulations the requirement for business to meet six or seven different standards, we are achieving fundamental gains in efficiency.

... this activity amounts to the most ambitious plan, the most rapid pace, and the most comprehensive sweep of micro-economic reform this country has ever seen. Productivity is increasing, and new investment is taking place – all without industrial disruption.

And here we are witness to a paradox. Those who for more than a generation in office entrenched the inadequacies of the past and themselves effected no change whatsoever, now with an hypocrisy that is truly breathtaking, clamour for even faster change.

They bear an onus, which they simply cannot discharge, of showing how in a practical way this could be achieved without poisoning the better industrial relations and investment environment we have created – without, in short, bringing the whole reform process to a grinding halt.

It is a matter of our results versus their rhetoric.

We will press ahead with further reform, to increase competition and efficiency within Australia. For the consumer, competition means lower prices and a broader range of better quality goods and services; for producers it provides the spur to better performance – at home and abroad.

We want to see the whole domestic economy opened up to this kind of positive structural change. And we have established a sub-committee of Cabinet's Structural Adjustment Committee to examine systematically the whole economy for opportunities to promote this process.

The Trade Practices Act is our principal legislative weapon to ensure consumers get the best deal from competition. But there are many areas of the Australian economy today that are immune from that Act: some

Commonwealth enterprises, State public sector businesses, and significant areas of the private sector, including the professions.

This patchwork coverage reflects historical and constitutional factors, not economic efficiencies; it is another important instance of the way we operate as six economies, rather than one. The benefits for the consumer of expanding the scope of the Trade Practices Act could be immense: potentially lower professional fees, cheaper road and rail fares, cheaper electricity.

This has to be done – and I have initiated the process, by today writing to the Premiers urging a positive examination of all we can do, at the May Special Premiers Conference, to widen the ambit of the Trade Practices Act to bring such excluded areas within the scope of a national framework of competition policy and law.

3. Investment for the 1990s
... to secure sustainable economic growth and the living standards to which we aspire, we need to ensure that there is a fertile environment for investment.

Our efforts to repair the macro-economic fundamentals underpinned rapid investment growth in the late 1980s – through the Accord, through floating the dollar, and through cutting Government spending. There is, however, one other fundamental which is crucial to investment: inflation.

It is vital that Australians understand the debilitating nature of the inflation disease. High inflation has brought high interest rates and a higher cost of capital than in our trading partners. This, in turn, undermined investment and made it harder for Australian firms to compete overseas. It has also discouraged productive investment in areas that would generate jobs and exports in favour of speculation in real estate. But today we have the opportunity, as I have said, of putting Australia on a low inflation path.

Australia's inflation is now below the OECD average: ours is 6.9 per cent and just 5.4 per cent in underlying terms and theirs is 7.2 per cent. A continued lowering of inflation is, without doubt, the major contribution this Government can make to the climate for investment in the 1990s.

Of course new investment, combined with lower tariffs, has meant, and will mean for a time, higher imports and a higher current account deficit. This becomes even more obvious at times when commodity prices are falling, as they are now due to the slowdown in world economic growth.

But this is a short term cost we must bear if we are to wind back the current account deficit in a sustainable way and thereby reduce our foreign indebtedness permanently. We are taking the essential steps to build an economy that is stronger in the longer term.

And there are other important areas where we can take action to foster productive investment.

The Government is very concerned at the difficulty which small and medium-sized Australian companies face in raising long term funds. We are pursuing discussions with major financial institutions aimed at overcoming this difficulty by ensuring a readier flow of such funds.

The development of new industry and the rejuvenation of the old depends on ready access to appropriately skilled labour – access which is increasingly difficult in our sprawling cities, with their often inefficient transport systems. These factors also reduce the quality of life for the residents affected. We are cooperating with State and local governments to develop effective approaches to these issues.

... this Government has done more than any other to reform the taxation system so that, as far as possible, tax considerations do not distort investment decisions.

Today I announce:

- A substantial widening of exemptions from sales tax for business inputs used by manufacturers, primary producers and miners. The cost to revenue of this measure will amount in 1992–93 to $375 million. But the cost benefits to producers, allowing for the effects of mark-ups as goods pass along the production chain, will in that year total around $700 million.

- We have radically overhauled depreciation provisions to bring them more in line with business realities. The reforms to be announced provide, for the first time, a definition in the Act of effective life and, importantly, it will allow self-assessment by the taxpayer. This will result in savings to business of the order of $100 million in 1992–93.
- Expenditure on environmental impact statements will be fully tax deductible over 10 years.

An industry which will benefit from these new tax provisions is tourism, which has generated over 100,000 new jobs during the 1980s and has the potential for very substantial further expansion.

One sector of the Australian economy is unique in terms of the investment environment in which it operates – the forest industries. This Government's consistent commitment is to the proper protection of our precious native forests. This has been, and remains, fundamental to our approach to Government.

But we recognise that – in part due to this commitment – there has been a contraction of the forest resource allocated to existing operations in the industry. Concern about future access to the resource has made new investment uncertain. Accordingly, the Government has decided to provide resource security for major new wood processing projects

- where the project involves a capital-intensive, value-adding investment of $100 million or more and is directed to export or to import replacement;
- where the proponent of the project makes a commitment to adhere to environment, heritage and Aboriginal policy requirements; and
- where the State Government agrees to enact parallel resource security legislation.

Resource security will involve undertakings, backed by legislation, guaranteeing an agreed volume of timber supply from an identified catchment area. There will also be provision in the legislation to establish plantations to provide for long term timber supply. The objective is to phase out woodchip exports by the year 2000 or soon after, and replace them with value-added products. This new emphasis on plantations will also, over time, take pressure off our native forests.

... the Government decided on resource security legislation only after receiving unqualified legal advice that it was the sole way the Commonwealth could provide a binding undertaking of the kind necessary to get major projects started which will provide new exports and new jobs.

Government has a duty to listen to and understand all legitimate community interests. It has a responsibility then to seek as far as possible to balance those interests where they compete. It should, where appropriate, establish processes aimed to achieve that purpose. In the end, Government must do what it was elected to do and make the necessary decisions. This will mean facing up to tough issues and it will rarely entail universal approbation.

So it is in this case where I believe my Government has struck the correct balance between environmental concerns – to which our commitment remains vital and unambiguous – and the interests of one of Australia's largest industries.

4. Becoming a clever country

... I said at the outset that securing the future of the country is in the hands of each one of us. To achieve change, we must mobilise our most valuable resource: the talents of the Australian people.

This does not necessarily mean working harder; in Germany and Japan, both highly successful competitive countries, working hours are actually falling. But it does mean working smarter – working more effectively, using new materials, new production technologies and new management methods. It means being, like Germany and Japan, a clever country.

During the last election campaign I said Australia needed to become a clever country. The centrepiece of my commitment to that goal was the creation of a network of Cooperative Research Centres. I said that these Centres would draw together outstanding research groups to provide new drive to our national research effort.

Today I announce that the Government has selected the first fifteen Cooperative Research Centres. These Centres will focus their research effort on projects in the following key areas:

- resource based industries;
- manufacturing and information industries;
- the environment; and
- medical research.

My colleague the Minister for Science and Technology (Mr Crean) will provide details of successful projects this week.

The Government has also decided to continue indefinitely the tax deduction for spending on research and development at 125 per cent.

Cooperation with our talented neighbours in the region is important if we are to remain at the frontiers of technology. The Multi-Function Polis provides an opportunity to do this. Next month the Government will receive the report of the MFP–Adelaide Management Group which was set up to assess the economic and social viability of the MFP.

Cleverness is not confined to our universities and 'hi-tech' firms. Cleverness is something that should permeate the entire society – and especially our workplaces. And the foundation of a clever country is its education system. I have repeatedly, as you know, stated my pride in our achievements in virtually doubling the school retention rate, and expanding the number of tertiary places. Quite simply, unless we give our young people the motivation and the opportunity to bring out the best in themselves through education, we shall never be able to bring out the best in ourselves as a nation.

Today I announce

- an increase in the number and average value of Australian Postgraduate Research Awards;
- extra funding of $15 million over three years for the Country Areas Program to focus on greater rural school retention; and
- $10 million over three years in a community project to identify the key elements of good schooling.

Ours is a dynamic region, in a world of ceaseless technological innovation and burgeoning knowledge-based industries. In a clever country, all of us, as workers and managers, need to upgrade our job skills regularly.

A recession can savagely damage the job skills of a nation. Apprentices have been hit particularly hard in the past – young Australians seeking to acquire and improve their job skills have been laid off with their training incomplete. Accordingly, I announce a new program of assistance so that employers can retain and improve the skills of apprentices and other workers who would otherwise be working reduced hours or have been retrenched.

We will also spend $74 million over two years to provide work experience opportunities for people unemployed for more than six months; we will commit $50 million over the next fifteen months to provide additional pre-vocational training places, and we will seek State cooperation in this. We will provide $6 million over three years to strengthen management skills.

Education is clearly a vital preparation for the work force in a clever country, but it is in the workplace itself that the skills must be developed if they are to yield the productivity dividend we so desperately need in our enterprises.

Our trade union movement has made an enormous contribution to the creation of a more efficient Australia. Union amalgamations involving workers in metals, the public service, health, textiles, timber products and telecommunications have already been concluded. There are some 50 other amalgamations currently under way. The Government will commit a further $1.5 million to assist this process in 1991–92. I also pay tribute to those employers who, in partnership with the trade unions, have secured major gains through award restructuring and workplace reform.

My Government has provided financial assistance to this process and we will virtually double our financial support over the next few years.

The Business Council of Australia has proposed a major research project on international performance benchmarks of business input services. We have directed the Bureau of Industry Economics, with the cooperation of the BCA, to undertake this project at a cost of $1.8 million over four years.

The Pappas Carter Report commissioned by the Australian Manufacturing Council, and recent publications by EPAC, have placed particular emphasis on the importance of changing the workplace culture. In cooperation with the AMC, we will develop a program to raise the efficiency of Australian enterprises to world standards. We will draw on the experience of our own world class companies together with the best practice that can be found anywhere in the world in this endeavour.

I am particularly pleased to announce that John Prescott, Managing Director of BHP and Chairman of the AMC, has agreed to chair the board that will oversee the new program. We have earmarked $25 million over two years for the program.

... the measures I have announced today are absolutely vital for the continued transformation of the Australian economy. At the same time, they compromise neither our demonstrated commitment to fiscal restraint nor our medium term objective to maintain the structural integrity of the Budget. Their total costs in outlays and forgone revenue are $33 million in 1990–91, $446 million in 1991–92 and $854 million in 1992–93.

... this Government has never been in doubt about the kind of Australia we wish to build – a modern, growing, prosperous and competitive economy, within a tolerant and fair society; a nation where quality of life counts for as much as quantity of output; an outward-looking community, enmeshed with the dynamism of the Asia–Pacific region, and capable of taking on the best the world has to offer – and winning.

These are not short-term goals; they are not transitory values. They are deeply embedded in the character of this Government and of the Party I have the honour of leading.

This process of modernisation, of adaptation to the changing world economy, is not something that has some future cut-off point. It must be a continuing process. There is no point at which we can say, reform is finished – because there is no point at which the world will stop changing.

And this is the essential point … We live in a world of unprecedented, indeed breathtaking, change. Our own region is a crucible for change. We can no longer afford the easy simplicities, the costly complacencies of the fifties and sixties and seventies. I say 'costly' because we are now paying the price for the neglect of those decades.

Our task now is to make sure that future generations are not called upon to pay a similar price for any neglect or complacency on our part, in this make-or-break decade.

We need the habit of adaptation – because the lesson of international competitiveness must be constantly learned and re-learned.

If we get the basics right in these critical years we need not set limits on our prospects. I do not avoid the fact that I hold these prospects out to you at a time of recession. But we should understand that Australia comes to this task with two great advantages – enduring advantages that transcend the temporary, but real, difficulties of the recession.

First, we bring to the task our great natural and acquired endowments as a nation – our vast material resources, our vibrant multicultural community, our strengths as a free and prosperous people, our proximity to the fastest growing regional economy in the world.

Second, in meeting these tremendous challenges that lie ahead, we are not, in 1991, starting out from scratch. We are not, in this decade, coming to the task cold. We have already taken many of the essential decisions, we have already learned many of the vital lessons, we are already enmeshing ourselves with our region, we have already mastered many of the skills that we will need, to enter the next century with well-founded confidence that we will reach our goals.

But we must face the fact unflinchingly that we need, as a nation, to equip ourselves further, to meet the challenges of exposure to international competition. That has been central to the endeavour of this Government. It is central to the theme of this statement. It is the central purpose of the measures that I have announced today. It must remain the central challenge of this great nation for decades to come.

I restate my belief with which I began: the involvement, the commitment of all Australians is the vital ingredient to success in the challenge ahead. It is a challenge that, together, we can face and meet with confidence.

APPENDIX TWO –
MICRO-ECONOMIC REFORM

There is universal acceptance that the period of government between 1983 and 1991 produced the most extensive micro-economic reform in Australian history. The major decisions up to 1987 were the float of the dollar, the removal of foreign exchange controls and domestic interest rate direct controls, and the introduction of foreign competition in the banking sector.

The period 1987–89 saw the following reforms:
- a decision to abolish the two airline policy and removal of fare and capacity restrictions;
- the reinvigoration and utilisation of the Industry Commission as the principal tool for establishing the parameters of reform of industry policy;
- removal of a range of export controls on bulk commodities;
- removal of controls over crude-oil marketing;
- removal of bilateral air freight restrictions;
- removal of rail reservation restrictions and related reforms following the Royal Commission into Grain Storage and Handling;
- removal of Passenger Motor Vehicle (PMV) quotas and tariff phase-down;
- general tariff reductions – tops down to 15 per cent and 10 per cent by 1992;

- removal of restrictions on competitiveness of Government Business Enterprises, implementation of rate of return, corporate planning targets;
- Telecommunications Reform Package May 1988: allowed effective competition in the provision of customer premises equipment (eg PABX), value-added services (eg answering machines) and other telecommunications services (eg phone maintenance, installation of second and subsequent phones) through regulatory changes and the establishment of AUSTEL. This independent body subsumed Telecom's regulatory functions, so allowing effective competition;
- the shipping industry reform process which reduced manning on Australian vessels to internationally competitive levels without loss of a day in industrial disputes;
- the waterfront reform process;
- award restructuring, enterprise bargaining and workplace reform;
- reform of Commonwealth agricultural support, including phasing out dairy levies and conversion of assistance to sugar, dried fruit, tobacco and citrus industries to tariffs and phase-down along with manufacturing;
- introduction of a permits system to allow some competition on coastal shipping routes;
- reform of airport development and airways charging by introducing 'user-pays' pricing and allowing industry-driven investment in aviation facilities;
- liberalised negotiation of Air Services Agreements to allow for rapid growth in tourism and increased competition on international routes.

These extensive reforms were followed in the period 1990–91 with these further decisions:

- direct, full network competition in telecommunications and unrestricted resale competition;
- further tariff reform with all rates to be reduced to 5 per cent by 1996 – the cumulative result of tariff decisions taken during the period of the Hawke Government will mean that the effective rate of assistance to

manufacturing will have fallen from 25 per cent to 5 per cent by the end of the decade;

- the removal of textile, clothing and footwear (TCF) quotas and phase-down of tariff protection for motor vehicle and TCF industries accelerated; and

- as a result of the Special Premiers Conference process:
  - a single-gauge national rail system under the National Rail Corporation,
  - mutual recognition legislation creating a national market for goods,
  - reform of electricity and gas industries commenced,
  - road transport reform,
  - reform of Commonwealth–State environmental assessment procedures.

APPENDIX THREE –
ABORIGINAL AFFAIRS

Some of the more important advances in areas specifically affecting Aboriginal Australians during the period 1983–91 were:

FUNDING
Government funding for Aboriginal programs increased in constant (1991–92) dollar terms by 96 per cent from $513 million in 1982–83 to $1005 million in 1991–92.

HEALTH
There are now eighty-four Aboriginal community-controlled health services, compared with twenty-seven in 1982–83.

In 1990, the Commonwealth secured the agreement of all States and Territories to the National Aboriginal Health Strategy (NAHS), which, for the first time, joined the Commonwealth, State and Territory Governments and Aboriginal communities in developing services for Aboriginal and Torres Strait Islander people.

In December 1990 the Government decided to contribute up to an additional $232 million over the next five years to implement the strategy in conjunction with significant contributions by the States and Territories.

The funds were principally directed to public health matters, housing and infrastructure.

HOUSING

In 1991–92 the Government provided $176 million for Aboriginal housing programs, compared with $71.1 million in 1982–83. The funding included the purchase and construction of about 1550 houses and renovations to a further 500 houses.

EDUCATION

Aboriginal enrolment in secondary schools increased from 20000 in 1982 to 30344 in 1990. Retention rates have risen from 10 per cent in 1982 to 28.9 per cent in 1990. Enrolment in higher education courses (excluding TAFE) increased from 845 in 1982 to more than 3000 in 1990.

The Aboriginal and Torres Strait Islander Education Policy was developed with State and Territory Governments and Aboriginal and Islander people in 1988 and $241 million was allocated in the first triennium. The Commonwealth has committed $266 million to the policy over the period 1990–92.

EMPLOYMENT

The Government introduced the Aboriginal Employment Development Policy (AEDP) in August 1986 to help achieve employment and income equity with other Australians for Aboriginal and Torres Strait Islander people by the year 2000, while reducing welfare dependency.

As a major part of the community-based employment strategy of the AEDP, the Community Development Employment Projects (CDEP) scheme expanded rapidly between 1986 and 1991.

In the early stages the scheme involved fewer than twenty communities and 1500 participants. By the end of 1990–91, largely as a result of its post-1986 expansion, the scheme had grown to involve over 170 communities and more than 17000 participants.

The scheme provides grants to Aboriginal and Torres Strait Islander communities and groups to employ people to work part-time on projects within their own community. People participating in the scheme receive wages in lieu of Job Search or Newstart allowances from the Department of Social Security. In addition to the wages component, up to 40 per cent of the grant is made up of funding to cover administration costs and the purchase of materials and equipment for projects.

HERITAGE PROTECTION

The Government established the first federal legislation to protect important Aboriginal sites and cultural property and objects. The *Aboriginal and Torres Strait Islander Heritage Protection Act* 1984 ensures areas and objects of significance to Australia's indigenous peoples are protected. Two declarations have been made for the long-term protection of significant sites near Alice Springs and Broome.

INFRASTRUCTURE

Commonwealth expenditure on infrastructure programs for Aboriginal and Torres Strait Islander communities – including for water, sewerage and other facilities – increased from $32 million in 1983–84 to $90.1 million in 1991–92.

LAND

In 1985 the Government granted title to Uluru National Park to an Aboriginal Land Trust, which leased the area back to the National Parks and Wildlife Service as a national park for all Australians. A similar agreement applies to Kakadu National Park.

On 10th September 1989 the Government granted about half the Nitmiluk (Katherine Gorge), which was a national park established by the Northern Territory Government, to the traditional owners – the Jawoyn people.

All land in the Warumungu land claim involving land around Tennant Creek has now been returned to traditional Aboriginal owners.

In September 1989 the Commonwealth and Northern Territory Governments agreed to provide secure title to living areas for Aboriginal people in pastoral districts. Twenty areas have been secured from the Northern Territory Government and the Commonwealth had by 1992 delivered title to all thirty-six areas on stock routes and reserves forming Commonwealth land.

In 1990 the Merapah station on Cape York became the first Queensland pastoral lease to be openly transferred to Aboriginal control. The property was purchased with Commonwealth funds by the former Aboriginal Development Commission.

ATSIC may also make grants to Aboriginal and Torres Strait Islander corporations for the acquisition of land.

NOTES

1 United States, Japan, Germany, France, Italy, United Kingdom and Canada.
2 See p. 41–2.
3 In 1956 the Arbitration Court became the Conciliation and Arbitration Commission.
4 See p. 39
5 It was open to workers to seek over-award payments through industrial action but they were inhibited by penal sanctions within the arbitration system and the possibility of action for damages in the civil courts.
6 Blanche d'Alpuget, *Robert J. Hawke: A Biography*, Reed Books Australia, Melbourne, 1982, p. 185.
7 Junie Morosi, Jim Cairns' personal assistant.
8 On 2nd October 1948 *The Economist* reported: 'Of the 62,000 Arabs who formerly lived in Haifa not more than 5,000 or 6,000 remained. Various factors influenced their decision to seek safety in flight. There is but little doubt that the most potent of the factors were the announcements made over the air by the Higher Arab Executive, urging the Arabs to quit ... It was clearly intimated that those Arabs who remained in Haifa and accepted Jewish protection would be regarded as renegades.'

The Jordanian newspaper *Falastin* wrote on 19th February 1949: 'The Arab States encouraged the Palestine Arabs to leave their homes temporarily in order to be out of the way of the Arab invasion armies.'
9 Neither Israel nor the world had to depend on their interpretation of these intentions. On 18th November 1965 President Nasser said: 'Our aim is the full restoration of the rights of the Palestinian people. In other words we aim at the destruction of the State of Israel. The immediate aim: perfection of Arab military

might. The national aim: the eradication of Israel.'

And in case anyone should have been left in any doubt, Nasser said on 26th May 1967 as the Arab States prepared for the attack which was defeated by the Israelis' pre-emptive strike: 'I have always known that we will be in a position to demand the removal of the UN Emergency Force when we have completed our preparations. And this is exactly what happened. Now the war will be general, and our aim – the destruction of Israel.'

[10] See Appendix One.

[11] 'Bob played a big role in preventing a faction-feud. While he had strong personal views about Hartley, and while he would have liked to pursue them, he didn't. He backed off very quickly from the idea that Hartley be expelled. He kept that executive under a tight rein for two days, determined to elicit all possible information about what had happened, determined to get a genuine, non-factional discussion. If only Whitlam had handled the Loans Affair in the same way that Hawke handled that executive – getting everything out in the open, admitting there had been an error – then the Loans Affair would never have damaged us the way it did, with bits and pieces of information dragged out like teeth, and the suspicion in everyone's mind that the full story was never revealed.' Blanche d'Alpuget, op. cit., pp. 299-300.

[12] For a detailed account, see Blanche d'Alpuget, op. cit., pp. 347-348.

[13] Blanche d'Alpuget, op. cit., pp. 343-345.

[14] See pp. 364–5.

[15] 1973 – Amalgamated Metal Workers Union; 1976 – Amalgamated Metal Workers and Shipwrights Union; 1983 – Amalgamated Metal Foundry and Shipwrights Union; 1985 – Amalgamated Metal Workers Union; 1991 – Metal and Engineering Workers Union; 1993 – Automotive Metal Engineering Union; 1994 – Automotive Food Metal and Engineering Union.

[16] Ross McMullin, *The Light on the Hill: The Australian Labor Party 1891–1991*, Oxford University Press, Melbourne, 1991, p. 234.

[17] See pp. 405–6.

[18] 'The Resolution of Conflict', 1979 Boyer Lectures, Australian Broadcasting Commission.

[19] See Paul Kelly, *The Hawke Ascendancy: A Definitive Account of its Origins and Climax 1975-1983*, Angus and Robertson Publishers, 1984, North Ryde, p. 329, ff.

[20] Some authors writing about the period of my Government pretend to be able to repeat with absolute precision words used by various characters in this ongoing saga. I make no such claim. What I have given here in quotation marks is my best recollection of a memorable effort by the inimitable Freudenburg.

[21] Hazel Hawke, *My Own Life: An Autobiography*, The Text Publishing Company, East Melbourne, 1992, p. 146.

[22] *Business Review Weekly*, 15th May 1987.

[23] Arthur as minister and we as government were helped by having as head of the Returned Services' League that very great Australian, Sir William Keys, a man reasonable in his demands and broad in his vision.

[24] Labor MP from 1937–66 and Minister for Commerce and Agriculture, 1946–49, in the Chifley Government.

[25] The popular tag for the Economic Review Committee under the Coalition.

[26] Monthly working days lost per thousand employees fell from 49 in 1976–82, to 19 in 1983–91.

[27] Harvey Barnett, *Tale of the Scorpion*, Allen & Unwin, Sydney, 1988, p.197.

[28] ibid., p. 189.

[29] David Marr, *The Ivanov Trail*, Thomas Nelson Australia, Melbourne, 1984 p. 301.

[30] Henry Kissinger, *Years of Upheaval*, Weidenfeld & Nicolson and Michael Joseph, London, 1982, pp. 80 – 81.

[31] See Chapter Twenty.

[32] See pp. 93–4.

[33] Membership of the South Pacific Forum in 1983 was: Australia, Cook Islands, Fiji, Kiribati, Nauru, Niue, New Zealand, Papua New Guinea, Solomon Islands, Tonga, Tuvalu, Vanuatu, Western Samoa. The Federated States of Micronesia was an observer. It became a member in 1987, as did the Republic of Marshall Islands.

[34] The members of the Association of South East Asian Nations (ASEAN) are: Indonesia, Malaysia, Philippines, Singapore, Thailand and Brunei.

[35] See pp. 110–111.

[36] Paul Dibb, *A Review of Australia's Defence Capabilities*, Report to the Minister for Defence, AGPS, Canberra, 1986.

[37] Tindal, in Katherine; Curtin, in Derby; Scherger, on the Cape York Peninsula, is under construction.

[38] Australia, House of Representatives, *Debates* (Hansard), 8th May 1984, p. 2026.

[39] Ross Garnaut, *Australia and the North East Asian Ascendancy*, AGPS, Canberra, 1990, pp. 6-7.

[40] Paul Kelly, *The End of Certainty: The Story of the 1980s*, Allen & Unwin, Sydney, 1992, pp. 86-87.

[41] 9th May 1984.

[42] '1929 and all that ...', the Shann Memorial Lecture 1984, delivered at the University of Western Australia on 27th August 1984.

[43] See pp. 472–3.

[44] After the 1984 election, the next two Parliaments ran the greater part of their three-year terms.

[45] See Chapter Eighteen.

[46] Hazel Hawke, op. cit., p. 166.

[47] ibid., p. 167.

[48] Morgan Gallup poll taken on the weekend of 15th and 16th September 1984, in *The Bulletin*, 2nd October 1984, p. 40.

[49] 'Labor in Power', ABC Television, broadcast on 15th June 1993.

[50] Australian National Opinion Polls, Labor's polling agency at the time.

[51] David Lange, *Nuclear Free – The New Zealand Way*, Penguin Books, Auckland, 1990.

[52] See p. 265.

[53] David Lange, op. cit., p. 90.

[54] 'Labor in Power: Taxing Times', ABC Television, broadcast on 15th June 1993.

[55] Australia, House of Representatives, *Debates* (Hansard), 2nd October 1984, p. 2719.

[56] Australia, House of Representatives, *Debates* (Hansard), 1st June 1984, p. 2720.

[57] *Inflation and Taxation: Report of the Committee of Inquiry into Inflation and Taxation*, AGPS, Canberra, 1975.

[58] See pp. 117–8.

[59] Australia, House of Representatives, *Debates* (Hansard), 2nd October 1984, p. 1335.

[60] The nine principles of tax reform were: no increase in the overall tax burden; provision of further cuts in personal income tax in any reform; the elimination of tax avoidance and tax evasion; simplification of the tax system; a fairer tax system; the removal or reduction of poverty traps; reforms, including changes to indirect tax, must be acceptable to the entire community; reforms must be optional for investment, growth and employment; and any reforms must include widespread community support and endorsement from the National Tax Summit.

[61] 'Labor in Power: Taxing Times', ABC Television, broadcast on 15th June, 1993.

[62] I am indebted to Labor historian Brian McKinlay for his reflections on Hughes in the ABC Radio series 'Prime Minister: The Labor Prime Ministers', broadcast on 'Broadband' 16th September 1980.

[63] 'Four Corners', ABC Television, broadcast on 19th August 1991.

[64] Paul Kelly, *The End of Certainty*, op. cit., p. 174.

[65] See Appendix One.

[66] Australia, House of Representatives, *Debates* (Hansard), South Africa Statement, 21st August 1986.

[67] Australia provided one of our ablest officials, Tony Cole – later Secretary of Treasury – to head this group which was generously assisted by further input from Jim Wolfensohn. The initial impact of their work was enhanced when it was published, on our initiative, in book form in 1989 – Ruth Ovenden and Tony Cole, *Apartheid and International Finance*, Penguin, Melbourne. For an assessment of my initiative, see Gareth Evans and Bruce Grant, *Australia's Foreign Relations in the World of the 1990s*, MUP, Melbourne, 1991, p.275.

[68] See Chinese People's Institute of Foreign Affairs, *Foreign Affairs Journal* No.28, June 1993, pp. 6-7. '... In China, the historical 14th Party Congress had achieved two major accomplishments, the endorsement of the goal of establishing a socialist market economy and the election of a younger party leadership, including a new Central Committee, a Political Bureau and its Standing Committee.

The establishment of a socialist economy represents a significant breakthrough in China's economic theory. The shift from 'planned commodity economy' to 'market economy' will bring about a fundamental restructuring of the country's economic system, providing necessary conditions for China's economy to be gradually integrated with that of the world, and gaining faster and better results in her economic reforms. As to the younger Party leadership, nearly half of the Central Committee members are new faces, three-fifths being under the age of fifty-five. This will ensure continuity of Party policies into the next century. A striking feature of this congress is that economic construction will continue to be the nation's most urgent and fundamental task and the Party's basic line of economic construction has been institutionalised with the inclusion of many younger representatives in the central leadership...'

[69] See pp. 89–92.

[70] See pp. 77, 89–92.

[71] **Australia's Manufactured Exports to Japan**

	1983	1984	1985	1986	1987	1988	1989	1990	1991
Manufactured exports ($A million)	6302	7041	9054	9045	9661	11489	12441	13441	14820
Manufactured as % of total exports	5.1	9.0	8.9	9.0	13.8	17.6	17.2	14.8	14.0

These figures graphically demonstrate how Australian industry responded to the challenge I set out in a speech to the Kansai Federation of Economic Organisations in Osaka on 3rd February 1984:

'The Australian trade relationship with Japan is at something of a cross-roads. Growth projections for raw materials and energy resources, the traditional sources of much of the strength in Australia's trading relationship with Japan, have been substantially modified because of the combined impact of slower Japanese economic growth and associated adjustments in the patterns of Japanese demands.

'This imposes on Australian exporters a need to explore carefully new opportunities in the Japanese market. We have begun to identify new opportunities in industrial and consumer products and services, and to register Australian interests in future Japanese trade liberalisation packages... It is now widely recognised in Australia that there is a need to improve the relative performance of Australia's manufacturing industry.'

72 'Labor in Power: Taxing Times', ABC Television, broadcast on 15th June 1993. Keating: '... it wasn't designed to be shattering to the Government. As it turned out, it was.'

73 'Labor in Power: Taxing Times', ABC Television, broadcast on 15th June 1993.

74 'Labor in Power: Taxing Times', ABC Television, broadcast on 15th June 1993.

75 Edna Carew, *Keating: A Biography*, Allen & Unwin, Sydney, 1988, p. 168.

76 'Labor in Power: Taxing Times', ABC Television, broadcast on 15th June 1993.

77 Barry Cohen, Minister for Home Affairs and Environment 11th March 1983 to 13th December 1984; Minister for Arts, Heritage and the Environment 13th December 1984 to 24th July 1987.

78 'This pledge, the most specific social commitment of the century, has been the subject of a historic package to provide a guaranteed minimum income for poor children whose parents earn less than about $300 per week.

'We congratulate the Federal Government on its work on child poverty, which represents a historic breakthrough in the national attack on child poverty. The Federal Government has now built a solid foundation of income security for Australian families.'

Brotherhood of St Laurence, 'Promise the Children' Campaign, 4th May 1989.

79 Clive Bean and Jonathan Kelley, 'Partisan Stability and Short-Term Change in the 1987 Election: Evidence from the NSSS Panel Survey', in *Politics*, 1988, Vol. 23, pp. 80–94.

80 See pp. 232–3.

81 The fourteen countries came from Latin America (Argentina, Brazil, Chile, Colombia and Uruguay); Asia (Indonesia, Malaysia, Thailand, the Philippines); the Pacific (Australia, New Zealand and Fiji); North America (Canada); and the Eastern Bloc (Hungary).

82 See pp. 265–6.

83 APEC's ten work areas were: trade and investment data; trade promotion; expansion of investment and technology transfer in the Asia–Pacific region; human resource development; regional energy co-operation; marine resource conservation; telecommunications; fisheries; transportation; and tourism.

84 See Appendix Three for a record of these achievements.

85 That great Australian, Colin Hayes, the master trainer, deserves much credit for his strong representations on behalf of the Australian racing industry.

86 In Episode 3, broadcast on 22nd June 1993, he recalls his comments in this way: 'This Government's got two leaders within it, and I'm the other one, and you don't treat me like that.'

87 See p. 428.

88 *Report of the Commission of Inquiry into the Lemonthyme and Southern Forests*, Vols I and II.

[89] Gareth Evans and Bruce Grant, op. cit., p. 158.

[90] See Appendix Two.

[91] Australia, House of Representatives, *Debates* (Hansard), 13th April 1989, I said: '... the most interesting statistic around this Parliament at the moment is the number 34, the current tally of votes the shadow Treasurer has in the attack that he is making upon the leadership of the Leader of the Opposition. If any figure is likely to rise in the next few days it will be the number 34 because the intelligence is that gradually the shadow Treasurer is increasing his numbers. I hope that he does.'

[92] The original levy, in February 1984, was 1 per cent; it increased to 1.25 per cent in December 1986 and to 1.4 per cent in July 1993.

[93] In August 1983 support for Medicare was 44 per cent. This grew to 64 per cent by 1987 and to 71 per cent by 1990. (Source: Commonwealth Department of Human Services and Health.)

[94] This organisation has developed in recent years from a narrow sectorally-based interest group into a major contributor to the national debate on a range of important issues, e.g. the environment and Aboriginal affairs.

[95] The blueprint covered biological diversity; endangered species; introduced plants and animals; international co-operation agreements; preservation of habitat; ocean and fisheries; the greenhouse effect; ozone depletion; soils; water; trees; historic, cultural and urban environment; waste management and industrial chemicals; coastal zone management; tourism; energy; and mining.

The One Billion Trees project included a Community Tree Planting Program to plant over 400 million trees, and a Natural Regeneration and Direct Seeding Program to establish over 600 million trees in the open areas of Australia.

[96] See pp. 274–77.

[97] *The Australian*, 19th March 1990.

[98] See Appendix Two.

[99] 'In the important growth area of telecommunications, we must significantly increase competitive influences so that benefits to the economy of the new technologies which characterise this sector are maximised... Further signals to the industry on our attitude to telecommunications growth will be provided by the decisions on mobile phones; competition between the public carriers; and the future viability of AUSSAT. If competition and the growth of the industry are to be fully advanced we will need also actively to address even wider issues. In this context we will also need to consider how we fund essential community service obligations.'

[100] Clem Doherty, Director of McKinsey and Co., said in *Australian Communications*, June 1993, pp. 53-54: 'Telecom Australia ... has become one model which is being assessed in great depth by European and Asian companies ... We have a

duopoly plus resellers, three mobiles and other players can line up in various parts of the business. It's actually more competitive than a duopoly and moving much faster than elsewhere... Its the best access arrangement in the world.'

[101] See Appendix Two.

[102] Paul Kelly, *The End of Certainty*, op. cit., pp. 665-668. The Statement containing the detailed decisions is reproduced in Appendix Two.

[103] See p. 10.

[104] See Appendix One, Statement to Parliament on 12th March 1991, for further details on Co-operative Research Centres.

[105] See Chapter Twenty-Nine.

[106] See p. 203.

[107] See Bede Nairn, *The Big Fella: Jack Lang and the Australian Labor Party 1891–1949*, Melbourne University Press, Melbourne, 1986, p. 2.

[108] Tom Mockeridge, Keating's Private Secretary at the time, said in the ABC series, 'Labor in Power: The Recession We Had to Have': ' ... he (Paul) used to sometimes I think tease us with a couple of ideas about a few outrageous things he might say ... and on this occasion he said "Now what say I say this, about leadership isn't about tripping over television cords in shopping centres", which was code for Bob's leadership style ...'

[109] See Paul Kelly, *The End of Certainty*, op. cit., p. 626.

[110] *The Age*, 25th May 1991.

[111] Australia, House of Representatives, *Debates* (Hansard), 28th May 1991.

[112] See pp. 112–3.

[113] Section 10 (4) of this Act.

[114] Report of the Resources Assessment Commission, paragraph 7.126.

[115] Report of the Resources Assessment Commission, paragraph 7.89.

[116] See p. 128.

[117] The progress achieved at the second Special Premiers' Conference, 30th July 1991, dealing with the New Federalism included:
   - creation of a National Rail Freight Corporation;
   - establishment of a national heavy road vehicle regulation scheme, together with uniform technical and operating regulations and nationally consistent changes;
   - establishment of a working group to investigate nationalising generation, transmission and distribution of electricity in the ACT and in the States except WA;

In the area of regulatory reform the conference also agreed:
   - that uniform food standards should apply across the country and be regulated by a National Food Authority;
   - that mutual recognition in the area of occupational licensing and qualifications would apply across all States and Territories i.e. acceptance in one State would by recognised in others.

- to establish national standards where that was seen to be essential to the efficient working of the Australian economy – as in food – and to accept the principles of mutual recognition in all other areas.

Agreement was also reached:

- to facilitate reform in the structure and ownership of government trading enterprises (GTEs) including acceptance of the principle of national performance monitoring of GTE's;
- to the co-operative development of a better way of achieving more integrated and more effective delivery of programs and services to citizens;
- to examine more efficient and equitable patterns of urban settlement including urban consolidation;
- to conclude an Inter-governmental Agreement on the Environment;
- in the area of industrial relations, to take steps immediately to maximise resource savings between the Commonwealth and the States through enhanced co-operative efforts, including co-location of industrial tribunals and greater shared use of facilities.

Most of these agreements have been concluded or are still being worked through.

[118] B. Galligan and D. Mardiste, 'Labor's Reconciliation with Federalism', Discussion Paper No. 5, Federalism Research Centre, ANU, Canberra, 1991, p. 5.

[119] The communiqué reflected this position: 'Leaders and representatives have agreed on the need for a fundamental review of Commonwealth/State financial arrangements by a committee of senior expert officials.

In this review the Commonwealth and the States recognise the need to address the question of vertical fiscal imbalance – with a view to reducing that imbalance while recognising the necessity for the Commonwealth to have adequate means to meet its national responsibility for effective macro economic management... This will embrace ... an assessment of the distribution of Commonwealth and State Government taxation powers and examine the efficiency of the present allocation of such powers. All options for reform of the distribution of taxation powers will be considered in the course of this review, including the place of Local Government in the structure of taxation.'

[120] See pp. 532–3.

[121] See pp. 532–3.

[122] Paul Kelly, *The End of Certainty*, op. cit., p. 647.

[123] 'Labor in Power: The Recession We Had to Have', ABC Television.

[124] HAWKE: Any claim that I was consulted about that phrase beforehand is an absolute lie. (Transcript, 'Labor in Power: The Recession We Had to Have', ABC Television.)

[125] See p. 472–3.

[126] In *The Age*, 30th September, under the heading 'Keating In Call For Economic Policy Shift', reporter David Humphries said: 'The former Treasurer, Mr

Keating, wants to scuttle the tight economic policy he guided and replace it with an emphasis on growth and job creation.'

127 See pp. 475–6.

128 See pp. 298–305.

129 Real GDP fell by 2.4 per cent in the recent recession compared with a fall of 5.9 per cent in 1982–83.

130 'I believed by that time due to the way I was handling the media, that I thought that was probably a proper decision. And it wasn't one I particularly resisted.' 'Labor in Power: The Sweetest Victory of All', ABC Television.

PICTURE CREDITS

1–12 From the private library of RJL Hawke; **13–14** Courtesy of the *Age*; **15** From the private library of RJL Hawke; **16** Courtesy John Crowther, Department of Foreign Affairs and Trade (DFAT); **17–18** From the private library of RJL Hawke; **19–20** Courtesy of the *Age*; **21** From the private library of RJL Hawke, photographer John Knight; **22–23** From the private library of RJL Hawke; **24** Courtesy of the *Age*; **25–26** Courtesy of the *Canberra Times*; **27** Courtesy of the *Age*; **28** Courtesy the White House, Washington; **29** Courtesy of the *West Australian*; **30** Courtesy of John Crowther, DFAT; **31** Courtesy of Bartho/John Fairfax Group; **32** From the private library of RJL Hawke, photographer Peter Mars; **33** From the private library of RJL Hawke, photographer Alex Gall; **34** From the private library of RJL Hawke; **35** Courtesy of the *Age*; **36** From the private library of RJL Hawke; **37–38** Courtesy of Michael Jensen, DFAT; **39–41** Courtesy of John Crowther, DFAT **42** Courtesy of Michael Jensen, DFAT; **43** Courtesy of John Crowther, DFAT; **44** KN 7/3/89/417, DFAT; **45** KN 2/6/88/666, DFAT; **46** KN 2/6/88/680, DFAT; **47** Courtesy of the *Canberra Times*; **48** KN 28/7/89/198, DFAT; **49** Courtesy of Reuters Australia Pty limited; **50** Courtesy of the *Age*; **51** Courtesy of Michael Jensen, DFAT; **52** Courtesy of Stevens/ John Fairfax Group; **53** Courtesy of Richard Briggs/the *Canberra Times*; **54** Courtesy of the *Age*; **55** Courtesy of Pearce/ John Fairfax Group.

INDEX

congresses 93, 94
Hawke presidency 45, 47–68, 81–4,
  92–5, 96–7, 100, 104
and pilots' strike 458, 459
and Tax Summit 306–9
uranium policy 93, 94
white collar unions affiliation 54–5
Australian Electoral Commission 275
Australian Federation of Air Pilots
  (AFAP) 457–61, 463
Australian Labor Party (ALP)
and ASIO 188
communist influences 33–4, 49
conferences 92, 107, 111, 112, 138,
  253, 492
environment policy 138
foreign policy 110
Hawke presidency 64–72, 78–80,
  82–4
the split 33–4, 41, 48
uranium policy 92, 111–12
Victorian branch 34, 48, 56, 61, 95,
  98
Australian Labor Advisory Council 64
Australian Manufacturing Council
  (AMC) 584
Australian Mining Industry Council
  (AMIC) 508–9
Australian Security and Intelligence
  Organisation (ASIO) 187–201

Baker, James 520
Baker, Major-General John 521
Balderstone, Simon xi, 477
banks see financial deregulation
Bannon, John 310
Barblett, Alan 9–10
Barnard, Lance 66–7, 145
Barnett, Harvey 187–93, 198, 200
Barron, Peter 162, 164, 165, 242, 302,
  414–15

Barwick, Sir Garfield 69, 294–5
Baume, Peter 388, 410
Bavadra, Timoci 329
Beahan, Michael 523
Beazley, Kim 160, 487, 552
as Defence Minister 228, 329
as Telecommunications Minister
  490–2
and Hawke leadership battles 504,
  553
Bechtel Corporation 208, 209
Beetham, Richard 236
Bennett, Ken 78
Bicentenary celebrations 443–5
Bjelke-Petersen, Sir Joh 8, 185, 308,
  387, 401
Blewett, Neal 160, 429, 475–6
Block, David 420–1
Bolkus, Nick 273, 419, 504, 553
Bourkes-ACTU 57, 58
Bourkes Stores 57
Bowan, John 167, 231
Bowen, Lionel 110, 123–4, 156,
  193–4, 367, 373–4
Bradley, Bill 429
Briese, Clarrie 267
Brogan, Brian 66
Brown, Bill 49, 50
Brown, Bob 394, 396
Brown, Horrie 38
Brown, John 161, 440
Budgets see economic affairs
Burke, Brian 310, 365, 496
Bush, George, 427–9, 471, 554
and Gulf War 513, 515, 516, 520,
  521, 524, 525
Business Council of Australia 182,
  307–8, 583–4
Button, John 121–2, 123, 157, 378,
  465, 497